Mathematical Research

Computers in Science and Higher Education

edited by

Jan Grabowski

Volume 57

AKADEMIE-VERLAG BERLIN

In this series original contributions of mathematical research in all fields are contained, such as

- research monographs
- collections of papers to a single topic
- reports on congresses of exceptional interest for mathematical research.

This series is aimed at promoting quick information and communication between mathematicians of the various special branches.

In diese Reihe werden Originalbeiträge zu allen Gebieten der mathematischen Forschung aufgenommen wie

- Forschungsmonographien
- Sammlungen von Arbeiten zu einem speziellen Thema
- Berichte von Tagungen, die für die mathematische Forschung besonders aktuell sind.

Die Reihe soll die schnelle Information und gute Kommunikation zwischen den Mathematikern der verschiedenen Fachgebiete fördern.

Manuscripts
in English and German comprising at least 100 pages and not more than 500 pages can be admitted to this series. With respect to a quick publication the manuscripts are reproduced photomechanically. Authors who are interested in this series please turn directly to the 'Akademie-Verlag'. Here you will get more detailed information about the form of the manuscripts and the modalities of publication.

Manuskripte
in englischer und deutscher Sprache, die mindestens 100 Seiten und nicht mehr als 500 Seiten umfassen, können in diese Reihe aufgenommen werden. Im Interesse einer schnellen Publikation werden die Manuskripte auf fotomechanischem Weg reproduziert. Autoren, die an der Veröffentlichung entsprechender Arbeiten in dieser Reihe interessiert sind, wenden sich bitte direkt an den Akademie-Verlag. Sie erhalten dort genauere Informationen über die Gestaltung der Manuskripte und die Modalitäten der Veröffentlichung.

Computers in Science
and Higher Education

Mathematical Research · Mathematische Forschung

Wissenschaftliche Beiträge
herausgegeben von der
Akademie der Wissenschaften der DDR
Karl-Weierstraß-Institut für Mathematik

Band 57

Computers in Science
and Higher Education

Computers in Science and Higher Education

Contributions to the Conference BIT '89,
held in Berlin, GDR, June 19–23, 1989

edited by
Jan Grabowski

Akademie-Verlag Berlin 1990

Herausgeber:

Prof. Dr. Jan Grabowski
Humboldt-Universität zu Berlin
Organisations- und Rechenzentrum

Die Titel dieser Schriftenreihe werden vom Originalmanuskript der Autoren reproduziert.

ISBN 3-05-500774-3
ISSN 0138-3019

Erschienen im Akademie-Verlag Berlin,Leipziger Str.3-4,Berlin,DDR-1086

Lizenznummer: 202.100/551/89
Printed in the German Democratic Republic
Gesamtherstellung: VEB Kongreß- und Werbedruck,Oberlungwitz,DDR-9273
Lektor: Dr. Reinhard Höppner
LSV 1085
Bestellnummer: 764 088 1 (2182/57)
04200

P r e f a c e

The present volume contains the contributions to the conference on "Computers in Science and Higher Education" to be held 19-23 June, 1989, at Humboldt University, Berlin (GDR). The conference is the third in the series "Berliner Informatik-Tage (bit)".
The Computing Centre of Humboldt University, on the occasion of its 25th anniversary, has the pleasure to organise this conference as a contribution to the international scientific life in the field of computer science and academic computer applications.
The volume contains those contributions the final versions of which arrived before the deadline: five invited papers, and 25 communicatios. The latter had been subject of refereeing and revision.
The contributions can be roughly grouped into the following topics:

Computers in Education
Document Processing,
Networking,
Languages, Tools, and Technology,
Problem Solving Environments and Knowledge Based Systems,
Human Factors.

The editor thanks all authors for their interesting contributions. He expresses his gratitude to the members of the international Programme Committee and the referees for their good co-operation. On behalf of all participants of the conference I thank the organising staff, especially Conrad Piens and Bodo Hilger, for their efforts in preparing the conference and the present volume.

Berlin, April 1989

Jan Grabowski

Table of Contents

Mathematics and Computer Science

Lothar Budach
Akademie der Wissenschaften der DDR
Forschungsbereich Mathematik und Informatik
Rudower Chaussee 5
DDR - 1199 Berlin

Abstract

Mathematics and computer science are intimately related. Beside many attributes which are common in mathematics as well as in computer science as formula manipulation, the reduction of problems to simpler problems, considerations in structures and abstract reasoning the major link between these sciences is algorithmic thinking. The relationship between mathematics and computer science can be demonstrated by many interesting examples. This exemplification will be given in the talk along the following items.

1. **The development of mathematics is from its very beginnings intimately connected with man's struggle against nature,with his efforts for a better understanding of the real world, and his endeavour to extend his restricted organic bounds.**

   The natural numbers have not, as Kronecker said, been created by God. They are the result of the necessity to compare finite sets and to denote the size of these sets. The comparison of sets of goods led to the notion of measure. The definition of cardinality and measure, the need to note these concepts and to operate with them extended to the determination and comparison of time intervals. Geometry originated in land surveying and topography. Notations, still used nowadays like digits stemming from the ten fingers of our hands, calculus (calculi = little pebbles which were used as means for addition and subtraction) and abacus (=calculating machine using balls gliding on wires) resemble the origins of mathematics.

2. **With the formation of mathematics arose simultaneously the main method to apply mathematics. Comprehension of quantities and geometric properties and modelling of reality enables the simulation of real processes which is a source for forecasting.**

So f. i. building a house it was possible to design the ground plan and to predict the number of necessary bricks, the number of craftsman and the amount of food for these.

The observation of sun, moon and stars helped man to explore regularly returning time intervals and the prediction of them. Some of the greatest mathematical discoveries as algebra and arithmetic arose from the man's need to develop the calendar.

3. Basis of all mathematization is the method to assign numbers - or, more general, abstract **computable** values - to natural phenomena.

   This method reduced mathematical forecast to computational problems. In the development of mathematics this method always led to unifying approaches which have their roots already in the Pythagorean mathematics. As an example of this approach can serve the analytic geometry of R. Descartes in [7],

   which overcame the distinction between geometry, the greek science of the continuum, and the babylonian-indian-arabic algebra and arithmetic of al-Khwârizmî.

4. The mathematical theorem with its proof presents a universal method for **generalization** and **transfer** of experiences.

5. Modelling, simulation, generalization, simplification and transfer of experiences - this arsenal of methodologies and tools made mathematics always to an indispensable science for the development of technic.

   But for a long period of the development of mankind the use of mathematics was restricted to simple calculation, to problems in building, ship building, clock making and hydraulics. Refinements made by I. Newton in the computation of trajectories respecting the resistance of air were far from being used in his century. The inaccurate guns of his time made that the skill of the gunner had greater influence to good shooting than the exact mathematical calculation of the trajectory. (The first application of these methods stems from the time of World War I.)

6. Never before the importance of mathematics for application especially in technology has been greater than today.

   Exact observations, calculations and predictions as they characterized only astronomy in the past centuries - astronomical objects are relatively simple and of low complexity - are now the basis of every technical design. Technology is a driving force for the development of mathematics.

Many applications of mathematics are made by users of mathematics: physicists and engineers. The mathematization of science is the major source for the increase of the actual importance of mathematics.

Nevertheless: the high precision and complexity of modern machinery, manufacturing systems and electric appliances raises mathematical problems which belong to the most difficult and partially unsolved problems. Problems of this type need the specific mathematical consideration and argumentation. As a result the arsenal of mathematical problems and methodologies enriches and the development of mathematics proceeds. This can be seen in many examples: network-simulation and numerical methods for differential equations, vision and two dimensional algebraic topology, partition and routing and simulated annealing, dynamics of the head on hard disc drives and computational mechanics, computer tomography and operators, and so forth.

7. Computation has ever been and will ever be an essential part of mathematics.

The word *algebra* and the word *algorithm* have a common root. They both stem from one of the most famous mathematical books, the *Kitâb al-jabr wa'l-muqâbala* of al-Khwârizmî, certainly one of the most influential textbooks on algebra and arithmetic in the middle age. (12th century).

Formalization of algebraic manipulation by Vieta (1540 - 1603), the introduction of decimal numbers by Stevin (1548 - 1620) and the logarithmic tables of Napier (1550 - 1617) reduced long computation times significantly. This raised the problem whether these calculations can be done by mechanical calculation. The construction of a mechanical adding machine by Pascal (1642) and a multiplying machine by Leibniz (1670) led to the design of an mechanical difference engine (1823) and analytical engine (1835) by Ch. Babbage (1792 - 1871). The importance of these endeavors can not better be characterized than by the following notes of K. Marx [13] to [1]:

> "D. Theilung der Arbeit erlaubt uns in den Operationen des Geistes u. d. Körpers leicht zu erhalten und anzuwenden auf jedes besondre Detail die präcise Qualität v. Geschicklichkeit u. Instruktion, welche diese Arbeit erfordert. So z. B. bei der Rechenmaschine, vermeiden wir den Verlust, der Statt hat, wenn man den Geist eines gelehrten Mathematikers auf die einfachsten Operationen der Arithmetik verwendet. "

8. The principle of electro-mechanical working Relais made already in the thirties the development of programable digital computers possible. K. Zuses **Z1** (1937), H. H. Aikens **Harvard Mark.I** (1944) are electro-mechanical computers of that time. The cathode-ray tube led to the first generation of purely electronic computers. The first computer of this type was constructed in 1946 in Pennsylvania (U. S. A.). It was the Electronic Numerical Integrator and Computer (**ENIAC**) which offered 5000 operations/sec and which was presented by J P. Eckert, J. W. Mauchly and H. H. Goldstine. 1953 followed S. A. Lebedev's **BESM** which, with 10 000 op/sec, was at that time the speediest computer all over the world. The discovery of the transistor effect at the end of the forties by J. Bordeen, W. H. Brittain and W. Stockley led to the next generation of electronic computers followed by the third and fourth generation computers with LSI- and VLSI-circuits. The successes of VLSI-technology have enabled computer speed and storage capacity to grow in an astounding way, confronting mathematicians and other scientists with a continually widening range of opportunities. Continued improvement in magnetic recording densities, chips for specialized high resolution graphic display, for signal analysis, data communication, data retrieval, and so on allow the construction of comfortable and attractive computers.

9. The growing power of computers gave rise to a whole new scientific discipline which makes the computers and all that what can be done by these machines a new object of scientific curiosity and intellectual effort.

   This discipline, called **computer science** in the U. S. A. and other english speaking countries, Informatique in France, where the German Informatik came from, and Kibernetika or Prikladnaia Mathematika in the Soviet Union deals with the comprehension, classification, storage and processing of information and knowledge and with the development and the design systems which are able to process this information automatically. The concepts, formalizations and theories describing the communication of computers also belong to this new science.

10. Computer science is primarily the study of algorithms ([12]).

    There are many attributes which are common in mathematics as will as in Computer science: formula manipulation, the method to reduce problems to simpler problems, structural considerations and abstract reasoning are examples for common types of thinking. But the major link between mathematics and computer science is the algorithmic thinking. We have seen that algorithms played an imported rôle in a long period of the development of mathematics. Elementary computation where already intimately connected with the very first steps of this discipline. But it took thousands of years in the development of mathematics until different formal definitions of algorithms could be given independently by Post, Kleene and Turing in 1936 - 1937. It could be proved that all these algorithmic notions are mathematically equivalent and Church stated the general (philosophical) hypothesis that all formalizations of the notion of algorithm are equivalent to each other. All these algorithms can be realized on a Turing machine - an abstract machine which was the basis of Von Neumanns architecture of real computers. The von Neumann architecture is computationally universal, any computational paradigm is accessible to it, so that it can be improved in speed and size only, never on fundamental capability. The dynamics of a computer is characterized abstractly by algorithms. Therefore algorithms are the central concepts of computer science.

11. Computer science is a technical science.

    J. Hartmanis expressed this as follows in [8]: "In computer science we must first imagine or build what we want to study. We must develop the intellectual tools not only to explore the existing but to study the possible, to help us imagine it, to build and analyze it or analyze and build it".

12. Contemporary computers are a novelty of historic dimension. It is the first time in history of mankind that not only physical but also intellectual parts of human work can be realized by technical means.

    The development and application of computers technology based on a very high standard of microelectronic has broadened rapidly: Its widening range of opportunities ranks from databases, decision processes, control of flexible manufacturing systems, artificial intelligence, to communication technology. Therefore computer technology is one of the most important technologies of our time.

13. Not only that computers allow to implement algorithms, they have the ability to deal successfully with the irreducible complex.

    Perhaps this complexity of problems and processes which have to be described and formalized by computer science separates computer science from mathematics: Computer science is beginning to blaze trails into the zone of complexity whereas mathematics has to simplify: "To find the simple in the complex, the finite in the infinite - that is not a bad description of the aim and essence of mathematics" (J. T. Schwartz [11])

14. Concepts, formalizations, structures and theories of information processes and systems have already been studied and developed long before the advent of computer science as a scientific discipline. Take the representation of knowledge by language and the coding of this knowledge by written texts as one of the oldest and most decisive information techniques. The practical necessity to bring order in collection of plants f. i. in botanic gardens led K. Linné to his classification system and to questionnaires as a universal method to classify by sequence of questions which have to be answered according to certain attributes (see [15] and [4]).

15. Efficiency, productivity and power of computers depend significantly on the quality of software.

    Costs for purchase and development of software rank already over these for hardware. (The sum total purchase of western countries in software 1987 amounts to 75 billion US$.)

16. Further progress in the power of computers can only be realized by innovative parallel architectures.

    Though the von Neumann architecture is computational universal, it can be improved in speed and size especially by parallel working processors as a supplement to the von Neumann processor as computer kernel. Remark that contemporary von Neumann computers are of a very low standard if we compare them with industrial structures. They are comparable with classical handicraft productions where one craftsman realizes all necessary operations in the flow of work. As opposed to this situation there are already experiences in the division and parallelization of computational processes which reach back to the time of the french revolution where the director of the Bureau des Cadastres, M. de Prony, used the manufactory (which he found described by A. Smith in [14]) as paradigm for parallel computation: he computed tables by parallel calculation of 80 persons which had only to add and to subtract columns of numbers in a well defined manner. This ancient manufactory principle is going to be applied right now in modern parallel computers. (vector processors, RISC, cache-memory, connection machine, neural networks, ...) Cheap processor chips will make new generations of computers enormously powerful and economically feasible.

17. An appropriate decomposition of the production process into different phases is the supposition of an effective production. In the same manner the effective decomposition into parallel executable steps is possible only on the basis of an analysis of the problem.

    This analogy indicates how difficult it is to parallelize algorithms and to create adequate architectures for circuits and computers. This is one of the most important problems of theoretical computer science. Special design procedures can be used for the on-chip parallelization of algorithms (see [3] and [6])

18. Parallelism is not imaginable without communication.

    Non sufficient communication can limit the effect of highly parallel processes Consider as an example circuits with bounded fan-in and fan-out in comparison with neutral nets with nearly unrestricted fan-in and fan-out; rather than the abilities of the single neuron, the large number of dendrites in neural nets is presumable the crucial reason for the enormous capabilities of the human brain. A well organized computer net communication may cause a remarkable profit of efficiency (Computing in a net, distributed processing; Example: Factorization of large numbers).

19. Design and analysis of algorithms, in particular with respect to parallelization is one of the hardest problems at the boarder line between mathematics and computer science.

    Further work in this direction is indispensable for further progress in software and hardware development. In computer science a large collection of techniques for the design of algorithms has already been developed: data structures, divide-and-conquer, recursion, evolution algorithms, greedy-algorithms, simulated annealing, dynamic programming, and so forth.

20. The proof of principal lower bounds for the size of hardware and software products forces novel concepts.

    In designing high integrated circuits the problem arises to guarantee a fastest solution with respect to a given amount of chip area. If no such solution exists, then compromises for this have to be formulated. This corresponds in a unique fashion to research for lower bounds for defined complexity measures (space = memory, time, tradeoff between space and time, tradeoff between area of a chip and quadratic time).

The proof of lower bounds is one of the most attractive and difficult problems of theoretical computer science.

Artifacts as circuits and computers become now independent objects of scientific research. Examinations of this kind direct to mathematical problems of the following kind: One has to prove that it is impossible to execute predefined procedures using only restricted resources (see [10], [2] and [5] as examples).

21. J. Hopcroft draws our attention to a new direction of computer science (see [9]):

"Over the past 20 years, theoretical computer science has developed the mathematical foundations to support algorithm design, compiler technology, language specification, distributed processing and other computer subdisciplines. During the next 20 years, computer science will broaden its horizons and develop the theoretical fondations to support a broad spectrum of engeneering applications. Robotics, computer aided design and electronic prototyping will be among these applications. These areas will require simulation systems capable of representing physical objects and their behavior under external forces."

References

[1] CH. BABBAGE, On the Economy of Machinery and Manufactures, (II. Auflage, London 1833).

[2] L. BUDACH, Automata and Labyrinths, *Math. Nachr.* **86** (1978), 195–282.

[3] L. BUDACH, Mathematische Probleme beim Entwurf von VLSI-Schaltkreisen, *Mitteilungen der Math. Gesellschaft der DDR* **2** (1983), 5–23.

[4] L. BUDACH, Klassifizierungsprobleme und das Verhältnis von deterministischer zu nichtdeterministischer Raumkomplexität, *Seminarbericht der Sektion Mathematik der Humboldt-Universität zu Berlin* **68** (1985), 1–64.

[5] L. BUDACH, A lower bound for the number of nodes in a decision tree, *Elektron. Inf. verarb. Kybern. EIK* **21** (1985), 221–228.

[6] L. BUDACH, E.-G. GIESSMANN, H. GRASSMANN, B. GRAW, CH. MEINEL, B. MOLZAN, U. SCHÄFER, P. ZIENICKE, Recursive VLSI-Design Theory and Application, *Bull. of the EATCS* **37** (1989), 131–150.

[7] R. DESCARTES, Discours de la méthode, (Paris 1637).

[8] J. HARTMANIS, Observations about the Development of Theoretical Computer Science, *20th Annual Symposium on Foundations of Computer Science* (1979), 224—233.

[9] J. HOPCROFT, The Promise of Electronic Prototyping, *LNCS* **238** (1986), 128—139.

[10] J. KAHN, M. SAKS, D. STURTEVANT, A topological approach to evasiveness, *Combinatorica* **4** (1984), 297–306.

[11] M. KAC, G. -C. ROTA, J. T. SCHWARTZ, Discrete Thoughts, (Birkhäuser, Boston Basel Stuttgart, 1986).

[12] D. E. KNUTH, Algorithms in Modern Mathematics and Computer Science, *LNCS* **122** (1981), 82—99.

[13] K. MARX, Excerpte über Arbeitsteilung, Maschinerie und Industrie, Historisch-kritische Ausgabe, Transkribiert und herausgegeben von R. Winkelmann, (Frankfurt/M-Berlin-Wien 1982).

[14] A. SMITH, An Inquiry into the Nature and Causes of the Wealth of Nations, (London, 182.).

[15] S. UNGER, F. WYSOTZKI, Lernfähige Klassifizierungssysteme, (Akademie-Verlag, Berlin 1981).

HETEROGENEOUS NETWORKS

R.F. Hille
ETH Zürich
on leave from
The University of Wollongong
Australia

Abstract

The recent past has seen the development of a large number of wide area communication networks that are functionally different so that communication between them is possible only through gate ways which perform complex translation services. A conglomerate of heterogeneous networks has developed and the need for integration is obvious. The digitization of communication services formerly carried by analog signals is the first step towards the integration of services on the same network. There remains the integration of wide area networks into one transport medium. Fast packet switching has the potential to be that uniform transport medium. This paper discusses performance characteristics and protocol requirements of a fast packet switching network. Conventional packet switching protocols are not suited to a fast packet switching environment and a completely different approach to the problem of protocol design is needed. Particular emphasis is placed on the design of fast packet switches as their performance determines the feasibility of fast packet switching and the detail of protocols.

1 Introduction

During the past two decades a large number of different wide area communication networks have been developed that are functionally incompatible so that communication between them is possible only through gateways which perform more or less complex translation of protocols, addresses and formats. A conglomerate of different networks has developed and the need for integration is obvious.

There are two fundamentally different switching mechanisms, circuit switching or packet switching, where the word *switching* is used in the sense of establishing a connection between two stations and ensuring continued delivery of the signal. The public telephone network is a circuit switching network. A number of packet switching networks are dedicated to computer communication (UUCP net, ARPAnet, TYMNET, TRANSPAC, etc.). In packet switching the information flow between communicating entities is broken up into small portions, the packets, which are transported by the network as individual entities to their destinations where they are re-assembled into messages.

New services have been grafted onto existing networks whose original purpose was different. An example is the introduction of an electronic mail service on top of the file transfer utility provided by the UUCP network. Various add-on services are offered by the operators of public telephone networks in addition to the normal telephone service. The packet switching service offered by European PTTs is an example of this. Its implementation may vary between countries, making inter-networking difficult. Again, this highlights the need for standardization of networks and services.

The digitization of the public telephone network began about two decades ago and the existence of digital encoding methods for services which were formerly transmitted by analog signals is one necessary prerequisite for the integration. Digital telephone networks use time division multiplexing which sometimes is called *asynchronous time division multiplexing* if there is no common reference frequency on th network. Synchronization between receiver and transmitter is then achieved by the insertion of additional bits (stuffing bits). The term *synchronous* time division multiplexing also describes the situation in principle because each time slot in a multiplex belongs to a particular communication channel. Multiplexing is organized into a hierarchy of levels with well-defined band width. The basic unit of band width is provided by the DS-0 channel of 64 kbit/s, which is one digital telephony channel. Usually 24 telephony channels are multiplexed together and transmitted on a standard 1.544 Mbit/s DS-1 carrier. The next levels are DS-2 at 6.312 Mbit/s and DS-3 at 44.736 Mbit/s. There are several other bit rates up to about 1.7 Gbit/s. The *integrated services digital network* (ISDN) is based on circuit switching and the interface to the user equipment has two B-channels of 64 kbit/s each and one D-channel of 16 kbit/s which is for signalling purposes. The B-channels can carry a variety of services to be provided by the terminal equipment. Up to eight separate devices can be connected to the user terminal of which two can communicate simultaneously on the two B-channels. It is planned to extend ISDN by the addition of 4 channels of 2 Mbit/s each and one channel of 150 Mbit/s. This is called Broadband ISDN or in short B-ISDN.

The International Consultative Committee for Telephony and Telegraphy (CCITT) has accepted *asynchronous transfer mode* (ATM) as the basis of future development of B-ISDN. Traffic of any bit rate is assembled into cells of fixed length which consist of a header and an information field. The cells are inserted into the 150 Mbit/s channel of the circuit switched digital network. The effect of using asynchronous transfer mode is to de-couple the function of multi service terminal equipment from that of the underlying network. Asynchronous transfer mode is compatible with fast packet switching and it is therefore possible to make the transition from the circuit switched digital network to a fast packet switching network quite easily.

The main weakness of circuit switched networks is that band width can be allocated only in integer multiples of basic units which are determined by the multiplexing hierarchy of the network. In a packet switching network, band width allocation is completely flexibility. The development of new encoding and compression algorithms for digital video and other services using high band width will result in new band width requirements that are difficult to predict and may not be compatible with the existing multiplexing hierarchy in circuit switched networks. Once allocated, a communication channel in a circuit switched network is the exclusive property of the communication session which requested it, no matter how lightly or heavily the channel is used, until the session is terminated. In packet switching there is no exclusive allocation of circuits or channels and unused band width remains available to all communications. Streams of packets are multiplexed by interleaving them in the arbitrary order of their arrival, hence the name of *statistical multiplexing*.

The hardware of circuit switched digital networks is very complex and therefore expensive and difficult to maintain. Fast packet switching on the other hand requires a potentially simple hardware and this will lead to a reduction of the connection cost per subscriber. In wide area packet switching networks, fast packet switching can remove the bottleneck that is formed by the backbone and replace it by a reliable transport mechanism that is sufficiently faster than the devices it connects.

2 Network Structure

With the introduction of optical fibre technology the transmission speed increases relative to the speed of processors and a dramatic shift in favour of the transmission speed has occurred recently. the result is that complex protocol functions cannot be implemented in the backbone network and must be moved to the perimeter of the network where the bit rate is small enough. The backbone network will simply be a fast reliable relay with only minimal protocol functions. Differentiation between types of service will be possible and indeed necessary only at the end points of communication paths, and that is where it should be done.

We distinguish between local and long distance traffic. There are far fewer trunk lines than local access lines. Many individual communications are bundled together at the exit of a local region to be transported over large distances on few trunk lines to other distribution points at which they again become part of the local traffic. The *backbone network* carries the long distance traffic and provides the communication paths between a number of *local area networks* which are access networks. The structure of the network is shown in Figure 1.

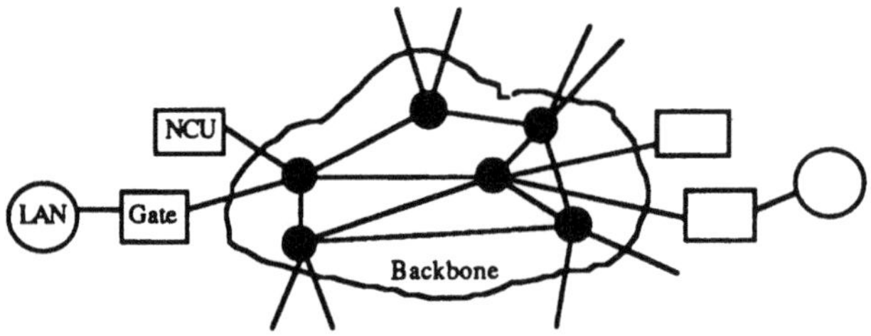

Figure 1 The Packet Switching Network

The architecture of the distribution networks may be different to that of the backbone. Therefore, there are bridges or gateways between the backbone and the distribution networks. One network control unit (NCUs) is associated with each backbone node. The NCUs take care of connection establishment, band width allocation and network management functions in general.

The introduction of two levels of hierarchy makes it possible to limit the number of switching ports of the backbone nodes. This may be necessary so that switches can be built that can handle the required band width per link. The ratio between the band width of the backbone and that of the distribution networks determines the detail of communication protocols. The aim is to make the backbone as fast and simple as possible so that the detail of any communication protocol is entirely up to the communicating stations.

In conventional packet switching networks the band width of the backbone (typically 50 kbit/s) is *much* smaller than that of any of the local area networks attached to it. They are usually designed for a nominal band width from 1 to 10 Mbit/s. This speed mismatch between periphery and backbone, coupled with variable server rates in the backbone nodes and the possibility of high bit error rates on the links, has led to the design of very complex flow and error control protocols and routing strategies. A reversal of the ratio of backbone and perimeter device speed (coupled with the substantially lower bit error rates of optical fibre links) means that conventional link-by-link flow and error control is both impossible and unnecessary. The more complex protocol functions have their rightful place at the end points of communication paths where the degree of multiplexing and hence the transmission speed is small enough for the processors to keep pace. The backbone network is only a basic relay mechanism and because of the multiplexing it must have a much higher speed than the distribution networks.

3 Switch Fabrics

The backbone nodes must be as simple as possible in order to achieve high link speed. Switching is based on self routing datagrams. They are packets whose address header sets the path through the switch and each switch removes that part of the address header which it used.

There seems to be no agreement about the required size of switches and the argument reduces to whether there should be only one level of hierarchy in the packet switching network. In that case switches must play a role similar to that of telephone exchanges which are usually hybrids between local and trunk exchanges, where the mix between local and trunk traffic capability is variable.

However, internally the two functions are performed by separate building blocks. A local exchange must support a large (10^3 to 10^4) number of subscribers whereas a trunc exchange supports only a small (about 10^1) number of high capacity links.

3.1 Switch Size

The two level hierarchy of the packet switching network makes it possible to keep small the number of links incident on backbone nodes. In existing backbone networks or in the public telephone network it is unlikely that a trunk exchange has more than sixteen neighbours (16 is a convenient choice because it is a power of 2). For the purpose of this discussion we assume that the switch size is $N \leq 16$, but we allow for modular extension of switches so that the network capacity can be adapted to changing conditions.

3.2 Multiple Stage Switches

A survey of switch fabrics for a variety of different applications has been given in [Feng, 1981] and some of them are important for packet switching networks. In multiple stage switches each packet must pass through several switching elements before it reaches the desired output channel. Each additional stage multiplies the switch size (i.e. the number of possible output ports) by the degree d of the elements. Thus, a switch of i stages of degree d has $N = d^i$ output ports. Multiple stage switches permit easy modular extension. Their main weakness stems from the fact that they have fewer than N^2 internal paths. This introduces the possibility of contention between packets inside the switch fabric, even though the packets may be heading for different output ports. Buffers are required to resolve the conflicts and avoid packet loss. If the buffers are placed outside the switch fabric, that is, either before the input ports or at the output ports, a multiple stage fabric behaves essentially like a single stage fabric. There are switch designs based on multiple stage fabrics which use pure input buffering in conjunction with processing of packets before they enter the fabric [Uematsu, 1988], [Anido, 1988]. However, because of their geometry we treat them as multiple stage fabrics. In the next section we consider multiple stage switches with buffering in the elements.

3.2.1 Banyan Switches

The members of the class of *banyan switches* are composed of binary elements with two input and two output ports. At each stage a packet selects its path to the next stage by the leading address bit such that the value 0 guides it to the upper and the value 1 to the lower output port. These switches are also called *delta networks* or *butterfly networks* [Brooks, 1987]. A banyan switch of size $N = 8$ is shown in Figure 2. It consists of $\log_2(N)$ stages of binary elements.

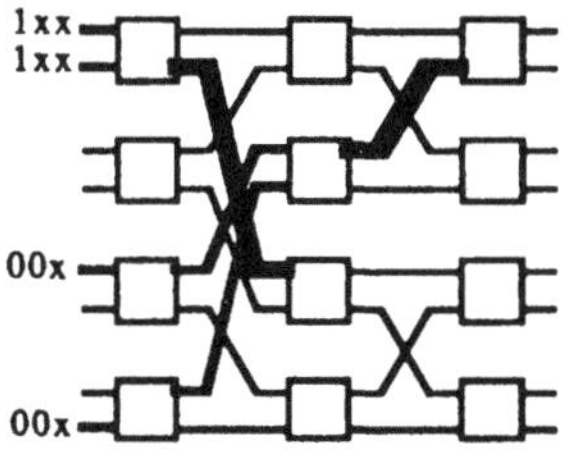

Figure 2 A banyan switch of size $N = 8$

The banyan switch suffers from the phenomenon of internal contention. Pairs of packets that arrive within one packet length of each other at input ports, where the ports belong to the same group of size 2^i, collide after at most i switching stages if they have a common address prefix of i bits. Output contention between simultaneously arriving packets that request the same output port is equivalent to internal contention as the collision may occur before the final switching stage.

The buffers may be located at the input ports or at the output ports of the switch elements. The two alternatives are shown in Figure 3.

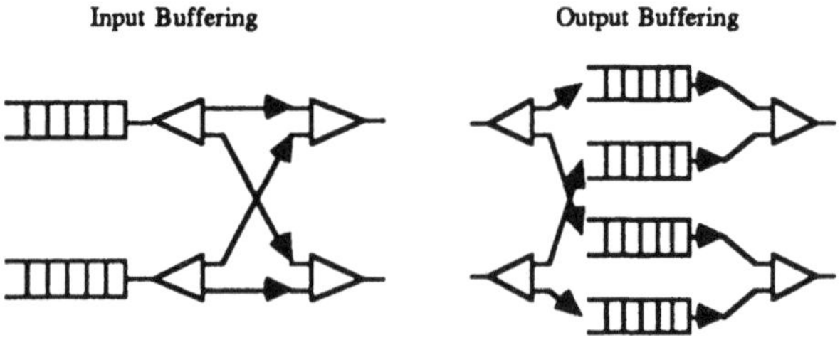

Figure 3 Buffering in Binary Switching Elements

All input buffering suffers from a phenomenon called *head-of-line* blocking [Hluchyj, 1988]. If two simultaneously arriving packets request the same output channel one of them must be buffered. It can then block the advance of a packet following on the same line which is destined for the other (free) output channel. Output buffering avoids this at the expense of twice as many buffers per element. However, the buffers may be much smaller. To obtain a fair comparison one would make the total buffer space equal in both cases.

3.2.2 Batcher-Banyan Networks

In an effort to preserve the modularity of the switch fabric and avoid internal contention a different switch fabric, the Batcher-banyan Network, was introduced. The first of these and perhaps the best known is the *Starlite Switch* which is described in [Huang, 1984]. Several variations have been proposed since [O'Neill, 1988], [Palmer, 1987], [Hui, 1987] which differ only in detail like the buffering scheme or different processing requirements for the packets. A diagram of the Starlite switch architecture is shown in Figure 4.

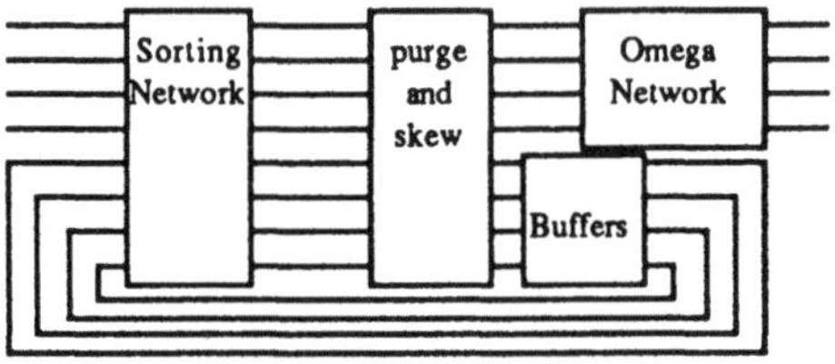

Figure 4 The Starlite Switch Architecture

Arriving packets are sent through a bitonic sorting network [Batcher, 1968], where the term *bitonic* refers to the mathematical properties of the number sequences on which the sorting algorithm is based. A bitonic number sequence consists of two monotonic sequences, one increasing and one decreasing. After the packets have been sorted by address and and packets with repeated addresses have been removed, the remaining packets are passed through an *omega* network which is a banyan switch with slightly different connection pattern between stages. The omega network is the actual switch and the sorter is only a pre-processor. The point is that there is no internal contention in the omega network if the simultaneously arriving packets are sorted by address and if there are no repeated addresses. The packets with repeated addresses are stored in a recycling buffer and can enter the switch again later.

The switch must operate in cycles because the sorting network compares pairs of packets in each stage. When the packets have been sorted by address it is easy to trap the ones with repeated addresses because equal addresses appear on adjacent lines. The remaining packets with unique addresses are offered to the omega network that routes them to the appropriate output channels. The sorter alone would not suffice as a switch because it cannot produce the required bijective mapping of addresses to output ports unless there is a packet on each input line and the packets have unique addresses.

An omega network of size $N = 8$ is shown in Figure 5. It is equivalent to the banyan switch of Figure 3 and can be obtained from it by exchanging the two middle elements of the second stage and arranging the input lines of the first stage in the same way as those of the other two stages.

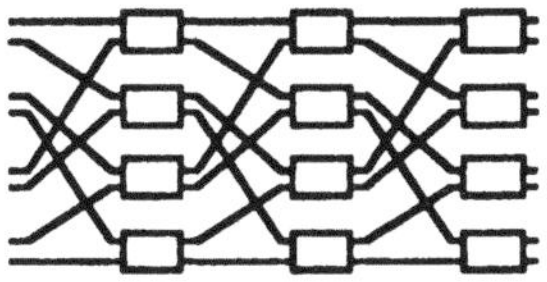

Figure 5 An Omega Network

The re-circulation buffering may get packets out of sequence. The solution of this problem introduces additional complexity into the higher level protocols of backbone network using this switch design. It is important not to re-circulate packets too often while others with the same address are not re-circulated. This requires keeping track of the re-circulation age of packets and the necessary processing further complicates the switch operation.

3.2.3 Other Multiple Stage Networks

Other multiple stage designs are rearrangeable Benes networks [Benes, 1962]. Because they have more than the minimum number of stages there exists more than one path between a given pair of input and output channels. This fact can be used to reduce the probability of internal conflict at the expense of additional processing of packets. Conflicts must be recognized and resolved before the packets enter the switch fabric. In [Newman, 1988] a multiple stage switch in the form of a Benes network composed of elements with degree $d = 8$ is described and its performance is analyzed. The necessary processing per packet limits the band width per input channel to about 50 Mbit/s with present VLSI technology. Paths through the fabric are set at call setup time and the appropriate address headers must be substituted on each packet. The same idea is used in [Anido, 1988] where the switch fabric consists of two banyan networks arranged back to back so that N different paths are available between each pair of input and output port.

3.3 Single Stage Switches

In a single stage switch with N inputs and outputs the path to the requested output port is set in *one step* by the packet's address header. There are N^2 internal paths between the input and the output side.

3.3.1 A Simple N^2 Switch

A very simple switch can be constructed as follows. Each input offers an arriving packet to all output ports. The filter elements at the N^2 cross connections permit only those packets to pass which have the correct address. Since the requested output port may be busy when a packet arrives, there must be provision for parallel buffering. One buffer is located after each filter element. This means that each of the output ports has $N-1$ parallel buffers, one for each of the other inputs (Note: no packet will ever go back on the way it came). Figure 6 shows a diagram of the switch.

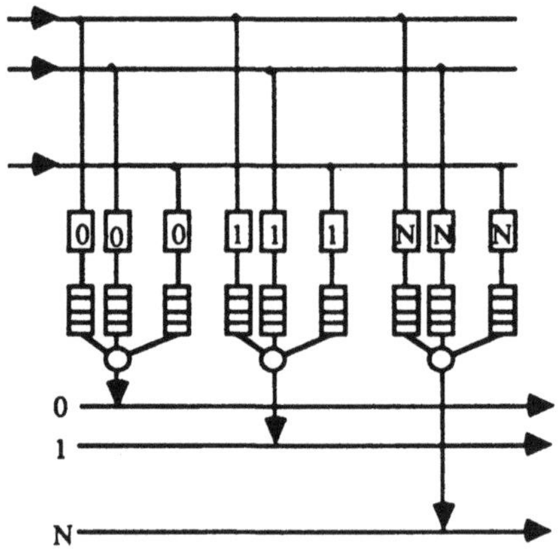

Figure 6 N^2 Switch with Output Buffering

In terms of delay and packet loss this switch performs better than the banyan switch with output buffered elements. The main drawback is the quadratic dependence of the number of buffers on the switch size N which makes modular extension difficult.

3.3.2 The Knockout Switch

The *knockout switch* [Yeh, 1987] avoids the problem of quadratic growth of the number of parallel output buffers at the expense of some small additional packet loss. It is essentially a single stage N^2 switch with a constant number L of parallel buffers at each output. The name is due to the fact that packets with the same address compete in a knockout tournament for access the L parallel buffers. The losers are discarded to reduce the number of contenders to L. If $i \leq L$, all i packets are winners. The switch operates in cycles. All packets present at the input when a cycle begins are processed during that cycle. The winners of the knockout tournament are passed through a shifting network so that storage of packets in the parallel buffers of each output port takes place cyclically, ensuring even occupation of the buffers and thus reducing the probability of buffer overflow.

The inventors [Yeh, 1987] of the knockout switch claim that an increase of N, the number of input ports, provided that the packet addresses are uniformly and randomly distributed, leaves almost constant the probability of the arrival of more than L contending for the same output during one cycle. The theoretical analysis in [Yeh, 1987] shows that packet loss due to the knockout mechanism remains below 10^{-6} for $L = 8$ and a load factor of 90%, even if $N \rightarrow \infty$.

3.4 Switch Performance

Large buffer delay and relatively high packet loss rates effectively rule out switches with pure input buffering. The queues are long and the mutual blocking at the head of the queue leads to the onset of congestion at a load factor as low as 58% [Hluchyj, 1988]. Congestion is usually described as the uncontrolled growth of a queue when the packet arrival rate exceeds the server rate.

Simulation studies of the banyan switch, the simple N^2 switch and the knockout switch have shown that the simple N^2 switch with pure output buffering performs best. This is no surprise because internal contention in multiple stage fabrics occurs in addition to output contention. The knockout switch also performs well if the number of buffers per port is large enough. The packet loss in the banyan switch with output buffered elements is about 5 times higher than in the corresponding single stage switch fabrics at the same load factors. However, it does have the advantage that it permits simple modular extension.

3.4.1 Packet Loss

Some packet loss can be tolerated in telephony and, depending on the coding algorithm, also in video communication. Digital telephony uses a sample rate of 8 kHz and 8 bit encoding. If one assumes the data field of packets to be 60 octets long (CCITT Study Group 18), then the loss of one packet corresponds to the loss of 60×125 μs = 7.5 ms of audio signal, provided that the gap is not closed. An investigation of the effect of packet loss on the quality of transmission [Seneviratne, 1987] showed that the substitution of pink noise is preferable to simply leaving a silent gap which would come across as a short sharp clicking sound.

The packet loss probabilities as determined by a simulation study of four different switch fabrics are shown in Table 1. For each type of switch and each load factor there were 10 simulation runs of 10^6 packet arrivals each.

load factor	60%	70%	80%	90%
SW1	2×10^{-7}	5×10^{-6}	2×10^{-4}	4×10^{-3}
SW2	0	9×10^{-7}	2×10^{-5}	5×10^{-4}
SW3	0	0	0	0
SW4	0	0	7×10^{-7}	1.8×10^{-5} (± 1.1)

Table 1 Packet Loss Probabilities

The numbers shown are the averages computed from the ten runs. The packet arrivals were derived from the exponential distribution but were pre-processed by a queue so that no two packets could arrive within one packet length of each other. This is more realistic than a pure exponential process as it takes into account that the packets have already passed through other queueing networks. SW1 is the output buffered banyan switch, SW2 the N^2 switch with the same total buffer capacity, SW3 the same as SW2 but with cyclic parallel access to one buffer per output channel (as in the knockout switch), and SW4 the knockout switch with $L = 8$ parallel buffers per output. The size of all switches was $N = 16$. In the knockout switch the combined loss due to buffer overflow (which takes over at 90 % load) and to the knockout mechanism is listed. Each time the number of parallel buffers of the knockout switch is decreased by one, the packet loss due to knockout increases by about one order of magnitude.

3.4.2 Packet Delay

The buffering delay in fast packet switches is proportional to the packet length (in time units) and inversely proportional to the band width. At an assumed band width of 1 Gbit/s and a packet length of about 0.5 kbit (60 octets plus address field) the buffering delay is small enough compared to the propagation delay on the links to be neglected. In a banyan switch with four stages and output buffering (each packet passes through four buffers) the expectation value of the delay ranged from 1.2 packet lengths at 50% load to 10.9 packet lengths at 90%. The maximum delay observed among 10^7 packets was 69 packet lengths at 90% load. With a band width of 1 Gbit/s and a packets length of 0.5 kbit the largest delay observed was 35 μs. During that time interval the optical signal travels less than 10 km. This was the largest delay observed and it occurred only once in 10^7 packets. Therefore, the buffer delay can be neglected compared with the propagation in wide area networks operating at 1 Gbit/s.

4 Protocols for Fast Packet Switching

The detail of the communication protocol is determined by the performance parameters of fast packet switching networks. A communication between two stations in a connection oriented network consists of three phases:

1. connection establishment,
2. the data transfer phase,
3. connection termination.

Of these the data transfer phase is affected most by changes of the transmission speed. In the connection establishment phase agreement must be reached between the communicating stations about the type of the communication, a path must be selected and permission to use the required band width must be obtained from the network. The network control units maintain information about the current network load, available paths, etc. The connection is refused (blocked) if sufficient resources are not available. When a connection is terminated the network control units must be notified of the freed band width. Certain error recovery procedures are required. The network must be able to recognise an abnormal termination due to some error after which the normal notification of freed band width is not received by the network control.

Any protocol functions to be performed during the data transmission phase must match the transmission speed. How much protocol is required depends on the type of the communication, that is, the sensitivity to errors or to delay. Therefore, these protocols are a matter for the communicating stations. The question is, how much data transmission protocol in the form of error and flow control must be done by the backbone network.

4.1 Data Transmission

The data transmission protocol has the task to ensure safe delivery of messages (packets) across an imperfect network, that is, a network in which errors may occur and in which packets may be lost. In conventional packet switching networks a communication between two stations (hosts) consists of a string of communications on the transmission links which form the selected path. The network uses a *store and forward* mechanism to transport packets from node and on each link flow and error control procedures are in operation. Each node holds arriving packets in a transmission queue until the appropriate outgoing link is available and until save receipt of the transmitted packet has been confirmed. It is clear that these protocol functions require too much processing power and buffer space to remain viable in fast packet switching.

Flow control is indispensable in conventional packet switching protocol for two main reasons: (1) the backbone operates at relatively low link capacities and could easily be overrun by local networks on the perimeter; (2) the server rate may vary between nodes because different node processors may have to service different numbers of virtual routes. The transmission speed is limited by the link speed, the complexity of the required protocol and the processor speed. A vast increase of the link speed to about 1 Gbit/s has two consequences:

1. The quotient a of propagation delay on the link and the packet length changes from $a < 1$ (as in conventional packet switching networks) to at least 10^3 in fast packet switching, assuming a packet size of about 10^3 bits and a link of 250 km length. One thousand packets may be in transit on the link at any time and another one thousand may be transmitted during the time it takes for an acknowledgement to travel in the opposite direction. This means that buffering for at least two million bits must be provided in the nodes per link for the purpose of conventional flow and error control protocols.
2. The available processors are much too slow to be able to perform the necessary processing of individual packets.

4.1.1 Error Control

The network must deal with transmission errors and with packet loss due to buffer overflow. Transmission errors could in principle be handled by forward error correction, i.e. the inclusion of error correcting codes in the packets so that they can be corrected at the receiving end, provided that the error rate is not too high. This may be preferable to requesting the re-transmission of faulty packets which would result in a substantial loss of throughput, particularly as $a \gg 1$. However, a re-transmission mechanism is necessary in any case to deal with packet loss and one may argue that forward error correction together with the re-transmission of packets would be wasteful.

Optical fibre links are insensitive to electro magnetic interference and very low bit error rates between 10^{-11} and 10^{-9} have been reported for single mode optical fibre links of 50 km length [Heidemann, 1988]. This is at least three orders of magnitude lower than the error rate of good quality electrical transmission lines. Assuming a packet length of 10^3 bits, only one in 10^8 to 10^6 packets will contain a bit error on the average. Since a link may be an order of magnitude longer than the distance between repeaters, one can expect 10^{-7} to 10^{-5} packet errors per pair of nodes. If a path across the backbone has 10 links, there will be 10^{-4} faulty packets end-to-end at the worst. The probability of transmission errors is constant and determined by the quality of the hardware, but the probability of packet loss can be controlled by band width allocation. Thus it is possible to limit the packet loss rate to the rate of faulty packets due to transmission errors.

To some extent, the telephony and video services can tolerate packet errors and packet loss. The tolerance of these services to packet loss and error has been investigated by some authors and the results show that surprisingly high packet loss rates can be tolerated. In 64 kbit/s telephony a bit error rate of 10^{-7} would result in the generation of one short crackling sound every two and a half minutes. The loss of packets in telephony can be handled in a variety of ways, see for instance [Seneviratne, 1987]. In video communication the tolerance to packet loss depends on the decoding algorithm. The investigation reported in [Crosthwaite, 1988] shows that video communication, like telephony, can tolerate packet loss rate much higher than we estimated in the previous paragraph.

There remains the question of what to do in the case of address errors. The address field is only a small part of the whole packet and the probability of address errors is correspondingly smaller than the probability of packet errors generally. A packet with a faulty address may either be sent to an inactive station (where it can do no harm), or it may stray into another communication. Since the packet address is removed during the passage through the backbone network and wrongly routed packets cannot be recognised by the backbone and this must be done in the application specific protocol. The data field of the packet transmitted across the backbone still contains an address field to be used by the local distribution network. Because the switch fabric will probably have to operate with 16 or 32 bits in parallel, one can use one of the well-known parallel error recognition and correction methods imlemented in hardware. In a 16 bit address field up to two simultaneous errors can be recognized and corrected with the aid of a check word of 6 bits.such chips have been available commercially for a number of years.

4.1.2 Flow Control

The main purpose of flow control is to provide speed matching between transmitter and receiver. The mechanism of band width allocation in the fast packet switching backbone network ensures that no receiving node can be overrun by too much traffic from another node upstream or by a local area network on the perimeter. That leaves end-to-end flow control the prerogative of individual communications and perhaps of communicating local area networks.

In telephony on a packet switched network one must ensure that the next packet is ready when decoding of the previous one has finished. A small number of voice packets can be buffered before the decoder is started in order to cover the delay fluctuation across the network. If the clock of the receiver is a little too fast the buffer will eventually run out of packets and a short gap must be left or a dummy packet inserted until there are again enough packets in the receiving buffer. On the other hand, a slower receiver will eventually have its buffer overflow and lose a packet. In this way a speed mismatch between transmitter and receiver can easily be handled [Bradlow, 1988] without serious loss of transmission quality.

If other types of communication like file transfer an end-to-end flow control mechanism may be necessary. Because of its substantially higher band width the backbone network is completely transparent and the detail of the flow control protocol depends entirely on the requirements of the communicating stations. At the end points of a communication path the quotient of propagation delay over packet length may still be significantly greater than one despite the lower transmission speed after de-multiplexing, rendering conventional flow control protocols unsuitable. For such situations in high speed networks a dynamic window flow control mechanism with selective re-transmission of packets has been proposed [Bux, 1988].

4.1.3 Service Classes and Discard Priorities

Because occasional packet loss during transitory overload appears to be inevitable, it has been proposed by several authors to use a selective discard mechanism which ensures that only those packets are discarded which belong to loss insensitive services or which have low priority. These ideas were first discussed in the context of token rings and similar local area networks for integrated services, but they are not suitable for the type of wide area backbone network discussed here. The only viable mechanism for congestion control in the backbone network is a tight band width allocation strategy in the connection establishment protocol.

4.2 Resource Allocation

Since there can be no link-by-link flow control in the backbone the control of network resources must take place during the call establishment phase as it is done in circuit switched networks. The difference is that the actual band width used by individual communications in packet switched networks is not fixed and the possibility exists to use some of the band width which would otherwise be wasted in circuit switching. The aim of band width allocation schemes would be to utilise the network optimally and one would therefore try to *oversell* the network's band width as measured against the sum of all maximum band width requirements.

The band width requirement of a communication must be specified by at least two measures, the *average* and the *maximum* band width. Allocation of the maximum requested band width for the duration of the call would be wasteful as is demonstrated by the example of telephone traffic where the average line utilization is clearly below 50% [Brady, 1968]. Some communications may have a low average band width with very short occasional bursts of high band width. This problem has been addressed by several authors, see [Hui, 1988] and [Pattavina, 1988], for example. One proposal is to allocate band width on the basis of the *average* requirement and seek special permission to transmit bursts of higher band width. While this appears reasonable at first sight in certain types of network, it is hardly feasible in large backbone networks where the control is distributed over many nodes which would have to be notified of such short term changes.

The situation is problematic only when the total band width of a link in the network can be exhausted by very few (say, two or three) individual communications. In that situation the coincidence of bursts may cause temporary overload and result in excessive packet loss. If, on the other hand, the band width of the network is much larger than the requirement of individual communications, statistical multiplexing works much better. The fluctuations due to bursts are easily absorbed by the margin of band width that is kept in reserve to safeguard against congestion. Consider a backbone network with a link band width of 1 Gbit/s in which the strategy is to allocate up to 80% of the transmission capacity on the basis of average band width requirements. That leaves 200 Mbit/s for short term fluctuations. Compressed full motion video, assuming 30 frames per second and 250000 pixels per frame has 5 Mbit/s average and 10 Mbit/s peak bit rate. A total of 160 video communications could be allocated on the basis of their average band width requirement. It would require a coincidence of 40 band width maxima at a time in which no minima occur in the remaining communications to overload the network.

Little is known about the variability of the band width in different types of communication. One can expect the detail to depend, as in the example of compressed video, on the encoding algorithm, and on other aspects of more complex communications like multi-media conferences in which voice, data files and graphics in some form are transmitted and updated in real time. New encoding algorithms are under development and the average band width requirements and fluctuation are impossible to predict. Ultimately, the solution will require experimentation as well as theoretical investigation.

5 Conclusion

In the recent past many different networks have developed independently, originally without regard for communication between them. Different network architectures and operational modes developed more or less independent of each other. The need for inter-connection is now generally recognised and a variety of bridges, gateways and inter-network communication protocols have been developed. In parallel to this another development took place which resulted in the recent introduction of the integrated services digital network. We have argued that the integration and unification of these different communication media and of the services offered on them can be carried out by means of fast packet switching.

The structural and operational properties of a fast packet switching network are determined by the performance of the switches which form the network nodes. In Sections 2 and 3 we discussed the design and performance of several switch designs. Simplicity of switch operation is a necessary prerequisite for the construction of a backbone network with sufficient capacity to be able to carry the communication load that can be expected to result from the introduction of multi-service terminal equipment.

The introduction of a packet switched backbone network of high transmission capacity poses entirely new problems for the design of communication protocols and a discussion of the associated problems was given in Section 4 where it was argued that optical transmission equipment with its very low bit error rates and high transmission speed makes it possible to omit flow and error control from the backbone links and leave these protocol functions to the terminal equipment at the ends of communication paths. An additional argument in favour of this comes from the fact that different services require different levels of freedom from errors and pose different constraints on the rate of traffic flow.

The absence of flow control mechanisms from the backbone network makes it necessary to exercise tight control over the allocation of band width. This is an area of active research as it is not yet clear what types of communication services will be offered in the future, what their band width requirements will be and how much the average and peak data rates can be permitted to differ.

Fast packet switching is potentially the principal agent for the integration of different communication services on one homogeneous network and the acceptance of asynchronous transfer mode as the basis for future developments of B-ISDN can be seen as the first step in that direction.

Literature

Anido, G. and Seeto, A., 'Multi-path routing techniques of multi-stage fast packet switches', *1988 International Zürich Seminar on digital Communications*, IEEE catalog no. 88TH0202-2.

Batcher, K.E., 'Sorting networks and their applications', *AFIPS Conf. Proc.*, 1968 Spring joint Computer Conference, 307-13

Benes, V., *Mathematical theory of connecting networks*, Academic Press, N.Y., 1965

Bradlow, H., 'The design of an integrated voice/data terminal and voice trasnport protocol', *3rd ATERB FPS Workshop*, Melbourne, May 19-20 1988

Brady, P.T., 'A statistical analysis of on-off patterns of speech', *Bell Syst. Tech. J.*, vol. 44 (Jan. 1968)

Brooks, E.D. (III), 'A butterfly processor-memory interconnection for a vector processing environment', *Parallel Computing*, vol. 4 (1987) 103 - 110

Bux, W., 'Protocols for high speed communication', *European Telecommunications Workshop*, Montpellier, France, September 1988

Crosthwaite, P., 'Fast packet video', *Third ATERB FPS Workshop*, Melbourne, 19-20 May 1988

Feng, Tsu-yun, 'A survey of interconnection networks', *IEEE Computer* (Dec 1981) 1-27

Heidemann, R., 'Investigations of the dominant dispersion penalties occurring in multigigabit direct detection systems', *J. Lightwave Technol.*, vol. 6, no. 11, Nov. 1988, 1693-7

Hluchyj, M.G. and Karol, M.J., 'Queueing in high-performance packet switching', *IEEE Journal on selected areas in communications*, vol. 6, no. 9 (Dec 1988) 1587-97

Huang, A. and Knauer, S., 'Starlite: a wide band digital switch', *IEEE Global Telecommunications Conference (GLOBECOM '84)* November 1984, pp. 121 - 125

Hui, Joseph Y. and E. Arthurs, 'A broadband packet switch for integrated transport', *IEEE Journal on selected areas in communications*, SAC-5, 1987, no. 8, 1264 - 73

Hui, Joseph Y., 'resource allocation for broadband networks', *IEEE Journal on selected areas in communications* vol. 6, 1988, no. 9, 1598 - 1608

Newman, P., 'A fast packet switch for the integrated services backbone network', *IEEE Journal on Selected Areas in Communication*, vol. 6, no. 9, December 1988, 1468-79

O'Neill, C., Palmer, R., Tirtaatmadja, E.,, 'The application of multistage interconnection networks to fast packet switching', *private communication* (1988)

Palmer, R., 'Some fast packet switching architectures using sorting networks', *Fast Packet Switching Workshop, Telecom Research Laboratories*, Melbourne, May 1987

Pattavina, A.P., 'Multichannel bandwidth allocation in a broadband packet switch', *IEEE Journal for Selected Areas in Communication*, vol 6, no. 9, December 1988

Seneviratne, A., 'Factors influencing the quality of packet voice', *Fast Packet Switching Workshop, Telecom Research Laboratories*, Melbourne, May 1987

Turner, J., 'Design of an integrated services packet network', *IEEE Journal on selected areas in communications*, SAC-4 (1986) 1373-9

Uematsu, H. and Watanabe, R., 'Architecture of a packet switch based on banynan switching network with feedback loops', *IEEE Journal on selected areas in communications* vol. 6, no. 9, December 1986, 1521-7

Yeh, Y.S., Hluchyj, M.G., Acampora, A.S., 'The knockout switch: a simple modular architecture for high performance packet switching', *IEEE Journal an Selected Areas in Communication*, vol. 6, no. 9, December 1988, 1274-83

SOLVING SELECTED R & D PROBLEMS BY LEARNING FROM EXAMPLES

Z.S. Hippe, A. Kerste and M.Mazur -

Department of Physical & Computer Chemistry,
Technical University, 31-041 Rzeszow, Poland

Abstract. Some selected problems of machine learning have been briefly discussed, as a background for broader presentation of a new concept in learning from examples. Basically, the model presented constitutes of logical connections of the following type:

Cause A and Cause B gives Result C

being an example of a solution to a given problem. Such examples have been used as a convenient mechanism of knowledge representation in recently developed in our group family of expert systems. One of them (SCANMIX) is discussed here with some details. The model presented has been successfully implemented to solve some real-world problems of surprisingly different domains, like: battle management, materials engineering, metallurgy, mineralogy, rubber industry, optimization of various industrial processes and technologies, etc.

The practical application of some basic c o n c e p t s of artificial intelligence (AI), creates increasingly growing interest. Among them, the idea of expert systems technology plays an important role in development of many useful applications, giving for the first time impressive outcomes and real commercial successes for this part of computer science [1]. Beyond doubt, expert systems (further called ES) present the new approach to the problem-solving in many domains of science, industry and management [2-4].

A thorough analysis of the accessible literature has shown that recently various professional programming tools are available and some new are rapidly emerging, to support automatic design of expert systems and knowledge bases. A brief summary of these tools (for microcomputers) is shown in Fig. 1. In the lowest level, we have various computer languages (usually compiled), and some special utilities called here tool-boxes, for example computer gra-

L A N G U A G E S

AND T O O L S

FOR EXPERT SYSTEMS

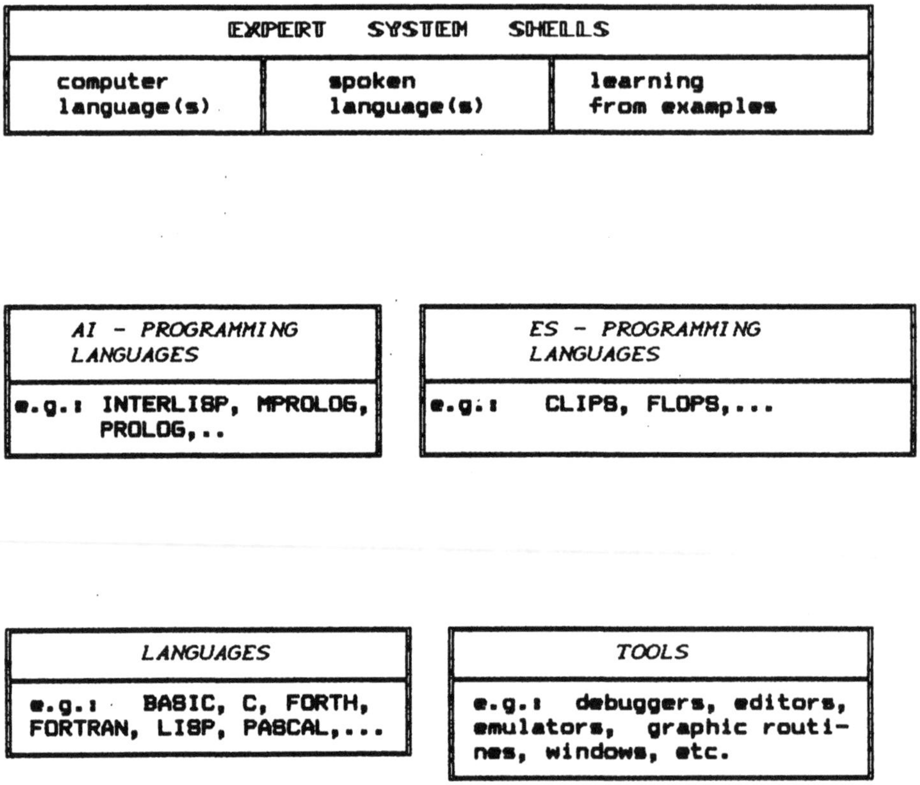

Fig.1 Tools for designing expert systems (see explanation in the text).

phics, intelligent editors, terminal emulators, debuggers, code analyzers and optimizers, windowing routines, etc.

More elaborated seems to be the collection of AI-languages and specialized ES-languages: the latter address directly the automatic design of expert systems. Tools of the lowest and medium levels are used for designing of dedicated expert systems (suitable to solve problems in one domain only), and also - for development of expert system shells (upper level). An expert system shell is a software package that distinctly simplifies the effort involved in building an expert system. The architecture of these tools and their action have been described elsewhere [5]. Here, it is just to notice, that the concept of shells has the great impact on the broad acceptance of the expert system technology. Having properly designed expert system shell, one can create a prototype of a decision support system or an expert system rapidly, and inexpensively, because the design is restricted to the development of the knowledge base only. The methodology of creating the knowledge base itself, constitutes the main point of expert system technology: procedures used here (for capturing knowledge and/or expertise), determine the scope of automatic design of expert systems, in any domain. Let us focus for a while the attention on the composition of a knowledge base.

According to the latest view in this respect [6], the knowledge base should consist of five distinct parts: text base, data base, rule base, model base, and common sense base.

Text base - is not structured, built using open vocabulary. It stores general knowledge about the domain. The aim of the text base is to display questions, messages and comments on the monitor screen during the consultation. The action of the text base may be probabilistic what means, that in some cases various outputs may be obtained for the s a m e or similar inputs);

Data base - is structured; it stores specific knowledge about the domain (numeric data: parameters, coefficients and also functions or equations). Information retrieved is always stylized. The data base operates deterministically;

Rule base – here, a special formalism of knowledge representation in the form of so called production rules, is meant. The first part of a rule (between the keywords IF .. THEN), contains a list of logical conditions, that must be fulfilled (with a given confidence level) to conclude a hypothesis (X, Y, ..) or to undertake a given action, both enumerated in the second part of the rule (after THEN....). The rule base may contain n production rules (where n should not exceed 10000; practical size of the base is usually maintained in the region <50, 2000> [7]). The formalism presented permits rather simple updating of knowledge in the base, or even some operations on the production rules, like their generation, specification, combination, or generalization. The knowledge representation discussed describes a basic fact (or event) as:

a triplet O-A-V (object-attribute-value), or

a pair A-V (attribute-value).

Other methods of knowledge representation are also used in expert system technology, for example frames, semantic networks or some special logic structures. However, a thorough overview of accessible literature pointed out, that about 85% of shells available use production rules formalism for knowledge representation, whereas only in 13% frames are applied.

Model base – contains the full or partial model (models) of the domain, provided such model was correctly formulated. Thus, this part of the knowledge base may influence distinctly the q u a l i t y of solutions offered by the expert system. In presence of the model base, the results (conclusions, hypotheses) might even constitute a discovery, or unprecedented knowledge. When the model base is missing the system is able only to reproduce the knowledge stored in the base, having no capacity to create anything new.

Common sense base - is considered as an indispensable part of future expert systems. According to [8], the first American expert system to have a common sense base as a part of the knowledge base, will be released in the 1992-1994 time limit. It seems, the common sense may be displayed (to some extent) by systems with knowledge base built from examples, supplied by a human expert.

There are some different methodologies used to design knowledge bases for expert systems, comprehensively covered in the literature, e.g. in [7]. We will focus our attention on a very special methodology in which the automation of creating the knowledge base relies on the transfer of information hidden in data into a decision tree, using the process of machine learning. How we can describe generally that process? To give an idea of what's involved in modeling learning with computers, let us examine very briefly just what learning is. According to [9], a dictionary definition of learning is the process of acquiring skill or knowledge, whereas in psychology is the modification of behavior through training. Various types of learning have been described, for example rote learning, learning by being told, learning by analogy, learning from examples, and learning from discovery [10].

In rote learning, as a matter of fact, the computer makes no special effort to learn. This type of learning does not involve inference. Simply, it is the storing of knowledge, and - as a secondary process - the retrieval of knowledge when it is required.

In learning by being told (or learning by instruction) the general knowledge is modified and then stored in the form of machine recognizable rules for further induction or deduction, and for applying these rules to generate new patterns.

Learning by analogy relies on acquiring new knowledge to represent a pattern in a way successfully used in the past. Here, the knowledge given to the computer may not be necessarily directly relevant, and the machine must hypothesize analogous cases to assist in solving the problem at hand.

Learning from examples (known also as learning with a teacher, or supervised learning), is based on knowing the class membership of patterns. Patterns known to be assigned to a given class, are then used to learn about the model of the class. In other words, that type of learning can be seen as a task of developing a classification rule (or tree) from several examples of proper membership in the investigated class.

Learning from discovery (without a teacher) seems to be a step forward on the way of machine learning. It was shown, that a necessary and sufficient condition to learn from discovery is that a certain amount of a priori knowledge is required, and that the classes be linearly independent. Hence, rules used to learn by discovery must impose such a priori knowledge on the problem.

Recently, a modification of learning process from examples has been developed in our group. For any object regarded, a connection is created that exhibits logical relations between sets of parameters describing important features of a n y technological process, in various domains of science and technology. An example of that connection is given below:

mixture (physical or chemical) of materials	->	steering parameters of the process	->	properties of a given product
[A]		[B]		[C]

Thus, the connection constitutes a convenient formalism to describe precisely divergent technological processes, for example in material engineering, rubber or polymer industry, glass industry, metallurgy, etc. Using the example of rubber industry, we may say that a given mixture of selected elastomers, plasticizers, carbon black, sulfur, antioxidants, fillers, and so on, [box A], described by means of selected attributes, treated in a given way (described by another set of attributes, say: type of the vulcanization machine, pressure, temperature, time, etc., [box B]), yields the specific type of product (rubber), [box C], displaying strictly defined properties (attributes), like Young module, shear resistance, elasticity, stiffness, etc.

It is to emphasize the generality of the elaborated model. For example, the same type of connection (A + B --> C) may be used to describe other problems, met e.g. in environmental protection, or in exploitation of a mineral resources, for example sulfur. Here, attributes in the box [A] may constitute important descriptors of the deposit: its composition, sulfur content, level of water table, etc. In the box [B] we insert such attributes as the depth of melting site, diameter of melting pipes, temperature and pressure of the technological (overheated) water, pressure of air, and so on. Finally, the product (sulfur) may be described by various parameters, like color (expressed numerically), melting point, density, type of the unit cell, together with some attributes of the well itself, say its yield and registered downtime.

The discussed formalism may be treated as a relation of the cause-result type:

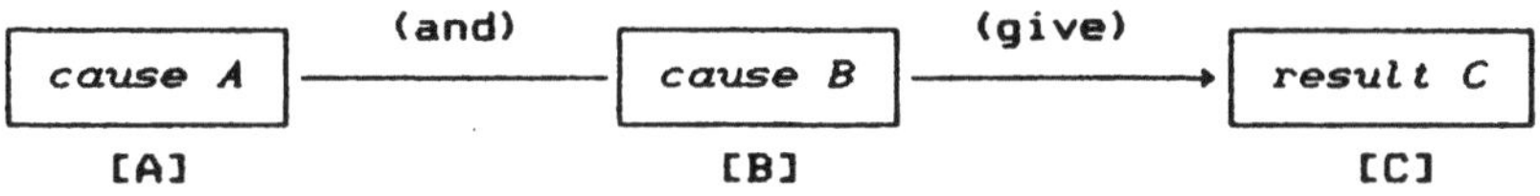

Only the user's experience and intelligence determine which attributes should be placed in the box A, B and C, respectively. Usually, in the box C the attributes describing the main goal(s) of the optimization process, should be located. On the other hand splitting of attributes among the boxes A and B (causes, generally), do not play any role. We may, for example, more all attributes from the box B to the box A, what yields the one-step association (with the logical product):

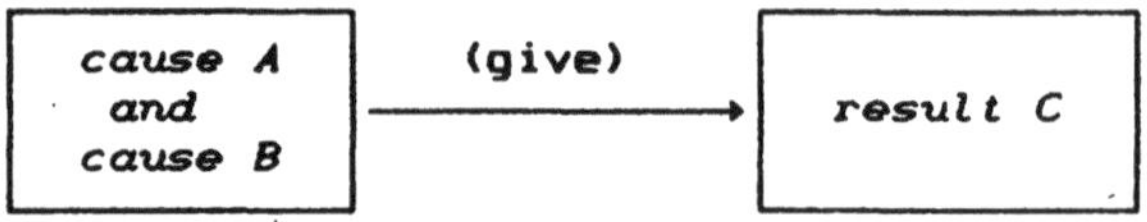

An ordering effect is clearly seen here, if - without the change of attributes values in the box A - we will change the attributes (exactly speaking, their values) in the box B. That situation is represented by the following association:

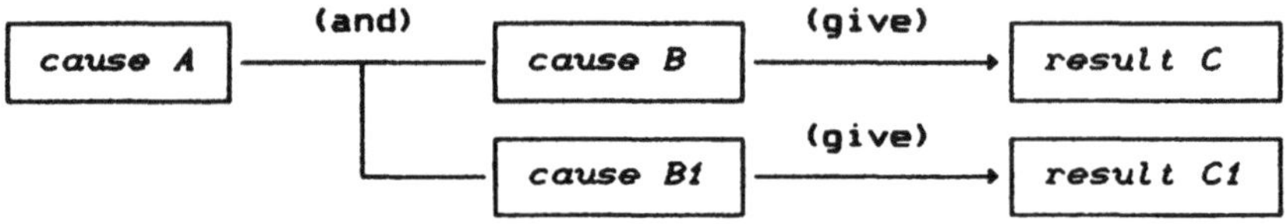

The example shown might be easily converted to two one-step associations:

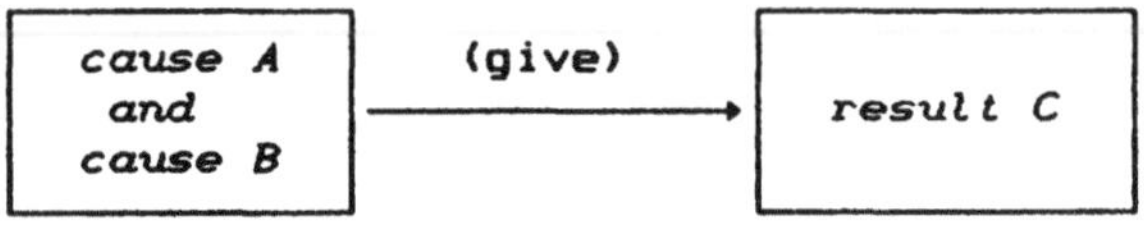

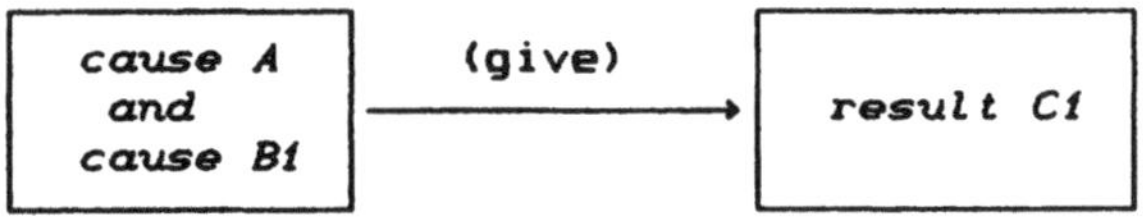

The model presented has been successfully implemented in expert system SCANMIX, designed in our group. Existing knowledge bases of the system serve to solve some real-world problems. In a given base, each record may contain up to 300 attributes, creating in this way an <u>example</u>: a set of relevant examples constitutes the body of a knowledge base. Some stand-alone utility programs have been designed to <u>learn</u> from these examples, hence the concept of the connection may be effectively used for classification of the unknown processes (not used for the construction of the knowledge base).

Some advanced features of the expert system SCANMIX should be briefly discussed. First, a very user-friendly menu-driven module (named DBM) has been designed for the creation of domain-oriented knowledge bases. Although any knowledge base can be very easy updated or extended, it is always secured by special protection mechanisms, and is treated as "untouchable" repository of knowledge and information about technological processes in a given environment.

A separate module of utility programs, WFC, is used for the development of so called working file. The file contains compressed and compiled information, extracted automatically from a given knowledge base. The formal structure of the working file is presented below:

<u>domain X (working file)</u>

	attribute 1	attribute 2	....	attribute 300
association 1	value 1,1	value 1,2	....	value 1,300
association 2	value 2,1	value 2,2	....	value 2,300
.	.	.		.
.	.	.		.
.	.	.		.
association N	value N,1	value N,2	....	value N,300

Additionally, the WFC module executes some useful operations, giving better insight into the data structure.For example, means, variances and alteration coefficients for the data set are automatically (column by column) computed; also, the strictly correlated attributes (for the entire array of data) can be sought. Thus, the redundancy hidden in data may easily be discovered.

The working file may then be used directly in learning process, using a modified K-nearest-neighbor method [11], or fast linear learning machine [12]. In that case, however, the working file may be adjusted by another stand-alone module, WFA, <u>before</u> the learning. The WFA module causes profound changes of data structure in the working file, enabling much more effective learning. Besides, this module executes some very powerful mathematical and statistical procedures, like data transform by means of selected math functions, autoscaling, calculation of weights, etc. Applying the enumerated operations, the learning process may be interactively improved by a knowledgeable user.

Particularly, the expert system SCANMIX may be used to solve the following questions:

1. (forward chaining)

   given:
   mixture composition and parameters of the process

   taxonomy:
   what type of product will be obtained, in sense of its properties?

or

2. (backward chaining)

   given:
   required product with specified properties

   prediction:
   how we should formulate the mixture (components and their concentration), and how parameters of the technological process should be settled?

It was found, that in both directions (forward and reverse) SCANMIX supplies optimal solutions. This approach seems to be very useful in such fields, where reliable mathematical model(s) do not exist or may not be elaborated, owing the inherent complexity of the problem being solved (huge size of the solution space, or its very large dimensionality). The strategy described is effective, provided that do not exist two (or more) examples having exactly the same values of all attributes, but belonging to different categories. In this very case it is assumed, that the list of attributes (used to describe the relations in the base) is not sufficient to perform the classification (or prediction).

References

[1] W.B. Gevarter: Artificial Intelligence - Expert Systems, Computer Vision, and Natural Language Processing, Noyes Publications, Park Ridge 1984

[2] R. Forsyth (Ed.): Expert Systems. Principles and Case Studies, Chapman & Hall, London 1984

[3] Z.S. Hippe: Proc. Int. Conf. "Analytiktreffen 88", Neubrandenburg (in printing)

[4] N.J. Nilsson: Principles of Artificial Intelligence, Tioga Publ. Comp., Palo Alto 1980

[5] Z.S. Hippe: Artificial Intelligence in Chemistry: Structure Elucidation and Syntheses Design, Elsevier/PWN, (in printing)

[6] R.K. Belev, in: L.B. Methlie, R.H. Spraque (Eds.): Knowledge Representation in Decision Support Systems, Elsevier, Amsterdam 1985

[7] F. Hayes-Roth, D.A. Waterman, D.B. Lenat: Building Expert Systems, Addison-Wesley Publ. Comp., Don Mills 1983

[8] D.B. Lenat: 2nd Artificial Intelligence Satellite Symposium (Texas Instruments Inc.), June 1986

[9] R.S. Michalski, in: R.S. Michalski, J.G. Carbonell, T.M. Mitchell (Eds.): Machine Learning II, M. Kaufmann, Los Altos 1986

[10] A.T. Kolokouris: Machine Learning, Byte 11: 225-231, 1986

[11] Z.S. Hippe, A. Kerste, M.Mazur: Res. Report, TU Rzeszow, 1985

[12] Z.S. Hippe, A. Kerste, M.Mazur: Res. Report, TU Rzeszow, 1987

A Knowledge Based Program Understanding for An Intelligent Programming Environment for Novice Programmers

Haruki Ueno
Department of Systems Engineering
Tokyo Denki University
Hatoyama, Saitama 350-03
Japan

This paper discusses the concept and techniques of the ALPUS system which is an algorithm-based program understander, and its application to the INTELLITUTOR system which is a knowledge-based programming environment for novice programmers. INTELLITUTOR attempts to work as a human programming tutor to guide a user, i.e., a student, who is trying to write programs, to detect logical errors, and to make an advice not only for fixing them but also for letting him notice his misunderstandings. These intelligent functions are achieved by a knowledge-based program comprehension ability of the ALPUS system. The key knowledge used to understand user's programs is represented in a form of hierarchical graph called Hierarchical Procedure Graph-(HPG). HPG is an abstract representation of knowledge about an algorithm. In addition, the system attempts to work as an intelligent CAI system for programming education by combining these functions and computerized manuals attached with some teaching strategies. It should be stressed that the knowledge represented in the HPG graph is shared for multiple purposes in the system, and that the HPG-based knowledge representation is one of the candidates for deep knowledge representations, and that the way of program comprehension by means of the HPG graph is a kind of model-based reasoning. This paper discusses concepts and the outline of the system, and relatively detail methodologies for program comprehension and its application to logical error detections. Although the experimental system is handling PASCAL programs most knowledge included is applicable to other programming languages. The system is implemented in the knowledge engineering environment ZERO on a LISP machine.

1. INTRODUCTION

Artificial intelligence technologies have been applied to a variety of domains and have demonstrated interesting functions. Although most trials are still on a research and prototyping stage[16], the new technologies brought us innovations for, especially, man-machine environments. A knowledge-based intelligent programming environment must be one of the most attractive and useful applications of AI concepts and technologies[1]. By an intelligent programming environment we mean that a computer comprehends user's intentions from texts entered by him through an interactive terminal device, makes advices for fixing errors included, not only for syntactic errors but also for semantic ones, and helps him program more comfortably. These intelligent functions can only be achieved by a knowledge-based approach, i.e., an AI technology. It should be stressed that this kind of interactive programming environments should include an intelligent CAI system as a subsystem. This means also that this kind of systems should be useful for an intelligent CAI system for novice programmers.

The key issue in realizing knowledge-based intelligent programming environments is that the system has the ability of program comprehension. Advanced programmers can understand semantics of computer programs, detect logical errors, guess programmer's intentions from erroneous programs, and fix these errors. An intelligent programming assistant system is required to have these abilities. Knowledge about topics, algorithms, coding techniques and programming languages play a key role in this kind of situation. Several approaches for program comprehensions have been tried. In PROUST[3] programming plans and discourse rules are applied. A graph model, called 'program model', is used in LAURA[7]. In PA[ref] programming plans are employed. The plan in PROUST is, however, different from the one in PA. The program comprehension applied to PROUST is based on the concept of cognitive psychology. In PA a formal model is intended rather than the cognitive psychology oriented model. In INTELLITUTOR the knowledge about algorithms plays a key role, and the knowledge about plans supports it. A cognitive modeling approach is also applied.

The key knowledge used to understand user's programs is represented in a form of hierarchical graph called Hierarchical Procedure Graph(HPG). HPG is an abstract representation of knowledge about an algorithm. It should be stressed that the HPG graph represents a semantic structure of a program, while a flowchart represents just a sequence of operations. Therefore the knowledge represented in the graph is shared between multiple purposes in the system, i.e., as a program template to guide user's programming, for program comprehensions, and for program teaching. For this reason the HPG-based knowledge representation is one of the candidates for deep knowledge representations[13], and its method of program comprehension is a kind of model-based reasoning which is much more flexible and powerful than rule-based reasoning used in ordinary knowledge-based systems. The key concept in the INTELLITUTOR system is a cognitive psychology-based design. By this concept we mean that a computerized system can understand user's intentions from erroneous program texts entered by the user in an interactive situation just as an advanced programmer or tutor can.

In this paper we discuss the concept and techniques of the program understanding system ALPUS and its application to INTELLITUTOR, the knowledge-based intelligent programming environment for novice programmers. INTELLITUTOR attempts to work like a human programming tutor, with its intelligent functions being achieved by a knowledge -based program comprehension ability of the ALPUS system.

The system is written in a frame-based knowledge representation language ZERO, which has been developed in our laboratory for developing a variety of AI applications[12], working on a LISP work station for feasibility study.

2 Program Understandings

Program understanding is an important theme both in AI and in knowledge-based software engineering, since "understanding" is in general a major issue in intelligent problem solving. However, few efforts have been tried on program understandings, in contrast to the amount of work done on automatic program generations and mathematical program verifications. It is easy to understand that program comprehension plays a key role in most phases of program development if one watches the actions of an expert programmer. Expert programmers use a variety of programming knowledge both in writing and reading programs. This knowledge may be divided into several abstract levels, and has some semantic structures. Program comprehension may also be divided into several levels of abstraction according to the levels and structures of the knowledge, because knowledge and comprehension have strong relationships. In this chapter we discuss the basic idea about meanings(i.e. semantics), understandings, programming knowledge, and knowledge-based program comprehensions.

2.1 Meaning of Program

It may be defined that understanding is the process to reason about the meaning of things. The meaning of things may be represented by means of a data structure, i.e., a cognitive model, of the object. This data structure can be called semantic data structure, or simply semantic structure. Understanding can be achieved by pattern matching of an object to the semantic structure associated with it. Program understanding is similar to natural language understanding, because both of them handle sentences. Yet, there are major differences between them. Natural language sentences are used to express events and situations and therefore include ambiguity, while programming language sentences are used to express the precise procedure of data manipulation and therefore ambiguity is not allowed. In addition, the sequence of sentences is strictly defined in programs, while it is not in natural sentences. The strictness of the sequence of the program sentences comes mainly from the algorithm associated with the problem to be solved.

The meaning of programs might be divided into four semantic levels of hierarchy. For convenience of discussion we call them the basic data handling level, the data processing technique level, the algorithm level, and the data solving notion level, from the bottom to the top of the hierarchy. The semantics of a programming language comes under the basic data handling level. In this level actions and/or effects of commands constitute the semantics. For example, the semantics of the WRITE command is the action of moving the data stored within the main memory to an external file. We focus on the four levels of the programming semantics later in this paper. The semantics of programs has a strong relationship with programming knowledge because the semantics can be extracted by reasoning using the knowledge associated with it as mentioned before. Therefore we should discuss programming knowledge next.

2.2 Programming Knowledge

The meaning of a program can extracted by knowledge-based reasoning. Programming knowledge is used in writing, reading, testing, debugging, and modifying a program. In other words, the quantity and quality of programming knowledge result in programmer's ability in program comprehension. Expert programmers seem to have a large amount of programming knowledge, by which they understand a given program, analyze it, design an algorithm for it, design a program, code it, comprehend it, debug it, and so on.

Programming knowledge is classified into semantic knowledge, and syntactic knowledge. The first one is the knowledge about programming methods, and the second one the knowledge about programming languages. These two classes of knowledge should be independent from each other. The knowledge on programming methods seems to be organized in a four-level hierarchical structure just like the semantics of programs. The knowledge about basic data handling includes value assignment to a variable, comparison between two data, conditional branching and so on. Any complex algorithm can be implemented by proper combinations of the basic data handling commands. The knowledge about data processing techniques consists of such things as techniques in exchanging values between two variables, counting the number of data, and getting the largest value in an array. Programs written by expert programmers are easier to read because they have enough of this type of knowledge and use them in writing programs. It is very impressive that even if a systematic training on coding techniques has not been given to a group of programmers their knowledge about coding techniques becomes similar through long experiences in programming[1,10].

The knowledge about algorithms consists of a set of typical data processing algorithms for basic problems such as an algorithm to compute a product of two arrays and to sort the data stored in an array. Since a unit of knowledge in this level is relatively large, only an abstract framework of an algorithm is stored within the memory, and details are referenced from associated external memories when they are needed. Pointers and related attribute information might be attached for reference. The knowledge about data solving notions is a declarative notion about a typical data solving method such as a notion to compute a product of two arrays, and a notion of sorting a set of data. It should be noted that this is a declarative knowledge, while other three levels of knowledge are procedural. There exist higher level notions which include lower level notions as subnotions. For example we can define a complex problem solving notion such as a notion of file maintenance which includes the notion of sorting a set of data as a subnotion.

It is important that higher level knowledge is more declarative than lower level knowledge, and can be expressed by a set of lower level knowledge. It seems that expert programmers have a much more structured knowledge than novice programmers. From the point of view of program comprehension and their applications to logical error detections, error fixing advices, and intelligent CAI systems for teaching programming knowledge, the knowledge on algorithms and the knowledge on data processing techniques are important. This is the major reason why we have developed the HPG graph formalism to represent programming knowledge and to comprehend programs.

3 Outline of INTELLITUTOR System

INTELLITUTOR attempts to work like a human programming tutor in a situation of a practical programming education. In this situation the human tutor watches the texts on a display screen which is entered by a student to understand his intentions and to detect syntactic and semantic errors. According to these data the tutor gives advices for proper operations and for fixing the errors, and teaches him correct programming knowledge. The INTELLITUTOR system attempts to perform these functions just like a human tutor by watching user s texts behind the screen.

Figure 1 shows an overview of the INTELLITUTOR system. The system consists of four main knowledge bases, three main modules and user interface as in the figure. The knowledge bases consist of the knowledge on syntax which is based on the syntax graph for a Pascal tutor, the knowledge on semantics which is represented in a HPG graph formalism, the knowledge on students which is represented as a student model and the knowledge on teaching methods.

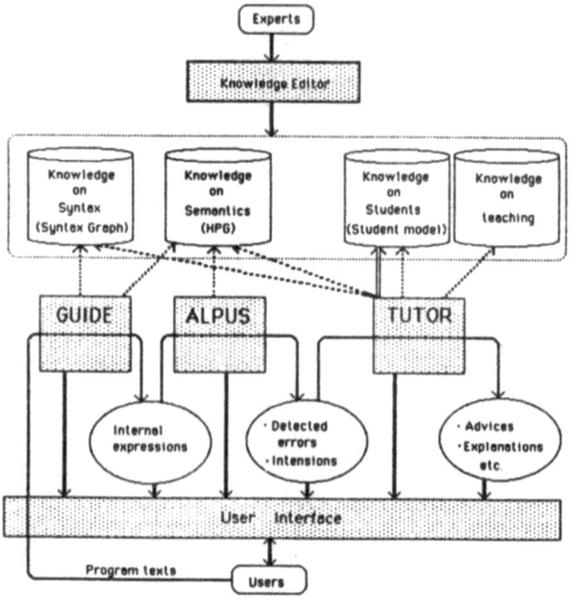

Fig. 1 An overview of the INTELLITUTOR system.

Three major modules, i.e., GUIDE, ALPUS, TUTOR modules, perform intelligent tasks of INTELLITUTOR. The GUIDE module is a knowledge-based guided editor. This subsystem guides and assists a user who is trying to write a program in an interactive environment by using the knowledge on syntax for general usage and the knowledge on semantics, i.e., HPG graphs, for topic-oriented program editing. Source programs entered by the user are converted into an internal representation form which is an input for program comprehension by ALPUS. The ALPUS module includes not only correct knowledge about algorithms and their implementations but also the knowledge on how novice programmers make confusions and mistakes which is necessary to infer user's intentions. The knowledge about mistakes has been obtained by observing novice programmers' programming activities. The TUTOR module is a knowledge based programming CAI system embedded in the INTELLITUTOR system. This module is activated by the system monitor just after the ALPUS module terminates. The TUTOR system receives the detected errors, intentions and advices produced by the ALPUS system, and infers and decides advices and contexts for teaching a user the appropriate knowledge about programming using all the knowledge in the knowledge bases. That is, the knowledge on syntax, the knowledge on semantics, the knowledge on students and the knowledge on teaching methods are referenced according to the contents to be taught. In addition the TUTOR system has its own textbook files for teaching which stores manual-related information in a hierarchy.

4 Algorithm-Based Program Understandings

The central module of the INTELLITUTOR system is the ALPUS module which is an algorithm-based program understanding system. Currently ALPUS receives user's program written in the Pascal language. There are two types of understandings. One is "understanding the thing which one knows before". The other is "understanding the thing which one does not know before". Program understandings done by ALPUS is of the first type. That is, the system is able to understand the semantics of a program written by a user by means of the knowledge about the algorithm which is associated with the program. This is according to the assumption that a human tutor understands a program using his knowledge about the algorithm associated with it. Therefore, the knowledge about algorithms must be represented in a machine readable form.

From the point of view of the semantics in program design and program comprehension, an advanced programmer considers at least major variables and their roles, major operations on the variables and their roles, and a proper sequence of the operations. An identification of the specific role of each variable, of each operation on the variable, and the location of the operation in a program are, therefore, issues in program comprehension by a computer. An algorithm gives a major constraint to these elements, and for this reason we have chosen an algorithm-based program comprehension approach.

4.1 Knowledge Representations in HPG

Knowledge is needed to understand user's programs. ALPUS uses an algorithm-based programming knowledge. This knowledge is represented in a hierarchically structured graph called the HPG graph, Hierarchical Procedure Graph. The HPG graph works as a program template and consists of algorithm-related program attributes such as procedures, variables, statements and structural and semantic relationships among these components. A QUICKSORT program written in the Pascal language is used as an experiment. The QUICKSORT program was chosen because the algorithm was popular and useful in both programming education and business applications, and because the program was not too complex. There are two types of implementations, i.e., recursive procedures and non-recursive procedures. The non-recursive version is understandable for novice programmers. It is, however, not smart and attractive in terms of programming techniques. The recursive version is relatively hard to understand for them, although it should be learned for the sake of advanced techniques.

The QUICKSORT algorithm is an algorithm to sort a random sequence of data which is stored in an array memory by a repetitive division of the sequence. By single division cycle one sequence of data is divided into a smaller value group and a larger value group. The division cycle is applied again and again so that every group member becomes single. The QUICKSORT algorithm gives a procedure, i.e., a sequence of operations on the array of data so that the initial state of the array is properly converted to the goal state. A set of variables to store the data, pointers and intermediate values and an operation sequence must be defined appropriately.

Figure 2 shows a skeleton of the HPG graph for SORT procedure of the QUICKSORT algorithm. As in the figure the SORT procedure consists of three major processes which are initialization process, search-and-exchange process and recursion control process, in this sequence. It should be stressed that the operations to achieve the QUICKSORT algorithm by the recursive processing technique are divided into three major groups and that operations related to these processes are not mixed together between different processes. This is an important difference between program comprehension and natural language comprehension although these two have several similar characteristics as mentioned before[1].

The initialization process is divided into three parallel subprocesses which are left-pointer-setting process, right -

pointer-setting process and base-value-setting process. The search-and-exchange process, the second process, consists of two serial subprocesses which are search process and exchange-and-judge process in this order. The search process is a process to find two elements to be exchanged and is divided into two parallel subprocesses which are left search process for finding the first value element smaller than the base value from the left hand side of the array and right search process for finding the first larger value element from the right. The exchange-and-judge process is a process to exchange the two elements which have been found by the search process and then to narrow the width of the sequence by two and check the termination of the process. The subprocesses are structured as in the figure. The third major process which is the recursion control process controls the recursions and consists of two subprocesses as in the figure.

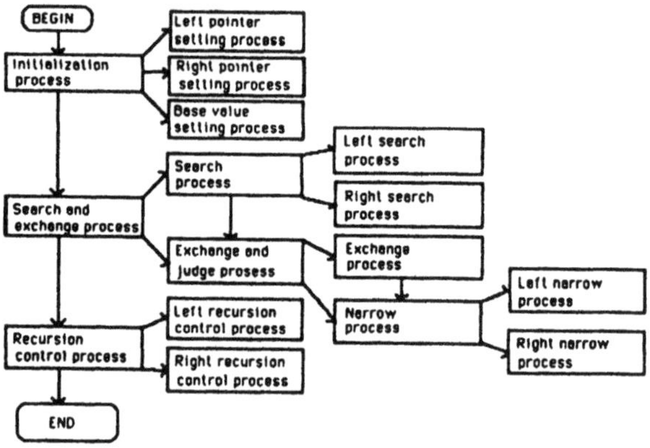

Fig. 2 The HPG graph for the QUICKSORT algorithm.

The attribute informations for typical control strategies and operations are attached to each related process node of the HPG graph as in figure 3. For example, for the search-and-exchange process REPEAT or WHILE commands are typically applicable. In the case of the REPEAT command a proper template is given as in the figure where v3(variable-3) and v4 are referenced as shown. These two variables appeare within the left search process and the right search process where other control strategies and operations are given as the templates as in the figure. These attribute informations are represented as abstracted procedure-oriented knowledge which is referenced by the knowledge-based pattern matching module of the ALPUS system in the program comprehension process.

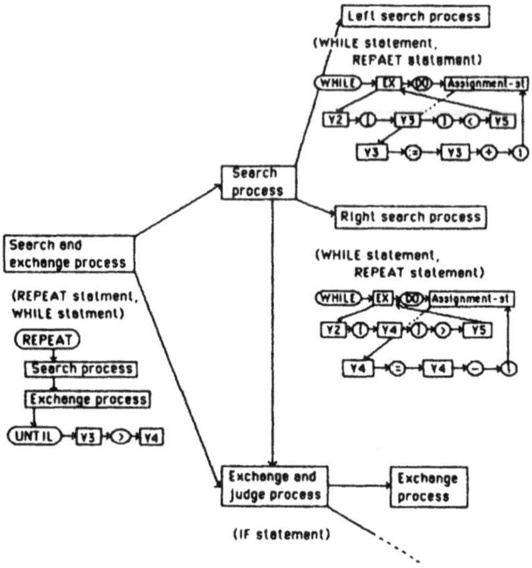

Fig. 3 Attached information to the HPG graph.

In addition to the typical patterns of knowledge discussed above the HPG graph includes several acceptable patterns and error patterns as shown in figure 4. These additional informations could make the performance of the program comprehension more powerful and flexible. This knowledge have been extracted by cognitive psychology-based examinations applied to novice programmers at our school. Detailed discussions will be given in the following sections.

4.2 Knowledge Representation in ZERO

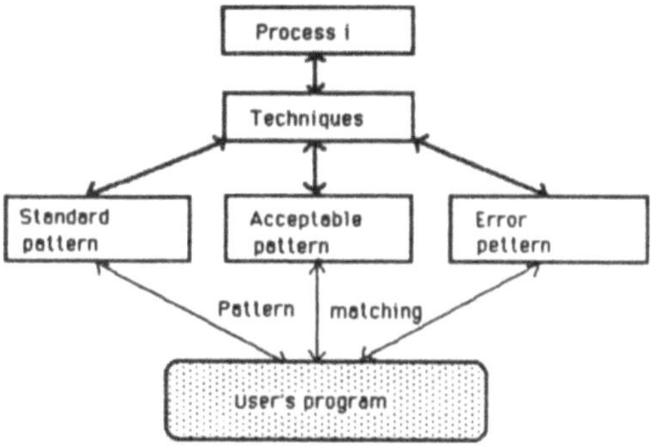

Fig. 4 Template patterns for understanding user's codes.

The INTELLITUTOR system is implemented in ZERO which is a frame-based general purpose knowledge engineering environment[12]. Each process, i.e., node, in the HPG graph is represented using a frame. Figure 5 shows an example of the frame representations in the ZERO formalism for the right-search process node in figure 2. As in the frame the available implementation techniques and possible erroneous techniques are registered in the Technique slot and the Error-Technique slot respectively. The first technique in the Technique slot is a standard one and the rest acceptable ones. In this example the right-search-technique by the WHILE statement is the standard. Every process node in the HPG graph is represented like this as a class frame, i.e., a template frame. The associated instance frames are generated by the system for pattern matching reasoning at the time of program comprehensions as shown in the next section. Each technique registered in the process node frames are defined in a technique frame. The right-search-by-WHILE technique is defined as a class frame as in figure 6. In this frame the detailed information, i.e., knowledge, for the technique is described for understanding an associated program segment. As in the frame the associated attribute informations shown in figure 3 are defined in the Template slot. In the Message-Rules slot a set of rules to generate advice messages for users is stored. Appropriate messages may be generated accoding to the results of understanding. The other template informations are used at the time of program comprehensions as shown in the following section.

4.3 Method of Understanding

The program understandings are done by a knowledge-based pattern matching. That is, a user's program in an internal representation is checked against an associated program template represented in the HPG graph. Because variables that appear in the program would be different from those which are defined in the graph a reasoning to identify the role of each major variable is the first task. This task is done by combining bottom-up and top-down reasoning. Since ALPUS has the knowledge about the variables, which includes types of the variables, their roles and their locations to be referenced and to be handled, it is possible to identify the role of each variable by checking these attributes between the data, i.e., hypotheses, and the template, i.e., knowledge. Normalization of program representations is done prior to this task. Normalization is very important, but for the current version of the system the power of normalization is not sufficient, and the identification of an algorithm is rather simple. We are currently trying to develop a

```
Process:右側からの走査

frame name : Process:右側からの走査  frame type : CLASS

A-kind-of            FRAME     ProcessDescription
DDescendants         FLIST     (Process:右側からの走査0087 Process:右側からの走査0106)
Description          STRING    *UNDEFINED*
Created-by           STRLIST   ("NAKA" "19-Apr-88 12:09:47")
Modified-by          STRLIST   ("NAKA" " 6-Feb-89 16:50:56")
Technique            FLIST     (Technique:右側からの走査-WHILE Technique:右側からの走査-REP
                               EAT)
Error-Technique      LIST      (Error-Technique:右側からの走査-ARRAY
                                              Error-Technique:右側からの走査-REPEAT)
```

Fig. 5 Frame representation of right-search-process template in ZERO.

```
Technique:右側からの走査-WHILE

frame name : Technique:右側からの走査-WHILE  frame type : CLASS

A-kind-of            FRAME     TechniqueDescription
DDescendants         FLIST     (Technique:右側からの走査-WHILE0088
                                            Technique:右側からの走査-WHILE0107)
Description          STRING    *UNDEFINED*
Created-by           STRLIST   ("NAKA" "19-Apr-88 14:45:28")
Modified-by          STRLIST   ("NAKA" "23-Feb-89 19:34:05")
Template             LIST      ((1 WHILE (EXPRESSION < &BASED-VALIABLE
                                            (&ARRAY (&RIGHT-INDEX)))
                                   (2 ASSIGNMENT &RIGHT-INDEX := &RIGHT-INDEX -
                                      /CONST1)))
Matched-Template     LIST      NIL
Missing-Template     LIST      NIL
Most-Inportant-Factor
                     LIST      (1 WHILE)
Technique-Point      INTEGER   0
Setting-Point-Rules
                     LIST      (((1 ALL)
                                 -20)
                                ((2 ALL)
                                 -20))
Message-Rules        LIST      [(RULE IDENTIFY1 (IF (1 -1))
                                      (THEN (MESSAGE$ Pattern1)
                                            (REMOVE$ IDENTIFY1)))
                                (RULE IDENTIFY2 (IF (1 0))
                                      (THEN (MESSAGE$ Pattern1)
                                            (REMOVE$ IDENTIFY2)))
                                (RULE IDENTIFY3 (IF (1 OTH))
                                      (THEN (MESSAGE$ Pattern16 &ARRAY OTH WHILE文 右
                               側 &BASED-VALIABLE)
                                            (REMOVE$ IDENTIFY3)))
                                (RULE IDENTIFY4 (IF (1 WHILE))
                                      (THEN (MESSAGE$ Pattern30 &ARRAY LINE-NUMBER
                                                      ERROR-OBJECT &BASED-VALIABLE)
                                            (MESSAGE$ Pattern31 LINE-NUMBER)
                                            (MESSAGE$ Pattern32)
                                            (MESSAGE$ Pattern3
```

Fig. 6 Frame representation of right-search-by-WHILE technique template in ZERO.

system that gives better performance. The following pattern matching processing is done by top-down reasoning. Since the knowledge base of the system that is the HPG graph includes several patterns for each technique which is attached to each process node in the graph as shown in figures 5 and 6, this reasoning does not require complicated processing techniques. Pattern matching is done by way of segment to segment matching. If the user's program segment matches the standard pattern, then the system understands this segment as a complete one. If it matches one of the acceptable patterns, then the system is able to make an advice to the user for writing better programs. It is also possible to rewrite the segment into the best one, a standard-like form. If it matches one of the error patterns then the system is able to assume the user's intention using informations attatched to the pattern, and can make an advice for fixing the error or for letting him know his confusions, mistakes or misunderstandings. Further advices are given by the TUTOR system according to the output informations of this

```
Process:右側からの走査0087
frame name : Process:右側からの走査0087   frame type : INSTANCE

A-kind-of               FRAME     Process:右側からの走査
DDescendants            FLIST     NIL
Description             STRING    *UNDEFINED*
Created-by              STRLIST   ("NAKA" "23-Feb-89 19:37:14")
Modified-by             STRLIST   ("NAKA" "23-Feb-89 19:37:44")
Most-Possible-Technique
                        FLIST     (Technique:右側からの走査-WHILE0088)
Technique-Instance      FLIST     (Technique:右側からの走査-WHILE0088
                                        Technique:右側からの走査-REPEAT0089)
```

Fig. 7 Instantiated frame of the right-search-process.

```
Technique:右側からの走査-WHILE0088
frame name : Technique:右側からの走査-WHILE0088   frame type : INSTANCE

A-kind-of               FRAME     Technique:右側からの走査-WHILE
DDescendants            FLIST     NIL
Description             STRING    *UNDEFINED*
Created-by              STRLIST   ("NAKA" "23-Feb-89 19:37:14")
Modified-by             STRLIST   ("NAKA" "23-Feb-89 19:42:02")
Matched-Template        LIST      ((1 13))
Missing-Template        LIST      ((2 20))
Technique-Point         INTEGER   -20
Data-Area               LIST      ((20 (RIGHTINDEX := RIGHTINDEX - 1)
                                       代入文 6)
                                   (1 (PROGRAM QUICKSORT %( INPUT , OUTPUT %))
                                      PROGRAM 1)
                                   (2 (VAR A : ARRAY %[ 1 .. 100 %] OF INTEGER)
                                      VAR 2)
                                   (3 (I : INTEGER)
                                      VAR 2)
                                   (4 (PROCEDURE SORT %( LEFTPARAMETER , RIGHTPARAMETER
                                                 : INTEGER %))
                                      PROCEDURE 2)
                                   (5 (VAR LEFTINDEX , RIGHTINDEX , BASE , WORK :
                                           INTEGER)
                                      VAR 3)
                                   (6 (BEGIN)
                                      BEGIN 3)
                                   (14 (RIGHTINDEX := RIGHTINDEX + 1)
                                       代入文 6)
                                   (15 (IF LEFTINDEX <= RIGHTINDEX THEN)
                                       IF文 5)
                                   (16 (BEGIN)
                                       BEGIN 6)
                                   (17 (A %[ RIGHTINDEX %] := A %[ LEFTINDEX %])
                                       代入文 6)
                                   (18 (A %[ LEFTINDEX %] := A %[ RIGHTINDEX %])
                                       代入文 6)
                                   (19 (LEFTINDEX := LEFTINDEX + 1)
                                       代入文 6)
```

Fig. 8 Instantiated frame of the right-serach-by WHILE technique and intermediate results of program understanding.

system. A part of comprehension will be discussed in more detail next.

As in figure 2 an algorithm is represented by a hierarchical organization of the processes, and as in figure 3 the knowledge to understand program segments associated with the processes is attached to associated nodes. The detailed information of each node is represented in template frames as in figures 5 and 6. As in figure 5 for the right-search process, a standard pattern, one acceptable pattern, and two error patterns are registered. These informations have been extracted through programming examinations done to a number of students.

The detailed information for each technique is represented in another template frame as mentioned before as in figure 6, where the standard technique for the right-search process is registered. The right-search process should consist of two segments as shown in the Template slot, which are a WHILE statement segment and an assignment statement segment. This means that the right-search process is recommended to be implemented in this pattern of program statements for it to be the best one. In the Most-Important-Factor slot the key segment number of the template is specified. In this example, the WHILE segment of the pattern plays a key role in understanding the part of program statements associated with this process. Variable names and constants are checked in this formation.

The pattern matching is done using the instantiated informations generated from the template frames. Figure 7 shows an instance frame generated from the template frame which is shown in figure 5. Figure 8 shows an instance frame for the WHILE-based right search technique which is generated from the template frame shown in figure 6. Intermediate results are stored in these frames. As in figure 7 acceptable patterns are generated as code numbers 0088 and 0089, and the first one is recognized as the standard pattern.

Figure 8 shows the detailed information for the 0088 pattern. As the intermediate result of a partial pattern matching, matched segment pairs and mismatched segment pairs are assigned into the Matched-Template slot and the Missing-Template slot respectively. Then the matching score of the user's program codes to this pattern is assigned to the Technique-Point slot. The segmented user's program statements to be understood are stored in the Data-Area slot in the internal representation. In this case the first template segment of this technique is matchd to the 13th program segment and the second template segment is mismatched to the 20th program segment. The technique point assigned is -20 which means that although a segment associated to the template segment is included in the program, an missing structure has been detected. This score is assigned by the setting-score rules in the template frame. Prior to the pattern matching, user's codes are normalized so that the number of the template pattern is minimized and the flexibility of the pattern matching capability is maximized.

If neither the standard pattern nor any available patterns match the user's code then the system assumes that logical errors exist in the user's program. In cases of simple errors such as missing of binary operators or condition codes the system can detect them using the standard or acceptable template patterns. In other cases the system tries to identify an error by matching the code to the error patterns registered in the template frame. If one of the error patterns matches then the system comprehends it as the logical error and assumes the user's intention assosiated with it. Messages are generated according to the matching test and displayed as an advice. If no error pattern matches then the system assumes that some errors exist within the program but theiridentifications failed. In this case error messages are not enough as advices.

Figure 9 shows an example of an error detection by the ALPUS system and advices produced by the system for a user. As shown in the figure the system shows the precise error location in the algorithmic structure of the program, the type of the error, the possible error cause, advices for fixing, and so on.

5 Related Works

Soloway's PROUST[3] is a knowledge-based programming aid for novice programmers. This system can detect multiple logical errors and can infer user's intention from erroneous programs. The major

```
ZERO : ACTIVATOR
1    PROGRAM QUICKSORT ( INPUT , OUTPUT )
2     VAR A : ARRAY [ 1 .. 100 ] OF INTEGER
3     I : INTEGER
4     PROCEDURE SORT ( LEFTPARAMETER , RIGHTPARAMETER : INTEGER )
5      VAR LEFTINDEX , RIGHTINDEX , BASE , WORK : INTEGER
6      BEGIN
7       LEFTINDEX := LEFTPARAMETER
8       RIGHTINDEX := RIGHTPARAMETER
9       BASE := A [ ( LEFTPARAMETER + RIGHTPARAMETER ) DIV 2 ]
10       REPEAT
11        WHILE A [ LEFTINDEX ] < BASE DO
12         LEFTINDEX := LEFTINDEX + 1
13        WHILE A [ RIGHTINDEX ] > BASE DO
14         RIGHTINDEX := RIGHTINDEX + 1
15        IF LEFTINDEX <= RIGHTINDEX THEN
16         BEGIN
17         WORK := A [ LEFTINDEX ]
18         A [ LEFTINDEX ] := A [ RIGHTINDEX ]
19         A [ RIGHTINDEX ] := WORK
20         LEFTINDEX := LEFTINDEX + 1
21         RIGHTINDEX := RIGHTINDEX - 1
22        END
23       UNTIL LEFTINDEX > RIGHTINDEX
24       IF LEFTPARAMETER < RIGHTINDEX THEN
25        SORT ( LEFTPARAMETER , RIGHTINDEX )
26       IF LEFTINDEX < RIGHTPARAMETER THEN
27        SORT ( LEFTINDEX , RIGHTPARAMETER )
28      END
29      BEGIN
30       FOR I := 1 TO 100 DO
31        READ ( A [ I ] )
32       SORT ( 1 , 100 )
33       FOR I := 1 TO 100 DO
34        WRITE ( A [ I ] )
35      END


"One logical error has been detected in this QUICKSORT program. "

The error occures within the [Right-search] process  in  the [Search]
 process  in  the [Search-and-exchenge] process  in SORT proceduer.

"Intentions infered from your statements, types of errors and suggestions for
 fixing the errors are as follows:"

It is infered that you might intend to search a bigger value than the BASE
 value from the right hand side for array A using the WHILE
 statement in line 13 . However, the search from the right hand side
 will be failed by this statement. The index variable RIGHTINDEX
 must be subtracted by one for this operation.
Therefore, it is recomended that you should exchenge the '+' operation to the
 '-' operation to fix the error.

"Causes of the errors are supposed as follows: "
1: You might copy line 12 for ease and change the variable names, and forget
the change of the operation.
2:Although you intended to write a correct statement you might make a careles
s mistake by considering only the form of a indexing operation and the variab
le names since the statement in line 12 is almost same.
```

Fig. 9 An example of advice statements generated by ALPUS. (Translated from Japanese statements)

difference of PROUST from ALPUS is that a plan-based knowledge is used for program comprehensions. They are supposing that a program consists of plans, i.e., program segments. Examples of plans are Counter Plan, Running Total Variable Plan, and Running Total Loop Plan. The plan-based program understander seems to be more flexible than the algorithm-based counterpart. It seems, however, difficult to manipulate complex programs by means of plans. Programming technique templates used in ALPUS are similar to plans in some ways.

Ritch's Programmer's Apprentice[2] is another plan-based programming environment. However, plans in PA are not program segments like PROUST's plans, but abstract representations of program codes combined from data flows and control flows. They are considering formal representations of the plans but not programmer's psychlogy. PA does not have program comprehension abilities in the sense of ALPUS's way, although attractive features have been demonstrated by the system.

Adam's LAURA[7] is a debugging system for novice programmers, and has an ability to detect multiple logical errors using a program model. The program model is a directed graph of a procedure of a program, where operations are represented by nodes and sequences of operations by arcs. The LAURA system has modules to convert program codes to the graph formalism and to normalize it to a standard representation of the graph, i.e., the template. LAURA can detect multiple logical errors by pattern matching processing between a user's program and a standardized program model. LAURA is not based on cognitive psychology.

Ruth's Intelligent Program Analysis system[17] comprehends user's programs and detects multiple logical errors. IPA uses an algorithm representation scheme called PGM (Program Generation Model) for program comprehensions, where a program is represented by a list of specially designed actions, i.e., basic operations. The comprehension is done by pattern matching between a PGM which is a standardized list of actions and the list of actions which is generated from a user's program. He calls this process reverse synthesis. IPA is an interesting system from the point of view of software science, although it is not based on cognitive psychology.

6 Conclusions

Understanding is an important, basic and common issue in Artificial Intelligence. In the area of software engineering, however, much more effort has been spent in Automated Program Generation. The lack of basic research on Program Understanding has inevitably resulted in very poor products. A person who cannot understand the semantics of a program cannot write any valuable programs. Although a variety of approaches are applicable to program understandings I believe that the most important one must be based on the concept of cognitive science. Only an intelligent human being could accomplish sophisticated problem solvings such as program comprehensions and generations. For this reason we should do much more work on this theme.

We have been trying to develop a deep knowledge-based expert system for more than five years for next generation expert systems[13]. Our efforts in representing programming knowledge by the HPG graph is an attempt in this direction. One of the important characters of deep knowledge is that it can be independent from specific application and can be shared by a variety of applications. In this sense the HPG graph is independent from a logical error detection application and is shared by GUIDE, ALPUS and TUTOR. We hope that in the future a knowledge base which includes many typical algorithms in the HPG graph may be shared by many users for a variety of applications.

Although the ALPUS system has demonstrated interesting functions in program comprehension the ability of the current ALPUS system is limited. We are trying to extend the performance of the system.

Acknowledgement

This work is supported in part by The Science Research Foundation of Ministry of Education, NTT Software Institute and Tokyo Denki University Research Center. The author would like to thank Chikahito Nakajima and Hirosi Murayama for implementing ALPUS, Hirosi Takahasi for implementing GUIDE, Hitomi Usiyama for obtaining cognitive data, and Masami Yano for implementing TUTOR, and other laboratory students for system implementations and discussions. The author would like to express sincere gratitude to Jan Grabowski for his comments and suggestions for my earlier draft. The author would like to thank Kotaro Hosokawa for editing the draft.

[References]

[1] Ueno, Haruki, " Knowledge Based Intelligent Programming Environments", Information Processing, Vol.28, No.10, pp.1280-1296, Information Processing of Japan, 1987(in J.)
[2] Ritch, C., A Formal Representation for Plans in the Programmer's Apprentice, Proc. 7th IJCAI, pp.1044-1052, 1981
[3] Jonson, W.E. and Soloway, E., "PROUST: Knowledge-Based Program Understanding", IEEE Trans. on Soft. Eng., Vol.SE-11, No.3, pp.11-19, 1985
[4] Jonson, W.E., "Intention-Based Diagnosis of Novice Programming Errors", Morgan-Kaufman Publishers, 1986
[5] Shapiro, D.G. and McCune, B.P., "The Intelligent Program Editor", IEEE, pp.226-232, 1983
[6] Ruth, G.R., "Intelligent Program Analysis", Artificial Intelligence 7, pp.431-441, 1976
[7] Adam, A. and Laurent, J.P., "LAURA: A System to Debug Student Programs", Artificial Intelligence 15, pp.72-122, 1980
[8] Hukunaga, K., "PROMPTER: A Knowledge Based Support Tool for Code Understanding", Proc. IC on Soft. Eng., 1985
[9] Nakajima, C. and Ueno, H., "Knowledge-Based Program Understanding by Means of Algorithm Oriented Hierachical Procedure Graph", EIC SIG AI88-31, pp.1-6, 1988(in J.)
[10] Soloway, E. and Ehrich, K., "Empirical Studies of Programming Knowledge", IEEE Trans. on Soft. Eng., Vol.SE-10, No.5, pp.595-609, 1984
[11] Ueno, H. and Nakajima, C., "Logical Error Detection by Means of Program Understanding", Proc. 1st JSAI Conference, pp.449-452, 1987(in J.)
[12] Ito,H. and Ueno,H., "ZERO: Frame + Prolog", Logic Programming '85, LNCS221, pp.10-17, 1986
[13] Ueno, H., "Object Model for A Deep Knowledge System", Preprints of 7th IC on MCDM, Kyoto, pp.792-800, 1986
[14] Ueno,H., "INTELLITUTOR: A Knowledge Based Intelligent Programming Environment for Novice Programmers", Proc.COMPCN89 Spring, pp.390-395, 1989
[15] Minsky, M., " A Framework for Representing Knowledge", in The Psychology of Computer Vision(P.H.Winston, ed), McGraw-Hill, 1975
[16] Ueno,H.,"Expert Systems", Information Processing, Vo.28,No.2,pp.147-157, Information Processing Society of Japan, 1987(in J.)
[17] Ruth,G.R., "Intelligent Program Analysis", Artificial Intelligence 7, pp.431-441, 1976
[18] Schneiderman,B and Mayer,R., "Syntactic/Semantic Interactions in Programming Behavior: A Model and Experimental Results", Int.J. of Computer and Information Sciences,Vol.8,No.3,pp.219-283, 1979

Evolution of Brussels Free Universities Computer Centre (BFUCC) during the period 1984 - 1989 : from computers to services.

W.P. De Wilde,
Civ. Eng., Ph.D., Prof.
Chairman of BFUCC
Pleinlaan, 2
B-1050 Brussels.

Abstract

The present paper tries to show the evolution of computing resources and services at the Brussels Free Universities. The BFU Computer Centre (BFUCC) has now been run jointedly by two Universities since twenty years and it has evolved qualitatively during the last five years. The author tries to underline the reasons behind the taken policy decisions.

1. Introduction : the situation up to 1984.

Up to 1984, BFUCC has been running mainframes, connected in a "star"-type network and interconnecting about 500 TTY- like terminals. Based on its original network protocol, that was designed in 1975 by G. Destrée and P. Lenders, it was doing its best to give access to a community of more or less 2000 academics and 20000 students (of whom, of course, only an estimated 20% ever wanted to access such a network). This network has been discussed in previous papers (eg. [1]).

Roughly speaking, following mainframes hab been installed in 1984, practically all of them still present in BFUCC today :

i) 1 CYBER 855, scientific "all-purpose" powerful number cruncher (~ 2 Mflops)
ii) 1 CYBER 815, running PLATO®, a computer assisted learning system (~ .7 Mflops)
iii) 1 WANG installation for the VUB administration (financial system, word processing, personnel databases, student registration)
iv) 2 PR1ME computers for the ULB libraries
v) 1 interconnected network of VAX computers

The whole area covered by these computers had a diameter of approx. 25km, so that extensive use has been made of RTT lines, which were (standard in Belgium) at 9600 or sometimes 19200 bps.

As written previously, this network gave full satisfaction, but ... with the provision, by BFUCC, of the basic needs, new ones soon appeared !

If one tries to remember, 1984 can be viewed as a turning point in the evolution of computers : for the first time the computers not only are accessible to more people (massive penetration of the PC and introduction of really user friendly hard- and software, attracting more people to these tools), but also does the scope of computer applications open tremendously : the introduction of the concept of LAN, combined with its financial affordability, really makes computers open to everyone[1]. Confronted with a whole set of new possibilities, the user wants more and more. It will surprise nobody when one writes that a University community should have been among the most exacting in its requests: indeed it was...

Taking into consideration what were the new possibilities, a large number of users started to complain about the technical limitations of the installed network (essentially speed limitations in multiplexed lines). Confronted with the problem, the author was charged, together with a few colleagues[2], to make a recommendation for the development of a renewed computer infrastructure, to be installed in a period of 4 years from then. Today, in 1989, practically everything that was included in the recommendation has been installed and a review of taken decisions can be done. Some lessons can also be learned from the past...

2. 1984 : evolution of needs...

Like written previously, 1984 will mark an evolution of the needs of the Universities communities, more precisely in the following directions :

i) in the first place, an evolution is felt in the needs of the users towards more fast transfers from/to of data (one of the triggers may have been the University administration and its huge amount of information stored in databases : for these VUB files, about 1 Gbytes are on-line !). Not only administration feels this need, but also some users in the scientific world (for instance, involved in finite element techniques, requesting transfers of large amounts of (output)data and graphics). *High-speed networking* is the word one hears more every day!

ii) *computer graphics* get more attention; with the installed configuration they are virtually impossible to be used (think of the technology and the software in 1984 : the centres who are acknowledged with GKS and have fully implemented and exploited such systems, at that moment, can be counted by tens, not hundreds...).

iii) *powerful workstations* appear on the market, allowing new types of applications, especially in the field of simulations, graphical pre- and postprocessing of finite element packages, computer aided design, the latter in architecture, chemical engineering, electronic design, civil engineering etc...

iv) *high speed computing* also interests more people, especially when one considers that large (industrial) contracts are drawn to the University by departments like fluid dynamics, chemistry, materials, to name just a few.

v) *an irreversible dynamic* is initiated, as much by academic personnel as by students, in the field of PC's, which show ever decreasing prices for ever increasing performance. Add to this that major breakthroughs are made in the field of user-friendly software and nobody will be surprised when the actual figure of approx. 1750 individual computers on the campuses is cited.

---

[1] The author himself remembers very well being more than reluctant to introduce, at that moment, a PC in his house and, today, not being able to support the least crash with his home computer...

[2] It is sure that today's computing environment at BFU's has been largely contributed to by people like Prof. J. Tiberghien, former president of BFUCC, J. Sacton, also a former president of BFUCC, M. Goossens, T. D'Hondt, P. Raeymaekers, G. Destrée, R. Binon, and many others who, although not nominally mentioned, made this possible.

vi) *innovative techniques and aspects of computing* are started, in particular artificial intelligence, knowledge based systems, which require very specific equipment (for its LISP machines the department of AI chose SYMBOLICS).

To technically cover all these aspects and to respond to all these demands, several actions were undertaken by the Computer Centre, the most important of all being the design of a new network infrastructure. Although the Computer Centre should cover the needs of two Universities and, up to now, always has implemented policy decisions which were common to the two Universities, in the field of networking a discrepancy in opinions was felt.

3. Evolution of networks at BFUCC.

3.1. The situation at VUB :

The VUB (University of the author) was very strongly influenced by a team of young professors, M. Goossens essentially, J. Tiberghien and T. D'Hondt, each of them very skilled and aware of all the technical problems involved in networking. They had implemented (successfully) a network of mini's in the Faculty of Engineering, which had provided them with experience and they felt confident that they would be able to implement a complete network for the two Universities. They proposed, and it was generally accepted, that they would base this implementation on the UNIX® operating system and that they would act in several steps :

i) in a first step, the students, who were using too many resources from the CYBER mainframes would be directed to other types of equipments, essentially PC's. Considering the different characteristics of the equipments both PC-compatibles and MacIntosh' s were bought[1]; the latter equipment was selected because of its graphical possibilities (elementary level CAD-techniques and teaching). It was decided, to make all this operational, to develop, on the main campus of the VUB, three local area networks based on the following equipments :

- a set of PC's (or Mac's) interconnected in local area network (Ethernet or Appletalk);
- a file server, or disk server : SUN workstations were used for that purpose;
- other equipments like print servers,...

These local area networks were installed starting from 1986. They are fully operational to-day, but it has to be admitted that it took some time[2] to reach this stage.

ii) a second step consisted in the design of the interconnection of the existing LAN's and the effective inclusion of the mainframes in this network. This was a much more difficult problem taking into consideration the extreme heterogeneity of the machines. It was clear, among other things, that it was an illusion to try to provide the users with a service up to level 7 of ISO ! In this step, the first objective was to allow file transfers from and to the mainframes to the local networks. The implementation took much time, for some people too much, but it is honest to mention that the main responsibility of this lies with RTT. The latter organism does not allow to interconnect

[1]They implemented Olivetti M24 (about 100 are in public locations to-day) and Mac SE's (about 30 in public locations).

[2]A probable policy mistake, made by VUB, was to allow academics to interfere with what should have remained pure logistics ! On the other hand, it gave the VUB a leading edge in the field of networks.

different locations with private lines and, as they are somewhat retarded from a technical point of view, the connection of eg. the CYBER computers to the main campus of VUB (some 4 kms further) with high speed lines was delayed. Recently, the problem has been solved (a 2 Mbps line, using an optical fiber has been made operational).

The interconnection of the LAN's was more easily solved, as the location is centralized, and a star-network, also based on optical fibre technology, interconnected the three LAN's.

To-day the VUB network (logically called VUB-NET), has more or less the following characteristics : it interconnects three campuses (as recently the Faculty of Medicine was included), hundreds of small computers, mainframes on the level of file transfer.

3.2. The situation at ULB :

The decisions taken by ULB were technically very different and based on X25 protocols in networks. In the opinion of the author, one of the decisions at least was sound : ULB decided to give the technical responsibility of the implementation to a commercial partner; unfortunately, this partner did not achieve the proposed goals, with the result that, here also, the aid of the academics was called for. Even today, the implementation is not complete, but it can be stated that, although it was the first time that VUB and ULB decided to follow different roads, the result is rather complementary than competitive : VUB gives an opening to the UNIX world, while the access to public and private networks is guaranteed by the ULB-network.

The ULB has also its own characteristics which probably have been the basic reason of their technical choice : a rather large amount of PC's in the student and academic communities[1], an IBM 4341 (now 4381) of the National Science Foundation, giving access to the EARN network and the IBM community[2], access to the same mainframes described above, and which are shared with VUB.

4. Evolution in the scientific departments.

An evolution of needs in the various scientific departments was also felt : especially two characteristic applications were not very well accepted by this type of network : interactive applications and (of course also interactive) computer graphics. The latter particularly has known an explosive development during the last years, especially in the field of computer aided design.

More users got equipped with workstations, generally provided through their industrial contracts. Unfortunately, the majority of this equipment introduced one or more degree(s) of heterogeneity in the types of machines to be interconnected[3]. The need of interconnection between this type of equipment and the mainframes was strongly felt, and faced the Computer Centre with additional demands.

---

[1] Although probably more oriented, at least up to recent times, to PC compatibles than to Apple equipment.

[2] IBM is practically not represented at VUB, which, in the eyes of the author, is a pity !

[3] Especially the APOLLO equipment, which, at that moment, did not easily fit into a Unix network.

5. A necessary evolution for BFUCC : from centre of computers to services.

One can say that, till approximately 1988, most of the computer centres have been providers of raw computer power and large volumes of data storage. The situation was anyway not very much different in BFUCC : the image of the Centre was one of very powerful CPU's and a huge amount of disks. Some of the people on the Board of BFUCC felt that if this situation was to continue too long, a certain death of the Centre was to be foreseen. Indeed, considering the large decentralisation of equipment (individual computers, workstations,...), it was to be feared that there would be a scattering of expertise, part of which would have flown from the Computer Centre. Some departments in the Faculty of Engineering of VUB, backed by industrial contracts were already thinking of developing their own (though smaller !) computer centre...

It was thus necessary to redefine the exact role of BFUCC, common to two Universities; this was not an easy task. Nevertheless, more than two years later, one can say that the face has changed very much; one can have an overview of the most important decisions :

i) it was decided to increase significantly the computer power, the gap in computing power between the used mainframes (essentially CYBER 855) and available workstations (type SUN, APOLLO, equipped with RISC architecture) getting too small (whereas the gap in price was continuously increasing !). Belgium also showed a dramatic arrear in the field of supercomputers : up to 1988 not a single one was installed ! This was probably one of the first actions to undertake, especially when taking into consideration the needs of industry. Some of the members of the Board, among which the author, proposed to use the existing network facilities and to install a few minisupercomputers[1], also decentralised over the various campuses. This proposal could come in due time, due to the intention of the belgian government to equip different universities with very high capacity computers. The final decision was taken by the two rectors of the Universities, who, among several proposals, decided for the acquisition of a CRAY XMP-14. This computer was installed in february 1989 and is now fully functional[2]. It is temporarily attacked by three front-end computers, which are a SUN 4, the CYBER 855 and the IBM 4381. As will be seen further, this situation is to change in the future.

ii) it was decided to open up the catalog of services provided by BFUCC, with the creation of what was called µShop : a shop, open for students and Universities staff, providing them with individual computers (with significant educational discounts) and also additional services like maintenance and repair of these. This was made possible by signing agreements with some manufacturers, which helped µShop in taking off. An additional extension of the services would be in the field of software and accessories, but in the Universities this market has restricted possibilities[3].

iii) the next policy decision is to shift from a network, which still has a somewhat hierarchical structure (one can think for instance of the front-end computers on

[1]The field of minisupercomputers, most of them based on CRAY-like architecture, was exploding; moreover, some of them had the raw computing power of approx. 0.2 CRAY XMP-14 for purchasing prices under the 10^6 US$.

[2]Meanwhile two high capacity systems were also installed in Belgium : an IBM 3090/600 with vector facilities in Leuven Catholic University and an ETA 10P in the Ministery of Health, the latter for the exploitation of the mathematical model of the North Sea (pollution).

[3]Anyone knows that a University student does not buy software, but rather copies it...

the CRAY) to a more flexible "backbone" structure, using a "channel-like" communication link :

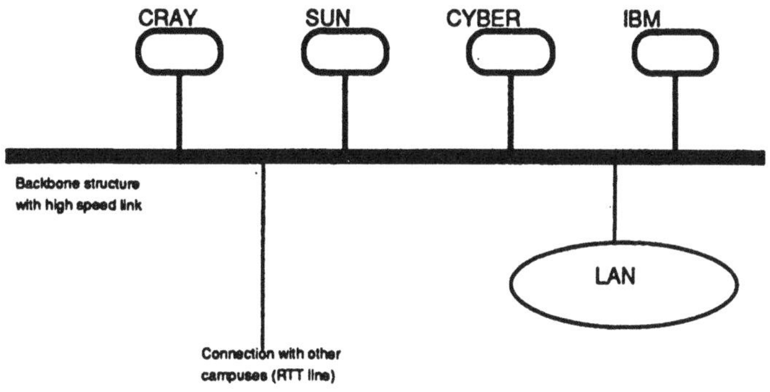

As can be seen in this structure, the end-user would be selecting his mainframe either than being channeled into a CRAY through the other machines. This structure, which is essentially non-hierarchical is more flexible and does not subordinate the functionality of the CRAY to that of its front-ends[1]. Most of the industrial users have shown a strong preference for this type of approach of the network and the functionality it provides.

6. Conclusions.

The survival of a "classical" computer centre, in the sense that it provides its users with computer power and disk space, seems endangered : the end-user wants more. It will be necessary to shift the attention to provision of services by developing more functional and accessible structures. Taking into consideration that a lot of expertise is concentrated in computer centres, which in general can count with a "critical mass", they could very well be the best suited to organise themselves this shift.

7. References.

[1] **De Wilde, W.P.**
Various papers in previous issues of "Computer at the University", organized by University of Zagreb Computer Centre.
Cavtat, 1979-1987.

[1]Of course, there is a reason for the actual, intermediate structure : today, the IBM is still the nodal point of the EARN network and the SUN is the access to the UUCP (Unix) network; two of the machines thus play an important role in providing the CRAY to the EARN and UUCP community.

INFORMATION DISSEMINATION TO USERS WITH HETEROGENEOUS INTERESTS. MODEL OF SPLIT PROFILES

Witold Abramowicz
Academy for Economics Poznan / Poland
Humboldt University Berlin / GDR

Abstract

Context oriented dissemination of information or CODI brings a new concept to the dissemination of information for computer users who teach or do research. Information users or *consumer* need integrated communication and information systems, which are tailored to their individual information needs. CODI was a system developed for the following purposes:

first, for the automatic dissemination of homogeneous documents (for example, software packets [Abramowicz85a] or bibliographic information [Abramowicz85b] or patents or news) from the information producer (software or bibliographic information distributor, Patent Office etc.) located in the network node to all the other nodes and their respective consumers (like a scientist or an engineer), with special attention to their heterogeneous information needs;

second, for the consumers' interactive evaluation of documents automatically selected by the producer;

and finally, for the organization and re-retrieval of documents in the individual consumer's own single-user information retrieval system.

CODI makes use of two-way communication between the producer and the consumers in a computer network. The producer provides each consumer with context relevant documents and relevance information in the following three new categories:

- how relevant the document is for the consumer (this information is usually in information retrieval systems);
- why the document is relevant for the consumer;
- what can augment the relevancy of the document for the consumer.

Lastly in this paper, a theoretical approach called model of split profiles will be presented.

1. INTRODUCTION

The interchange, analysis, storage, and retrieval of information in the setting of research and academic education is influenced by many factors.

Many computers located in workplaces are interconnected in LAN and/or WAN. This is necessary for the quick and easy interchange of information within a research group, a university or, for that matter, across the globe.

The new hardware properties such as large capacity, erasable optical memories, and high-resolution monitors allow for user-friendly analysis as well as the ability to store a great deal of information.

Plenty of new computer based services are available today. Multimedia information, such as text, graphics, audio and video as well as source codes, can be incorporated in computer readable form for interchange (or process by groupware), analysis, storage and retrieval [Conklin87].

The are two separate trends in the process of scientific information.

First, there are a great deal of heterogeneous data bases. More often than not, one finds that there are too many data bases with very different access modes and query-languages to find the information one needs easily. If one information item would be located in any of the data bases, nobody could be certain of finding that needed item for up to possibly three months, because the re-organisation of a data base doesn't respect a particular user's information needs. In other words, everyone working in research and education receives a great deal of information to analyse and certainly far too much to evaluate.

On the other hand, many of us need private information [Abramowicz85b], that is, a collection of relevant information items, which are specifically for that person. The owner can always find available information, edit and organize it. He can treat this information as his own, insofar as he is legally entitled to do so.

In my judgement, both research and education should be united for the purpose of achieving the best satisfaction of a user's information needs. The user should be continually provided with new information items from all the data bases he needs. The justification which the user gives for having access to the relevant body of information is wortlly of special consideration.

This article proposes a solution to this problem by means of CODI - the context oriented dissemination od information.

2. CODI IN COMPUTER NETWORKS

Here we consider a special class of information items. They should be available in a computer readable form and their contents should be describable. They shouldn't be jointly connected or sensitive from the point of view of security [Schmidt89]. Such information items will be called *document*. Examples of such documents are bibliographic and patent descriptions, judicial judgements, news releases ... etc.

The documents will be processed by two groups of subjects the *producers* and the *consumers*. Everyone who belongs to one of these groups is connected with one particular node in the computer networks.

The producer - a computer system - is responsible for the dissemination of documents in the context of the consumers' information needs. The producer can create documents (i.e. be the author of a document in the legal sense), but he can also merely be a distributor of documents (e.g., as with a patent office). From the consumers' point of view, this is unimportant. The primary concern for a consumer in a research or education capacity is the following: can I receive the information (documents) I need and only such information. The secondary concern for him is where does the information come from.

The fundamental problems of CODI are as follows: how does one choose the proper method for representing, acquiring, and retaining information. I don't think it's necessary in this paper to consider this matter in detail because there are many AI and IR publications about [Salton83, Barr83]. It is important to emphasize that: knowledge is available as a set of terms (i.e., words or phrases); the terms are vital for the information content of documents and for converting the consumers' interests; the semantic relationships between terms comprise the other component in knowledge. Some of the methods which represent and satisfy this account of knowledge include classifications, thesauri, semantic nets and so on.

The producer automatically forms the information content of a document by extracting the proper terms from a knowledge representation based on the document being analysed. The importance of each of the chosen terms can be specified by a weight (an attribute from a set of importance factors); consequently the information content of a document will be represented as a set of weighted terms, otherwise known as the document profile. Every document will be considered separately and independently by the producer. The AI and IR methods for describing the content of a document are well known, particularly for textual documents [Salton89].

Using the terms of knowledge repesentation every consumer should be able to interactively construct a descriptor of his information needs. He can choose a set of terms relevant for his interests. Every selected term could be additionally qualified by a weight. This set of weighted terms would then be called his consumer profile as it is the only representation of that particular consumer's information needs. The producer then will be responsable for the acquistion, storage, and care of the consumers' profiles.

The pivotal problem to consider regarding the dissemination of documents is to whom should a particular document be sent? In other words, how does a producer know which document is relevant for which consumer? This question could be answer by matching the document profile against the consumers' profiles. An algorithm is necessary in oder to match the relevant consumers' profiles with a particular document profile. This is contrary to the common way of addressing IR-problems, that is, by finding the relevant document descriptors (documents' profiles) for a query (a consumer profile). There, the documents' descriptors are permanent but the query is temporary. With our method, the consumers' profiles are permanent while the document profile is temporary.

In the common IR-systems the retrieval of relevant documents is approximative. The user first formulates a query; the system then retrieves the set of relevant documents; next, the user evaluates this retrieved set of documents; finally, based on the evaluation of the retrieved documents , only then can the query be improved by the user himself or by the system (relevance feedback); in the latter case, the system automatically retrieves a set of documents until the set of retrieved documents satisfes the user.

Our method is different. Every document could be analysed by the producer only once. Possible improvements in the consumer profile will have no influence over the dissemination of document once they already have been analysed. Every consumer should be desirous of formulationg a *perfect* consumer profile, that is, one that ensures that only the relevant documents will be sent to the consumer. Of course to formulate a *perfect* profile is utopian. The formulation will be a compromise between the precision and recall of information [Salton83]. The simple statement: "a document is relevant for the consumer" isn't sufficient for constructing a *perfect* consumer profile. I think the producer should provide each consumer with the following information concerning what constitutes relevant, matching profiles, that is, between consumers and documents (the latter two being newly defined):

1. how relevant is the document for the consumer (the correlation between the consumer and the document profile is mapped into a single value);

2. why the document is relevant for the consumer (which terms from the consumer and document profile are responsible for determing relevancy, and how these terms determine relevancy);

3. what can augment the relevancy of the document for the consumer (the terms of which belong to the document profile but don't belong to the consumer profile)?

The first one of the above mentioned information items gives a synthetic hint; it could be, for example, useful in the scheduling of documents by the consumer.

The second and third of the above mentioned information items are very useful for the ad hoc evaluation of documents and for the improvement of the consumer profile.

All categories of relevance information are sent to consumers by the producer with the correspondimg document.

The producer can't assume that consumers are always available to receive the relevant documents. For the dissemination of documents should be used a computer-based mail system [Vervest87]. A separate mail unit should be created for every document and the envelope should be automatically edited by the producer. A document and, connected with it, the three categories of relevance information items constitute a single mail unit.

Consumers can check their mail boxes in the mail system at any time. Using the first relevance information the user can choose more relevant documents. Using the second and third relevance information items the user can examine a document more closely. If a document is of special interest for the consumer, he could include it in his private collection of documents. The second and third relevance information items are the integration and search criteria for documents in the private collection.

Using the second and third relevance information items a special subsystem (profile editor) allows the user to re-edit (improve) his consumer profile. The new version of the consumer profile will be automatically sent to the producer with the computer based mail system. Before the producer disseminates a new document he should search his mail box for new versions of consumer profiles.

3. MODEL OF SPLIT PROFILES

There are many theoretical approaches to information systems. The idea presented of an information system called "model of spit profiles" applies to CODI and is related to work done by Marek and Pawlak [Marek76], Codd [Codd70], Wong and Chiang [Wong71].

Let us consider a set of terms T (like at point 2) and a set W of well-ordered weights. The set of indices IND is T x W. A pair:

$$(T_k, W_k) \mid T_k \in T \ \& \ W_k \in W$$

is called an index.

We shall take *information system of consumers' information needs* to mean a 4-tuple:

$$S_I = (I, A_I, V_I, R_I)$$

where:

I - is a finite set of consumers' information needs,

A_I - is a pair of consumers' information needs attributes:

A_I = {Name, Indices}

Name - is a set of unique identifiers of the consumers' information needs,

Indices- isolates a set of representations of the consumers' information needs (a set of consumers' profiles),

V_I - is the domain of A_I: $V_I = V_{name} \cup V_{indices}$

V_{name} = Strings

$V_{indices} = 2^{IND} - 0$

R_I - is a function from I x A_I into V_I:

for the attribute Name: R_I: I x Name -> Strings

for the attribute Indices: R_I: I x Indices -> $2^{IND} - 0$

The function R_I is totaly defined.

Let us consider an example:

T = {$term_1$, $term_2$, $term_3$, $term_4$}

W = {$weight_1$, $weight_2$}

I = {$needs_1$_of_consumer_A, $needs_2$_of_consumer_A, $needs_1$_of _consumer_B}

R_I: {$needs_1$_of_consumer_A, $needs_2$_of_consumer_A, $needs_1$_of_consumerB} x Name -> {$needs_1$, $needs_2$, $needs_3$}

R_I: {$needs_1$_of_consumer_A, $needs_2$_of_consumer_A, $needs_1$_of_ consumerB} x Indices -> { {($term_1$ $weight_1$), ($term_2$ $weight_2$)}, {($term_2$, $weight_1$)}, {($term_3$, $weight_2$), ($term_4$, $weight_2$)}

On the other hand we should consider an information system with only one document, which should be able to be disseminated by the producer at the moment.

We shall take *information system of a document* to mean a 4-tuple:

$$S_D = (D, A_D, V_D, R_D)$$

where:

D - is a single document,

A_D - is a pair of document's attributes:

A_D = {Name, Indices}

Name - is a identifier of a document,

Indices- isolates the contents of a document (a document profile),

V_D - is the domain of A_D: $V_D = V_{name} \cup V_{indices}$

V_{name} = Strings

$V_{indices} = 2^{IND} - 0$

R_D - is a function from D x A_D into V_D:

for the attribute Name: R_D: D x Name -> Strings,

for the attribute Indices: R_D: D x Indices -> $2^{IND} - 0$

The function R_D is totally defined.

Let us follow our example: D is only one document in the S_D system.

R_D: D x Name -> name_of_document

R_D: D x Indices -> {(term$_1$, weight$_2$), (term$_3$, weight$_1$), (term$_4$, weight$_2$)}

Let a composition S_P of S_I and S_D be *an information system of producer*:

$$S_P = S_I \cup S_D = (P, A_P, V_P, R_P)$$

where:

P - is a set of objects (this set inclueds all consumers' information needs and only one document): P = I ∪ D,

$A_P = A_I = A_D$ = {Name, Indices},

$V_P = V_I = V_D = V_{name} \cup V_{indices}$

R_P - is a function from P x A_P into V_P:

for the object from I: $R_P = R_I$

for the document in D: $R_P = R_D$

The value of the attribute Indices is called a profile O_1 over an object P_1 from P in the information system of the producer. O is a set of all profiles over objects of S_P.

In our example:

P = I ∪ D = {needs$_1$_of_consumer_A, needs$_2$_of_consumer_A, needs$_1$_ of_consumerB} ∪ {document}

We can denote four profiles:

O_1 = {(term$_1$, weight$_1$), (term$_2$, weight$_2$)}

O_2 = {(term$_2$, weight$_1$)}

O_3 = {($term_3$, $weight_2$), ($term_4$, $weight_2$)}

O_4 = {($term_1$ $weight_2$), ($term_3$, $weight_1$), ($term_4$, $weight_2$)}

O_1, O_2, O_3 are consumers' profiles and O_4 is a document profile.

Two profiles O_i and O_j from the set O are said to be similar (indicated as $O_i \sim T_k O_j$) iff:

$$(\exists T_k \in T \mid (T_k, W_m) \in O_i \ \& \ (T_k, W_n) \in O_j \ \& \ O_i <> O_j) \Leftrightarrow O_i \sim T_k O_j$$

i.e. the term T_k also describes the object P_i (with profile O_i) as the object P_j (with profile O_j). The weights of the term in both profiles (W_m and W_n) are irrelevant and could be different. P_i and P_j could belong to I as well to D.

In our example:

$$O_1 \sim T_1 O_4, \qquad O_1 \sim T_2 O_2, \qquad O_3 \sim T_3 O_4, \qquad O_3 \sim T_4 O_4$$

The set of profiles O is said to be split up iff:

$$(\forall O_{T_k} \in O : O_{T_k} = \{O_i \mid O_i \in O\}) \Rightarrow O_i \ \& \ O_j \in O_{T_k} \Leftrightarrow O_i \sim T_k O_j$$

i.e. every split subset O_{T_k} of the set O contains only similar profiles (profiles with the comman term T_k).

In our example:

$O_{T_1} = \{O_1, O_4\}$ $\qquad$ $O_{T_2} = \{O_1, O_2\}$

$O_{T_3} = \{O_3, O_4\}$ $\qquad$ $O_{T_4} = \{O_3, O_4\}$

If an object P_i from P is the document D, then the profile over this object is denoted as OD. OD is a document profile. In our example OD = O_4.

The set of profiles O is called normally split up iff the set of profiles is split up and:

$$\forall O'_{T_k} \in O : OD \in O'_{T_k}$$

i.e. every normal split subset O'_{T_k} of the set O contains profile OD (and at any rate one other profile).

Because the set O contains only one document profile, and every normal split subset of O contains one document profile, and also because split subset of O contains at least two different profiles, every normal split subset of O contants only one document profile and one or more consumer profiles.

In our example O_{T_1}, O_{T_3}, O_{T_4} are normal split subsets of the set O.

If the consumer profile P_i belongs to the normal split subset O'_{T_k}, than the document D described by profile OD is relevant for the consumer profile P_i based on the term T_k. The term T_k belongs to indices in the profile OD and in the profile P_i. In this case there exists a document-consumer path denoted DC_i. The existence of the DC_i means that the document is relevant for the consumer profile. While we don't know how relevant, we can speak about a qualitative relevance. Algorithm 1 shows how qualitative relevance will be estimated.

```
FOR ∀ O'_{T_k} DO
  FOR ∀ P_i ∈ O'_{T_k} DO
    IF ¬DC_i THEN set DC_i END;
  END;
END;
```

Algorithm 1

In our example: document is relevant for O_1 (because of O_{T_1}) and is relevant for O_3 (because of O_{T_3} and O_{T_4}) and is irrelevant for O_2. DC_1 and DC_3 are created.

If indices (T_k, W_u) belongs to P_i and (T_k, W_d) belongs to OD, than the value of a function A with parameters W_u and W_d explains the contribution of the T_k for the relevance of the OD for the P_i. This contribution is called the term related document-consumer path DC_{T_k}. The algorithm 2 (the extension of the algorithm 1) shows how these contributions will be estimated:

```
FOR ∀ O'_{T_k} DO
  FOR ∀ P_i ∈ O'_{T_k} DO
    IF ¬DC_i THEN
      set DC_i;
      initiation of a set B_i;
    END;
    DC_{T_k} := A(W_u,W_d);
    insert DC_{T_k} to B_i;
  END;
END;
```

where:
B_i - is a set of term related document-consumer paths for the document profile OD and the consumer profile P_i.

Algorithm 2

The set B_i denotes the second relevance information and tell us why the document is relevant for consumer (because of all analysed O'_{T_k}), which terms from the consumer and from the document profiles are responsible for the relevancy, and how they participate in the relevancy (by the value of DC_{T_k}).

In our example:

$B_1 = \{DC_{T_1}\} = \{A(weight_1, weight_2)\}$

$B_3 = \{DC_{T_3}, DC_{T_4}\} = \{A(weight_2, weight_1), A(weight_2, weight_2)\}$

Obviously the first relevance information is the function over all elements of the set B_i, e.g. it is a function over the contributions of every term for the relevance of the document profile OD for the consumer profile P_i. The algorithm 3 (the extension of algorithm 2) shows us how the first relevance information will be estimated.

```
FOR ∀ O'_{T_k} DO
  FOR ∀ P_i ∈ O'_{T_k} DO
    IF ¬DC_i THEN
      set DC_i;
      initiation of R_i;
      initiation of set B_i;
    END;
    DC_{T_k} := A(W_i, W_d);
    insert DC_{T_k} to B_i;
    R_i := F(R_i, DC_{T_k});
  END;
END;
```

where:

R_i - is a variable which denotes the first relevance information for the consumer profile O_i

Algorithm 3

Considerations of the nature of the function A and the function F are less important for this shortend presentation of the CODI idea.

R_1 is function over $\{A(weight_1, weight_2)\}$ and R_3 over $\{A(weight_2, weight_1), A(weight_2, weight_2)\}$.

The third relevance information (what can angment the relevancy of the document for the consumer, which terms belong to document profile OD, but don't belong to consumer profile P_l, and how they are important for the document) is a set of weights definted as:

$$\{T_k \mid (T_k, W_d) \in OD \ \& \ OD \in O'_{T_k} \ \& \ P_l \notin O'_{T_k} \ \& (\exists\, O'_{T_l} \mid OD \ \& \ P_l \in O'_{T_l})\}$$

In our example the third relevance information for O_1 = {$term_2$} (because of ($term_2$, $weight_2$)) and for O_3 = {}.

4. CONCLUSION

The CODI based information system ensures information users of heterogeneous interests of always receiving actual information they need. The presented idea has been verified in some implementations.

References

[Abramowicz85a] W.Abramowicz, Computer Added Dissemination of Information on Software in Networks, in: Compas'85, Standard Software, Berlin West, VDE-Verlag, 491-505.

[Abramowicz85b] W.Abramowicz, Context Oriented Dissemination of Information, PhD Thesis, Technical University of Wroclaw, 172pp.

[Barr83] A.Barr, E.A.Feigenbaum, The Handbook of Artificial Intelligence, Vol.1, Pitman Books Ltd.

[Conklin87] E.J.Conklin, Hypertext: An Introduction and Survey, IEEE Computer, Sept., 17-41.

[Codd70] E.F.Codd, A RElational Model of Data for Large Shared Data Banks, Communications of the ACM, Vol.13, 377-387.

[Marek76] W.Marek, Z.Pawlak, Information Storage and Retrieval Systems - Mathematiacl Foundations, Theoretical Computer Science, No.1, 331-354.

[Salton83] G.Salton, M.J.McGill, Introduction to Modern Information Retrieval, McGraw-Hill Book Company, 448pp.

[Salton89] G.Salton, Automatic Text Processing. The Transformation, Analysis, and Retrieval of Information by Computer, Addison-Wesley Publishing Company, 530pp.

[Schmidt89] S.Schmidt, Buero-Informationssysteme - Ein Ueberblick, Informatik-Spektrum, Feb., 19-30.

[Vervest87] P.H.M.Vervest, Innovation in Electronic Mail, Noth-Holland, 212pp.

[Wong71] E.Wong, T.C.Chiang, Canonical Structure in Attribute Based File Organization, Communications of the ACM, Vol.14, 593-597.

The Text Database Management System SIGMA: An Improvement of the Main Engine

S. Arikawa*, M. Haraguchi§, H. Inoue**, Y. Kawasaki**, T. Miyahara*, S. Miyano*, K. Oshima+, H. Sakai†, T. Shinohara††, S. Shiraishi+, M. Takeda**, S. Takeya‡, A. Yamamoto**, H. Yuasa**

* Research Institute of Fundamental Information Science, Kyushu University 33, Fukuoka 812, Japan

§ Department of Systems Science, Tokyo Institute of Technology, Yokohama 227

** Department of Information Science, Kyushu University 39, Kasuga 816

\+ Department of Applied Mathematics, Fukuoka University, Fukuoka 814-01

† Information Science Center, Kyushu Institute of Technology, Iizuka 820

†† Department of Artificial Intelligence, Kyushu Institute of Technology, Iizuka 820

‡ Computation Center, Kyushu University 36, Fukuoka 812

Abstract

This paper describes a general purpose text database management system SIGMA that exploits very fast and efficient one-way sequential processing of text files. For the implementation, a fast pattern matching algorithm which can deal with multiple keys is designed to realize commands for searching, replacing and extracting keys. The algorithm also copes with Japanese texts containing both 1-byte and 2-byte characters with shift codes. A new file system is also designed to manage large text files efficiently. The system SIGMA is now working at the Computer Center of Kyushu University for large scale text databases, natural language analysis and bibliographic retrievals. It is also sketched how the main engine may be improved for finer processing.

1. Introduction

In contrast with the usual information retrieval systems [18], [20] and database management systems [25], the text database management system SIGMA stores data simply as the form of text files, i.e., strings of characters, and exploits very precise and fast one-way sequential processing methods.

The recent spread of personal computers and word processors has been producing quite large amount of text files stored in external storage devices or in floppy disks. These files are, for example, documents written in English, Japanese texts, DNA files, the whole volumes written by a novelist, etc. Especially, the increase of Japanese text files which consists of both 1-byte and 2-byte characters with shift codes is remarkable.

The system SIGMA is designed to cope with these text files. Perhaps the structure of strings is the simplest and most basic data structure which allows complicated retrievals, editing and refiling of retrieved records. Moreover, texts are the most common data that users of word processors supply.

```
#@
#0300907 DIE <GESCHICHTE <HANS <CASTORPS , DIE WIR ERZ=AHLEN WOLLEN ,
 - NICHT UM SEINETWILLEN  ( DENN DER <LESER WIRD EINEN EINFACHEN , WENN
AUCH ANSPRECHEN DEN JUNGEN <MENSCHEN IN IHM KENNENLERNEN  ) , SONDERN UM
DER <GESCHICHTE WILLEN , DIE UNS IN HOHEM <GRADE ERZ=AHLENSWERT SCHEINT
( WOBEI ZU <HANS <CASTORPS <GUNSTEN DENN DOCH ERINNERT WERDEN SOLLTE , DA$
ES SEINE <GESCHICHTE IST , UND DA$ NICHT JEDEM JEDE <GESHCICHTE PASSIERT
> :
DIESE <GESCHICHTE IST SEHR LANGE HER , SIE IST SOZUSAGEN SCHON GANZ MIT
HISTORISCHEM <EDELROST =UBERZOGEN UND UNBEDINGT IN DER <ZEITFORM DER
TIEFSTEN
<VERGANGENHEIT VORZUTRAGEN .
#@
#0300917 DAS W=ARE KEIN <NACHTEIL F=UR EINE <GESCHICHTE , SONDERN EHER EIN
<VORTEIL ;
#0300917 DENN <GESCHICHTEN M=USSEN VERGANGEN SEIN , UND JE VERGANGENER ,
K=ONNTE MAN SAGEN , DESTO BESSER F=UR SIE IN IHRER <EIGENSCHAFT ALS
<GESCHICHTEN UND F=UR DEN <ERZ=AHLER , DEN RAUNENDEN <BESCHW=ORER DES
<IMPERFEKTS .
#0300921 ES STEHT JEDOCH SO MIT IHR , WIE ES HEUTE AUCH MIT DEN <MENSCHEN
UND
UNTER DIESEN NICHT ZUM WENIGSTEN MIT DEN <GESCHICHTENERZ=AHLERN STEHT :
SIE IST
VIEL =ALTER ALS IHRE <JAHRE , IHRE <BETAGTHEIT IST NICHT NACH <TAGEN , DAS
<ALTER , DAS AUF IHR LIEGT , NICHT NACH <SONNENUML=AUFEN ZU BERECHNEN ;
#0300926 MIT EINEM <WORTE : SIE VERDANKT DEN <GRAD IHRES <VERGANGENSEINS
NICHT
EIGENTLICH DER <ZEIT ,  - EINE <AUSSAGE , WOMIT AUF DIE <FRAGW=URDIGKEIT
UND
EIGENT=UMLICHE <ZWIENATUR DIESES GEHEIMNISVOLLEN <ELEMENTES IM
<VORBEIGEHEN
ANGESPIELT UND HINGEWIESEN SEI .
#@
```

....

Fig. 1: Thomas Mann File: from "Zauberberg"

The text in Fig. 1 is taken from Thomas Mann File [12], [13]. If we choose some words in the text and take them as delimiters, for example **#@**, then the text is regarded as a collection of records, where a record in this case is a paragraph. This collection of records varies depending on the choice of delimiters. In this sense, a text file can represent various kinds of collections of records. Moreover, if we use another delimiters within records, for example a blank (␣), it allows extremely fine searches. This is a remarkable feature in one-way sequential processing of text files that is not found in another systems. It should be also stated that the current technology makes one-way sequential processings in feasible time. For example, it is possible to search a 2MB file (1,000,000 2-byte characters) in 1CPU second or in 5 seconds even if disk accessing time is included.

SIGMA has two specific features.

- Powerful and fast operators on text files (multiple key retrieval, multiple key replace, sorting, etc.). Some of commands are shown in Table 1.
- A new file system for text files that makes file constructions easier and more efficient.

SEARCH	:	search multiple keys
REPLACE	:	replace multiple keys
SORT	:	extract records and sort them
REFILE	:	make a text file from an index file
CATENATE	:	catenate files
COPY	:	copy a file
DELETE	:	remove a file and add it to BACK-UP
GET	:	move a file to WORK
KEYIN	:	write onto WORK
LOAD	:	load a file onto WORK
MOVE	:	move a file
PUT	:	put the top work file
SAVE	:	store the top work file
LOOK	:	show the topmost work file

Table 1: A list of commands

The first item is achieved by a fast efficient multiple key pattern matching algorithm for Japanese texts. With this algorithm, ten thousands of keywords can be searched and replaced both space and time efficiently. This pattern matching algorithm for Japanese texts keeps the speed even for texts only with 1-byte characters.

The file system enables a simple but practical realization of a learning system. It always keeps communications between the system and a user in a log file. This log file is also a text file consisting of a sequence of commands and inputs given by a user. It can be directly used as a program that executes the same commands. This idea helps users to construct programs rather easily.

SIGMA was first implemented on FACOM M-780 OS IV/F4 MSP at the Computer Center of Kyushu University and has been serving for researchers. It is also used in the main bureau of Fukuoka Prefecture for retrieving and organizing governmental documents.

SIGMA made a noticeable contribution to the natural language analysis. Higuchi [12], [13] constructed in SIGMA the Thomas Mann File (26MB; 11,000 pages; 400,000 lines) from the complete volumes of Thomas Mann (S. Fischer Verlag, in 13 Bänden, 1960) and investigated the usages of words by Thomas Mann. He made some discoveries and *proved* them by SIGMA [11], [12]. This was possible since it takes only one minute to *read* the whole volumes. He also constructed Goethe File (15MB) from Goethes Werke (Hamburger Ausgabe in 14 Bänden) [14]. A new style of research in Literature is going with SIGMA. Further, Tadauchi [21] has organized a database of insects reported in major journals in Japan (KONCHU; 12,000 records) in SIGMA. As far as data are prepared and organized as text files, SIGMA can work and help in another fields in various ways.

2. The file system

The files in SIGMA consists of three parts which are called a *MEMO space*, a *SIGMA space* and an *EXTERNAL space* (Fig. 2(a)). Each user can have these three spaces. A user makes files in a MEMO space for his/her own use. The files in a MEMO space are not shared with other users. The files in SIGMA space are for sharing data with other users. A SIGMA space simply consists of SIGMA and SIGMA-BACK-UP sections (Fig. 2(c)). The SIGMA-BACK-UP section forms a stack of files. The depth of the stack is currently set

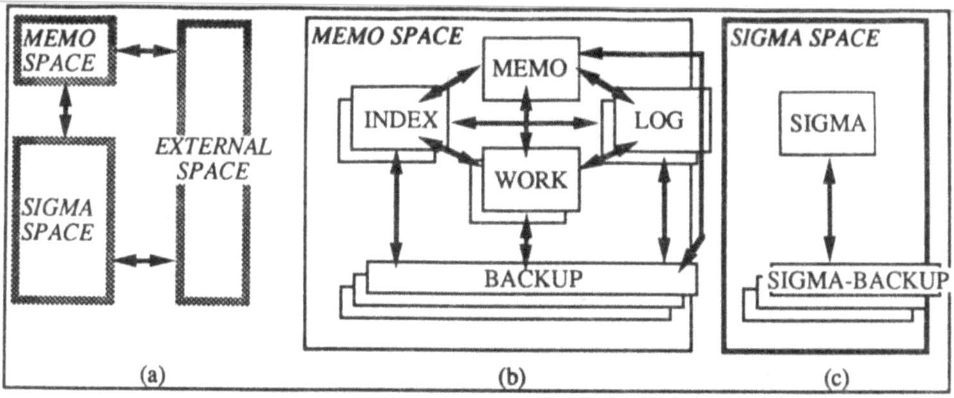

Fig. 2: Spaces and sections in SIGMA

900. The EXTERNAL space are the files under the operating system, terminals, printers, etc.

The files in a MEMO space are further classified into five sections MEMO, WORK, LOG, INDEX and BACK-UP (Fig. 2(b)). Each section except MEMO section is also a stack of files of bounded depth. The roles of these sections are as follows:

1. MEMO: Private files of a user are stored.

2. WORK: This is the work area for a user. A file in this section is called a *work file*. Usually, a file in another sections are moved or copied onto a work file for processing.

3. LOG : All but some communications between SIGMA and a user are recorded in a file called a *log file*. This file, for example, helps to construct a command procedure from a sequence of commands which is already tested for correct run. In this sense, the use of log files realizes the learning ability in the system.

4. INDEX: An execution of SEARCH command produces a file called an *indexing file*. Such files are stored in this section. The files in INDEX section are the only files which are not text files.

5. BACK-UP: The files flowing over from the stacks in WORK, LOG and INDEX sections and the files deleted from MEMO section are collected in this section. Some of the files in BACK-UP are deleted only if all space in a MEMO space is exhausted.

Since 1973 some of the authors have been concerned with the special research project on information systems for researchers [2], [4], [15]. The project concluded and proposed a view that scientific information systems consist of three levels data, namely, *private researcher files*, *user data library* and *center data library* [15]. Prior to SIGMA, an experimental system MIR-RF that deals with private researcher files and user data library was developed [2], [4]. The system SIGMA is mainly based on this view and the experiences from MIR-RF.

3. Multiple key pattern matching algorithm for Japanese texts

For one-way sequential processings of text files, pattern matching algorithms play the key role in extracting keywords from a text and replacing multiple keywords simultaneously.

The pattern matching problem is, given a text file T and a collection of keywords $K = \{k_1, ..., k_n\}$, to find all locations of occurrences of each keyword k_i for $i = 1, ..., n$. The most important techniques are pattern matching algorithms due to Knuth, Morris and Pratt [17], Boyer and Moore [10] and Aho and Corasick [1], respectively. The first two are for locating all or the first occurrence of a *single* keyword and the third for *multiple* keywords.

The system SIGMA is designed to satisfy the following item:

- 30 thousands of keywords shall be searched very fast at a time.

We adopted Aho-Corasick pattern matching machines [1] for searching because of the following reasons. First, multiple keywords must be simultaneously processed. The Boyer-Moore method is understood that it is the fastest way. Moreover, it can be extended for multiple key pattern matchings [22]. However, this method is not applicable to Japanese text processings since Japanese texts consists of both 1-byte and 2-byte characters with shift codes.

To achieve the above requirement with Aho-Corasick pattern matching machines, we had to overcome the following three difficulties:

(1) The Aho-Corasick pattern matching machine (pmm for short) is a finite automaton which locates all occurrences of given keywords. It consists of three functions; *goto*, *failure*, *output* (Fig. 4). In order to speed up the pmm, it is realized as a deterministic finite automaton by transforming the failure function to the goto function and using the state transition table by the technique so called *table look-at* [16]. If the number of the states in the pmm is s and characters are coded by 8 bits, then the size of the transition table becomes $256 \times s$. When the number of keywords is large, even on a large scale computer, we face memory shortage. Further, the problem becomes more serious since Japanese texts use about 7,000 of characters and require 2-byte codes.

(2) Let $P = \{(x_1, y_1), (x_2, y_2), ..., (x_n, y_n)\}$ be a set of pairs of patterns. The problem of replacing keywords $x_1, ..., x_n$ by specified words $y_1, ..., y_n$ seems to be similar to the pattern matching problem. However, the problem is not so simple since the patterns $x_1, ..., x_n$ may have overlaps.

(3) Texts in Japanese use Japanese alphabet *kana* and Chinese letters *kanji*. Kanji characters are represented by 2-byte codes. On the other hand, the usual 1-byte characters are also used together with special escape sequences. Without loosing the efficiency, the pmm is required to run on mixed occurrences of 1-byte and 2-byte characters.

The first problem (1) was solved in Arikawa and Shinohara [6]. The idea is dividing each character code into two subcodes and replacing each transition by two consecutive transitions. This simple idea surprisingly reduces the amount of memory. With this idea $256 \times s$ size table can be reduced to $2^4 \times 2 \times s = 32 \times s$, even in the worst case. The amount of space is just 1/8 while the running speed is only 2/3 slowed down at most. The experiments on various pattern matching machines showed that this technique is most suited for multiple key pattern matchings [6].

For the multiple key replacement problem, we devised a new algorithm [3], [7]. Our algorithm searches a given text T from left to right for the longest possible first occurring keyword x_i in

$$P_T = \{x_i \mid (x_i, y_i) \in P\}$$

and replaces it with the paired word y_i. This algorithm is also based on Aho-Corasick pattern matching machines.

Finally we have to cope with Japanese texts. According to Japanese Industrial Standards (JIS C 6226), the code system for Japanese texts is basically described as follows:

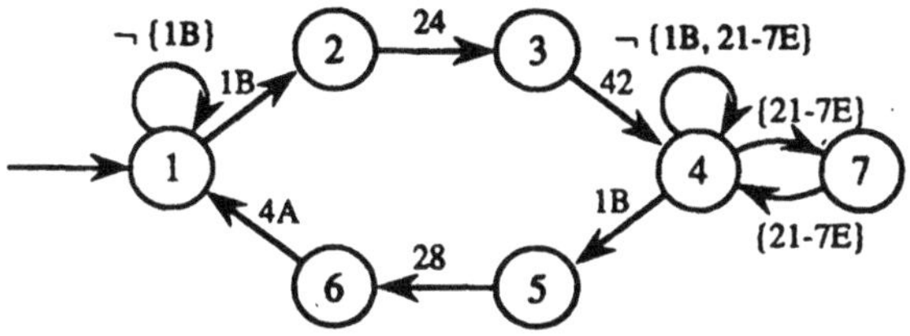

Fig. 3: Finite automaton accepting Japanese texts

1. 1 byte is 8 bits. 1-byte characters are from $00_{(16)}$ to $FF_{(16)}$, where numbers are represented in hexadecimal. Hence there are 256 1-byte characters.
2. A 2-byte character consists of two bytes. Both the first and last bytes are from $21_{(16)}$ to $7F_{(16)}$. There are 94×94 2-byte characters.
3. A switch to 2-byte characters is designated by the 3-byte escape sequence 1B 24 $42_{(16)}$ (KI for short).
4. A switch to 1-byte characters from $21_{(16)}$ to $7F_{(16)}$ is designated by 1B 28 $4A_{(16)}$ (KO for short). At the beginning of a text no designation is required.
5. 1-byte characters except $21_{(16)}$ to $7F_{(16)}$ are always designated.

For simplicity, we assume that no escape sequence other than KI and KO is used and no redundant occurrences of KI and KO are allowed. Formally, only strings accepted by the finite automaton in Fig. 3 are correct Japanese texts. We just mention the pattern matching machine for keywords k_1 =カナ (consisting of two characters "カ" and "ナ"), k_2 =KIab, k_3 =カナab, described Fig. 4. It should be noticed that the left part of the pmm is the same as the finite automaton accepting Japanese texts in Fig. 3. The details of constructions are shown in [19].

The commands `SEARCH`, `REPLACE` and `SORT` (that extracts keywords and sorts them according to the order specified by extracted keywords) in SIGMA are all realized with the algorithms and techniques developed above.

4. Using SIGMA

As stated in Introduction, a text can be regarded as various collections of records according to purposes. For example, in Thomas Mann File, words can be regarded as records by setting the blank symbol (␣) and other unnecessary symbols to be delimiters. On the other hand, sentences and paragraphs can also be taken as records using delimiters `#` and `#@`, respectively.

Let us explain how the command `SEARCH` works. The following is an example of search for Thomas Mann File.

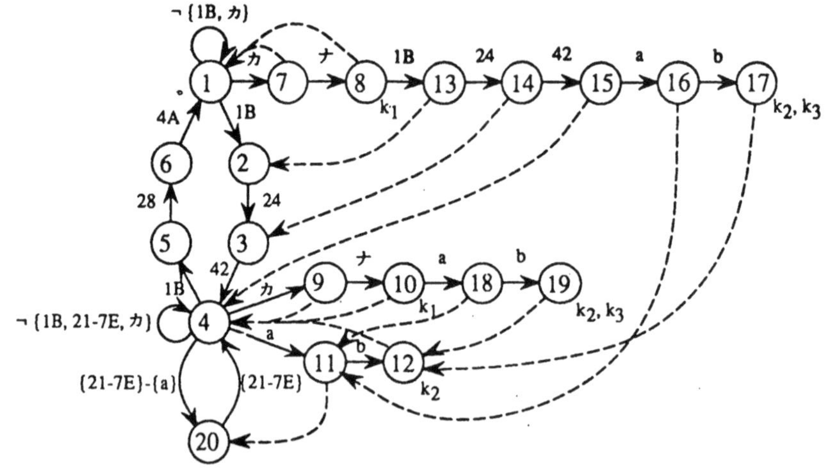

The solid arrows and the broken arrows (ϵ-moves) represent the goto and the failure functions, respectively. The strings k_i below the states mean outputs from them.

Fig. 4: The pattern matching machine for {カナ, KIab, カナab }

```
SEARCH
FILE:=MANN.ZB
    RECORD DELIMITERS
D1:=#
    KEYWORDS
A1:=⊔UM⊔...⊔ZU⊔
A2:=⊔WENN⊔...⊔AUCH⊔
A3:=⊔UN
A4:=⊔UND⊔
    LOGICAL FORMULAS
Z1:=A1
Z2:=A2
Z3:=A3
Z4:=A3.^ A4
Z5:=A3>A4
```

· The choice of the delimiter # specifies that records are sentences. **A1, A2, A3, A4** are called *keyword variables* each of which gets a keyword. The *triple dot* "..." in **A1** and **A2** represents a wild card and ⊔ represents a blank symbol. With each keyword variable **Ai**, a counter is associated to count the number of occurrences of the keyword assigned to **Ai** in a record. **A1**, ..., **A4** also denote these numbers. These counters shall be reset everytime the next record comes.

Z1, ...,**Z5** are called *formula variables*. A *logical formulas* is composed by using keyword variables (**A1**, **A2**, *ldots*), formula variables (**Z1**, **Z2**, ...), integers, logical operators ("," (or), "." (and), "^ " (not)), comparison operators (<, >, ...), arithmetic operators (+, −, ∗, /) and parentheses. A logical formula is assigned to each logical variable.

For each logical variable, the SEARCH command retrieves the records defined by its logical formula but simultaneously for all logical variables. For example, after the execution

```
\#@
\#0300907 Die Geschichte Hans Castorps, die wir erz=ahlen wollen,
 - nicht um seinetwillen  (denn der Leser wird einen einfachen, wenn
auch ansprechen den jungen Menschen in ihm kennenlernen), sondern um
                              .....
\#@
\#0300917 Das w=are kein Nachteil f=ur eine Geschichite, sondern eher ein
Vorteil;
                              .....
```

Fig. 5.

of SEARCH, **Z1** is the set of sentences containing the form "␣UM␣...␣ZU␣" and **Z3** is the set of sentences containing a word with prefix "UN".

The following search is possible by SEARCH that cannot be achieved by information retrieval systems based on inverted files:

Example 1. In Thomas Mann File, find all sentences which contains a word that has "UN" as its prefix but is not "UND".

It should be noted that **Z4:=**A3.^ **A4** does not satisfy our requirement since a sentence which contains both "UND" and "UNTER" cannot be retrieved by this formula. Example 1 is simply solved by **Z5:=**A3>A4 that retrieves the sentences in which the number of words with prefix "UN" is greater than the number of "UND".

When the text file to be searched is quite large, the REPLACE command executing multiple replacements of keywords is as useful as SEARCH.

The command REPLACE is very powerful in the following case:

Example 2. Change the sentences in Fig. 1 to Fig. 5.

Example 2 can be processed in the following way:

REPLACE
FILE:=MANN.ZB
X1:=<A
Y1:=A
X2:=A
Y2:=a
.....
X52:=<Z
Y52:=Z
.....

Since the multiple keyword replacement algorithm replaces the first found longest keyword, the above replacement correctly works.

The command SORT also plays an important role in organizing files. It extracts keywords from records in a way to REPLACE and sorts them according to the order of chosen words. Therefore, it allows various sorting orders.

The use of a log file is very useful in constructing command procedures. It consists of prompts from the system and responses from a user. While we are working on the system this file is automatically and uncosciously constructed.

Exploiting these commands, we can make very fine retrievals, conversions of files and sortings of records. Intensive usages of SIGMA are found in [9], [11], [12], [13], [21].

5. An improvement of the main engine

In order to realize more flexible and finer processing on texts, we improve the main engine, i.e., the pattern matching machine. The Aho-Corasick machine searches simply string patterns. Here we consider patterns with pictures. For example, let A be a picture for a, b, ..., z, and N for 0, 1, ..., 9. Then we treat patterns such as aA, a7$NNNNA$, ..., etc.

For these patterns, the naive method is to construct a machine from all strings in the patterns. That is, for the pattern aA we build a machine from strings aa, ab, ..., az. This method, however, increases the number of states exponentially. We have already invented an algorithm to construct an efficient machine for multiple patterns with pictures [23]. A machine can be built easily and quickly, and the number of states is decreased as we possibly can, without the state minimization technique. After the construction, it runs in linear time proportional to the text length as the Aho-Corasick achieves.

Unfortunately, the method of dividing each 1-byte character into two subcodes can not be used. But we can treat some pictures for 2-byte characters, for example *Hiragana*, *Kanji*, etc., by taking them as concatenations of two pictures.

This algorithm is available not only for the command SEARCH but also for the command REPLACE [24]. Suppose that we want to change 1967, 1979, 1985, ... to '67, '79, '85, ..., respectively. By the command REPLACE, we have to give all pairs (1967, '67), (1979, '79), (1985, '85), ... On the other hand, by using pictures, we may simply give a pair of patterns with pictures as follows:

$$19NN \Rightarrow \text{'}NN .$$

We are improving the main engine with this algorithm, to realize more powerful commands for text processing.

References

[1] A.V. Aho and M.J. Corasick, Efficient string matching: An aid to bibliographic search, Comm. ACM **18** (1975) 333-340.

[2] S. Arikawa and T. Kitagawa, Multistage information retrieval system based on researcher files, *Proc. 2nd USA-Japan Computer Conf.* (1975) 149-153.

[3] S. Arikawa, One-way sequential search systems and their powers, Bulletin of Mathematical Statistics **19** (1981) 69-85.

[4] S. Arikawa, S. Kano, T. Kitagawa and S. Takeya, Organization and use of private researcher files in scientific research works, Scientific Information Systems in Japan (H. Inose, ed.), North-Holland, (1981) 43-50.

[5] S. Arikawa, T. Shinohara, S. Shiraishi and Y. Tamakoshi, SIGMA - An information system for researchers use, Bull. Informatics and Cybernetics **20** (1982) 97-114.

[6] S. Arikawa and T. Shinohara, A run-time efficient realization of Aho-Corasick pattern matching machines, New Generation Computing **2** (1984) 171-186.

[7] S. Arikawa and S. Shiraishi, Pattern matching machine for replacing several character strings, Bull. Informatics and Cybernetics **21** (1984) 101-111.

[8] S. Arikawa and T. Shinohara, String pattern matching algorithms, Computer Software **4** (1987) 2-23 (in Japanese).

[9] S. Arikawa et al., A text database management system SIGMA: Version 2, Koho **20** (1987) 517-581, Computer Center, Kyushu University (in Japanese).

[10] R.S. Boyer and J.S. Moore, A fast string searching algorithm, Comm. ACM **20** (1977) 762-772.

[11] T. Higuchi, Über den Gebrauch von „bis“, Doku-Futsu Bungaku Kenkyu **36** (1986) 183-210, Kyushu University.

[12] T. Higuchi, On Thomas Mann File, Research Reports in Computer Science **4** (1987) 37-39, Computer Center, Kyushsu University (in Japanese).

[13] T. Higuchi and T. Shinohara, Completing and reorganizing a text database "Thomas Mann File", Koho **20** (1987) 582-596, Computer Center, Kyushu University (in Japanese).

[14] T. Higuchi, Completing a text database "Goethe File", Koho **22** (1989) 1-5, Computer Center, Kyushu University (in Japanese).

[15] H. Inose (ed.), Scientific Information Systems in Japan, North-Holland, 1981.

[16] D.E. Knuth, The Art of Computer Programming, Vol. **3**, Sorting and Searching, Addison-Wesley, 1973.

[17] D.E. Knuth, J.H. Morris Jr. and V.R. Pratt, Fast pattern matching in strings, SIAM J. Comput. **6** (1977) 323-350.

[18] G. Salton and M.J. McGill, Introduction to Modern Information Retrieval, McGraw-Hill, 1983.

[19] T. Shinohara and S. Arikawa, Pattern matching machines for Japanese texts, Research Report No. 110, Research Institute of Fundamental Information Science, Kyushu University, March, 1986.

[20] T. Shinohara, S. Futamura and F. Matsuo, On revised version of an in formation retrieval system AIR, Koho **20** (1987) 211-238, Computer Center, Kyushu University (in Japanese).

[21] O. Tadauchi, A public database of entomology KONCHU and its usage, Koho **20** (1987) 597-614, Computer Center, Kyushu University (in Japanese).

[22] M. Takeda, A proof of the coprrectness of Uratani's string searching algorithm, RIFIS-TR-CS-7, Research Institute of Fundamental Information Science, Kyushu University, October, 1988.

[23] M. Takeda, A fast matching algorithm for patterns with pictures, RIFIS-TR-CS-11, Research Institute of Fundamental Information Science, Kyushu University, March, 1989.

[24] M. Takeda, Efficient multiple string replacing with pictures, RIFIS-TR-CS-13, Research Institute of Fundamental Information Science, Kyushu University, March, 1989.

[25] J.D. Ullman, Principles of Database Systems, second edition, Computer Science Press, 1982.

MARS - Multimedia Archiving and Retrieval System: An Algebraic Specification of the Document Model

Helmut Eirund

Universität Oldenburg
FB Informatik
Postfach 2503
D-2900 Oldenburg

Abstract:

This paper presents an informal discussion and an algebraic specification of a model for multimedia documents. It satisfies the requirements formulated for conceptual modeling of unstructured documents, supporting efficient retrieval and flexibility in dynamic applications. The mapping of the syntactic clauses of the query language to operator expressions are discussed. The model is employed within the MARS project at University of Oldenburg. A first application is developed for the radiologic department of a district hospital.

1. Introduction

Documents are the basic information sources in various office applications, e.g. in management, engeneering or clinical environment. Electronic documents are no longer restricted to alpha-numerical data or strict formatted forms. In this paper we refer to *documents* as information units in electronic representation with a not neccessary formular structur. It consists of multimedia content units, like alpha-numeric character sequences (text), graphics, bit-map images or audio annotations.

Examples of documents coming from several application fields are accounting forms (strong formatted), product offers (free formatted), radiograms (image with inclosed data fields), reports (complex) or memos (simple).

With the variety of structural information that can be observed, two questions arise:

(i) *What structural information is to be described* ?
Documents are normally manipulated as one unit by the end-user, i.e. the document is a single *user object*. Heterogenous structural information can be observed that describes different views of the document, supporting different utilizations:
- a document represented in pages, blocks etc. enables the presentation of the document content on an output-medium
- partitioning of the document content in e.g. chapters, paragraphs, subparagraphs supports the intelectual comprehension of the document content
- naming and describing semantic components of a document (independent from layout and logic objects) serves for accessing documents by qualifying those components.

(ii) *How is the structural information to be represented* ?
Splitting document units into several different relations (i.e. one document represented as a set of *model objects*) according to their structural properties, needs a lot of expansive joining operations to reconstruct the *user object* each time a document is manipulated by the user. Furthermore, giving structural information implicitly through a relational schema tends to be too unflexible to describe all occurences of structural relations in office documents.

The different utilizations presented above motivate three different views of document structure: (a) the *layout structure*, (b) the *syntactic structure* and (c) the *conceptual structure*.

All these views can be represented in a tree like manner, where inner nodes include structural information and are described by more simple objects, their subnodes. Leaf nodes are associated to content portions. Layout and logic structure of multimedia documents can be efficiently described within the ODA standard (Office Document Architecture). The Standard is specified in [ECMA85].

In this paper a model for the conceptual view is formalized. The MARS Project (Multimedia Archiving and Retrieval System) at University of Oldenburg follows this specification. Influences came from the modeling approach first presented in [Barb85] and from the ESPRIT project MULTOS that makes use of conceptual structures for multimedia document retrieval [Cons86], [Bert88].

The syntactic structure of this paper is as follows: In the second chapter the problem of representing document semantics is discussed and on that basis requirements of a document model are formulated. Furthermore, a general view of the document model employed in MARS is given. Chapter 3 very briefly introduces some fundamentals of a usual algebraic specification formalism (readers familiar with this specification method may skip the chapter). In chapter 4 the specification of the model is given and the semantic specifications of some selected operations are discussed. A test application currently developed within a clinical environment is presented in chapter 5. Chapter 6 concludes with a summary.

2. Requirements for a Conceptual Document Model

In many papers requirements have been defined for designing office models or data models specially suitable for office applications with different emphasis, e.g. - [Abra87] propose an extension of the ER model for software engeneering; - many suggestions are based on the NF^2-model [Sche82], appropriate complex operations are given in [Sche83]; - semantic information of office documents were discussed in [Sacc84]; - [Förs88] analysed requirements of archiving systems in the office and give a classification of models; - involving knowledge bases for document representation are proposed in many papers, e.g. in [Crof86], partially implemented in [Appe87]).

Concepts for document modeling and manipulation are influenced from at least three sides:

- database theory with a practicable relational calculus,
- information retrieval with its homogenous view of the data object "document" and appropriate access methodes and
- knowledge engeneering with the issue of representing complex user objects through model objects in a suitable way.

The following list describes the main requirements that have influence on the MARS document model:

(a) Provide an *abstract view* of document semantics: describe document semantics by naming conceptual units, i.e. application relevant units, and specifying hierarchical relations between them, like aggregation or specialization.

(b) Associate values (content portions) to conceptual units and permit *fact retrieval* by qualifying documents through document values.

(c) Support a systematic and consistent process of modeling document semantics: typical semantic properties of documents are generalized to *document types* that serve as templates and support query formulation as well as evaluation.

(d) Allow *flexibility* of describing document semantics and types.

Informal Discussion of the MARS Model

Tree structures are well suited for representing document semantic strutures. In the MARS model *document conceptual structures* are defined as trees. It identifies and allocates a name to all those components of a document that are relevant for further processing [Eiru88].

A conceptual structure is composed of *conceptual components* (also denoted as *concepts*). It contains *basic* conceptual components as leaf nodes, possibly with content portions associated as values, and *complex* conceptual components constructed by subcomponents. The construction mechanism may be *aggregate* to describe a concept by those concepts participating in its definition, or *specialize* to describe a concept as a whole. The next figure visualize[1] a document conceptual structure that can be observed in a clinical environment.

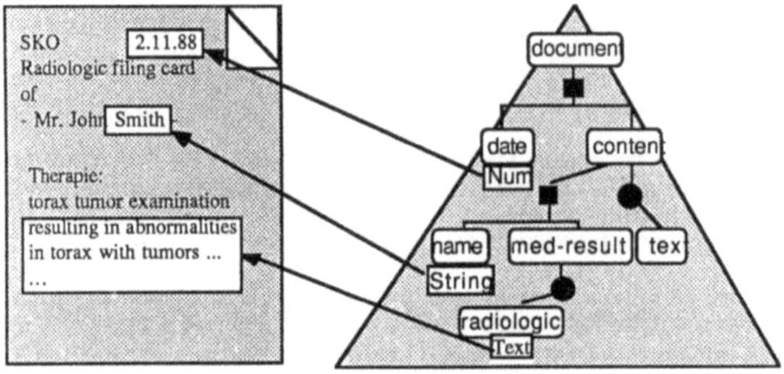

Figure 1: Document with its conceptual structure

Classes of similar structured documents can be described by document types. A type conceptual structure is a generalization of the document conceptual structures associated to it. Thus, basic concepts in type conceptual structures are not further described by associated values but have value *domain specifications* . Furthermore, a varity of concepts specializing one concept can be formulated (*choice-specialization*). Document conceptual structures are instances of the appropriate types. Figure 2 visualizes[2] a possible type conceptual structure with the document structure of fig. 1 as one of its instances.

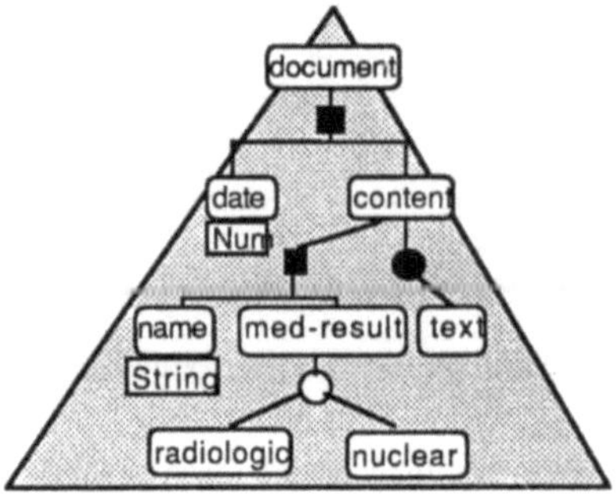

Figure 2: Type conceptual structure

Document conceptual structures of one type are not required to be identical. This is denoted *weak typing* opposed to strong typing. Refinement of types also can produce new types (subtypes). According to this refinement relation that specifies inheritance of type conceptual structures to subtypes the set of types can be organized in a directed acyclic graph. Both, weak typing and multiple inheritance provide the flexibility demanded above.

These data structures together with a defined set of operations for creating, modifying and selecting them, is the basis of the MARS document model.

---

1 The graphic representations are: - aggregate constructor / black square, specialization / black circle, value / arrow to value box, value domain / associated box.

2 The graphic representation for choice-specialization is an unfilled circle.

3. Some basic statements on the specification of the MARS model

There are several specification techniques for abstract data types, e.g. specification by intuition, example or implementation. These are all straight forward, but often things become complicated when investigating some more sophisticated questions.

We present an abstract specification that should describe, how document semantics is represented and manipulated. In [Gutt77], [Henh87] and others the algebraic specification formalism is recommended for describing data structures and the appropriate operations. It helps to present syntax and semantics of both, supports verification of model properties and a consistent model specification. Furthermore, properties difficult to express in a data model (e.g. "well defined" conceptual structure, "value" of a concept) can be shifted into the specification of the appropriate operations (modification and value operations, resp.).

Trying to follow the enhancements proposed in the algorithmic specification formalism by [Loec87], we specify the semantics of most of the MARS operations through recursive functions.Thus the existence of an implementation and its freedom of contradictions can be simply derived.

In the rest of this section we introduce two basic definitions and a small example to make the formalism employed in chapter 4 more understandable.

An algebraic specification consists of two parts: a *syntactic specification* and the description of the *semantics of the syntactic elements*. The syntactic specification is fixed in a *signature* of the formal language or abstract data type. Similar to the interface specification a signature determines the descriptors of the relevant data domains and operator symbols, and defines the type of the operators. In the following the basic elements of the formalism used hereafter is presented. A more exact backround give e.g. [Klae83].

Elements of algebraic specification:

Definition: A *Signature* is a pair $<S, \Sigma>$, with S a set of sorts, Σ a family of sets of operator symbols. Each element O_k of Σ is linked to a sequence $(s1_k,\ldots,sn{+}1_k)$, $s_{ij} \in S$. An operator op is syntacticly defined by its symbol $op_s \in O_k$ and the association of the sequence of argument sorts $(s1_k,\ldots,sn_k)$ and its target sort $sn{+}1_k$.

The second part of the algebraic specification determines the semantic properties. For each sort a carrier set is defined, i.e. the set of its values, and for each operator symbol a mapping from the carriersets of the argument sorts to the carrierset of the target domain is given. This part is called a *Σ-algebra*.

Definition: Let $<S, \Sigma>$ be a signature, (C^s) denotes the carrierset of s and $C = (C^s)_{s\in S}$ is a family of sets. Let $C^{\varepsilon} =_{df} \{\}$ and $C^{ws} =_{df} C^w \times C^s$, with $w \in S^*$, $s \in S$.
For each op_s in each $O_k \in \Sigma$ a mapping op_{sC} is associated with $C^{(s1_k,\ldots,sn_k)} \rightarrow C^{sn+1_k}$.
The pair $(C, \{op_{sC} \mid op_s \in S\})$ defines a Σ-algebra.

Some extensions should be presented informally. We introduce variables by giving the corresponding *term-algebra* with defining *terms* by: each element of a carrier set, each operator expression and each variable. A set of equations implies equivalence classes on different syntactic elements with same semantics. Restricting operator specification to those classes abbreviates the specification process.

Example: - algebraic specification of the abstract data type "Set" -

The signature <S, Σ> is given by:

S= {Set, Int, Bool}

with constructors[3] for Set: emptyset: → Set, and insert: Set, Int → Set

Σ= {InSet: Int, Set → Bool}[4], tests the membership of an Int-element in a set

The Σ-algebra comes with:

C^{Bool} =df {true, false}

C^{Int} =df N

C^{Set} =df {"the set of words defined by constructors" [5] }

InSet (i, s) =df | true, if $\exists\, e_1,..,e_n \in C^{Int}, s_{n+1} \in C^{Set}$ with
$s = insert\,(..(\,insert\,(s_{n+1}, i), e_n)..), e_1)$
| false, else

Equations:

insert (insert (s, j), i) = insert (insert (s, i), j), with i, j∈ N, s ∈ Set

insert (insert (s, i), i) = insert (s, i), with i ∈ N, s ∈ Set

An algorithmic notation of the example above would change the definition of the mapping given for the operator by a recursiv function, e.g.

InSet (i, s) =df	| true,	if	s = insert (s' i)
	| false,	if	s = emptyset
	| InSet (i, s'),	if	s= insert (s', j), j≠i

4. Data Structures and Operators of the MARS Model

This section outlines the signature and the Σ-Algebra of the document model employed by MARS, as introduced informally in the 2nd chapter. We first present the set of sorts together with the description of their carrier sets as comments (in brackets "(* .. *)"). In the rest of this paper we will identify a sort with the respective carrier set for abbreviation reason.

```
S = {  CC,              (* descriptors of the conceptual components, denoted as concepts  *)
       Dom,             (* set of sort descriptors of the atomic value domains: "Num",
                           "Text", "String"                                               *)
       Num, Text, String (* atomic value domains, also denoted by Dom_i,
                           the carrier set of Text is arbitrary sequences of String-elements *)
       Bool,            (* = {true, false}                                                *)
       CS               (* any conceptual structures (e.g.document-, type-, sub-structure *)
    }
```

Elements of the sort CS are tree-like structures with concepts as nodes and constructors that define all the relationships between nodes. Latter describe the structural properties of the document semantics and will be given in the following list:

3 Constructors can be seen as unevaluable operators. The semantics of a constructor term is just the character sequence built according its definiton.

4 The target sort is prefixed with a "→"

5 The syntactic definition of a sort with constructors implies a context free grammar; here:
G= (Set, {emptyset, insert, N}, {Set}, {Set ::= emptyset | insert (Set , N) }) and
$L(G) = C^{Set}$

```
CS =df ( CC;              (* single node structure                                        *)
  agg (CC,CS+⁶)           (* concept with its aggregates and their substructures          *)
  spec (CC, CS+)          (* concept with a set of its specialisations and their substructures *)
  c-spec (CC,(CS+)+)      (* concept with possible (choice-) specializations, applicable only
                             in type structures, to make them more general                *)
  conc (CS+)              (* combination of different kinds of structure with same root - thus
                             it is used for technical reason and does not express any semantics
                             of the document content                                      *)
  iterate (CC, Num)       (* identical iteration of one concept with its substructures, applicable
                             only in type structures                                      *)
  domain (CC, Dom)        (* concept with associated value domain - establishes an attribute *)
  value(CC, Dom, Domᵢ)    (* concept with linked value from given domain                   *)
  )
```

The constructive definition of CS allows the definition of different structures although describing same properties. The following equations E help to minimize redundancy[7]:

$$
\begin{aligned}
E =_{df} (\ & \mathrm{conc}(\mathrm{Tree}, \mathrm{Node}) &&= \mathrm{Tree}, \quad \text{if } \mathrm{Tree} = \Phi(\mathrm{Node}, \mathrm{Arg}^{\rightarrow}) \\
& \mathrm{conc}(\mathrm{Tree}_1, \mathrm{conc}(\mathrm{Tree}_2, \mathrm{Tree}_3)) &&= \mathrm{conc}(\mathrm{Tree}_1, \mathrm{Tree}_2, \mathrm{Tree}_3) \\
& \Phi(\mathrm{Node}, \varepsilon) &&= \mathrm{Node}, \quad \text{if } \Phi \in \{\mathrm{agg}, \mathrm{spec}, \text{c-spec}\} \\
& \Phi(\mathrm{Node}, (\mathrm{Sub}_1^{\rightarrow}, \ldots, \mathrm{Sub}_n^{\rightarrow})) &&= \Phi(\mathrm{Node}, (\mathrm{Sub}_2^{\rightarrow}, \mathrm{Sub}_1^{\rightarrow}, \ldots, \mathrm{Sub}_n^{\rightarrow})), \quad \text{if } \Phi \text{ as above} \\
& \mathrm{conc}(\Phi(\mathrm{Node}, \mathrm{Sub}^{\rightarrow}), \Phi(\mathrm{Node}, \mathrm{Sub}^{\sim\rightarrow})) &&= \Phi(\mathrm{Node}, (\mathrm{Sub}^{\rightarrow} \oplus \mathrm{Sub}^{\sim\rightarrow})), \quad \text{if } \Phi \text{ as above} \\
).
\end{aligned}
$$

As we distinguish document conceptual structures from the generalized type conceptual structures, a further rule not expressed in the data structure specification nore hidden in the operation specifications should be given informally:

Type-Instance-Rule:

(a) Type conceptual structures do not contain "iterate" or "value" constructors
(b) Document conceptual structures (as instantiations of a type structure) have:
- a "value" constructor for each "domain" constructor in the type (a value is linked to each attribute-concept)
- no choice of specialisation ("c-spec" constructor)

The notation of a (simplified) conceptual structure is given in the following example. It referes to the structures given in fig. 1 and fig. 2, respectively.

Example: - referring to figures 1 and 2 above -

(a) type conceptual structure (-> fig. 2)

Let cs ∈ C^{CS} be defined:

cs = agg (document, (domain (date, Num), conc (spec (content, text), agg (content, (domain (name, String), c-spec (med-result, (radiological, nuclear)))))))

(b) document conceptual structure, instance of type in (-> fig. 1)

Let cs ∈ C^{CS} be defined:

cs = agg (document, (value (date, Num, 881102), conc (spec (content, text), agg (content, (value (name, String, Smith), spec(med-result, (value (radiological, Text, <offset,length>))))))))

---

6 the "S+" names a sort S that specifies all non-empty sequences of elements of sort S - to avoid introduction of new sort descriptors.

7 Notations: • Arg→ denotes the rest of an argument list
• ⊕ denotes concatenation of sequences

The Syntactic Specification of the Operators Σ

The set Σ of sequences of argument and target sorts with the appropriate operator symbols are presented in the following list. Again an informal description of the operator function is given in comments:

Σ = { (CS, CC -> CS)	view (* provides superstructure with given leaf node *)
	project (* provides substructure for given root node *)
(CS, CC -> Bool)	is-concept (* existence of a concept in a structure *)
(CS -> CC)	root-concept (* root concept of a (sub-)structure *)
(CS, CS -> Bool)	is-substruc (* existence of a substructure in a structure *)
	is-ref (* compares two structures for refinement *)
(CS, CS, CS -> CS)	subst (* substitutes substructure in given structure *)
(-> CS)	create (* initialize new structure *)
(CC, CS, CS -> CS)	ref (* refine given structure in a specified concept by a new substructure ("refinement-step") *)
(CS+, CC -> Dom_i*)	val (* provides all values related to a concept *)
(Dom_i, Dom_i -> Bool)	<, >, =, ≠, contains[8] (* relations on atomic values *)
(CS, CC, Dom_i -> Bool)	$select_\rho$ (* compare according to ρ ∈ {<, >, =, ≠, contains} the values of a concept with a given value *)
(CS+ -> CS)	merge (* combines a refined structure from given structures*)
}	

Semantics of the Operators

In this section the semantics of the operators defined within the model is described. As structure manipulation is only supported by these set of operations, much of the data model semantics is implied by the operations.

The operators can be grouped into three groups: we distinguish operators for
- creating (i.e. initializing) and modifying structures (create, ref, merge),
- restricting structures to subparts (project, view, value) and
- comparing constants and structures (is-ref, select and the constant relations: {<,>,=,≠,contains}).

Furthermore, some basic operators are used to help defining the operators above (is-concept, is-substructure, root-concept, substitute). The definition of the operations are mostly defined recursively. We do not want to discuss all of them in this paper, but give some examples for the most essential ones:

The Operators "create". and "ref":

In the specification of the sort CS all possible structures are defined. Although, not all of these elements describe <u>well defined conceptual structures</u> of documents or types. These consistency constraints are hidden in the "ref" operator. Its definition describes all cases of allowed refinement steps that leads again to a well defined structure. All well defined structures have the root concept in common (named: $root^o$), initialized by the operator "create":

create () $=_{df}$ ($root^o$)

Some of the constraints given in the "ref"-operator, are presented below:[9]

---

8 "t contains s" denotes inclusion of s ∈ String in t ∈ Text

9 Notations:
- Arg→ denotes the rest of an argument list
- ⊕ denotes concatenation of sequences

ref (RefNode, RefStep, Tree) $=_{df}$

(1) | Tree [RefNode / RefStep],
<u>if</u> project (RefNode, Tree) = RefNode

(2) | Tree [domain (RefNode, dom) / value (RefNode, dom, v)],
<u>if</u> project (RefNode, Tree) = domain (RefNode, dom)
and RefStep = value (RefNode, dom, v) and $v \in C^{dom}$

(3) | Tree [Φ (RefNode, (Sub_1,..,Sub_n)) / Φ(RefNode, (Sub_1,..,Sub_n)$\oplus$ RefTrees$\rightarrow$)],
<u>if</u> project (RefNode, Tree) = Φ(RefNode, (Sub_1,..,Sub_n)) and
RefStep= Φ(RefNode, RefTrees$\rightarrow$), für $\Phi \in$ {agg, spez, c-spez}

(4) | Tree [c-spec (RefNode, (($Sub1_1$,..,$Sub1_n$),..,($Subm_1$,..,$Subm_n$))) /
conc (c-spec (RefNode, (($Sub2_1$,..,$Sub2_n$),..,($Subm_1$,..,$Subm_n$))),
spec (RefNode, ($Sub1_i$)))]
<u>if</u> project (RefNode, Tree)
= c-spec (RefNode, (($Sub1_1$,..,$Sub1_n$),..,($Subm_1$,..,$Subm_n$))
and RefStep = spec (RefNode, ($Sub1_i$))[10]

...

(7) | undefined, else

The following table summaries the substitution rules given in the "ref"-specification. The labels are "n" (no substitution), "s i" (substitution according to rule i), "c" (concatenation with "conc" constructor) and "-" (not defined).

Φ RefStep / Tree	*CC*	*dom*	*value*	*agg*	*spec*	*c-spec*	*iterate*
CC	n	s 1	s 1	s 1	s 1	s 1	s 1
dom	n	c	s 2	c	c	c	s 6
value	n	-	-	-	-	-	-
agg	n	c	-	s 3	c	c	s 6
spec	n	c	-	c	s 3	c	s 6
c-spec	n	c	-	c	s 4	s 3	s 6
iterate	-	-	-	-	-	-	-

The Operators val, select and is-ref

val (Tree, Node) $=_{df}$

| { (dom, v) }, <u>if</u> project (Tree, Node) = value (Node, dom, v)

| $\cup_{(SubTree \in Sub)}$ val (SubTree, root -concept (SubTree)),
<u>if</u> Sub = {SubTree | is-substruc (SubTree, project (Tree, Node)
and SubTree $\neq$Tree}

| {}, else

$select_\rho$ (Tree, Node, c) $=_{df}$

| true, <u>if</u> ($dom_i \neq$ Text
and $\exists(v_i, dom_i) \in$ val (Tree, Node): $v_i \rho c$, and $\rho \in \{<,>,=\}$
or $\neg\exists(v_i, dom_i) \in$ val (Tree, Node): $v_i = c$, and ρ = "$\neq$")
or ($\exists(v_i, dom_i) \in$ val (Tree, Node): $v_i = c$, and $dom_i \neq$ Text
or $\exists(v_i, Text) \in$ val (Tree, Node): $v_i \rho c$) and ρ ="contains"

| false, else

10 without restriction according to equations

As stated before, document structures are refinements of appropriate types (and associated to those types), and the type catalogue itself defines a directed acyclic graph according to the refinement relation. Refinements are defined by applying the "ref" operator - thus, structures can be equivalently specified an appropriate sequence of "ref"-applications. The "is-ref" operator uses this notation for specifying two structures to be in refinement relation:

is-ref (TreeSpec, Tree) =df
| true, if $\exists$ {N_1,..,N_n}, {$RefStep_1$,..,$RefStep_n$} with $n \geq 1$ and
TreeSpec = ref (N_n, $RefStep_n$) ref (N_1, $RefStep_1$) (Tree)
| false, else

Query-Language

With the operations above the query language can be defined. The features of the query language are: qualifying documents by
(a) their type association, (*type clause*) and / or
(b) the existence of a concept, (*existence clause*) and / or
(c) the value of a concept (*value clause*) [11].

The expressions of (a) are defined with the "is-ref" operator, (b) is defined with the "is-concept" operator and (c) is mapped to appropriate applications of the "$select_\rho$" operator. The evaluation of the operation expression is to be interpreted against a state of the MARS document archive $\mathcal{A}$ enhanced by the state of type catalogue $\mathcal{C}$. We define such an extended state $s_{\mathcal{AC}}$ as follows:

Definition: An *extended state* $s_{\mathcal{AC}}$ of a MARS archive is a triple (A, T, L) with:
- A is a set of pairs (ldi, cs), with ldi $\in ID_{\mathcal{A}}$, a countable set of internal logic document identifiers and cs is a document conceptual structure and ldi is unique in A.
- T is a set of pairs (lti, cs_t), with lti $\in ID_{\mathcal{C}}$, a countable set of internal logic type identifiers and cs is a type conceptual structure and lti is unique in T.
- L is a totally defined function mapping each pair (ldi,cs)$\in$ A to a *best fitting* type (lti,cs_t)$\in$ T, i.e.: $\forall$ (ldi,cs) $\in$ A $\exists$ (lti, cs_t)$\in$ T: ((ldi,cs), (lti, cs_t)) $\in$ L and is-ref (cs, cs_t) and $\neg$ ($\exists$ (lti', cs_t') $\in$ T: ((ldi,cs), (lti', cs_t')) $\in$ L and is-ref (cs, cs_t') and is-ref (cs_t', cs_t))

The evaluation of the tree kinds of clause-expressions is defined in the following way:
(a) For each type identifier $lti_t \in ID_{\mathcal{C}}$ of the type clause the set
{(ldi_d, cs) | $ldi_d \in ID_{\mathcal{A}}$ and is-ref (cs, cs_t)}
is evaluated, if (lti_t, cs_t) $\in$ C, {} otherwise. Thus we get the transitive closure according to the refinement relation. Sets for different type identifiers in the clause are united.

(b) For each concept c given in the existence clause the set
{(ldi_d, cs) | $ldi_d \in ID_{\mathcal{A}}$ and is-concept (cs, c)}
is evaluated.
(c) For each comparison (c ρ val) given in the value clause the set
{(ldi_d, cs) | $ldi_d \in ID_{\mathcal{A}}$ and $select_\rho$ (cs, c, val)}
is evaluated.
The boolean relations AND and OR in (b) and (c) are mapped to union and intersection respectively.

---

11 A further qualification of documents is supported in MARS by restricting the search scope to documents of user defined collections (*collection clause*)- they may be created by former query-results. As it is not a special document qualification coming from the model it is not discussed here.

With the specifications of the operators and the state given above, optimized evaluation algorithms can be varified. E.g. for the evaluation of the type clause first evaluating the set of all types in the transitive closure of the given type and then inquiring the L-relation will propably provide the specified documents more efficiently.

An example query that will qualify the document given in fig. 1, may be:
FIND DOCUMENTS [OF TYPE xxx] WHERE date > 880101 AND med-result CONTAINS "tumors"

5. Test Application in a Clinical Environment

A first application of MARS that supports the manipulation of conceptual structures is developed for the radiologic department of the district hospital in Oldenburg (SKO: Städtische Kliniken Oldenburg). To provide basic storage and retrieval functions for a large amount of data (estimation: 20 GigaByte a year for approximately 60.000 documents of different types) a Picture Archiving and Communication System (PACS), specially developed for clinical applicatios, is to be installed. MARS is to be operated beside PACS to manage the type and document conceptual structures and provide their manipulation.

Although the rather static "document type world" in the radiologic department of SKO is not the typical application environment of the MARS system that aims to support frequently restructuring and enhancement of the type calalogue, the object oriented MARS-model gives an organizational advantage: as the flow of activities relies on the document and formular structures, it must not be changes, as those structures can be directly mapped onto appropriate type structures defined in the MARS model. This makes a shnapshot test more easier.

MARS Software Architecture

In fig. 3 we present the layered software architecture of MARS (the documentation is included in [BFBI89]). The bottom layer includes basic file system facilities (in addition to sequential file access this layer also provides efficient multikey access by the gridfile system [Niev84]). The Data-Handler Layer encapsulates all fundamental data types. The module for managing conceptual structures follows the specification given in chapter 4. Specialized functions, e.g. for manipulating the type catalogue, handling document insertion and deletion, managing user interface I/O or evaluating queries are partitioned in tools of the Tool Layer. The tools support the development of functions for the user interface. These functions are situated in the application layer.

To access and present documents on an appropriate output medium PACS functions are called from different layers through an interface with industrial standard [ACR/NEMA][12].

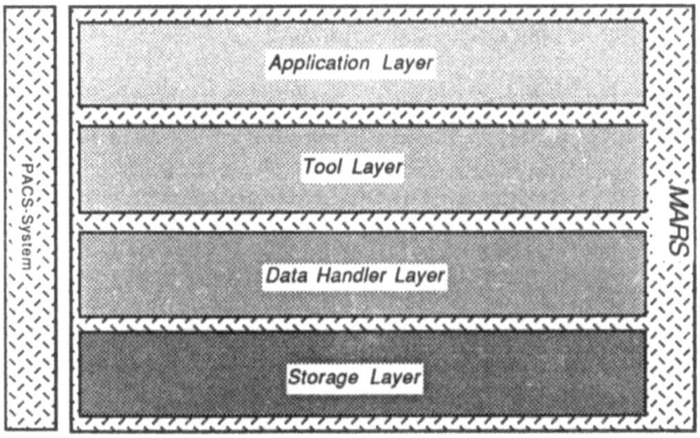

Figure 3: Software Layers in the MARS Architecture

12 simulated in the first prototype

6. Conclusion

Multimedia documents can be seen by a layout view, a syntactic view or a semantic view. This paper focuses on the last one, defining abstract representations of documents via tree like conceptual structures. It supports both retrieval by abstract concepts that take the role of descriptors known from Information Retrieval, and retrieval by facts as performed in bibliographic databases. Typical properties of classes of document structures can be generalized into type conceptual structures. With those types and their associations to documents complex retrieval functions can be supported. In the MARS project currently performed at University of Oldenburg appropriate facilities are implemented.

This paper concentrates on the specification of the model, i.e. both data structures and operations. It outlines the approach of an algebraic specification, suitable for describing abstract data types. While the syntactic specification with an informal semantic description is given in detail, presentation of the semantics of the operators is reduced to essential definitions.

In a clinical environment an application has been modeled. Ten document types represent a snapshot of the "document world" analysed in a radiologic department. Futher testing with the first implemented prototype will allow quantitative analysis of MARS.

Literature:

Abra87 K. Abramowicz, K.R. Dittrich, W. Gotthard, R. Laengle, P.C. Lockemann, T. Raupp, S. Rehm, and T. Wenner, *Datenbankunterstuetzung für Software Produktionsumgebungen*, IFB 136, Springer Verlag, 1987.

Appe87 H.-J. Appelrath, M. Ester, H. Jasper, and A. Ultsch, *KOFIS: ein Expertensystem zur integrierten Dokumenten- und Wissensverwaltung*, Proc. Expertensysteme '87, Teubner, 1987.

Barb85 F. Barbic and F. Rabitti, *The Type Concept in Office Document Retrieval*, Proc. 11th Conference on Very Large Data Bases, Stockholm, 1985.

Bert88 E. Bertino, A. Converti, H. Eirund, K. Kreplin, F. Rabitti, P. Savino, C. Thanos *MULTOS - A Filing Server for Multimedia Documents* , Proc. Euroinfo, Athens, May 1988

BFBI89 Interner Bericht Fachbereich Informatik, *Endbericht der Projektgruppe TEXIDOS / MARS*, Universität Oldenburg, März 1989 (to be published in German)

Cons86 P. Constantopoulos, H. Eirund, K. Kreplin, F. Rabitti, C. Thanos et al., *Office Document Retrieval in MULTOS*, Proc. 3rd ESPRIT Technical Week, North-Holland 1986.

Crof86 W. B. Croft, *User-specific Domain Knowledge for Document Retrieval*, Proc. ACM Conf. on Research and Development in Information Retrieval, ACM, Pisa, 1986.

ECMA85 European Computer Manufacturers Association, *Office Document Architecture ODA - ECMA-101*, Sept. 1985

Eiru88 H. Eirund, *Knowledge Based Document Classification Supporting Contend Based Retrieval and Mail Distribution*, Proc. IFIP TC6/TC8 Symposium - Sofia, North-Holland publ., May 1988

Förs88 F. Försterling, *Database Requirements in the Office*, Preprint of X.th int. Seminar on DBMS, Akademie d. Wiss. der DDR, Inst. f. Informatik und Rechentechnik, Berlin (DDR), Apr. 1988.

Gutt77 J. Guttag, *Abstract Data Types and the Development of Data Structures* , CACM 20 / 6, June 1977

Henh87 W. Henhapl, T. Letschert, *VDM - Vienna Development Method* , Informationstechnik it, 29 / 4, Oldenbourg Verlag München, 1987

Klae83 H. A. Klaeren, *Algebraische Specifikation - Eine Einführung* , Springer Verlag, 1983

Loec87 J. Loeckx, *Algorithmic Specifications: A Constructive Specification Method for Abstract Data Types* , TOPLAS 9 / 4, ACM Oct. 87

Niev84 J. Nievergelt, H. Hinterberger, K.C. Sevcik, *The Grid File: An Adaptable, Symmetric Multikey File Structure* , ACM TODS 9 / 1, ACM March 1984

Sacc84 G. M. Sacco, *OTTER - An Information Retrieval System for Office Automation*, Proc. 2nd ACM SIGOA Conference on Office Information Systems, Toronto, 1984.

Sche82 H.-J. Schek, P. Pistor, Data Structures for an Integrated Data Base Management and Information Retrieval System , Proc. VLDB Conf., MExico, Sep.1982

Sche83 H.-J. Schek and M. Scholl, *Die NF2-Relationenalgebra zur einheitlichen Manipulation externer, konzeptueller und interner Datenstrukturen*, Proc. Sprache für Datenbanken, IFB 72, Springer Verlag, 1983.

AUTOMATED PROTOCOL VALIDATION

Joachim Fischer
Eckart Holz
Peter Leipner
Klaus Ahrens
Hans-Dieter Burkhardt

bit '89
Humboldt University
P.O.Box 1297
Berlin - DDR 1086

Abstract. This paper presents a framework, called ATLANTIC, for the software development of distributed communication systems. The algorithmic specification is done in the CCITT language SDL. An overview of the functions of a protocol simulator is given. Two particular aspects of the validation of SDL specifications are presented in more detail: (i) an online verification by observing the system simulated and (ii) a possibility for analysing the reachability graph of a Petri net model of a specification in SDL. The analysis of SDL syntax and semantic and the optional transformation of the input specifications into corresponding models is done by programs developed by applying of UNIX tools. ATLANTIC is written in the language C.

Introduction

An increasing number of distributed algorithms (also called protocols) have to be designed and implemented. They provide such services as the transmission of information between sites (communication protocols), resource allocation, or consistency control in data bases, etc...
To prove that these algorithms work correctly is difficult because of their distributed, nondeterministic nature. Moreover, they usually communicate through an imperfect medium.

Communication protocols belong to the large mathematical model class of discrete event systems. Other examples of these systems are flexible manufacturing systems, process control systems, office information systems and VLSI circuits. The behaviour of all these systems can be characterised by moments at which their elementary activities start and end.

All these systems inherently involve the consideration of the notations of concurrency, nondeterminism, time and communication. Therefore, the formal description technique (FDT) used for the description of a discrete event system should be able to express these notions. A FDT has a formal, mathematical basis and can be used to simulate a specification or to prove the correctness of a specification. It also can be a basis for the implementation and for conformance testing. Usally a FDT does not replace an implementation language.
For some time, verification methods have been developed (see for example /IFIP 84,85,86,87,88/. But proving a protocol is still quite a difficult problem, and until now, proof systems cannot take into account real-sized protocols.

Being asked by designers of distributed systems in our research facilities to validate their real-sized protocols, we have prefered to limit our objectives to obtaining an acceptable degree of confidence. Therefore, we have accepted the view that a given protocol works tolerably well if it is proved to work correctly under various conditions, particularly when "dangerous" events happen.
Realizsed studies have shown that "specification testing" by simulated specification execution (as a special form of a simulation of a discrete event system) allows the detection of non-trivial errors. Furthermore in consideration of time dependencies of the protocol execution and transmission activities there are fundamental possibilities for a protocol performance prediction especially connected with optimization of needed timers.
This paper presents a tool box (written in the language C under MS-DOS/DCP or UNIX/WEGA), which can be used for debugging, validating and evaluating distributed algorithms.
The prototype of this system is the SIMULA package ATLANTIS /Fischer 88/.

Definitions

The production of high-quality communication protocols is a process which is based on consecutive stages: specification, verification, performance prediction, implementation, testing, certification and assessment, performance evaluation, documentation, and possibly synthesis and conversion.

Following /Piatkowski 86/ and /Sajkowski 87/ we will define here, for this paper, two stages of protocol production process only: specification and verification, and furthermore their relations to the protocol validation.

Protocol specification we have to understand of the description which defines the required behaviour of a protocol. The specification may be formal or informal. The formal specification uses a formal language to describe the protocol behaviour. The term "formal" means "expressed in a precise mathematical way using symbols with specific meaning" (/Løvengreen 85/).

Protocol verification is understood as the demonstration of the correctness, completeness and consistency of the protocol design represented by its formal specification. Two kinds of verification are distinguished in protocol engineering: general and special verification (/Drobnik 86/). The **general verification** proves general properties which have to be valid in any specified distributed system independent of the concrete protocol. Examples of such properties are absence of deadlocks, termination, no dead code,... In contrast to this **special verification** approach tries to show equivalence of the service specification and the realization of the underlying specified protocol.

The **validation process** consists of following steps:

1. verification of the specified system,
2. performance prediction of the specified system,
3. test of the implemented system,
4. performance analysis of the whole installed system,
5. certification (test of conformance, performance and robustness).

The ATLANTIC project

ATLANTIC offers a SDL oriented framework summarised in fig.1 to fig.3 .

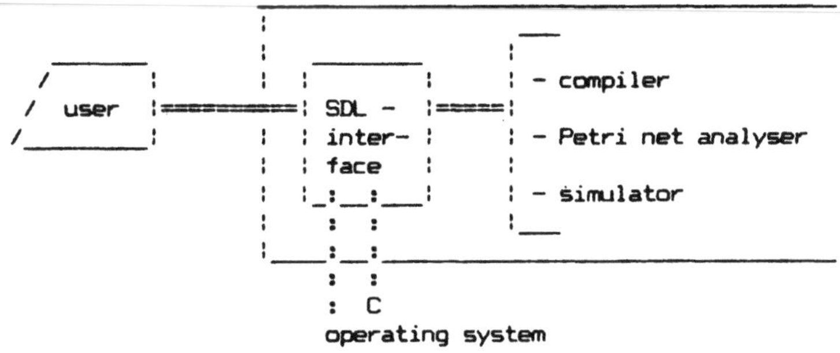

fig. 1 Structure of ATLANTIC

For next time other facilities are considered to be implemented, including a graphical syntax checker and a performance evaluator on the basis of extended queueing systems. In the following sections we shall briefly outline the system organisation.
The translation of SDL specifications into Petri net models uses

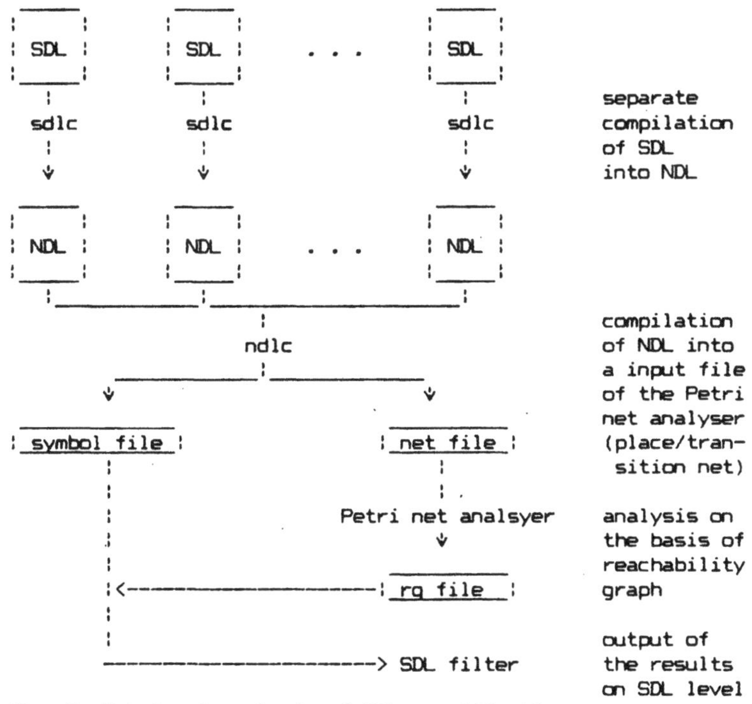

fig. 2 Petri net analysis of SDL specifications

a net description language NDL, whereby a compiler exists /Leipner 88/, which transforms a NDL model into a structure accepted by the Petri Net Machine /Starke 88/. The NDL compiler

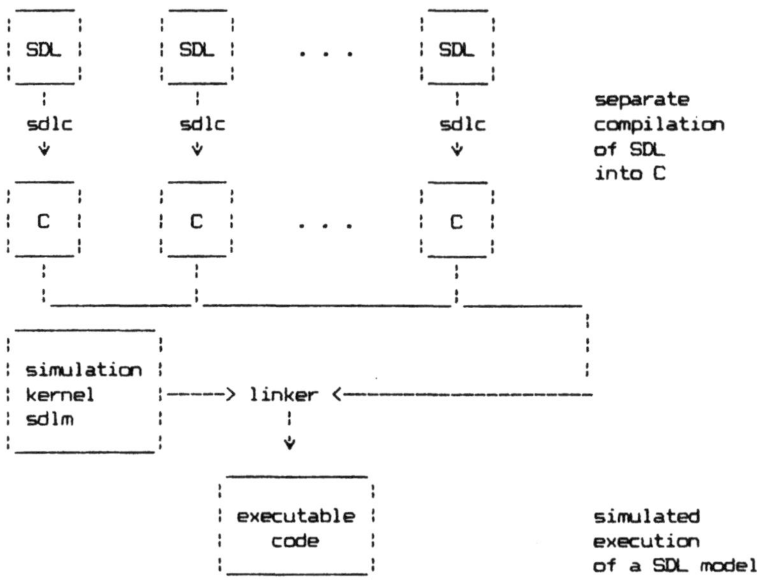

fig. 3 Simulation analysis of SDL specifications

generates a symbol table used by the filter program in processing the output files of Petri Net Machine. The main task of the filter is to output the results of the Petri Net Machine (like deadlocks, dead transitions,...) on user oriented SDL level.
Preposition for the simulation of SDL is a machine (sdlm) for executing SDL processes, which are specified by a SDL system. The main task of this machine is the organisation of a model-time driven execution of processes, timers and channels in quasi parallel manner.

The CCITT Specification and Description Language SDL

A short look on SDL

The language SDL is widely used for documentation of distributed systems at different levels of abstraction.
The SDL version used in our framework is based on the Recommendation Z.100 /CCITT 88/ with some usual extensions of the full SDL

(like i/o- procedures and random generators) and some restrictions in abstract data types.
A SDL specification consists of **blocks** of **processes**. Each process can be thought of as a finite state machine which is communicating asynchronously with other processes of the same block or other ones. The communication of processes of different blocks and the communication with a built-in process of the environment is done by signal exchange via infinite length FIFO channels. In contrast to this the communication of processes of the same block could be realised in two various forms, as directed signal exchange or by common variables.
A relative up-to-date description of SDL can be found in /Saracco 87/. Finally it should be remarked that two forms of the SDL-grammar are developed by the CCITT, a programming representation (SDL/PR) and a graphical one with a long practical tradition for more than 10 years (SDL/GR).

Graphical editing of SDL specifications

First steps were done in the development of a graphical editor of SDL with the aim of an automated transformation to the programming form of SDL. These works are realised by using GEM under MSDOS/DCP.

Compilation of SDL by sdlc

The parser of our SDL compiler **sdlc** (/Holz 88/) was built by application of the UNIX tool **yacc**. Besides of a syntactical analysis sdlc checks the statical correctness of the signal flow in SDL specifications.
The transformation of a SDL specification to discrete event model systems and to Petri net representations for the verification and performance prediction works on an internal representation of the input specification which is built up during the syntactical analysis. This internal representation is also a basis for the semantical analysis.
In present sdlc generates four output files optionally:

- a NDL file containing a Petri net model described in the net description language NDL,

- a C file containing a process oriented simulation model of the time driven system,
- a list file containing input, error massages and warnings of sdlc,
- a Cross-reference file of the input specification.

A generation of queueing models is planned.

General Verification of SDL specifications

Petri net representation

To obtain a place/transistion net from a syntactical correct SDL specification the following rules must be used:

(1) All process instances are levelled due to resolution of block structure.

(2) Each process instance is modelled by a NDL subnet with formal input and output places (cf. fig. 5). Each regular input message type a formal input place and each regular output message type per output process a formal output place will be assigned. If there is to model a dynamic process, the NDL subnet will get an additional call place.

```
                        Call  (_)
                               ↓
                     ----------------
            (_)---->|                |---->(_)  Output to
   Input            |                |---->(_)  process 1
                    |                |
            (_)---->|                |---->(_)  Output to
                    |                |---->(_)  process n
                     ----------------
```

fig. 5 Interface of a NDL subnet modelling SDL processes

(3) Procedures are handled as processes; recursions are not allowed.

(4) Each possible path of a state transition is represented by a local transition, unless rule (9) is applicable. So, this transition includes input of a message (INPUT), its processing (TASK), procedure calls, process calls, generation of output messages (OUTPUT) for each case fixed alternatives of SDL decision (DECISION).

(5) Each SDL state is modelled by a local place.

(6) Construction of input places of transitions (4) of a NDL subnet

depends on the type of the original SDL process.

(a) static processes: They have always one and only one state place and one and only one input message place as input places. (An exception will be transition with number 1, because the starting state of a process may go into the following state without message input.)

(b) dynamic processes: The input places of the first transition are a state place and a call place. All other transitions have input places like (a).

(7) Each transition has n (n >= 0) output places:

n = 0: process terminated

n = 1: output place is a state place (without OUTPUT)

n > 1: one and only one output place is a state place, all others are output places ((n-1) OUTPUT operations)

(8) All places (formal and local) of a NDL subnet are identified with the corresponding SDL identifier. Transitions are enumerated starting with 1.

(9) If there are k (k >= 2) transitions identically (i.e. they have the same input and output places), then they will be replaced by one transition.

(10) According to each state place additional transitions will be introduced. Their number per state place depends on each case unused (but possible) input message types. These transitions model the implicit DISCARD operations and are characterised to have only one output place which is identically with the input state place.

(11) SAVE operations are modelled implicitly. A message (the corresponding token) will be removed from the input place of a transition, if an INPUT or a DISCARD is modelled. Otherwise the message token remains at the input place and the process holds its current state.

(12) In order to prevent further expanding of model complexity SET and RESET operations are not modelled. In the same way explicit modelling of timer will be disclaimed. In general, their representation with Petri net models would be possible by introducing a timing of process runnings.

(13) Timeout signals are not produced by timer, they result from message transmission with loss. To each transition with message output an additional transition observing rule (9) will be introduced which has a so-called timeout place as message output place.

(14) To each message type (including timeout) per communication channel (block internal or block external over CHANNEL) a global place will be created. These global places are the actual parameters of the NDL subnet.

The up to now usage of the tools described, especially the performed analysis of concrete SDL specifications makes it possible to generalise following experience.

1. Because the derived Petri nets are abstract models of SDL specifications neglecting time and data dependencies, they include several possibilities of unconstrained growing of message buffers. First this unboundness is to recognise which is possible in analysing the coverability graph by the Petri Net Machine too.
2. In most cases there are some dead transitions, because on principle to each state transition all regular messages which have been handled neither by INPUT nor by SAVE will be removed from the related message input place using DISCARD.
3. The construction of reachability graphs very fast exceeds the limits of the used 16-bit and 32-bit computer systems referred to memory space and CPU time. Therefore, reducing complexity of the resulting Petri nets is the major task in analysing real specifications.

Because a translation of such SDL specifications is possible, which have a high degree of informal representations of the internal process structure, the main application of the Petri net analysis lies in the earliest design stages.

Simulated SDL execution

Implementing a protocol means translating its specification into a machine program. This program will interact with corresponding programs in other machines (or possible running on the same machine in the case of vertical communication between layers). The input and output operations for instance, which are to be found in the protocol specification, will translated into calls to some communications primitives of the underlying machine.
Once a protocol has been implemented, it can be tested. This is usally done by exercising it with some protocol drivers, which submit test requests or responses. The behaviour of the protocol driven test data in this way is then compared to its expected behaviour.

Simulation, as performed in ATLANTIC, applies another method. It works directly on the specification, not on a particular implementation. The environment of a protocol (the machine on which it runs, and the upper and lower layers surrounding the protocol) are modeled. The advantages of this approach are that:

- a simulation in virtual time is possible; in this way that the behaviour of a protocol can be tested in a time independend on the time in reality;
- it is possible to choose situations which occur seldom in reality, this comes from the fact that the SDL machine has a complete control over the environment;
- it is possible to study the protocol behaviour by varying of channel transmission times, channel failure rates, and dimensions of timers.

References

/CCITT 88/
Recommendation Z.100. CCITT Specification and Description Language SDL. CCITT 1988

/Drobnik 86/
Drobnik, O.: Softwaretechnologie für Kommunikationstechnik. in Informationstechnik, Oldenbourg Verlag, 1/1986

/Fischer 88/
Fischer, J.: Softwaretechnologie "Rapid Prototyping" bei der Entwicklung von Kommunikationssoftware verteilter sowie eingebetteter Systeme, Diss. B, Humboldt Universität zu Berlin, Berlin 1988

/Holz 88/
Holz, E.: sdlc - ein Compiler zur Generierung von Simulationsmodellen aus SDL Spezifikationen. Diplomarbeit, Humboldt-Universität zu Berlin, 1988

/IFIP 84,85,86,87,88/
Proceedings of th annual workshops on Protocol Specification, Verification, and Testing organised by IFIP/WG6-1.

/Leipner 88/
Leipner, P.: Nutzung erweiterter Petrinetze bei der Entwicklung von Kommunikationssoftware verteilter Systeme. Diss. A, Berlin 1988

/Piatkowski 86/
Piatkowski, T.,F.: The State of Art in Protocol Engineering. Proceedings SIGCOMM'86 Symposium, Stowe, 1986

/Saijkowski 87/
Saijkowski, M.: Protocol Verification Using Discrete-Event Models. Lecture Notes in Control and Information Sciences, No 103, (eds. Varaiya, P.; Kurzhanski, A.), Springer-Verlag, 1987

/Saracco 87/
Saracco, R.: Course on SDL. The CCITT Specification and Description Language. Centro Studi e Laboratori Telecommunicazioni, Turin, 1987

/Starke 88/
Starke, P.: Programmsystem Petri- Netzmaschine, (Version: März 1988), Humboldt- Universität zu Berlin, Berlin, 1988

DATA MODELLING ASPECTS FOR DISTRIBUTED OFFICE APPLICATIONS

Frank Foersterling

Academy of Sciences of the GDR
Institute of Informatics and Computing Technique
Rudower Chaussee 5
Berlin - GDR 1199

This paper gives a short overview of an information model in distributed office applications. The main characteristics of the information objects of the information model are sketched. A new data model - the Dynamic Object Model - is proposed as a modelling base for the information objects in the distributed office applications.

1. Introduction

The importance of office automation increases by the developments in the computer area. The feature of the office work demands a communication between many persons in an organization. Influenced by those observations the international standardization committees, like ECMA, ISO, CCITT started the development of a "Framework for Distributed Office Applications (DOA)" /1/, based on the OSI Reference Model /2/. Such services like

- message handling for the exchange of messages (MHS) /3/,
- the directory service (DS) /4/,
- document filing and retrieval (DFR) /5/,
- office document architecture and interchange format (ODA/ODIF) /6/

may be recognized as OSI applications that will fit in as members of a set of DOAs.

All mentioned services belong to the so called value-added services. Besides the communication task, value-added services include data processing and data storage facilities.

The information objects occurring in the above services (messages, directory entries, folders, documents), because of their highly variable structure, are a difficult class of objects to model. It may be pointed out, that the well-known data models (as the relational model or semantic data models like the NF2 model) have several disadvantages for this modelling task.

As a consequence, published proposals for a storage system of one of the considered services (e.g. /7/ /8/) represent special solutions, which are not suited for an integration of the information objects from the other services.

In this paper we propose a new data model - the Dynamic Object Model (DOM) - which overcomes the disadvantages of the known data models and may be used as a base to integrate the information objects of the mentioned servcices in the framework of DOAs.

2. The information model

Figure 1 shows an information model for a storage system of value-added services belonging to the DOAs.

3 classes of objects may be distinguished:

(1) "User-oriented" object class: User-oriented objects describe users having access to information objects of the third class.

(2) "Document-oriented" object class: The document-oriented object class •contains such information objects like documents, forms, messages, reports etc.

(3) "Filing" object class: Information objects of this class file document-oriented objects by predefind criteria. Examples are mailboxes, inlogs, or conferences.

Depending on the application, the classes form so called application-depending contexts. A context defines relationships between several objects of one object class (fig. 1):

(1') By means of the organizational context users may be grouped into user groups (e.g., a distribution list, participants of a conference, an office staff). A member of a group may be another group.

(2') The content-depending context defines relationships between several document-oriented objects by the help of special attributes (e.g., "comment to contribution", "regarding", "reply to").

(3') The administrative-technical context organizes the information objects of the filing class in a hierarchical manner (e.g., into archives, folders, file cabinets, etc.).

From the viewpoint of modelling an application (e.g. a mailbox system or a file cabinet for the office), all 3 classes of objects together with their contexts must be handled in a uniform way. In the real world, the user does not distinguish between these classes. He/she requires means to perform such complex objects in a quite intelligible way. Figure 1 shows the relationships between the 3 classes.

Unfortunately, the standardization efforts of services in the distributed office do not reflect the information model as a whole. Several standards bound their consideration to a subpart of the information model.

The standardized directory service /4/ is directed to the user-oriented object class and its organizational context.

The document filing and retrieval service /5/ standardizes the administrative-technical context of the filing object class.

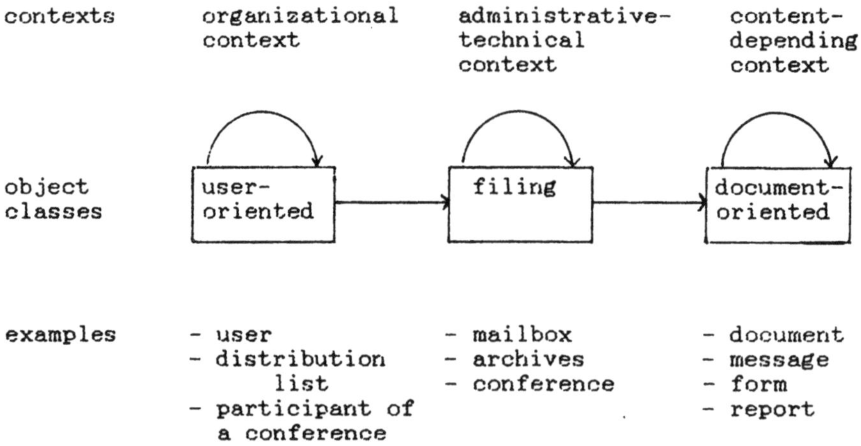

Fig. 1: Information model of a storage system for distributed office applications

The office document architecture and interchange format /6/ is oriented towards the standardization of documents as a special case of the document-oriented object class and its content-oriented context.

The sevice for message handling /3/ considers messages. Messages belong to the document-oriented object class. A message consists of a standardized envelope and a content. Normally, the content is uninterpreted. By one special part of the message handling, the interpersonal messaging, the content will be further subdivided into the standardized header and the uninterpreted body. The message store for storing messages is an optional information object. The message store belongs to the filing object class.

Several proposals to implement a storage system for one of the mentioned services are published /7/ /8/ /9/. The implementation proposals use well-known data models (like the relational model or the NF2-model) to represent selected information objects of the information model. These approaches must be considered as special solutions which cannot be expanded to the whole information model. The information objects mentioned above are distinguished by several characteristics being different from other applications and which are explained below.

3. Characteristics of the information objects

- Complexity

An object is described by a set of attributes. An attribute consists of an attribute type and an attribute value. The attribute value may be atomic (as in traditional applications), or complex, i.e., the attribute value is further substructured into a set of attributes. The information objects in the DOA-environment are characterized by complex attributes. They contain hierarchically structured (sub-)objects.

- Heterogeneity

Traditional applications are characterized by using a large amount of homogeneously structured objects. We find in distributed office applications a lot of objects with quite different structures. Especially, the information objects from the document-oriented class differ in their description by attributes.

On the other side, heterogeneous objects must be handled in a uniform way. A mailbox, e.g., contains such heterogeneously structured information objects like letters, telegrams, reports, etc.

- Semantic expressiveness

Considering complex objects, the user needs means to manipulate them as a whole (e.g., like the above mentioned mailbox). The underlaying structure is often unimportant for him. In other cases, the user wishes to access subobjects of more complex objects only (e.g., he is interested in all telegrams of his mailbox).

- Optionality

The aim of standardizing services for the distributed office is guarantee a worldwide interconnection of open systems. For this reason, the standards include a large amount of attributes. Only few of these attributes are mandatory. Most of the attributes are optional. As a consequence, an information object must be modelled by the present attributes only. It is undesirable to "hold place" for all valid but unused attributes.

Existing data models are unable to reflect the sketched characteristics of the information objects in distributed office applications sufficiently. Particularly, the optionality and heterogeneity requirements cannot be realized by the static schema assumption of the well-known (traditional and newer) data models.

4. The Dynamic Object Model

In this chapter the author proposes the Dynamic Object Model (DOM) which supports the presentation of information objects with characteristics mentioned in the previous chapter.

Describing a data model one has to take into consideration 3 aspects:

- the structural aspect,
- the operational aspect, and
- the integrity and consistency constraints of the data model.

4.1. Structural Aspects of DOM

Firstly, we describe the structural aspects of DOM.

The basic primitive of DOM is a subobject.

A subobject is a type/value pair. The type is an arbitrary string taken from a set of names. The value may be empty, atomic, a multiset of subobjects, or a list of subobjects.

Using the definition of the subobject we derive the following definitions:

An object is a subobject with a unique type, called the object identifier.

A structure is a subobject with non-atomic values.

An instance is a subobject with non-empty values.

An example of an subobject, is shown in figure 2a (to distinguish between the several value kinds the following symbols are used: {} for the multiset, <> for the list, () for an atomic value). The example shows an object of the type Mailbox (as its object identifier). Its value part is a multiset containing 4 subobjects (2 subobjects of the Letter type, one of the Report and one of the Telegram type). Every of these subobjects, again, has an non-atomic value part. All subobjects are further substructered (what is expressed by the dots). The subobjects of the Originator type contain atomic values.

In contrast with other data modelling approaches the subobjects of DOM have the following main features:

- The subobject is the only basic primitive in DOM for the structural description.
- The presentation of "incomplete information" by the usage of the empty value is possible.
- The presentation of the value part of a subobject as a multiset or list enables to construct complex structures.
- The subobject definition does not contain any boundaries for the usage of the subobject type. Therefore, the type may be used many times for describing different structures inside of a subobject. In this sense, the type possesses only a semantic meaning (for the DOM-user).
- The subobject integrates intentional and extentional aspects of the data description:
  - . The introduced structure definition of the subobject is comparable to the schema of traditional data models (fig. 2b).
  - . The instance definition of the subobject is comparable to an instance of traditional data models (fig. 2c).

Mailbox { Letter < Envelope < Originator (Miller), Recipient (Foersterling), ... >, Content < Header <...>, Text (...) >>,

Report < Originator (Miller), Title (...), ...>,

Telegram < Originator (Smith), Recipient (Foersterling), Text < ... >>,

Letter < Envelope < Originator (Young), Priority (urgent), Recipient (Foersterling), ... >, Content < ... >> }

a) Example of an object with the object identifier Mailbox

Originator < Country (GDR), Town (Berlin), Index (1199), Organization < Institute (IIR), Department (RK) >, Name < Surname (Foersterling), ChristianName (Frank) >>

b) Example of an instance

Originator < Country, Town, Index, Organization < Institute, Department >, Name < Surname, ChristianName >>

c) Example of a structure

Originator < Country (GDR), Town (Berlin), Index (1199), Organization < Institute (IIR), Department >, Name < Surname, ChristianName >>

d) Example of a subobject being neither an instance nor a structure

Fig. 2: Examples of subobjects in DOM

On the other side, there exist subobjects, which are neither a structure nor an instance (fig. 2d). Such subobjects are typical for office forms, but there is no equivalence in traditional data models.

- As a consequence, DOM does not know a rigid schema.

4.2. Operational Aspects of DOM

The applicability of a data model depends on a powerful data manipulation and retrieval language (DML). 3 main requirements can be formulated for the DML in the considered application context:

- The strong separation between the data definition language (DDL) for a schema and the DML for the instances in traditional data models must be abolished.

  The subobject definition in DOM automatically combines the DML aspects (via the "atomic value"-part) and DDL aspects (via the "empty value"-part). So, the DML includes the DDL aspects in a natural sense.

- The DML must be able to manipulate complex objects.

  If we find an appropriate DML approach for the subobject, DOM automatically fulfills this requirement, too. The subobject already includes the complex object character.

- The DML should be as powerful as the query language for relational models.

In this chapter we propose an approach fulfilling the above 3 requirements. A full description of the DML of DOM is beyond the scope of this paper.

For the development of a DML for DOM we use the logical approach.

We introduce the variable t as a "place-holder" for a subobject. Further we use the symbols

- TYP(t) to identify the type of a subobject t,
- VAL(t) to identify the value of a subobject t.

It follows the definition of an atom.

An <u>atom</u> is "true" or "false". Allowed atoms are

- $s \in VAL(t)$, where s,t are variables or subobjects, the value of t must be set-oriented (a list or a multiset);
- $VAL(s)\ \Theta\ VAL(t)$, $\Theta = \{ =, \neq\}$, the values of s and t may be compared by Θ (the list of the Θ-values may be extended);
- $TYP(s)\ \Theta\ TYP(t)$ is the same as above for types;
- H(s,t) means, that s is a subobject of VAL(t) in an arbitrary nested depth; this atom is quite similar to the s-

atom of /10/,

- Struct(s,t) means that s is the structure of t.

On the basis of the atom definition we introduce the definition of a formulae in the well-known way of the first-order logic:

(1) An atom is a formulae.

(2) If F, G are formulaes ===> ~(F), $(F \wedge G)$, $(F \vee G)$, (F --> G), (F <--> G) are formulaes.

(3) If F is a formulae, t is a free variable in F ===> $(\forall t)F$, $(\exists t)F$ are formulaes.

(4) A finite usage of (1) to (3) is a formulae.

Now we are able to present the retrieval instruction as

GET id(t): F;

where id is an object-identifier (a type unique in a set of names),
t is a free variable in F,
F is a formulae.

An example of this approach is given in fig. 3. The verbal task of this example is to find all letters and telegrams of the sender Miller from the example 2a.

In a similar way we may define instructions to insert, delete, or update subobjects, which is beyond the scope of this paper.

4.3. Integrity and consistency in DOM

The introduced formal approach to the operational aspects of DOM may be extended to the consideration of consistency and integrity constraints.

A constraint in DOM may be definded as a formulae with bounded variables only.

Figure 4 gives an example of a consistency constraint. The constraint requires that anonymous mail is not allowed in the object with the object identifier Mailbox of the example 2a.

In the field of distributed office applications we observe

- a frequent change of the constraints (especially, the access rights change frequently),

- extensive consistency requirements.

The trigger mechanism seems to be a well suited mechanism for embedding the integrity and consistency constraints in a flexible way.

"Find in Mailbox all letters and telegrams from Miller."

c) The verbal search requirement

```
GET TempBox (x) :
     x ∈ VAL(Mailbox)  ∧
     (( TYP(x) = Letter ) ∨ ( TYP(x) = Telegram ))
     (∃ y) H(y,x)  ∧
     ( TYP(y) = Originator ) ∧ ( VAL(y) = Miller );
```

b) The retrieval instruction

```
TempBox { Letter < Envelope < Originator ( Miller ),
          Recipient ( Foersterling ), ... >, Content
          < Header < ... > , Text ( ... ) >> }
```

c) The result of the retrieval

Fig. 3: An example of a retrieval of subobjects in the object with the object identifier Mailbox (fig. 2a)

"Anonymous mail is not allowed in Mailbox."

b) The verbal description of the constraint

$$\phi \equiv \forall x \, \exists y \; (\; x \in VAL(Mailbox) \wedge H(y,x) \wedge (TYP(y) = Originator \;) \wedge \sim(\; VAL(y) = 0 \;))$$

a) The formal description of the constraint

Fig. 4: An example of a consistency constraint for the object with the object identifier Mailbox (fig. 2a)

5. Conclusion

A new data model - the Dynamic Object Model (DOM) - for modelling information objects from the field of distributed office applications was presented. DOM realizes modelling facilities on the basis of the subobject primitive. The operational approach is logic-oriented. The presented data model is able to handle complex subobjects. A subobject may contain further heterogeneous subobjects which may be manipulated as a whole or seperately. Regarding to the application environment, optional parts of the information objects may be omitted because of the integrated type representation in the subobjects. As a consequence, DOM fulfills the characteristics mentioned in chapter 3. In this sense, DOM is suited to be a modelling base for the information objects of the services in the DOA environment or for application fields with information objects obeying similar characteristics.

Nevertheless, DOM is not a general-purpose model for all applications. Applications using a lot of homogeneously structured information objects are better modelled by conventional data models. Furthermore, DOM does not include facilities for modelling network-oriented structures.

References

1. Information Processing Systems - Text Communication - Distributed-Office-Applications Model, General Model, DP 10031-1

2. ISO, International Standard ISO/IS 7498, Information Processing Systems - Open Systems Interconnection - Basic Reference Model

3. CCITT, X.400 ff, Message Handling Systems

4. CCITT, X.500 ff, The Directory

5. Document Filing and Retrieval, in: The Open Systems Newsletter (OSN), Vol. 1, Issue 12, Feb. 1988, 8 - 10

6. ECMA, Standard ECMA 101, Office Document Architecture

7. J. Delgado, M. Medina, B. Butscher, M. Tschichholz: Use of SQL for Message Store and Retrieval. in: Proc. IFIP 6.5. MHS, Munich, FRG, 27-29 April 1987

8. H.-B. Paul, A. Soeder, H.-J. Schek, G. Weikum: Unterstuetzung des Buero-Ablage-Service durch ein Datenbank-kernsystem. in: H.-J. Schek, G. Schlageter (Eds.): Datenbanksysteme in Buero, Technik und Wissenschaft. GI-Fachtagung, Darmstadt, April 1987, Proceedings, Springer-Verlag (Informatik-Fachbericht 136)

9. R. Ruland, K. Kratzer: Verwaltung hierarchisch-strukturierter Dokumente mit DQL. in: Informatik Forschung & Entwicklung, Vol. 3, No. 1, 1988, Springer-Verlag, 34 - 45

10. B. E. Jacobs: On Database Logic, in: J. of the ACM, Vol. 29, No. 2, April 1982, 310 - 332

KNOWLEDGE BASED PROGRAM GENERATION USING ATTRIBUTED GRAMMARS

Peter Forbrig, Uwe Lämmel

bit'89
Wilhelm-Pieck-Universität Rostock
Sektion Informatik
Albert-Einstein-Str. 21
Rostock - DDR 2500

Abstract: The principles of the computer aided program generation environment FLR are described. The knowledge about already implemented parts of programs is stored as attributed grammar rules. New software can be composed in an interactive way with the system FLR.

1. Introduction

In recent years there have been many approaches using the computer as a tool in program development.
Nevertheless, until now most programs are written by hand. We believe that further assistance should be given for developing programs by the computer itself.
The computer should give support in using those programs which have already been implemented and even using parts of programs.

For some years we have been working with different kinds of attributed grammars for language description, compiler design and software development [3] [4] [5].
This induced our idea to use a new type of attributed grammars in the sense of knowledge representation of already implemented programs. The language generated by such a grammar is a set of programs. Programming means the user influenced generation of a word of the language. This is done by changing in an interactive way the value of special attributes controlling the generation of programs.
The idea was influenced by [1] where one attribute of each nonterminal has a general purpose. We have also defined a special purpose for two attributes of each nonterminal and believe that our approach can support program generation in a similar but simpler way as the approach in [2].
The same holds true for the development of specifications. In this paper, however, our attention is focused on the generation of programs.

2. Program generation environment FLR

2.1. Controlled simple attributed grammars

Context-free grammars have become more and more a fundamental concept in computer science. They are well studied and many theoretical results are proved. The main areas of application of context-free grammars are compilers and compiler compilers.
It is well known that grammars can be used to generate or accept sentences of a language.

Whereas the possibility of accepting a string by a grammar is often used in practice, the generational aspect is used in theoretical computer science only.
In our system FLR the generational aspect of attributed grammars for developing software is used.
To introduce the basic idea let us first recall the definition of a context-free grammar and have a look at a simple example.

Definition 1: Context-free grammar G

A context-free grammar is a tuple G = (N, T, S, R).
- N - finite set of nonterminals,
- T - finite set of terminals,
- S - start element, $S \in N$,
- R - finite set of production rules $A \text{ --> } B, \quad A \in N, \quad B \in (N \cup T)^*$.

#

Example 1: Context-free grammar G1

1. G --> A.
2. A --> "a", "+", A.
3. A --> "a", "-", A.
4. A --> "a".

The language L(G1) can easily be seen to contain the following terminal strings: a, a+a, a-a, a+a+a, a+a-a, a-a-a, ...

End of example.

There are many well-known algorithms, deciding for special context-free grammars whether a terminal string belongs to the corresponding language or not.
But it may also be interesting to generate special terminal strings of the grammar. Therefore, it is necessary to control the generation of terminal strings. A new type of attributed grammar will be used to support this process.

Definition 2: Controlled simple attributed grammar (CSAG)

An attribute grammar in the sense of Knuth is called controlled simple attributed grammar if the following properties are fulfilled:

- Attributes are attached to nonterminals only.
- Each nonterminal has at least two attributes.
  Thus, an occurence of $K \in N$ has the form
  K(a1, a2, a3, ... , an), n >=2,
  where a1, a2, ... , an are attributes of K and
  1.) The domain of a1 is the set C of characters.
  2.) The domain of a2 is the set ST of strings.
  3.) If K occurs on the left-hand-side of a grammar rule then a1 and a2 have to be constants. Whenever K occurs on the right hand side of a rule a1 may be a variable or a constant, and a2 is always irrelevant.
  4.) The start element has exactly two attributes.
- Semantic actions copy values only.

#

The value of the first attribute controls the derivation of a word. The second attribute gives some comment in order to support the interactive choice of the first attributes value.

Because of the special form of the nonterminals we can use a simpler notation of production rules. The following example is an ordinary rule of a CSAG:

K("f", "File-output", X) --> "b", T(Y,_,X).

--> - separates left-hand-side from right-hand-side,
',' - denotes a sequence,
'_' - denotes the anonymous variable, its value is without importance.
'.' - end of a grammar rule .

Terminals as well as character or string constants are enclosed in quotation marks. K, T are nonterminals and their attributes are enclosed in brackets. Variable names (e.g. X, Y) have local importance within a rule only. The same variable name within a rule represents the same value. Therefore, there is no need for an explicit notation of semantic actions.

The generation of a word of the language, described by a CSAG is slightly different from the usual derivation by a context-free grammar. Thus, another kind of derivation relation has to be defined.

Definition 3: Direct derivation

The string X is said to <u>directly derive</u> the string Y

$$X \overset{c}{\Longrightarrow} Y$$

if: $X = uK(a1,a2,a3,...,an)w$
$Y = uvw,$
$u \in T^*,\ v, w \in (N \cup T)^*,\ K \in N,$
ai - attributes of K, for i= 1,...,n,
a2 is the anonymous variable,
$c \in (C \cup \{\varepsilon\})$, ε - empty string,

and a rule K(b1,b2,b3,..,bn) --> v exists such that:

1. a) if a1 is already instantiated then b1=a1, c=ε.
   b) if a1 is a variable then the control character c determines the rule with first attribute b1=c to be applied.

2. The other attributes are evaluated according to their property: inherited - bi:= ai,
   sythesized - ai:= bi, for i=3,..,n.

#

Now it is possible to define a control character. These characters determine the generation of a word of the language described by a CSAG.

Definition 4: Control character
----

c is a <u>control character</u>, if two strings X,Y

$$X \overset{c}{\Longrightarrow} Y \quad \text{exist.}$$

#

Definition 5: Derivation

```
   The string X is said to derive the string Y
           s             *
        X =*=> Y  , s ε C ,

   if   s = cs' and  a string X' exists, such that
           c             s'
        X ==> X', and X' =*=> Y   .
```
#

The language generated by a CSAG is defined as usual. It is the set of all terminal strings derived from the start element S of the grammar:

Definition 6: Language of a CSAG

```
   The language of a CSAG  G  L(G)  is defined as:
                          *           s            *
     L(G) = { w ¦ w ε T ,  S(a1,a2) =*=> w , s ε C }
   S is the start element of the CSAG G .
```
#

The generation of a special terminal string is controlled by a sequence of characters the so called control string.

Definition 7: Control string

A string s is called <u>control string</u> of the CSAG G if a word w of the language L(G) exists which can be derived from the start element S by using s:

```
                 s
       S(a1,a2) =*=> w
```
#

Definition 8: Control language

The set of all possible control strings of an CSAG is called <u>control language</u>.
#

The generation process of an CSAG is to be demonstrated by extending the grammar of example 1 to a CSAG.

Example 2: Controlled simple attributed grammar G2:

```
 1.  G( "s", "G2")     -->  A( X, _).
 2.  A( "p", "Plus")   -->  "a", "+", A( X, _).
 3.  A( "m", "Minus")  -->  "a", "-", A( X, _).
 4.  A( "e", "Ende")   -->  "a".
```

The word a + a can be derived as follows:

```
              s          p                e
G("s","G2") ==> A(X,_) ==> "a","+",A(Y,_) ==> "a","+","a"
```

The control string s p e generates the word a + a .

Similarly the following control strings yield the outlined results:

```
   a)  s p p m e   :  a + a + a - a
   b)  s p p m m e :  a + a + a - a - a
```

If many terminal strings have already been generated it could be profitable to use one of the already existing control strings. A new terminal string can be generated by simply deleting or inserting some characters (according to the control language).

```
c) s p p   m m e :  a + a +     a - a - a
         A                  A
         !                  !
        p p               a + a
```

```
                                        *
The control language of G2 is   s ( m ! p ) e.
```

End of example.

The generation of terminal strings should be supported by the computer itself. That was the reason for implementing a program generation environment.

For practical reasons we extended our notation in order to have a more readable grammar in the case of string manipulation. It is sometimes necessary to concatenate string constants with string values of attributes. This possibility is described in the following grammar rule:

```
variabletext("v", "comment", Text) --> ["begin", Text, "end"].
```

During derivation all elements of a list enclosed in square brackets are concateneted.

Let us have a look at a more complex example generating Pascal programs in the next section.

2.2. Generation of Pascal programs

In this section the advantages of CSAGs are demonstrated by showing their application in generating programs, which have to calculate the wages of a company's staff.

Example 3: Calculation of wages

```
1. Calculation( "w", "calculation of wages") -->
       "PROGRAM wages;
        TYPE Namestr = STRING[20];
             Data    = RECORD
                          Name: Namestr;
                          Wage: REAL;
                        END;
        VAR",
    Inputport( X, _ ),
       "  Outtext: TEXT;
          Wage, Tax: REAL;
          I, Number: INTEGER;
          What: CHAR;
        BEGIN",
     Outputport( V, _ ),
       "  REWRITE( Outtext ); ",
     Wagecalculation( X, _ ),
       "  CLOSE( Outtext );
        END. ".
```

```
2. Inputport( "f", "wages are on a file") -->
      "File-of-dat:  FILE OF Data;
       File-record:  Data;
       File-name:    STRING[12]; ".

3. Inputport( "v", "variable dialogue input") -->.

4. Inputport( "d", "determined number of inputs") -->.


5. Outputport( "p", "printer") -->
     "ASSIGN( Outtext, 'LST:' ); ".

6. Outputport( "c", "console") -->
     "ASSIGN( Outtext, 'CON:'); ".

7. Outputport( "m", "menue") -->
     "REPEAT
        ClearScreen;
        WRITELN('Please choose: ');
        WRITELN('   p - printer');
        WRITELN('   c - console');
        WRITE('Decision: '), READLN(What);
        CASE What OF
           'p': ASSIGN( Outtext, 'LST:');
           'c': ASSIGN( Outtext, 'CON:');
        END;
      UNTIL What IN ['p', 'c']; ".

8. Wagecalculation( "f", "wages are on a file") -->
     "ASSIGN( File-of-data, 'TEST.DAT');
      RESET( File-of-data );

      WHILE NOT EOF(File-of-data) DO
      BEGIN
         READ(File-of-data, File-record);
         Wage:= File-record.Wage; ",

   Taxcalc( X, _, Wage, Tax),
     "   Name:= File-record.Name;
         WRITELN(Outtext, Name:15, Wage:8:2, Tax:8:2);
      END;
      CLOSE(File-of-date); ".

9. Wagecalculation( "v", "variable dialgue input") -->
     "REPEAT
        ClearScreen;
        WRITE('Name: '); READLN(Name);
        IF Name <> '' THEN
        BEGIN
           WRITE('Wage:'); READLN(Wage);",

   Taxcalc( X, _, Wage, Tax ),
     "     WRITELN( Outtext, Name, Wage, Tax );
        END;
      UNTIL Name = ''; ".
```

```
10. Wagecalculation( "d", "determined number of inputs") -->
      Determinenumber( X, _, Number),
       "FOR i:= 1 TO Number DO
        BEGIN
           WRITE(i:3,'Name: '); READLN(Name);
           WRITE(i:3,'Wage: '); READLN(Wage);",

      Taxcalc( V, _, Wage, Tax ),
       "   WRITELN(( Outtext, Name, Wage, Tax );
        END;".

11. Determinenumber( "c", "constant 100", Number) -->
       [ Number, ":= 100; " ].

12. Determinenumber( "d", "dialogue", Number) -->
       [ "Write('", Number,": '); READLN(", Number," ); " ].

13. Taxcalc( "1", "10 percent", Amount, Deduction) -->
      [Deduction, " := ", Amount, " * 0.1;
      "Amount, " := ", Amount, " - ", Deduction, ";"].

14. Taxcalc( "2", "20 percent", Amount, Deduction) -->
      [Deduction, " := ", Amount, " * 0.2;
       ",Amount, " := ", Amount, " - ", Deduction, "; "].

15. Taxcalc( "t", "table computation", Amount, Deduction) -->
      ["IF", Amount, " < 100 THEN", Deduction, ":= 0 ELSE
         IF", Amount , " < 300 THEN
             ", Deduction, ":=", Amount, "* 0.05 ELSE
          IF", Amount, " < 600 THEN
              ", Deduction, ":=", Amount, " * 0.1 ELSE
                ", Deduction, ":=", Amount, " * 0.2;
      ", Amount, ":=", Amount, "-", Deduction, ";"].
```

End of example.

The control language of this example is the following regular language:

w (((f¦v) (p¦c¦m)) ¦ (d (p¦c¦m) (c¦d))) (1¦2¦t)).

This language consists of 36 different control strings, that means that we would be able to generate 36 different programs using the knowledge coded in the CSAG of example 3.

The grammar of example 3 demonstrates the possible flow of information in a CSAG. Rules 13, 14 and 15 have no side effects. Propagating information is possible by attributes only. The other rules use global information.

Rule 1 demonstrates the propagation of control information via context conditions. The first attributes of "Inputport" and "Wagecalculation" have to be equal. Further generation is automatically restricted in this case.

2.3. Implementation of FLR

The name of the computer assisted program generation environment is FLR (Fast Laboratory for Recomposition - it may also be interpreted as Forbrig Lämmel Riedewald).

It is implemented in PROLOG and operates on a database, which is organised as a collection of controlled simple attributed grammar rules. The system supports the generation of various specifications (not only programs in a programming language).
The introduced notion of the rules of CSAGs is very similar to Prolog. Therefore, it is possible to store grammar rules straight forward in the database of the Prolog system. It is only necessary to introduce a predicate "@" handeling terminal strings.

```
The grammar rule          A("p", "plus") --> "a", "+", A(X,_).
has to be rewritten into
                          A("p", "plus") :- @("a"), @("+"), A(X,_).
```

This transformation is done by a special editor hiding the internal representation.
A metainterpreter manages the generation of terminal strings (e.g. Pascal programs). This metainterpreter works according to a control string, which is presented interactively or in a file.
If the user works in an interactve way with the computer it is also possible to store new grammar rules into the data base.

The system has some test fascilities too. It can look for some grammar rules which cannot be attained from the start element S. It looks for nonterminals at the right hand side of grammar rules, which are not defined on the left hand side of rules.
The system is also able to check some context conditions according to rule 1 of example 3, where a nonterminal must have the same first attributes as another nonterminal.

2.4. Using FLR in a two-level mode

The ideas of FLR to generate Pascal programs can be used for generating control strings, which in turn can be used as input to FLR.
The following example will demonstrate the two level approach in generating different programs according to example 3.

Example 4: CSAG G3 to generate control strings for example 3.

```
Start("c", "control strings for example 3") --> G(X,_).

G("a", "projekts for Africa") --> "w f p", A(X, _).
G("s", "project shipyard")    --> "w v p 1".
G("u", "project university")  --> "w d m 2".

A("a", "Angola")  --> "1".
A("e", "Egypt")   --> "2".
A("k", "Kenia")   --> "t".
```

There are 5 possible control strings. These strings and the corresponding generated strings have the following form:

```
c a a :  w f p 1        c a e :  w f p 2
c a k :  w f p t        c s   :  w v p 1
c u   :  w d m 2
```

End of example.

We have shown that FLR can be used for generating control strings of FLR. This may be important if many decisions have to be taken from different projects. In this case, the detailed decisions should be described by a metagrammar.

In our example we suppose all African countries want to have their information about wages on a file and they all want to have a printed list. The only difference between their projects is the different calculation of taxes. If we want to generate a project for Mozambique we can use this metagrammar und add a specific rule for tax calculation. This, of course, is important only if more powerful grammars and projects are available.

2.5. Controlled attributed grammars

Sometimes it may be necessary to compute attributes according to the value of others. This may be done by semantic actions. These semantic actions should be runnable in the Prolog environment.

Defintion 9: Controlled attributed grammar (CAG).

A <u>controlled attributed grammar</u> is a CSAG augmented with semantic actions within the left hand sides of grammar rules. The semantic actions are enclosed in curly brackets.
#

Semantic actions are invoked during derivation of a word. If X is a string X = ufx', with u c T and f a semantic function then f is executed and the derivation goes on with ux'(f is removed from X).

Example 5: Controlled attributed grammar G3.

```
G("s" , "G3") --> A( X, _, Z).

A("p", "plus", Z)  --> "a", "+",
                       { var(Z), X = "p", Z1 = 1; true },
                       A( X, _, Z1).
A("m", "minus", Z) --> "a", "-",
                       {var(Z), X = "m", Z1 = 1; true },
                       A( X, _, Z1).
A("e", "end", Z)   --> "a".
```

The generated language of G3 is:
a, a+a+a, a-a-a, a+a+a+a+a, a+a+a-a-a, a-a-a-a-a, a-a-a+a+a, ...

End of example.

In example 5 semantic actions are used to compute some attributes responsible for selecting further grammar rules.

Further research will have to investigate CSAGs. They may be important for restrictions in the generation process of terminal strings. During generation it might be possible to define the selection of the "best" next grammar rule by semantic actions. Some kind of artificial intelligence should be incorporated in such a way.

3. Summary

Attributed grammars have been introduced for knowledge representation in a program generation environment. Some properties of the program generation environent FLR, which has been implemented in our department, have been discussed. We have outlined some of our intentions to support the process of software development.

In the future we try to use FLR for the following problems:
a) Generation of programs in a programming language.
b) Generation of text documents.
c) Generation of attributed grammars for compiler writer.
d) Generation of formal specifications.
e.g. algebraic specifications.
Examples should be studied in all these directions.

It is also interesting to study how the generation of terminal strings should be controlled by semantic actions.

There exists another aspect of view of CSAGs, too. The generation may be defined in such a way that the grammar generates two languages.

I. The language of the underlying context-free grammar.

II. The control language.

The relation between both languages may be of interest from theoretical point of view.

4. References

[1] Christiansen, H.:
The syntax and semantics of extensible languages,
Datalogiske Skrifter, Roskilde, No 14, 1988

[2] Hrycej, T.:
A knowledge-based problem-specific program generator,
SIGPLAN Notices, 22(2)1987, p. 53-61.

[3] Knuth, D. a.:
Semantics of context-free languages,
Mathematical Systems Theorie, 2(1)1986, p. 127-145
and 5(1)1971, p. 1971.

[4] Riedewald, G.; Forbrig, P.:
Software specification and attribute grammars,
Acta Cybernetica, 8(1)1987, p. 89-114.

[5] Watt, D. A.; Madsen, O. L.:
Extended attribute grammars,
The Computer Journal, 16(2)1983

Gaertner, K. , Schreiber, Th.

Decision support system for mechanical ventilation control at ICU

1. Introduction

The optimization of mechanical ventilation on an intensive care unit (ICU) is an extremly complicated decision process because of the nature of the human organism (fig.1).

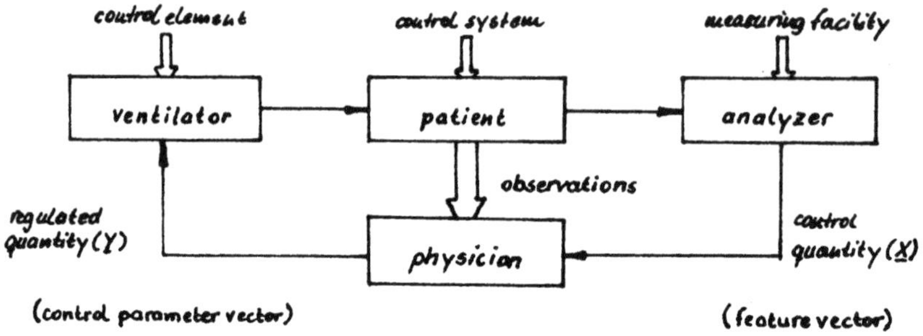

Fig. 1 : Blockscheme of the control system at the mechanical ventilation

The problems of this decision process are less on technical side but more on the side of the complicated human organism /1/:

1. There aren't any analytically describable connections between measured quantities and ventilator parameters.
2. These cause difficulties for the physician if he has to diagnose more than 6 equivalent symptoms.
3. During the registration he can obtain contradictory information about the patient's condition.
4. It is impossible to guarantee a permanent adaption between ventilator and patient with a reasonable number of medical personal.

These are the main reasons for offering a decision support system for mechanical ventilation control on ICU. This decision support system will use two different knowledge representation approaches:

1. production rules in a expert system consisting of two parts (rule interpreter 1,2)
2. statistical pattern classification and prognosis in a statistical classification system (prognosis optimization system - POS)

We begin with presenting the conception of the decision support system. A brief section will explain the main system components and then a short representation of the proposed operational function will follow.

2. System conception

The development of the decision support system intends to achieve a close connection between the two different approaches to knowledge representation and inference mechanism. The combination of both methods is to effect for medical users

- an essentially larger variety of the information to be processed (fig.1 -- i.e. observations of patient) and consequently an
- essentially increased probability that the results of the system consultations will be correct.

Further on it has to be emphasized that such an expert system has considerably increased interactivity compared with a black box - like statistical pattern classification. Fig.2 shows an architecture proposition for the decision support system.

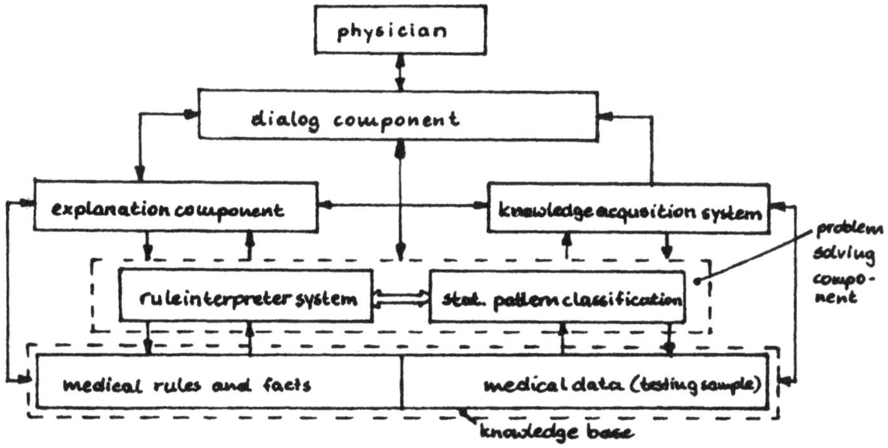

Fig. 2: Architecture proposition of the decision support system modul

The whole system has not only the component "Decision Support" but there will be also implemented three further components for

- knowledge acquisition (in proposing)
- sighting of data , files etc.
- maintaining the system , the knowledge bases , system adation to special users (change the user interface) etc.

Fig.3 shows a global overview about the whole system called IBEUS (IBEUS - abbreviation of Intensivtherapeutisches BeatmungsEntscheidungsUnterstützungsSystem).

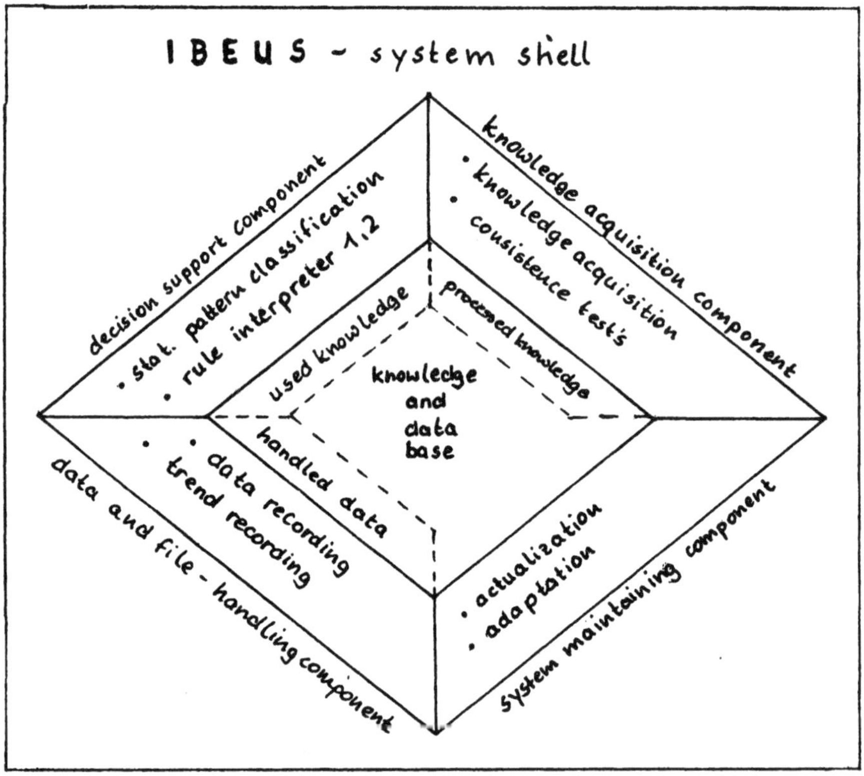

Fig.3 : IBEUS - components and tasks

For the IBEUS - system a uniformed HELP- and INFO-system is planed and the physician can use it during run-time.

In the decision support-modus the user can choose some other options , i.e.

- to see all generated important intermediate results,
- to break the runing and jump back to definite self-chosen marks,
- to interrupt the runing etc.

3. Rule-based system components

It has been told before that the rule-based system component consists of two parts. The first part is the rule interpreter 1, that will be need essentially to record the data of every special case (also additional information) and it will make decisions only for using the statistic component. The second part is the ruleinterpreter 2 . It will be generate the ventilator parameter-proposals. Than it will refine these proposals in according to the special case , if necessary with further additional information. This rule-based will be represented in the following two chapters.

3.1. rule interpreter 1

This component generates questions in accordance with the pathological findings recorded before. These questions find out important additional information about the patient's condition. By this the actual case will be classified into a special class of respiratory diseases. The result is a significant set of vital parameters important to that class of diseases to calculate the ventilator parameter propositions with them.
This modul disposes of an own knowledge base, essentially consisted of question sets. For problem solving-technique the simple data-driven forward chaining will be chosen. The question sets will be activated and processed there in a case data-driven manner. The expected size of the knowledge base allows to use such a simple solution for problem solving. Important intermediate results will be stored in a so-called working memory for the following components.
Important vital parameters - for instance :

- art. O2 partial pressure
- art. CO2 partial pressure
- heart rate
- tidal volume
- temperature
- inspired fraction of O2

and much more.

3.2. rule interpreter 2

Based on the pathological findings, vital parameter values, trend information about the patient's condition (special data file, actualized during every consultation) and additional information such as observations, medication and so on, the system finds out the minimal or maximal changing of ventilator parameters that will be aalowed to perform in this situation, the so-called ventilator parameter mask. Than it is compared value by value the POS-propositions with the ventilator parameter mask. The POS-propositions are classified into 3 groups depending on the number and degree of differences between mask and propositions. Alternatives will also be tested if the system was able to generate them. Therapy-supported activities will be offered if the system can generate them and these generated activities support the common aim of optimization or improvement of the patient's condition.
This modul also disposes of an own knowledge base. The great majority of knowledge concepts in this base will be production rules. If necessary it will be contain questions or little questionsets moreover.
The expected size of the knowledge base implicates an efficiant search and select-method. Therefore a combination of differential diagnosis and generate-and-test-strategy will be proposed. The range of rules and subrules corresponds to

commonly admitted and proved types of handling and heuristics of anaesthesists. The working memory-information will be used for generating intermediate results with the differential diagnosis. The check of usage these intermediate results will be realised by the generate-and-test-strategy. It's possible to use this search and select-method for more than only one hierarchical level.
If there isn't at least one solution the user can choose for searching a primitive selection. That will be the simple and time-consuming backward-chaining about the whole knowledge base. Another option for the user will be the turn-back.
Ventilator parameters :
- frequency of breathing per minute
- ventilation volume per minute
- positive end-expiratory pressure
- end-inspiratory plateau
- inspiration/exspiration
- inspiratory fraction of O2

4. Statistic-based component

4.1. Characterization of the model

The model statement gives rise to a system which obtains from features $\underline{X}$ the appropriate control-parameters $\underline{Y}$ which can be expected to optimize the condition of the ventilated patient after a certain period of time T (good prognosis).
The modification of the control-parameters are steady.

At the moment t_0 the condition of the patient will be registrated through the feature-vector $\underline{X}$ and the adjustment of the control-parameter-vector $\underline{Y}$ will be realized at the ventilator.

The condition of the patient at the moment $t_0 + T$ after the adjustment of the control-parameters will described through a so-called prognosis function PM. The model of the prognosis function PM($\underline{Z}$) will be built over the high-dimensional space

$$R^{N+M} = R^L \quad .$$

The vectors $\underline{X}$ and $\underline{Y}$ will be combined to

$$\underline{Z} = Z_1 \ldots Z_l \ldots Z_L = (X_1 \ldots X_N,\ Y_1 \ldots Y_M)^T .$$

Fig. 4 shows a model with one feature and one control-parameter in each case.
The prognosis function PM must obtain an optimum. This is the guaranty for a well-disposed following condition of the patient after the time T :

$$\underline{Y}^*(\underline{X}) = \arg_{\underline{Y}/\underline{X}} \min PM^*(\underline{Z}) \quad . \qquad (1)$$

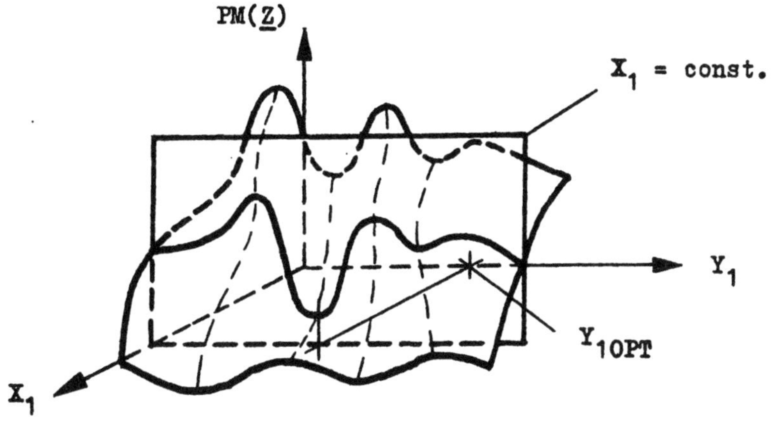

Fig. 4 : Model of a prognosis function

4.2. Model building

Information needed for the calculation of the model is obtained by a random sample of patients under clinical routine on ICU. This obtainment of informations from a random sample for the model building may be called learning.

The necessary learning sample has to be so determined that at the moment t_0 any given $\underline{X}$ will be allocated all regulated control-parameters $\underline{Y}$ and the true prognosis function PW, estimated at the moment $t_0 + T$ (judgement of the respiratory system's condition of the patients).
The learning sample also has to contain "non-optimal" examples, because the homogenity can be guaranteed only in such manner.
The project of the statistical system consists in the obtainment of weight-parameters with a suitable algorithm, which is able to learn.

For such non-parametrical information-processing-procedure was been chosen a distribution-free method of learning, the potential-functions-method /1,3/.

The algorithm of potential-function is suitable for the realization of very complex structures and for the approximation of functions with multidimensional variables. The structure of the model adapts oneself asymptotically to the objectiv function at increasing size of random test.

With the help of the potential-function-method the model gets the following form :

$$PM(\underline{Z}) = \sum_{j=1}^{J} G^j \; U(\underline{Z}, \underline{Z}^j) \,, \tag{2}$$

with G^j - weight-parameter of the j-th patient,
U - potentialfunction,
$\underline{Z}$ - vector of any patient,
$\underline{Z}^j$ - j-th vector .

The iterations interupt occurs after the obtainment of fixed testing thresholds. The necessary weight-parameters G^j for the basic algorithm of the model are the result of the system training after R-cycles under the use of the training sample.

4.3. Simulation

The simulation of the statistical system for prognosis optimization contains the search of the optimal control-parameter values $\underline{Y}$ at the model that was built by training under use of the Kiefer-Wolfowitz-method /1,4/.
It consists of a extrem value search at the L-dimensional model. This search is a minimum or maximum search according to the judgement criterion of the sizing "true"-prognosis-function PW. The task of the search is the finding of the prognosis-function's minimum, because during the control of the mechanical ventilation will be estimated the patients-endangerment.

The use of the control-parameters occurs cyclic during the peak-factor-search. One R-cycle contains M-steps of iteration. After finishing of R-cycle it forms the following algorithm of approximation :

$$Y_M^{R+1} = Y_M^R + \frac{ALFA^R}{2\ BETA^R} \left(PM1^R(\underline{Z}) - PM2^R(\underline{Z}) \right) . \qquad (3)$$

The calculation of the prognosis-function value occurs for :

$$PM1^R(\underline{Z}) \text{ with } \underline{Z} = (X_1 \ldots X_N, Y_1^{R+1} \ldots Y_{m-1}^{R+1}, Y_m^R - BETA^R \ldots Y_M^R) \qquad (4)$$

and $PM2^R(\underline{Z})$ with $\underline{Z} = (X_1 \ldots X_N, Y_1^{R+1} \ldots Y_{m-1}^{R+1}, Y_m^R + BETA^R \ldots Y_M^R)$. (5)

The connections between ALFA and BETA are realized by means of the conditions of convergence by NEIMARK /4/.
After the obtainment of conditions the iteration will be interupted. The optimal control-parameter-vector $\underline{Y}_{OPT}$ is contained.

At the begin of the iteration a start control-parameter-vector $\underline{Y}^0$ is to fix for $\underline{Y}^R$ with R=1. Because several local extrema must be supposed and we also should hold the number of iteration steps on low grade for the purpose of minimization of calculation time expense, the start control-parameter-vector $\underline{Y}^0$ will be ascertained out off the training sample with $\underline{Y}^0 = \underline{Y}^j$ from $LP(\underline{X}^j, \underline{Y}^j, PW)$ at $\underline{X}^j \approx \underline{X}$ of the testing sample (patient with similar condition) and good prognosis-value.

5. Operational function

The user can choose between three types of decision support :

1. REALTIME/EMERGENCY - for immediate decision ($t_{decision} \leq 1$ min)

2. DIALOG
   - for cases, that are not extreme situations concerning the decision time
   - it is possible to limit the information area for reaching additional information, observations, trend information, additional parameters about the patient's condition
   - possibility to generate high quality evaluation (valuated ventilator parameter offers, generating of therapy supporting activities etc.)

3. SIMULATION - a facility for teaching and test cases where user-own examples can be simulated

The decision support-modus "REALTIME/EMERGENCY" is distinguished by :
- limitation of dialog in rule interpreter 1
- with pathological findings generating the necessary important vital parameters for the POS-modul and vital parameter-input
- calculation of ventilator-parameter propositions and unvaluated output of this propositions.

The "DIALOG"- decision support-modus enables a bright investigation of the field of important information.
The significant features are :
- full dialog in rule interpreter 1 and generating of the necessary important vital parameters for POS
- storage of necessary important information for rule interpreter 2 (in the working memory)
- establish of at least one ventilator-parameter-mask under use of
  * working memory-information
  * vital parameter values
  * additional information by answering new questions
- comparison of ventilator-parameter-mask and POS-propositions and valuation of POS-propositions depended on number and size of the separate conformities between mask and propositions
- output of valuated POS-propositions inserted into the three groups
  * optimal suitable propositions
  * limited suitable propositions
  * not suitable propositions

  as well as, if generated therapy-supporting arrangements such like drug doses, physio-therapeutic activities etc.

Under "SIMULATION"-modus the user can choose two different main types :

1. Test of self-chosen ventilator-parameter propositions for fictive or actual patients and their valuation by the decision support system
2. Find out the ventilator-parameter propositions for a self-chosen patient (e.g. fictive) including the valuation by the decision support system for the purpose of teaching and learning

As operational function the user can choose some different ways, e.g.

* REALTIME / EMERGENCY
* DIALOG
* only rule-based
* only statistic-based
* vital parameter extraction

Fig. 5 shows the conception of the decision support in its basic operational function.

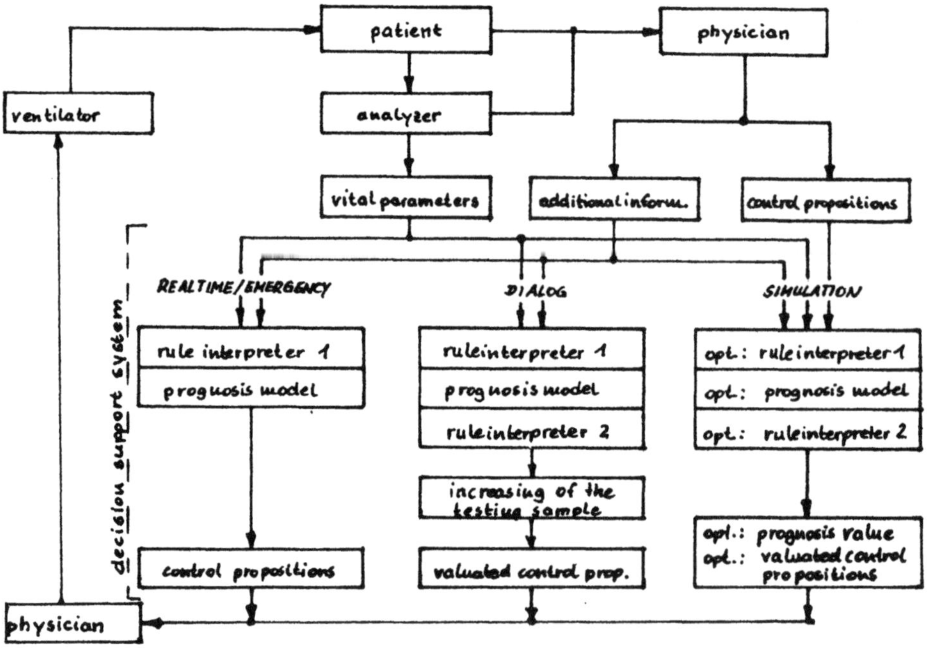

Fig. 5 : The basic operational functions of the decision support modus

In all three types of operation the user can claim an answer justification. Thus we hope to increase the system's acceptance.
In all situations the system can't make a decision with sufficient safety, it turns this decision back to the physician.

6. Current system realization

The following IBEUS-components will be realised on personal computer EC 1834 at present :

* the main control shell
* the decision support modus "REALTIME/EMERGENCY", that means, rule interpreter 1 and it's knowledge base (Prototyp)
* the POS-modul
* most of special functions like :
  - help
  - info
  - result listing
  - abort etc.
* parts of the data- and filehandling component

In processing are the following parts :

* the decision support modus "DIALOG" and "SIMULATION", that means, rule interpreter 2 and it's knowledge base (prototyp)
* the system maintaining component
* the knowledge acquisition system (in preparation)
* the rest parts of the data- and file-handling component

An easy to attend user interface has also been realised. This user interface will be accepted by our medical partners in the GDR.

The IBEUS-system is implemented in Prolog and Fortran-77 .

The system (first prototyp) will be tested at ICU from September 1989. Till Februar 1990 the knowledge bases will be extended stepwise intensivly. Behind this further measures for the practical realization will be fixed.

References :

/1/ Gärtner, K.:
Problemlösung für die Regelung der maschinellen Beatmung auf Intensivstationen unter Nutzung der rechnergestützten Entscheidungsfindung. - 1984. - Dresden, University of Technology, Informatics-Center, doctoral thesis.

/2/ Schreiber, Th.:
Entwurf von Beratungssystemen für die Optimierung der maschinellen Beatmung bei vorliegendem A-priori-Wissen in Form von Stichprobendaten und medizinischen Regeln.- 1987. - Dresden. University of Technology, Informatics-Center, submitted for diploma.

/3/ Fuchs, S.; Steinhagen, H.G.:
Objekterkennung. - 1.Auflage. - Berlin. Verlag Technik, 1976.

/4/ Neimark, Ju.I.:
Raspoznavanije obrazov i medizinskaja diagnostika. - 1972. - Moskau. Verlag Nauka.

/5/ Harmon, P.; Knig, D.:
Expertensysteme in der Praxis. - 1.Auflage. - München, Wien. Oldenburg-Verlag, 1985.

/6/ Fagan, L.M.:
Representation of dynamic clinical knowledge : measurement interpretation in the intensiv care unit. - Ph. D. thesis, Computer Science Depertment, Stanford University, 1979.

Burmese Computer-Fonts for a German-Burmese Dictionary

Dipl. Math. W. Dietmar Gellermann
Grünelinder Str. 26 , Berlin 1165
ORZ der Humboldt-Universität
zu Berlin

Dipl.Sprachmittler H. Fungk
Tucholskystr. 22 , Berlin 1040
Sektion Asienwissenschaften
Bereich Südostasien
Humboldt-Universität
zu Berlin

Summary and outlook

Using a computer for the edition of a Dictionary raises several problems. Which computer shall be used and which basissoftware is available? Which quality is achievable under reasonable conditions?

The choice was made for ATARI ST, NEC P6 respectively ATARI Laserprinter and SIGNUM, a product of the Application Systems Heidelberg. After a short period of practice with the computer, the project of the German-Burmese dictionary can be now finished.

The co-operation of linguists, language teachers and a computer specialist demonstrated how to save time in aquiring new techniques in social sciences. Although Mr. John Okell from the London School of Oriental and African Studies has developed a Burmese font in "Ethnofont" for MacIntosh computers this font cannot be used in the G.D.R. for lack of hardware.

The application of a computer for "typing" a dictionary ready for printing is, of course, only the first step towards using such efficient methods. In addition to textsystems like SIGNUM, WordStar and others, data-bases and other programs have to be used to fulfil the new and comprehensive tasks in social sciences.

Moreover, the example of the German-Burmese dictionary opens up new prospects in the co-operation between author and publishing house. With ever more convenient text programs the author can provide several lay-outs of his publications which are ready for printing.

Why use a computer for a German-Burmese Dictionary?

Dr. Annemarie Esche, former lecturer at the Department of Asien studies of Humboldt-University has started working on a German-Burmese dictionary twenty years ago. During her appointment at the embassy of the G.D.R. in the Union of Burma in Rangoon, she finished a Burmese-German dictionary which was printed in Moscow and published at Enzyklopaedie-Verlag Leipzig in 1976. Dr. Esche continued working on a German-Burmese dictionary, but the publishing house Enzyklopaedie—Verlag is not able to print Burmese characters and thus the manuscript remained unpublished until now.

In the late 1970s, the first group of students was matriculated for Burmese studies at Humboldt-University. This compelled the Department of Asien studies to provide new teaching material. Therefore, the work on the dictionary remains to be finished. Only by providing a manuscript ready for phototypesetting it became possible to publish other books like the "Lehrbuch des modernen Burmesisch (Umgangssprache)" (Manual of modern Burmese [spoken language]) by E. Richter(1983) and the "Burmesisches Übungsbuch" (Burmese textbook) by A. Esche, E. Richter in co-operation with U Khin Maung Saw (1988). Such a manuscript is very difficult to develop because it has to be typed with two typewriters – a German and a Burmese one. The typing alone took about one year for each book.

Meanwhile the German-Burmese dictionary contains about 30,000 entries. Preparing this manuscript for printing with the help of typewriters would last at least one year and the publishing house could only print an amount of about 15,000 entries. That is why we decided to use computer technology which has three major advantages for our purposes:

- we can provide a manuscript of high quality and with the full amount of entries which is ready for printing with phototypesetting,
- we can apply a new method to our scientific subject which will be extended in the future to save time and material,
- we can give fresh impetus to our colleagues in their work on similar problems (eg editing of non-latin characters).

Some special features of the Burmese alphabet and the requirements for the computer

The Burmese alphabet contains 39 main graphemes (eg က, ည, ပ) and 18 complementary graphemes (eg ေ-, ိ, ု, -ါ). Nearly every main grapheme can theoretically be combined with one or more complementary graphemes by putting them in front of, over, under or behind the main grapheme. Although not all combinations are used in practice with the grapheme က alone 35 combinations are possible:

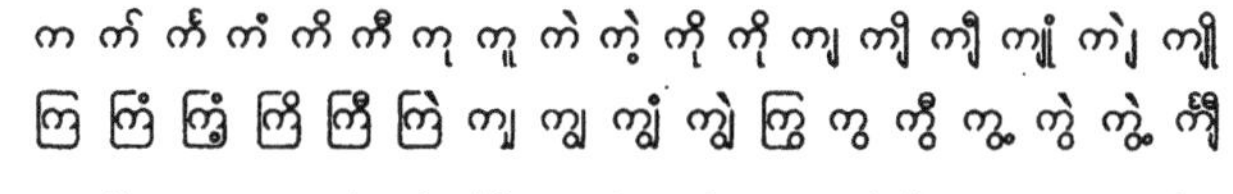

Moreover there are about 40 contractions and ligatures in the Burmese orthographic system (e.g., ဣ, ဍ္ဍ, ဏ္ဍ, ပ္ပ). Another problem for computer-based font edition: is due to the combination of complementary graphemes with main graphemes of two different sizes (e.g., ကြ, မြ). The two graphemes ြ and ြ may be used in the following combination:

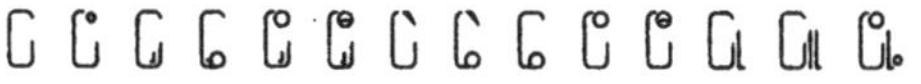

(nearly similar combinations can occur with the grapheme ြ).

For some main and complementary graphemes you can find two or three forms of appearance, eg:

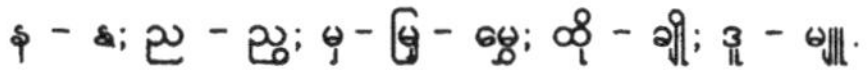

Taking account of all these questions we place three major demands on the computer:

1) universal definition of the keyboard,
2) use of several fonts at the same time (at least three – two for Burmese and one for German containing some characters for the phonemic transcription),
3) the combination of two fonts (for Burmese) must be possible.

A management of columns would be useful to save time and space for the work on a dictonary. It would enable us to provide different lay-outs for the publishing house.

Working on a Burmese font

The above-mentioned requirements create hardware as well as software problems. In the last few years publications in international computer magazines have dealt with the subject of Desk-Top-Publishing (DTP) and the use of 16-bit computers for font and text edition. We decided to go in this direction with

hardware: ATARI-ST computer, high-resolution monochrome monitor (640*400), hard-disc (20 Mbyte) and 24-pinwriter

software: SIGNUM/SIGNUM2.

Using the booting system GEM (Graphic Environment Manager), it is very easy to operate a computer. The SIGNUM-program is a convenient textsystem to design one's own font and which can use seven different fonts simultaneously. With a 24-pinwriter a matrix of 60*80 pixels (1 pixel=1/360 inch) is provided. An example for a printed grapheme in comparison with its definition in the design program is given below:

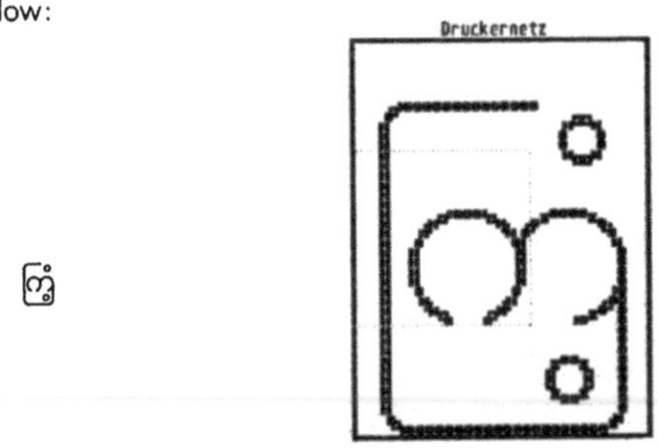

The main problem of a Burmese font is the large amount of combination. To produce every combination completely would mean to create several fonts. But it was already necessary to use Burmese and Latin characters and some characters for the phonemic transcription. This is also difficult for such systems like the Ventura-publisher for IBM-computers. SIGNUM provides the possibility using seven fonts containing 127 characters simultaneously. The WYSIWIG (What You See Is What You Get)- character of the editor supports this work and by the help of macros (defining a sequence of steps to one key) the combination of several graphemes is easier to manage. About 110 macros were programmed to combine the first Burmese font (which contains main graphemes, figures, ligatures and some frequently used combinations) with the second Burmese font (which contains complementary graphemes, some comination of complementary graphemes and reduced main graphemes for producing ligatures).

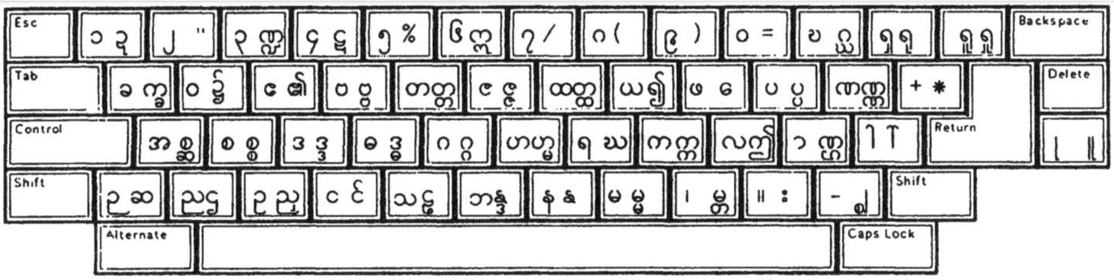

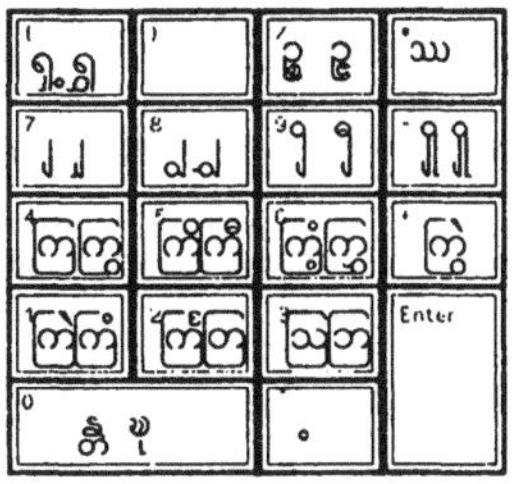

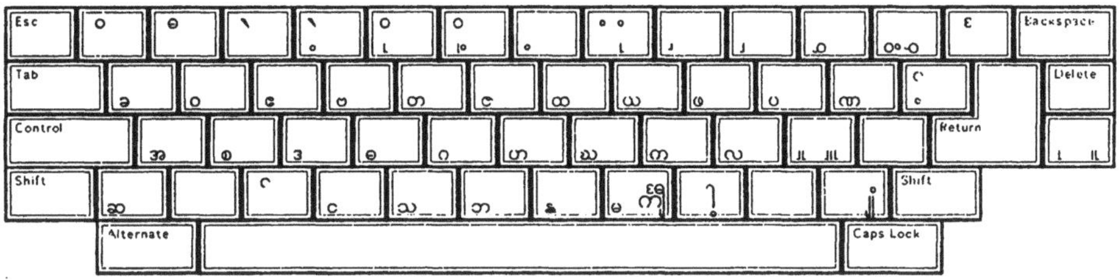

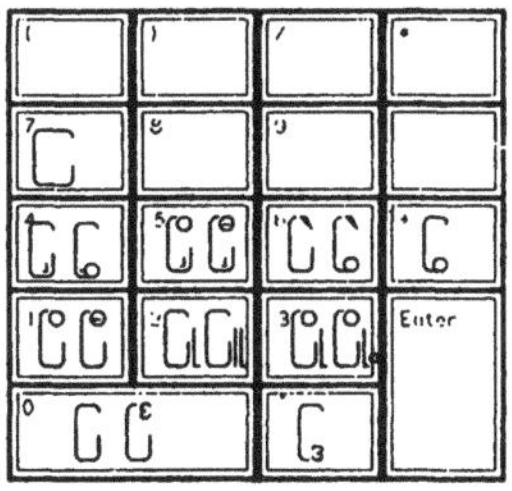

When defining the keys we followed the structure of the keyboard of the Burmese typewriter at the beginning. Later, we changed this practice and widely followed phonemic similarities between German and Burmese: e.g., the Burmese က /ka'/ lays on the key ‹K›.

After having designed the first Burmese font which was done by a software specialist from the Calculation and Information Centre at the Humboldt-

University, we continuously improved our fonts. A font for special application has also been designed.

Moreover, using the SIGNUM2-program makes the production of columns possible.

Tabaks|beutel *m* 4 ဆေးတံသောက်ဆေးအိတ်, ဆေးတံဆေးရှို့အိတ်, *orth V* ..ချို့အိတ်; **~dose** *f* 16 ဆေးတံသောက်ဆေးဘူး; **~pfeife** *f* 16 ဆေးတံ

Tabakwaren *f* 16 <*vorw Pl*> ဆေးလိပ်ပစ္စည်း

Tabaung *Eig* တပေါင်းလ [tə`bauŋla'] (12. Monat des burm Kalenders; etwa März)

tabellarisch *Adj* ဇယားကွက် ပြုလုပ်၍, အင်းစောက်ဇယားဖြင့်

Tabelle *f* 16 ဇယား, အင်းစောက်ဇယား

Tablett *n* 20 လင်ပန်း; (rundes ~ mit hohem Rand) ဗန်း; **~e** *f* 16 *Pharm* ဆေးပြား

Tabodwe *Eig* တပို့တွဲလ (11. Monat des burm. Kalenders; etwa Februar)

tabu *Adj* <*nur präd*> တားမြစ်ထား; **das ist ~ für dich** အဲဒါ မလုပ်အပ်တဲ့ကိစ္စပဲ; **für ~ erklären** ရှောင် မလေ့အဖြစ် ကြေညာ

Tachilek *Geogr* တာချီလိတ်[မြို့], တာချီလိပ် *orth V* (Grenzstadt im Shan-Unionstaat)

Tachometer *n* 23 *Tech* လည်နှုန်းပြ ကိရိယာ, *Kfz* အမြန်နှုန်းပြ ကိရိယာ, မိုင်/ကီလိုမီတာနှုန်းပြ ကိရိယာ

Tadel *m* 4 အပြစ်တင်ခြင်း; (strenger Verweis) ရှုံ့ချခြင်း; **einen ~ einstecken müssen** အပြစ်တင်ခံရ

tadellos 1. *Adj* အလွန်ကောင်း, ခြောက်ပြစ်ကင်း, သဲလဲစင်, ပြစ်မျိုးမဲ့မတင် *poet*; 2. *Adv* ခြောက်ပြစ်ကင်းသဲလဲစင်; (bei Übersetzungen u.ä.) အထစ်အငေါ့ မရှိပဲ

tadeln *vt* ရှုံ့ချ (*jmdn.* ကို; wegen [2] ကြောင့်); (beschuldigen) အပြစ်တင်; (*jmdn.* ကို) **wegen der schlechten Handschrift ~** လက်ရေးညံ့တဲ့အတွက်ကြောင့် ရှုံ့ချ; **~swert** *Adj* အပြစ်တင်ထိုက်

Tadshike [..'dzi..] တာဂျစ်လူမျိုး

tadshikisch [..'dzi..] *Adj* တာဂျစ်(နဲ့သက်ဆိုင်)

Tadshikistan [..'dzi:kista:n] *Geogr* တာဂျစ်ကစ္စတန် (Sowjetrepublik in Mittelasien)

Tafel *f* 16 (langer Tisch) စားပွဲရှည်; (Wand~) ကျောက်သင်ပုန်း; (gedeckter Tisch) ပြင်ထားတဲ့စားပွဲ; (königliche ~) ပွဲတော်; (Tabelle) ဇယား; *n* 23 ငွေထည်ဇွန်းခက်ရင်းစသည်တို့; **~tuch** *n* 22 စားပွဲခင်းကြီး; **~wein** *m* 1 ဝိုင်အပျော့စား

Täfelung *f* 17 သစ်သားပြားစီခင်းခြင်း

Taft *m* 1 *Textilw* တာဖတာ <*E*>

Tag *m* 1 (von Sonnenaufgang bis Sonnenuntergang) နေ့; (24 Stunden) ရက်; (~ des Monats) ရက်နေ့; (~ der Woche, an dem man geboren wurde) နေ့နံ; **am ersten ~** ပထမရက်မှာ, ပထမနေ့မှာ; **am dritten ~** သုံးရက်မြောက်သောနေ့တွင်, သုံးရက်မြောက်တဲ့နေ့မှာ; **ein schwarzer ~** ကြမ္မာငင်တဲ့နေ့, ဂြိုဟ်ဝင်တဲ့နေ့; **den ganzen ~ (lang)** တစ်နေ့လုံး; **ich habe heute den ganzen ~ verloren** ဒီကနေ့တစ်နေ့လုံးအလဟာသဖြစ်တာပဲ; **jeden ~** နေ့တိုင်း, နေ့စဉ်; **alle ~e** နေ့တကာ, နေ့အားလုံး, ရက်စုံ, အမြဲတန်း; **von ~ zu ~ , mit jedem ~ , ~ um ~** တစ်နေ့ပြီးတစ်နေ့, တစ်နေ့တခြား, တစ်ရက်ထက် တစ်ရက်, တစ်နေ့ထက် တစ်နေ့, တစ်နေ့နှင့်တစ်နေ့ *lit*; **bei ~e** နေ့ဘက်မှာ; **den lieben langen ~** တစ်နေ့လုံး; **pro ~** တစ်နေ့ကို *umg*, တစ်နေ့လျှင် *lit*; **am hellen lichten ~** နေ့ခင်းကြောင်တောင်မှာ; **sogar am hellen lichten ~ werden Sabotageakte verübt** နေ့ခင်းကြောင်တောင်/လင်းလင်းချင်းချင်းကြီးမှာတောင် အဖျက်လုပ်ငန်းတွေ လုပ်နေကြပြီ; **was für ein** (Wochen-) **~ ist heute?** ဒီနေ့ဘာနေ့လဲ; **freier ~** အားရက်, အားလပ်ရက်, နားရက်; **vor wenigen ~en** မကြာသေးမီရက်ပိုင်းအတွင်းက; **heute in fünf ~en** ဒီနေ့ကငါးရက်အကြာမှာ *umg*, ယနေ့မှစ၍ ငါးရက်အကြာ၌ *lit*; **ein bis zwei ~e** တစ်ရက်နှစ်ရက်, တစ်ရက်တစ်လေ *umg*; **in ein zwei ~en** တစ်ရက်နှစ်ရက်နဲ့; **~ und Nacht** နေ့ညမပြတ်, နေ့ရောညပါ; **auch ihre Meinungen unterscheiden sich wie ~ und Nacht** *übertr* အယူအဆခြင်းလည်းမိုးနှင့် မြေဆီနှင့်ရေပမာ ကွာခြားကြသည်, အယူအဆချင်း တစ်ယောက်တစ်ကမ္ဘာဖြစ် နေကြသည်; **~ für ~** နေ့စဉ်မပြတ်; **eines ~es** (Zukunft) တစ်နေ့တော့, (Zukunft) တစ်နေ့

TOWARDS SECOND-GENERATION LOGIC PROGRAMMING LANGUAGES FOR HIGH-LEVEL, KNOWLEDGE-ORIENTED PROGRAMMING

Jan Grabowski, Wolfgang Müller (Computing Centre)
Rainer Oehlke (Department of Mathematics)

Humboldt University
P.O.Box 1297
Berlin, DDR 1086

Abstract. This paper reports on work carried out within the Researchers' Workplace Project of Humboldt University. The work was basically devoted to Logic Programming and its capabilities for the practical development of knowledge-based systems. The following topics were considered:
- integration of term rewriting and semantical unification into logic programming,
- type concept for logic programming,
- export / import and authorization concepts for PROLOG,
- external database access from PROLOG,
- general-purpose user interface and knowledge acquisition facility for PROLOG,
- learning algorithms as a possible intelligent support for the knowledge acquisition facility.

1. Introduction

This paper reports on work carried out within the Researchers Workplace Project of Humboldt University. The work was basically devoted to Logic Programming and its capabilities for the practical development of knowledge-based systems. The motivation can be reconstructed as follows:

Data storage, manipulation, and retrieval has become a more and more typical business of the nonprofessional academic computer user. Data, in particular highly-specialized, "knowledge-representing" ones, become a more and more important part of computer software as a research product. Many naive computer users do not construct complex algorithms, and they do not use general-purpose programming languages at all. Instead they use high-level, easy-to-acquire tools such as database and spreadsheet systems.

This practice has obvious advantages, but it also has serious drawbacks due to limited flexibility in data structuring and limited problem solving capability. Therefore, once faced with the need for more flexible constructions, skilled users switch to traditional general-purpose programming languages, most often to BASIC, FORTRAN, and PASCAL with their low-level data handling facilities.

There seems to be a gap between these two approaches supported by available standard software. There is a third paradigm that may be suitable for filling the gap: the so-called knowledge-oriented programming paradigm, as supported by the AI programming languages. Cf. [06].

Logic Programming has been viewed as one of the most promising candidates for the role of a language for problem solving based on the knowledge-oriented paradigm. Throughout a decade, Logic programming has been employed in a form which may be called naive PROLOG. Naive PROLOG is basically a depth-first-search based goal reduction procedure based on equation solving in the Herbrand universe ("syntactical unification"). As the availability of random access computer memory rapidly increased and the basic algorithms were optimized, naive PROLOG proved a widely unexpected success as a programming language for (at least prototypes of) knowledge-based systems. However, as the complexity of applications becomes serious, the development process and its results suffer more and more from the drawbacks of naive PROLOG: defects of adequacy, bottlenecks in efficiency, and a general technological underdevelopedness.

Therefore, intensive research has departed from naive PROLOG into several directions, such as parallel inference and theory-based solution procedures. One direction starts from the viewpoint that the basic semantical properties should be preserved, but embedded into a richer system that takes into account more expressive and more adequate ways of program and data structuring suggested by theoretical insight, technological experience, and practical need. The intellectual sources of these approaches are: order-sorted logic, modular and parameterized algebraic-logic specification languages, semantical unification, polymorphically typed languages, and object-oriented languages.

The direction was marked by the EQLOG [03] project, and two of its typical representatives are TEL [08] and BABEL [07].

In our work we followed this approach. We started from the investigation of the following topics:
- integration of term rewriting and semantical unification into logic programming,
- type concept for logic programming,
- export / import and authorization concepts for PROLOG,
- external database access from PROLOG,
- general-purpose user interface and knowledge acquisition facility for PROLOG,
- learning algorithms as a possible intelligent support for the knowledge acquisition facility.

In the present paper we give a survey of the results. As a conclusion we formulate the requirements for the design of a second-generation logic programming language.

More detailed reports in German language are available from the authors.

We are indebted to Ulrich Geske and Hans-Joachim Goltz for their important suggestions.

2. Logic Programming with Functions and Equations

PROLOG has no direct support for evaluating functional expressions, except arithmetical ones. Function symbols are used for the construction of data structures only. This gives rise to inadequate constructions when essentially functional programming is required. The acceptance of logic programming could be improved if it would provide for functional evaluation, and a well-implemented evaluation technique would improve the overall efficiency. There are several approaches to this goal, most of which are summarized and evaulated in [02]. Our approach is based on defining a function by a conditional rewrite rule system. Literally, a conditional rewrite rule is a clause for the binary predicate '=>', the rewrite predicate. Example:

```
last([A,B|C]) => last([B|C]).
last([A]) => A.
```

We view these two clauses as defining the unary function 'last'. The procedural semantics of term rewriting is described by a reduction predicate '==>' which is evaluated by repeatedly replacing instances of left-hand sides of rewrite rules by the corresponding instances of their right-hand sides, following a prescribed order of application. E.g., we obtain the following result:

Goal: last([1,2,3]) ==> X.

Solution: X=3.

Conditional rewrite rules are a well-studied programming technique, see, e.g., [05]. In our case, the body, i.e. the condition part, may contain arbitrary goals. Application of a rewrite rule involves execution of the corresponding condition.

Every rewrite rule system gives rise to another predicate, the equation solving predicate, denoted ':=:'. "Substitution □ solves t :=: u " is intended to mean "t□ and u□ reduce to the same term". E.g., we intend to make the following correct:

Goal: last([1,2,X]) :=: last([3,4]).

Solution: X=4.

Operationally this can be realized in different, and more or less adequate, ways.

Our experimental system, called UNIFY, realizes both term reduction and unification with an outermost, "lazy" strategy. Equation solving is combined with reduction, which saves search space. Both procedures were programmed in several versions on top of PROLOG. The performance data for reduction are such that one can be optimistic for the performance of a reduction procedure to be built into the underlying inference engine (the PROLOG interpreter). The same could not be achieved for the equation solving procedure in the general case.

In future projects, we want to restrict ourselves to special kinds of term rewriting systems (such as the ones studied in [04]) and special variants of the equation solving predicate.

3. Types and Typechecking

The absence of a type system has often been said to be an advantage of PROLOG, since no restriction is imposed at compile-time on the sort of thing that may be assigned to a variable. From a software technological viewpoint, however, the total absence of types is a conceptual and technological deficiency. Using types wherever they are appropriate makes programming safer and saves search space. We constructed an experimental typed version of PROLOG, called PROFESS. PROFESS allows for defining subtypes and parameter-dependent (polymorphic) types. A user type declaration reads, e.g., as follows:

```
last(list(S)) :-> S.
```

which means that the type of last(l) is S if the type of l is list(S). Assuming that

```
[S | list(S)] :-> list(S).
[] :-> list(S).
```

are the implicit type declarations for the empty list and the list constructor, we see that the goal

```
write(last(8))
```

is ill-typed, since 8 is not a list. The typechecker of PROFESS checks if a submitted clause or goal has a correct typing, and rejects it otherwise. PROFESS allows also to insert type expressions into terms in order to guide and constrain typechecking. The typechecker operates nondeterministically in that it accounts for multiple declarations of the same functor. Similar to [08] we have a <u>containment predicate,</u> denoted '::', which calls typechecking at runtime. The subtype concept allows for describing partial functions. The typechecker can be used for checking if a particular function application is a "defined" one or not, if "undefined" expressions are "trapped" by supertypes, as explained in [09].

The subsort relation can also be used for expressing hierarchies of concepts (cf. [10]). An example of a subsort declaration is

bicycle 'ISA' vehicle.

This declaration implies that if t1 is of type bicycle and f(t) is well-typed for each t of type vehicle, then f(t1) is well-typed. This way of expressing inheritance gave rise to a frame preprocessor that translates expressions of a simple frame language into sets of PROFESS declarations.

Our experimental findings are: A polymorphic type discipline with its strong relation to syntactical unification is particularly adequate for a type-safe style of logic programming. The type discipline can be made as strong as necessary, or as liberal as desired. Subtypes are nice, especially if one makes the full power of order-sorted deduction available. However, this causes efficiency problems with stepwise constraining of types during computation. Undefined function applications should be handled by exceptions rather than by runtime typechecking.

4. Modules and Access Authorization

Modularity has become a standard feature in commercial PROLOG versions. Most often, modules are used as units for separate loading and compilation of program parts. They are also used for hiding program parts which are only of local interest, in order to improve readability, suppress name conflicts, and optimize code. PROLOG has this aspect of modularity in common with other languages. However there is one more point about modules in (interpreted) PROLOG: PROLOG modules exist not only during program development, they are runtime units handled by the interpreter in a way that is transparent to the user. E.g., each non-private predicate can be accessed explicitly by stating a goal on PROLOG top-level. We can see modules as "packages of knowledge". Consequently, it makes sense to assign to a module a runtime access status such as 'for reading', 'for writing', or 'for execution'.

We constructed (on top of an existing PROLOG system) a modular system called PROVISO. In PROVISO, each module has an "owner". The owner can entitle another user to access the non-private predicates of the module, using the 'export' predicate. The other user may, or may not, make each of these predicates available to his modules, using the 'import' predicate. A call to a predicate necessarily fails if the predicate was not imported. Of the three kinds of an access right mentioned above, PROVISO so far handles only the right of execution in this selective way. In further development, this principle shall be extended to all kinds of access and all types of modules. The experience with PROVISO allows the following conclusion: An access discipline as maintained by PROVISO can significantly support the safe development and use of complex, shared knowledge bases.

5. External Database Access from PROLOG

Coupling PROLOG with database management systems has been a popular subject of investigation, cf. [01]. In spite of the growing size of (virtual) internal data space that can be handled by PROLOG systems, the problem remains relevant, since database systems provide functions such as multi-access supervision and storage reorganization that are of independent value and interest, and routine tasks such as data acquisition, report generation, and backup / restore may be better performed within the DBMS environment. On the other hand, the problem solving capability achieved by accessing data through a deduction mechanism is challenging.

We constructed an interface PROMISE for accessing a relational database system (Berkeley INGRES) from PROLOG (CProlog). PROMISE makes all primary relations held in the database available for querying from PROLOG. In PROLOG a DBMS relation is represented by a predicate. Any call to this predicate is transformed into an appropriate database command. This consists, in the general case, in creating a working relation that contains exactly the solutions to the given goal. The relation is loaded pagewise into a buffer available to PROLOG. As the execution of the goal backtracks, one solution after the other is read and converted into PROLOG internal format. The procedure allows arbitrary nesting of uncompleted calls to the database system. The working relation is deleted when the corresponding goal is ultimately left, either due to search exhaustion or through a cut.
All code of PROMISE is written in PROLOG or as built-in extensions to the PROLOG interpreter.

The interface was tested with a small test database. People who are interested in constructing deductive databases are invited to use this product.

6. General-purpose user interface and knowledge acquisition facility for PROLOG

Designing a user interface is usually a time-consuming task for the non-professional programmer. Existing PROLOG systems provide no particular support for this task, except for basic window handling. There is a lack of standardization for user interfaces.

We constructed a module for prototypical, PROLOG oriented man-machine dialogue. The module was called PROPOUND.

We took the viewpoint that the user is part of the problem solving system and can be asked for solutions to goals, much like a PROLOG module. In particular, the questions posed to the user should be subject to backtracking (call for more solutions).

PROPOUND is activated (in the simplest case) by a goal

query(Goal).

It is assumed that Goal is a subtask that has to be solved by the user.

To get the solutions for query(Goal), it opens a window and asks the user:

Goal ?

The user has to enter the first solution to Goal. This solution is taken as the first solution to query(Goal). Upon backtracking, the window is re-opened, showing the goal Goal and the previously entered solution(s), and the user is asked for more solutions. While being asked for a solution, the user can in turn pose a goal to the system, by invoking a mechanism similar to PROLOG's 'break' predicate.

PROPOUND thus supports what may be called "interactive problem solving". It is designed as to fit into the procedural principles of PROLOG. The PROPOUND dialogue has a standard format which resembles the PROLOG top-level dialogue and is independent of the application. When used in an application, this format should be modified in an appropriate way, to get an application-specific interaction pattern.

We do not claim that this dialogue module can replace any particular, application-specific user interface. Rather, it can be used as a generally available prototype.

A typical, and interesting, application is testing an incompletely developed program (or: knowledge base), where the calls to undefined predicates are redirected to the user.

If we assume that the user is always able to give correct answers in these cases, we can go one step further and let the system <u>learn</u> from his answers. This means that the answers are stored, thereby gradually completing the incomplete knowledge. The effect, however, is only moderate if we do not introduce a step of <u>generalization</u>. This means that the answer should not be stored as it is, but in a more general form.

We constructed a knowledge acquisition facility for PROLOG predicates and functions that realizes this idea. We assume that there exists a number of predicates (or functions) that are not completely defined. Each time such a predicate (or function) is called, the goal is passed to the user. The user instantiates the goal by entering solutions. Now the instantiated goal is generalized. The result of generalizing fact B′ is an implication A -> B such that there exists a variable substitution ||| with B||| = B′. The implication A -> B is assumed to be a true and previously unknown clause. It is stored in the knowledge base. Finally, the goal A||| is called, since this is the resolvent of B′ and the newly introduced clause.

The open question is <u>how</u> to generalize, i.e. <u>how</u> to construct the implication A -> B. This is a task for <u>inductive inference</u>, and we might invoke Shapiro's model inference system to do the job.

In fact, Hans-Rainer Beick in our group studied systematically the algorithmic inductive inference of rewrite rule systems. He concentrated on learning non-recursive, i.e. explicit function definitions. We have not enough space to report on his results here. - Algorithms of inductive inference, however, essentially employ <u>overgeneralization</u>, which means that they construct false hypotheses that must be replaced by more special ones afterwards. It is an open question how to manage this hypothetical, and probably false, knowledge in a system that is normally expected to work correctly.

Our approach to generalization is more simple-minded. Instead of invoking an inductive inference machine, we invoke a dialogue with the user, which stepwise constructs more and more general hypotheses but avoids overgeneralization.

Example: We consider the unary predicates even_length and odd_length. Their meaning is that a list which is supplied as an argument has even or odd length, respectively. We assume that it is known to the system that these two predicates are defined incompletely. More specifically, let the definitions of both predicates be empty. Assume that the system has to execute the goal

even_length([a,b,c,d])

Since the predicate definition is unknown the following dialogue is invoked through PROPOUND:

<u>System:</u> even_length([a,b,c,d]) ?

<u>User:</u> yes

<u>System:</u> forwhich Cond : even_length([a,b,c,d]) 'BECAUSE'Cond ?

<u>User:</u> Cond = odd_length([b,c,d])

/* Somewhat sophisticated. Would you answer this way?*/

/* It follows a lengthy generalization dialogue,
we show only some steps */

...

<u>System:</u> forall A,B,C,D:
even_length([A,B,C,D]) 'IF' odd_length([B,C,D]) ?

<u>User:</u> yes

...

<u>System:</u> forall A,B: even_length([A|B]) 'IF' odd_length(B) ?

<u>User:</u> yes

/* No more generalization attempts */
/* This last implication is stored */

Now the goal odd_length([b,c,d]) is called. The predicate is also empty. In a similar way as above, the dialogue has the effect that the clause odd_length([A|B]) 'IF' even_length(B) is stored. The knowledge is now sufficient to further reduce the goal to even_length([]). The fact that the empty list is of even length is unknown, thus another dialogue starts.

<u>System:</u> even_length([]) ?

<u>User:</u> yes

<u>System:</u> forwhich Cond: even_length([]) 'BECAUSE' Cond

<u>User:</u> Cond = true

<u>System:</u> forall A: even_length(A)

<u>User:</u> no /* Overgeneralization rejected */

Now the generalization is completed. The most recently learned fact even_length([]) is stored in the knowledge base. The body is here trivial, and the initial goal is left with success. As a side-effect, complete definitions of the two predicates 'even_length' and 'odd_length' have been acquired.

This technique may be called "top-down program completion". It might be seen as an alternative way of developing a program (constructing a knowledge base), in which the user enters knowledge in the order it is needed during execution of a task. The example also shows that the generalization procedure is not as intelligent as to require only obvious answers from the user. In particular, the user has to recognize the need for a recursion step, and he has to construct it. It may take a naive user some time to find a good answer in these cases. (However, there are fewer recursive definitions in applicative knowledge-based programming than the hard-core PROLOG programmers suspect.)

<u>7. Requirements for the design of a second-generation logic programming language</u>

Our investigations helped us understand a few points of how to develop new paradigms for logic programming. Most of the ideas worked, and many further suggestions could be found in the literature. We feel that it is now time to switch from individual experiments with various ideas (mostly performed on top of existing PROLOG systems) to constructing a unified system that contains all these ideas. In other words, we are now aiming at the design and implementation of a new logic programming language. This should obey the following features:

- Programming with predicates and functions
- Equation solving at least <u>modulo the constructor-selector relations</u>
- Polymorphic typediscipline, automatic type inference, and

runtime typechecking

- Structured Programming with units, called classes, that contain predicates (and functions) as well as data, the latter being referred to by access methods. It should be possible to create more than one instance of a class, which means that the data exist more than once. This built-in mechanism shall serve as a basis for object-oriented knowledge representation
- Modular implementation with interface signatures, separate loading, detail hiding
- External data and program access facilities
- Development system that manages classes, modules, and users and supports the construction of applications
- Standard user interface
- Tools for knowledge-oriented programming, such as (executable) knowledge representation formalisms and knowledge acquisition tools.

References

[01] Appelrath, H.-J. Die Erweiterung von DB- und IR-Systemen zu wissensbasierten Systemen. ETH Zürich, Institut für Informatik, 1984

[02] Fribourg,L. Functional extensions to Prolog - are they needed? Algebraic and Logic Programming. Ed. by J.Grabowski, P.Lescanne, and W.Wechler. Akademie-Verlag 1988.

[03] Goguen,J.A., J.Meseguer: Eqlog: Equality, Types, and Generic Modules for Logic Programming. Logic Programming, Functions, Relations, and Equations. Ed. by D.DeGroot and G.Lindstrom. Prentice-Hall 1986.

[04] Goltz,H.J.: Functional Data Term Models and Semantic Unification. Algebraic and Logic Programming. Ed. by J.Grabowski, P.Lescanne, and W.Wechler. Akademie-Verlag 1988. 158-167

[05] Hu▲mann,H., Unification in Conditional-Equational Theories. MIP-8502. Fakultät Mathematik und Informatik. Univ. Passau 1985

[06] Lusk,E.L., R.A.Overbeek: Automated reasoning and knowledge base design in the scientific programming environment. Problem Solving Environments for Scientific Computing. IFIP WG 2.5 Working Conf.4, 1985. INRIA 1985

[07] Moreno-Navarro,J.J., and M.Rodriguez-Artalejo: BABEL: A functional and logic programming language based on constructor discipline and narrowing. Algebraic and Logic Programming. Ed. by J.Grabowski, P.Lescanne, and W.Wechler. Akademie-Verlag 1988. 223-232

[08] Smolka, G.: TEL (Version 0.9), Report and User Manual. SEKI Report SR-87-11, FB Informatik, Univ. Kaiserslautern, 1988.

[09] Smolka,G., Order-sorted Horn Logic: Semantics and Deduction. SEKI Report SR-86-17, FB Informatik, Univ Kaiserslautern, 1986.

[10] Smolka,G., H.Ait-Kaci, Inheritance Hierarchies: Semantics and Unification. MCC Technical Report AI-057-87. MCC, Austin 1987

ELLA, an Electronic Mailing System in Hungary

Borbála Háy, László Király and Tibor F. Liska

Computer and Automation Institute
of the Hungarian Academy of Sciences
Budapest 1132 Victor Hugo utca 18-22

Abstract. The ELLA Electronic Mailing system was developed in the Computer and Automation Institute of the Hungarian Academy of Sciences (MTA SZTAKI) as a project within the scope of the Hungarian Information Infrastructure Development Program (abbreviated as IID Program). The system operates regularly since September 1988. At the time of preparing the paper there are about 200 mailbox owners all over Hungary and more than 5000 electronic letters were sent in this way.

National IID Program in Hungary

The first stage of the National Information Infrastructure Development Program in Hungary was completed at the end of 1988. The aim of this program was to set up an information infrastructure based on a computer network in order to support research and technical activity in Hungary.

The IID Program can be devided into three separate parts:

- to establish an up to date computer hardware background to be used by researcher communities;
- to integrate these hardware resources into a wide area computer network (WAN) by the means of modern networking technologies;
- to develop different information services based upon the network mentioned before.

Within the frame of the project the participating institutes have recieved hundreds of IBM XT/AT compatible micros with a unified software environment (e.g the same operating system, text editor, database handling program e.t.c.)

SZTAKI has developed and the Hungarian PPT has set up the first public domain packet switching network in Hungary. At present approximatly 50 research institutes subscribe to that network. This means more hundred effective endpoints, since some of the institutes (especially the bigger ones) connect their whole local network to the X.25 network. According to our plans the network will be extended up to 200 participant. It means, that even more thousands of personal computers and severel mainframe computers will be integrated into one large network by the end of 1990.

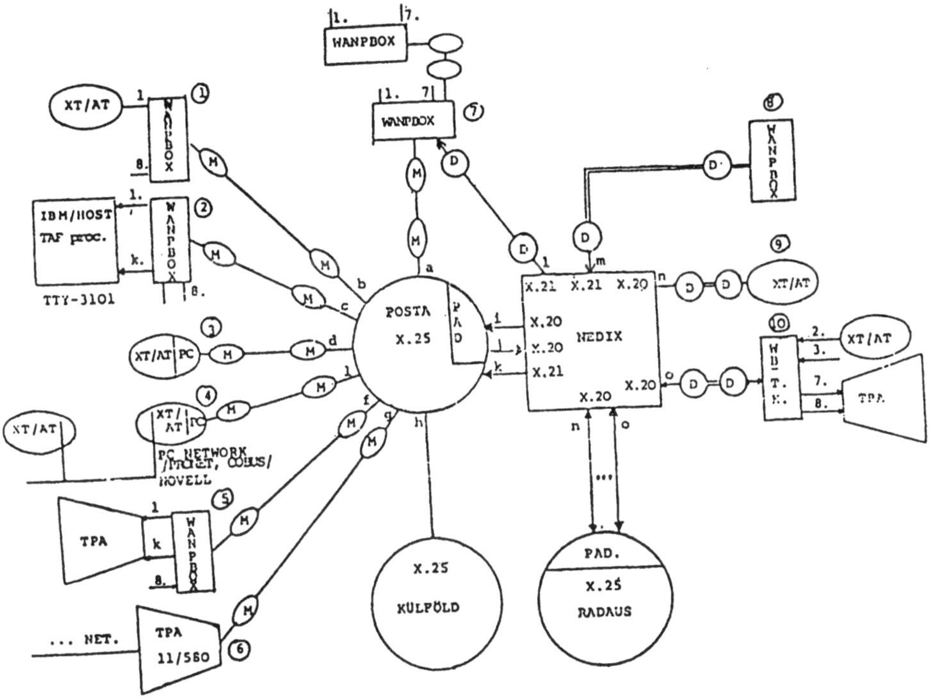

Parallel to the development of the X.25 network the first information services were also developed and put into operation by the end of 1988. These information services are briefly the following:

- there are about 40 databases operating on different mainframes. These databases can be accessed and retrieved through the X.25 network.

- as already mentioned, most of the end points of the network are IBM XT/AT compatible personal computers with

MS-DOS operating system. A program package was developed for these type of computers. This program, called UNI (User Network Interface) has a very user friendly interface, which hides the details of the network from the user. The only activity the user must do, is to choose a service from a menu (e.g. a remote database) and the program puts him immediately into the database query environment.

- the ELLA Electronic Mailing - which is the subject of this lecture - is an exclusive example for the network based information services. It was developed within the frame and by the support of the IID Program. The first version of ELLA was introduced in September of 1988. Since that time it has been improved according to the remarks and requirements of the ELLA users. Within a short time ELLA became one of the most popular service based upon the IID network.

Structure of ELLA

The ELLA system consists of two basic components communicating with each other through the IID packet switching network.

Whenever a mailbox owner wants to use the ELLA system, he calls up the ELLA Correspondence Program, which resides on his personal computer. The Correspondence Program connects to the ELLA Post Office Program running day and night on a mainframe computer under VM/SP operating system.

A so called channel box was developed, which connects the mainframe to the X.25 packet switching network via the byte multiplexer channel of the mainframe. The channel box handles 8 teletype lines and 8 lines corresponding to the ISO/OSI network layer (X.25) protocol. The ELLA communicates through the network interface, but other applications (e.g. databases) may use the teletype emulation.

The Correspondence Program (running on the PC under MS-DOS) is connected to the network usually through the asynchronous communication port of the PC. For network communication we use a well-defined device driver interface. The program can communicate in any other way, if one has an appropriate device driver. For example, in our institute a so called COMX card was developed which supplies a standard X.25 interface. The Correspondence Program can make use of it, because we have the proper device driver.

The network calling process, which establishes connection to the Post Office may be vary, too, depending on the location of the PC. For example, the computer may be part of a local network, or it may be attached directly to the X.25 network. The calling sequence is somewhat more complicated in the first case. To cope with this problem calling sequences are stored in a separate file using a simple language.

As to the relation of the two components of ELLA, the Correspondence Program is the component, that initiates the communication. Since personal computers are used for many other purposes, they cannot always be ready to catch external calls.

The way of sending an electronic letter to somebody else is the following:

- the sender starts the Correspondence Program on his PC invoking an appropriate MS-DOS command
- writes the letter (which is actually an ordinary ASCII file) using his own or the built-in text editor program;
- using an appropriate ELLA keystroke sequence he sends the letter through the network to the ELLA Post Office, working on a mainframe computer;
- the ELLA Post Office stores the letter in the mailbox of the addressee;
- the addressee starts the Correspondence Program on his PC;
- he notices, that he has mail in the mailbox:
- using an appropriate ELLA keystroke sequence he brings his letter across the network and puts it into an MS-DOS file on his personal computer.

ELLA mailboxes

Letters can be sent and received only by mailbox owners. The list of the mailbox owners (called Directory) is stored in the ELLA Post Office. Mailbox owners can inquire the Directory using the corresponding services of the Correspondence Program.

A mailbox owner can enter the system at any IBM microcomputer, that is connected to the network. The only thing he must know is his mailbox identifier, usually identical to his name, and his secret password, which can be altered by him at any time.

A one-line long information, the so called tag, can be put on every mailbox. For example:

I'm on holiday until August 20.

If somebody sends or trys to send a letter into this mailbox, he obtains this tag on his screen.

A mailbox can be "open" or "closed". If it is closed, then nobody can send a letter into it. The owner has the right to open or close the mailbox.

Addressing mechanism in ELLA

The address structure of ELLA is a hierarchical one. The following example may help to understand it.

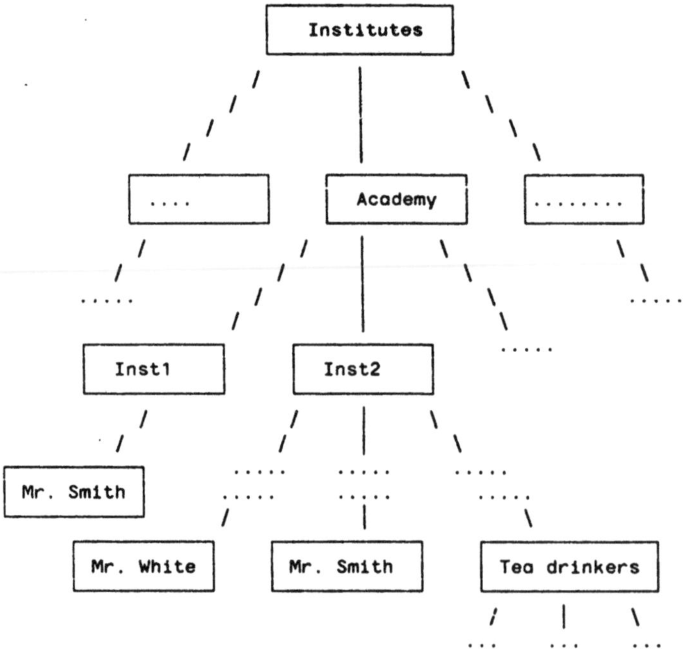

The hierarchy structure is flexible and is maintained by the supervisors of the ELLA system. At the bottom of the hierarchy there are the mailboxes of individuals. The nodes on the higher levels are called groups. Groups and boxes can form another group. The hierarchy isn't necessarily a tree, so a mailbox owner may be a member of two or more different groups. (However a circle is excluded.)

Letters can be sent to individual mailboxes as well as to groups. Sending a letter to a group means that all the members of the group will receive the letter. If a group contains another group, then the process is repeated until we reach the bottom of the hierarchy.

Boxes and groups can be addressed by their names, but sometimes this name isn't unique. In this case we can use the group names along the path in the hiararchy. For example

Academy>Inst2>Mr. Smith

is a unique address in the example above.

Whenever the ELLA supervisor creates a new mailbox or group entry in the directory, it gets a unique six digit number, called mailbox identifier, which can be used for addressing, too.

ELLA letters

Every MS-DOS file of at most 300 Kbyte, approximately 150 pages, can be regarded as an ELLA letter. The letter can be created and edited by a special text editor (built into ELLA), but any other editor may be used. The mailbox owner may change the default built-in text editor, when he configurates his Correspondence Program.

A special problem regarding electronic mailing in Hungary is the fact, that there are 18 accented characters in the Hungarian alphabet. Unfortunately there is no standard convention for their coding. ELLA takes care of the correct conversion and reconversion of these characters, even if the sender and the addressee use different coding scheme for the special Hungarian characters.

However, it is possible to send so called "code" type letters, which are transferred without any conversion. This kind of letter is very useful, if we send programs or special texts with editor or printer dependent elements.

The sender may require his letter to be acknowledged. If he does so, then he will receive a special message, called receipt. The receipt is a special letter, which informs the sender about the "fate" of his original letter, that is whether the letter was received, deleted or lost because of network malfunction etc.

ELLA Services

The ELLA Correspondence Program is a friendly menu-driven program. The list of all possible choices is on the screen and the user can choose from it by some simple keystroke. All the valid function keys are listed at the bottom of the screen.
How the main menu of ELLA looks like, is illustrated on the following figure.

Vis ——————— Elektronikus Levelező Program ——————— ELLA 2.2

Az aktuális postafiók neve: Visontay György Száma: 000116.
Jelenleg nyitva van. 1 levelet és 0 nyugtát tartalmaz.

Üzenet: Szabadságon vagyok 07.01 - 07.14.

Választék

Beérkezett levelek

Feladott levelek

Levélírás és -küldés

Iktató kezelés

Postafiók kezelés

Tudakozó

Postafiók választás

——————— F1=segítség F10=kilép Enter Esc ↑ ↓ ———————

As to be seen, the choices are marked generally by a single word only, but pressing the F1 (help) key one can obtain detailed instructions about the usage of the function.

You can configurate the Correspondence Program by the help of a simple utility program, called MODELLA. Among others the following attributes can be set or modified

- nick names,
- code conversion table,
- built-in text editor,
- formatting and coloring of the screen,
  etc.

When starting the Correspondence Program, the first thing one has to do is to choose a mailbox, provide the password, select a MS-DOS directory where the letters are stored. This procedure is called logon into the mailbox. (All of the necessary data may be stored in a special file, the use of which makes the logon procedure much simpler). After logging in the following menue appears on the screen:

Letters arrived
Letters sent
Edit and send
Register
Maintenance
Inquiry
Change mailbox

If we choose the "Letters arrived" function, then we get the list of letters and receipts arrived into our mailbox. Reading a letter means, that we transfer it across the network into our PC and store it as an MS-DOS file. Of course we can print it, or even discard it, if we want to do so. There is also a way to answer the letter immediately.

In the "Letters sent" function we get the list of those letters, which were sent, but the addressees hasn't received them so far. We can withdraw these letters.

We can handle our letters stored in a separate MS-DOS directory by the "Edit and send" function. We are able to create, to edit to delete or to send a letter. When addressing the letter, we can use a single name or group or list of them. Long and complicated names or lists of names can be substituted by a nickname.

When sending and recieving a letter or receipt the Correspondence Program updates a special MS-DOS file called Register. The Register contains one-line information about every letter sent or recieved (name and type of the letter, date of creation and delivery etc.).

By the maintenance function we can open and close our mailbox, change its password, or change the tag on it.

We can inquire the Directory stored in the Central Post Office by the "Inquiry" function of the Correspondence Program. One can list the names of mailbox owners, one can find out the path leading to a particular mailbox owner for resolving ambiguities, to find out the members of group etc.

The last function puts you into the main menu. One can choose another mailbox or leave the ELLA system.

Future enhancements

As already mentioned there are several institutes, where the PC-s are connected together by some kind of local network. The LAN-s are attached to the X.25 network by a special gateway. It is a quite natural aim to adapt ELLA to these systems. Now we are working on adapting ELLA for micros in DECNET and NOVELL type local networks.

The CMS version of the Correspondence Program is also under development. (CMS is the interactive operating system of IBM mainframes). When completed one can use ELLA from IBM mainframe terminaks.

The most important task in the near future is to connect to the great mailing systems common in Western Europe, as EARN, UUCP Mail etc. It is not only a technical problem, but also a legal one. As well known, western countries do not allow for socialist countries to use their computer networks because of USA embargo prescriptions.

At this moment there are chances to connect to the Unix based UUCP system. The task is to develop a gateway station which tranforms ELLA letters into UUCP letters and vica versa.

Knowledge Based Program Construction Using Domain Hierarchies

Rainer Hesse and Reinhard Klette

Zentralinstitut für Kybernetik und Informationsprozesse (ZKI)
Kurstrasse 33
Berlin, 1086, DDR

Abstract. The paper describes a knowledge based approach to problem oriented construction of domain specific software. The system performs the hierarchical construction of programs by scheduling operators for automatic and user controlled refinement and specification of the program to be constructed. A data base is used for accumulating the specification of the programming task, the knowledge base contains knowledge of how to construct programs. The knowledge consists of rules describing transformations for hierarchical refinement of program schemes. Constraint processing is used to consider interdependencies between operators and operands of the program space.

1. *Knowledge based approach to program construction*

The general structure of a program construction system which may be derived from our approach [*2,3,4*] is shown in fig.1. The *problem space* contains a model of the task to be solved by the program which is to be constructed. This model is formulated in terms of the domain of application and is stored within the domain specific *data base*. The *data base manager* acquires information from the domain oriented user considering semantic interdependencies of problem space items and domain specific user behavior to answer requests scheduled by the *inference machine*.

The actual program construction process takes place within the *program space* which is based on a specific domain independent language representing programming rules and partially specified programs. During this process, a diversity of possible hierarchical connections of rules of the domain specific *knowledge base* will be stepwise restricted to a unique characterization of a program. This restrictive process consists of repeated operations of refinement and specification.

The *connection table* specifies cross relations between program space and problem space. The program construction process and the interaction between program and problem space is controlled by the *inference machine*. Data base, connection table, and knowledge base determine the area of application of the program construction system and build the *target space* of this approach. The *strategy space* [8] as a whole is summerizing the meta-knowledge to select and schedule operators and operands of the design space to define a specific program construction system. The *design space* represents the potential program construction techniques. It contains *design operators* for specification and refinement during program construction, and *design operands* to control such a process.

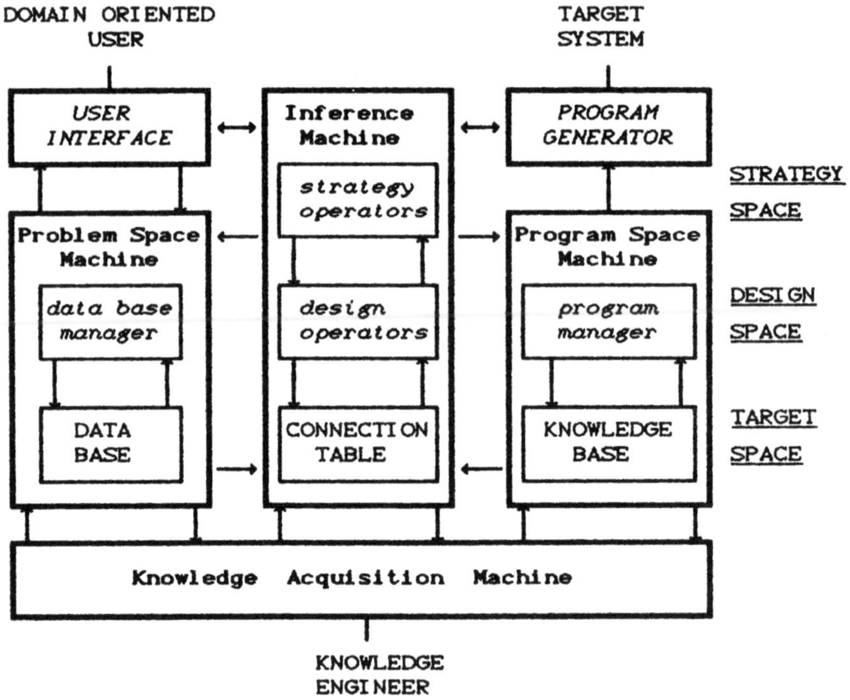

Fig. 1: General structure of a knowledge based program construction system.

Program construction systems are special approaches in the field of interactive programming environments [1]. In [5] the problem space is split into an application domain space and an example generation space, and a execution space is introduced for evaluating partially specified programs. Such further refinement of the system structure is obtained in our approach by defining special operators within design or strategy space. The use of time constraints as in [6] is not a standard mechanism in our approach because such constraints are hard to formulate for complex application problems. Instead, the complexity evaluation of syntactic structures is used for activity control. Algorithm design schemata as divide-and-conquer [7] are realized by special program construction rules in the program space.

Following the approach scetched in this paper, operational interactive program construction systems were realized for applications, e.g., in computer vision as analysis of microscopic slices or analysis of cardiologic images, or in office automation as data bank design.

2. *The Problem Space*

For an adequate represention of the problem which is to be solved by the constructed program, a representation tool is required to describe programming problems in terms of the application areas. This tool must be formal enough to meet the requirements of symbolic reasoning but also it must be comprehensive to the domain oriented user. Further it should include properties which allow the structuring of data base terms to semantic complexes to avoid permanent jumping between different points of view during user interaction. These requirements can be met by implementing a general relational representation of the problem space using an object-oriented representation of problem space items.

From these items, for the inference machine only lists (**key values**) are relevant, where **key** is a symbol which denotes an instance of a problem space item, and its value **values** is specifying the programming task. For example the lists (**run_number mult**), (**image_type greyvalued**), (**min_greyvalue 0**) and (**max_greyvalue 63**) describe the situation that a program is to construct which is to perform multiple processing runs on grey value images with greyvalues ranging from 0 to 63. The data base manager of the problem space has to answer requests of the inference machine receiving the **key**-symbol and sending back the actual **values**. With these lists, problem space conditions may be formulated. Here is a sample of such a condition:

```
and(or(not((sensor_view = LAO))
      (number_of_silhouettes > 2))
   (volume_calculation_method = cylinder_slices))
```

These conditions are used for triggering the application of program space operators.

3. The Program Space

Within the program space the hierarchical construction of programs takes place. Therefore, a representation of the actual state of the *design object*, i.e. of a partially specified program, is required as well as a representation of *construction knowledge*. The latter is the formal language of the knowledge base of the program space. *Program schemes* are words in an abstract *program scheme language*. Roughly, a program scheme may be characterized to be a collection of partially specified *operators* and *operands* which are linked by *control flow* and *data flow* relations, and between which certain dependencies are specified by *constraints*.

3.1. Domain Hierarchies

Operators of program schemes may be evaluated by *domains of operators* which are ordered within a tree of specialization (see fig.2). The specialization relation is denoted by « . Operands of program schemes may be evaluated by *domains of operands* which are also ordered within a tree of specialization (see fig.3). This evaluation allows to consider operators and operands at different levels of specification. Fully unspecified operators or operands are evaluated by variables.

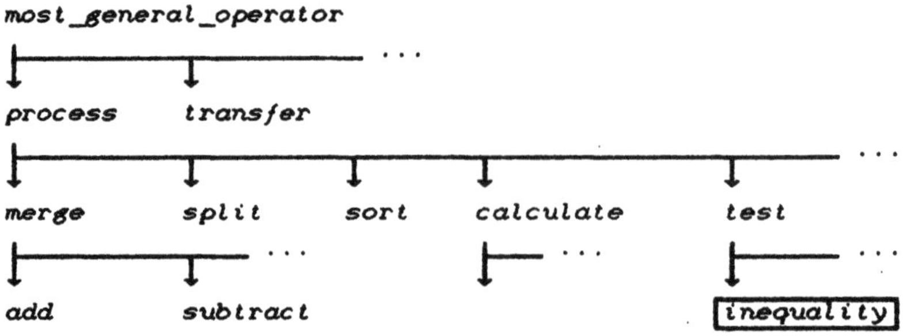

Fig. 2: Example operator domain tree ("inequality" is an example of a terminal domain).

3.2. *Program Schemes*

Program schemes are used to represent the refinement of operators and operands of the program space at different levels of construction and relations between those construction levels are relations between program schemes and their subschemes at subsequent levels of construction. A sample propram scheme is

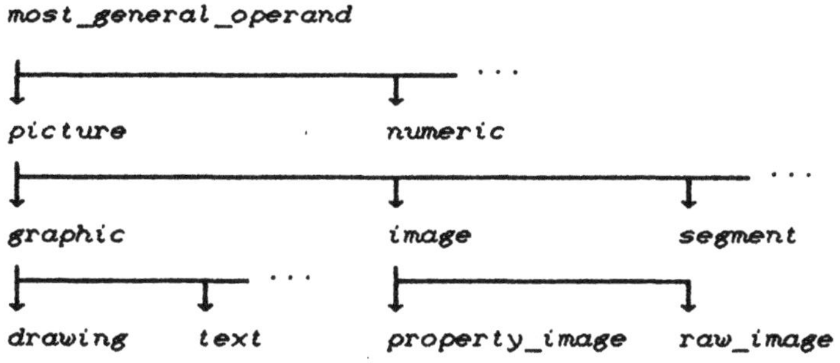

Fig. 3: Example operand domain tree.

given in fig. 4. In this scheme we are using operators **set**, **scan**, **process**, and **user_request** which are specified by operator domains **set_const**, **tv_scan**, **image_proc**, and **$F1** (what is equivalent to **most_general_operator**), respectively. The variable **$D1** is equivalent to **most_general_operand**. By **in**, **out**, or **inout** data-flow connections are specified.

```
begin
 set(set_const,[ans(boolean,out),val(true,in)]);
 while ans(boolean,in) do
  begin
  scan(tv_scan,[pict(image,out)]);
  process(image_proc,[pict(image,in),res($D1,out)]);
  user_request($F1,[request(string,in),ans(boolean,out)])
  end
end.
```

Fig. 4: A sample program scheme.

Altogether these program schemes are hierarchically ordered and this hierarchy characterizes the actual state of the program which has to be designed. Refinement operators of the design space are mapping operators of a given program scheme (*parent scheme*) onto program schemes (*child schemes*) which are informationally connected via common operands (*global data*) or are mapping operands of a parent scheme onto operands (*child operands*). The binding of unbound operator and/or operand domain variables of program schemes is restricted by *constraints* which are logical expressions over domain variables [3].

3.3. Complexity of Program Schemes

A complexity measure defined on the set of all program schemes is introduced by defining a complexity measure on the domain sets, then by defining complexities of program space operators and operands, and finally by defining complexities of program schemes. These complexity measures are used in the inference machine for several reasons.

The distance of specialization DISP(z,z') of two operand or operator domains z and z' is defined to be the length of the (shortest) path from z to z' in the relevant tree of specialization. A measure χ on the sets of operator or operand domains is *monotone* iff for two domain symbols z and z' with $z \ll z'$ it holds that $\chi(z) < \chi(z')$, and it is called *balanced* iff there exists a constant $\varepsilon > 0$ such that for any domain symbol z with the set $\mathbb{L}(z)$ of leaf nodes in its subtree (i.e. z as root) it holds that

$$\left|\chi(z) * \mathrm{card}(\mathbb{L}(z)) - \sum_{z' \in \mathbb{L}(z)} \mathrm{DISP}(z,z')\right| \le \varepsilon,$$

where ε is constant for measure χ on any tree of domain symbols. In the case of defining a measure χ by the maximum distance to the corresponding leaves,

$$\chi(z) = \max_{z' \in \mathbb{L}(z)} \mathrm{DISP}(z,z'),$$

this *maximum complexity measure* χ is monotone but not balanced. In the case of the medium distance to the corresponding leaves,

$$\chi(z) = (1/\mathrm{card}\ \mathbb{L}(z)) \sum_{z' \in \mathbb{L}(z)} \mathrm{DISP}(z,z'),$$

this *medium complexity measure* χ is not monotone but balanced with $\varepsilon=0$.

According to both definitions, for any leaf node z we have $\chi(z)=0$.

Now, according to the syntactic productions defining the language of program schemes [2,3,4], these complexity measures may be used to define the complexity of syntactic constructs. E.g., the syntactic production

selection ⟶ *then* **statement_1** *else* **statement_2**

corresponds to the complexity update operation

$$selection.\chi \longleftarrow k_{then\_else} * (statement\_1.\chi + statement\_2.\chi)$$

where k_{then_else} is a certain constant.

3.4. Construction Rules

The knowledge base contains *signature-structure rules* **(trans_1,cons,sem)** which are describing admissible refinements of program space operators, and *data-structure rules* **(trans_2,cons)** which are specifying admissible refinements of program space operand data types.

The left side of the transformation **trans_1** = (SIG→STRUC) is a program operator with its signature, the right side STRUC is a program scheme. The *constraint* cons restricts allowable bindings of domain variables. An informal description of the signature's semantics is represented by sem. The transformation **trans_2** = (DAT→STRUC) is mapping operand domains into compound data structures considering a constraint **cons**. The examples of fig.5 and fig.6 illustrate these definitions.

The actual state of the program to construct is characterized by a hierarchy of corresponding program schemes and a set of *global unresolved constraints* which were set up by design space operators during the program construction process.

```
trans:     cardio(img_proc,[pict(image,inout)])     ➡
           begin
            set(set_const,[ans(boolean,out), val(true,in)]);
            while ans(boolean,in) do
             begin
             scan(tv_scan,[pict($I,out)]);
             process(image_proc,[pict($I,in),
                                 res(histogram,out)]);
             user_request($X,[request(string,in),
                              ans(boolean,out)])
             end
           end.
cons:          specialization($X,yes_no_request)
sem:           'processing of %pict% by %cardio%'
```

Fig. 5: Example of signature-structure rule.

trans: **results ➡ list(record($D,features,statistics))**

cons: **or(same($D,patient_name),same($D,identification_key))**

Fig.6: Example of a data-structure rule.

The actual program created within the program space may be mapped by the *program generator* into the selected programming language of the target computer system. This modul may be considered as performing a special *interpretation* of program space objects, given in an abstract program scheme language, within a common programming language. So far, program generators into the languages C, FORTRAN 77 (including the IRIS image processing library), dBase III+ and LAMBA were implemented in our systems.

4. *The Inference Machine*

The design of computer programms may be considered to be an iterative and hierarchical process where the principle of subsequent decompositions of complex processing tasks into functionally relatively closed but cooperating subtasks represents the methodological basis. This design approach is performed by repeated application of the strategic operators **MATCH** (to find out the set of applicable design operators), **SELECT** (to schedule a subset of the design operators found), and **ACTivate** (to apply design operators following some general advice). See fig.7 for the used hierarchy of design operators.

In each decomposition or *refinement step* a complex task will be mapped onto a structure of functional and/or data nodes by selecting prototype operators and/or operands of the program space and instantiating the corresponding program subscheme (structure). Each refinement rule may be connected to a problem space condition. The connection table of the inference machine contains the links between corresponding refinement rules and problem space conditions. These conditions as well as the constraints connected to the rules are considered to be preconditions of applicability of rules. Applying refinement rules, program subschemes are created and unresolved but satisfiable constraints are set up as global ones.

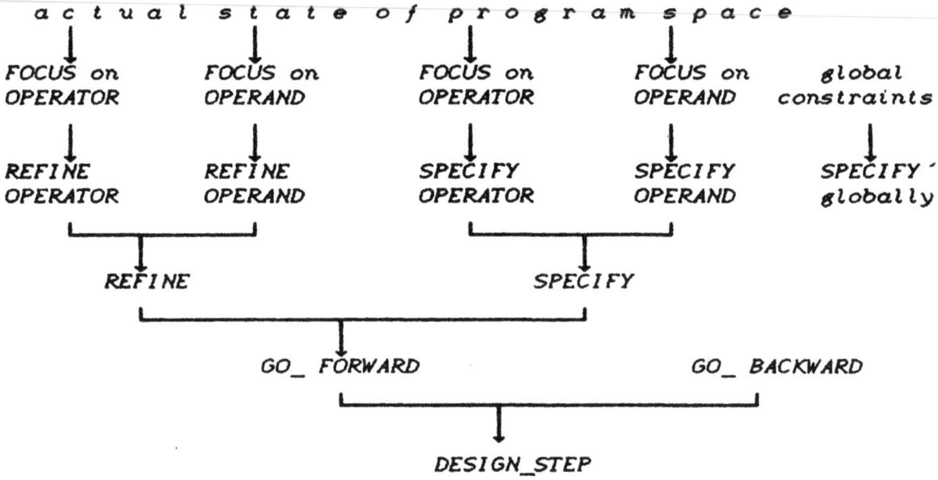

Fig. 7: Design operator hierarchy.

As an alternative to the decomposition of complex operators by refinement *specification operators* of the design space are reducing directly the difference of nonterminal program objects to terminal ones. Specification of program operators and operands may be performed locally by replacing unbound domain variables or less specific domain symbols by certain domain symbols or more specific domain symbols respectively. Global specifications are done by satisfying global constraints, i.e. by finding satisfiable variable bindings. If an over-constrained situation is reported then backtracking is performed to delete over-constrained instances of objects or operators as well as its refinement schemes.

The strategic desicions for scheduling design space operators are based on the available set of design operators and on quantitative measures characterizing the design state of the program and the possibilities of going forward in the program construction process like matching distance, constraint complexity, program scheme complexity (as defined in section 3.3), number of unresolved constraints.

For scetching mechanisms of one refinement step applied to a certain program space operator $\varphi = f(d, l)$ (after the application of the *FOCUS_ON_OPERATOR*-operator of the design space) we have to characterize the three basic cycles of the *REFINE*-operator.

In its MATCH-phase we find that the operator domain symbol *d* is labelling the root of a subtree having nodes with labels *d'*,*d''*,*d'''*,... Then, all refinement rules ρ,ρ',ρ''... are placed into the conflict set which are mapping such domains onto certain program schemes and where the signature of the left sides of these rules may be unified with the signature *l*, satisfying the set of global constraints $\mathbb{C}$ which was build-up so far and the local constraint of the rule.

Now, in the SELECT-phase the connection table is checked what condition of the problem space does support the application of what rule of the conflict set. If a unique decision is not possible for applying one of these rules, then in the strategy space one of the following strategies may be fixed:

(i) By interactive specifications of the next semantic complex in the problem space, a superset of evaluations is realized such that either a unique selection of applicable rule is possible, or there is at least a certain restriction of the set of applicable rules, or all rules of the conflict set are recognized as being not appropriate. In dependence on these situations, the ACT-phase may be entered, further activities in the SELECT-phase have to be scheduled in the design space, or the *GO_BACKWARD*-operator has to be activated, respectively.

(ii) Also, by decisions within the design space one rule of the conflict set may be selected for being applied in the ACT-phase of the *REFINE*-operator. Here, the complexities of the conclusions of the rules may be used, e.g. by the decision within the strategy space to favour the least-commitement strategy by applying the rule with minimum complexity for its conclusion. The complexity evaluation depends on the results during operator unification.

5. *Implementation*

During the elaboration of the approach described in this paper several versions of implementation were created each of them corresponding to the actual state of the concept at a certain time. The recent operational versions of the system are implemented in *Pascal* by taking care about the time complexity of subprocesses within the system, some essential progress could be realized in obtaining acceptable computing time behavior. The process of program construction is supported by displaying program schemes as graphical representation in one window and further windows on display are used for user-system interaction. The user has the special opportunity to generate partially (!) specified programs by calling the program generator and these programs run by replacing under-constrained domains of the program schemes by default or dummy symbols.

Favoring the aspect of using the system for testing mechanisms of program construction as described in this paper, further implementation activities are directed to a more sophisticated implemented version of the system taking care that the complete concept proposed in this paper will be met. The prototyping of the next version was started on the basis of *CommonLisp*.

Our further research is focusing on structuring the problem space for improved modeling of application domains and on increasing flexibility in design and strategy space for obtaining improved flexibility in the program space.

References

[1] Barstow, D. R., H. E. Shrober, E. Sandewall (eds.): **Interactive Programming Environments**. McGraw Hill, New York 1984.

[2] Hesse, R., R. Klette, Automatisierte Programmkonstruktion (1). ZKI-Information 3/1987, Akademie der Wissenschaften der DDR, Berlin.

[3] Hesse, R., R. Klette, Knowledge based program construction (2). ZKI-Information 3/1988, Akademie der Wissenschaften der DDR, Berlin.

[4] Hesse, R., R. Klette, Knowledge based program construction for computer vision. J. New Gener. Comput. Syst. **1** (1988) 1, 63-85.

[5] Kant, E., Understanding and automating algorithm design. IEEE Transact. on Software Engineering, **SE-11** (1985), 1361-1374.

[6] McCartney, R. D., Synthesizing algorithms with performance constraints. AAAI'87, Sixth Nat. Conf. on Artificial Intelligence, Seattle, July 13-17, 1987, Morgan Kaufmann, 149-154.

[7] Smith, D. R., Top-down synthesis of divide-and-conquer algorithms. Artificial Intelligence 27 (1985), 43-96.

[8] Stefik, M., Planning and Metaplanning (MOLGEN: Part 2). Artificial Intelligence Journal 16(1981), pp. 141-169.

A General Purpose Computer Teaching Room System*

Kazimierz Jojczyk Julian Kutrzeba Maciej Ślusarek

Department of Computer Science
Jagiellonian University
Kopernika 27
31–501 Kraków, Poland

Abstract. The TR'System supervises Computer Teaching Room users' work and keeps track of their results, especially those of didactical importance. A teaching schedule, which is defined for each student, specifies which lessons (educational programs), and under what conditions, should be carried out. The student is given much freedom in choosing lessons to work with, but the menu offered for a subsequent session depends heavily on the results obtained so far. A teacher may update schedule parameters between student's sessions, thus adapting its difficulty to his abilities. The System provides means for adjustment of any educational program to the TR environment, hence there are no restrictions on didactical methods used. Ordinary users need not have any computer experience to work with the TR'System, so its possible application ranges from primary school up to university.

1 Introduction

Various periods of the development of computer science and technology have had different impacts on applications of computers to teaching. In his influencing paper Hebenstreit [1] points out on three such phases.

During the first one (up to early sixties) computers were treated as more effective and cheaper substitutes for the men. For example, at that time a lot of programs for testing knowledge were developed, since the task of automatic, noncomplicated test can be done extremely effectively with the use of a computer.

Then the era of large multiterminal systems came. They made possible construction of educational software based on human-computer dialog. The famous example of such a system is Plato.

In the second half of seventies, when prices of computers sharply went down it became clear that computers need not eliminate the teacher, but they may be more effectively used as

*Research partially sponsored by Polish Ministry of National Education under grant RP.I.09

an everyday tool in teaching. A very good example of such a use is a computer classroom described by Nakayama [3].

The research partial results of which are presented in this paper is based on deep convince that each of the above trends still posseses a feature which can be implanted into a modern CAI system. Led by this idea we develop a project of a general purpose software for organization of teaching process for any kind of students or pupils.

The system makes possible to group educational programs and synchronize their successive undertakings by a student. This requires some kind of automatic evaluation of student's progress. We define tools for that, but also make possible doing it by the teacher individually. We also provide means for adjustment of difficulty level of educational software to student's abilities.

It must be stressed that we do not concentrate on a particular kind of computer education from the didactical point of view. Our goal is to build a lower-level software support for teaching process organization.

That is why we do not assume either presence or absence of a real teacher during student's work. This is only the matter of the type of educational programs used. Being rather against substituting the teacher by a computer we supply possibilities to teacher's intervention or even cooperation with the student either on-line, during educational program execution, or off-line (marking results of lessons, changing difficulty level). We also admit the use of highly advanced educational systems, like self learning ones (see for example [2]).

2 Teaching process organization

We describe general way of work in the Teaching Room for two main groups of users: students and teachers. As we mentioned above the areas of activity of both groups are strongly related to each other. Another feature of these groups is that they may intersect, which is explained further.

2.1 Students

The main group of TR'System users consists of students. Each student is assigned by his tutor an education schedule. The schedule states which computer lessons, in what order, and under what conditions may be undertaken by the student. It also decribes the way of evaluation (marking) of individual lessons.

In the data base of the System there is separate place for each user, called a journal, in which traces, including marks, of each lesson performed are stored. There is also other information, like parameters of the schedule, kept here.

The education schedule is created by a teacher. When doing this he has a library of computer lessons at his disposal. After choosing some of them he describes logical dependencies between the lessons chosen by defining an entry condition for each one. In general the condition is a logical function of the data base contents, date, time, the state of the System and others. Usually, the results of lessons already performed appear as operands of the function. Only when the condition is satisfied the lesson can be taken by the student.

For example, one can define the entry condition for a lesson in such a way that it it accessible only on Mondays. Or one can state that a particular lesson which performs final test of knowledge can be done only after successful passing of another two lessons which teach that material.

The second thing which must be defined by the author of the schedule for each lesson is data to be stored in the base after the execution of a lesson. Those data are called traces.

Each educational program is integrated with the System by means of a shell. At the shell level there are appropriate tools defined to make data exchange between the lesson and the System possible. Data produced by programs which do not use System facilities may be retrieved by the shell and then stored as traces in the base.

In order to construct a schedule a teacher can join lessons of a given subject into groups. Within each group he specifies entry conditions for all lessons used and in this specification he usually uses traces of the lessons. He also introduces special parameters which would serve as an evaluation of student's advance in the group—so called statuses Such a group is called a course.

A course can be used at the same way as a lesson in another course. This means that it has also an entry condition which is a function of user's journal, and its statuses can be used in the upper level course in defining entry conditions for lessons and other courses. Due to this nesting property we obtain a hierarchical treelike structure of a course. The root course of the structure, together with all courses and lessons it comprises, appropriately linked together, constitute a thing which is called a teaching schedule.

When a student logs into the System to start his next session he is presented his teaching schedule. It is done according to the schedule structure. At first the student sees only courses and lessons of the topmost level, in a form of menu.

Then he chooses an item from the menu. If it is a course, the System changes to the next level, and the next menu is displayed, according to the contents of the course chosen. Otherwise, the selected lesson is executed, and afterwards the menu of the last course proceeded is shown. That menu now may be different, since the lesson execution has changed journal contents, and consequently new lessons can be ready, while some of previously ready ones now may be inaccessible.

In every menu there is an option to return one step back, into the menu of the course previously visited (out of the TR' System in case of the schedule root). However, after choosing (starting) a lesson it must be executed according to its algorithm, and the student cannot leave it earlier.

The menus of the courses of a teaching schedule reflect current state of student's progress in the following way. Courses and lessons which are active (i.e. can be taken) are distinguished in the display. The others also can be observed, and in the case of courses also chosen, but no nonactive (inaccessible) lesson can be executed. The possibility of reviewing all the teaching schedule including nonactive courses enables the student to understand better what he is expected to do and what conditions should be met in order to have the whole schedule performed. All the needed information can be prepared by the authors of the courses and lessons in such a way that it is depicted during schedule overview.

2.2 Teachers

As we mentioned above the division of the TR'System users into the groups of teachers and students is not unambiguous. Not only a student may have several teachers for different courses (within his one teaching schedule). It also may happen that user X is taught history by teacher Y and biology by Z, and at the same time X as a very good computer programmer is a teacher of that subject for Y and Z.

The primary teacher's task is supervising and controlling the learning process of his student. To perform this he works with his student's teaching schedule: overviews subsequent menus, reads traces of the lessons and statuses of the courses. However—and this is really natural—he cannot execute any lesson (even a ready one). Instead, he is able to change parameters of the courses. These include statuses and other, local course attributes called options, but only a precisely defined subset of them. A status or option attribute can be modified by a teacher only when the property of modifiability was declared for that attribute by the author of the course.

Teachers in TR'System can be supported by various programs which make the task of students' courses control easier. For example, a program for quick overview of some specific lesson trace or course status could be such a tool. Programs like that can be created and introduced into the System as lessons, and grouped and scheduled within courses. We see then that the meaning of the terms *lesson* and *course* in TR'System is much broader than the usual one.

3 System administration

All the users must be known to the System. Among the users there are relations of three kinds.

Introducing of a new user can be done only by another user who posesses an appropriate privilege. The user who introduces a new one automatically becomes its superior and has the right to remove his subordinate from the System. The relation superior-subordinate has the form of a tree.

The superior defines a tutor for his subordinate. Each user has a uniqe tutor. Usually in case of a non-student he is also the tutor for himself.

The task of the tutor is to define teachers responsible for separate courses of student's teaching schedule. Each fragment of the teaching schedule of the student is assigned to a unique teacher. Notice that this last relation helps much to individualize teaching process.

4 Teaching Room structure

Briefly speaking, the Teaching Room is a collection of personal computers connected with each other by means of a network. There is one distinguished microcomputer having relatively more computational power, equipped with a fast hard disk of big capacity. We call it a host computer, to tell apart from the rest terminals of the Room. The network has a star-like configuration.

The host keeps the whole System. The data base is fully protected. It contains information about the users, and for every user there is a separate area called the journal. In that area the traces of all lessons' executions are stored, including information about all events which took place during the session, starting and finishing time etc.

TR users have also their private archives, in which they keep data needed for future sessions. Those data also can be stored only with the help of the System.

Other TR resources include libraries of general purpose programs as well as characteristical for TR libraries of lessons and courses. For example, a Pascal compiler needed for the course in programming is kept in the part devoted to ordinary programs. The System allows for its use, however it is protected against damaging.

5 *Course* and *Lesson* languages

One of the most important TR' System features is the possibility of describing how an educational program is implanted into the System and how lessons are coupled together to form a course. This description is made in two high level programming languages *Lesson* and *Course*.

Actually, the two languages have a lot in common, including Pascal like control instructions, so even there is only one translator for them both. Nevertheless, from the conceptual point of view they differ much, hence we present them separately.

5.1 *Lesson*

In the language *Lesson* the description of so called shell is made. A shell of a program (for example an educational program) is a sequence of commands which operate on simple local variables and call for execution of programs. Usually at least one of them is that of didactical interest but not always. In particular cases there can be no call, and the whole processing is done explicitly at the shell level.

Performing a call to another program does not require a special language. The problem lies in preparing a specific environment for the program, and after its execution preserving information obtained during the process. The shell language *Lesson* enables that and owing to its generality it makes possible multiple use of the same educational program in various circumstances.

Below a sample program in the language *Lesson* is presented. Its goal is to enable the student to execute his program written in assembly language of a didactic computer which has been translated earlier.

```
LESSON   DC2Interp;
   DESCRIPTION
      "The Didactic Computer interpreter; you can use the debug option.
       Afterwards you can decide to leave the program for evaluation
       and cease work on it; otherwise the file containing it will wait
       until your next session";
```

```
   TRACE
      decision : string;
   VAR
      tag, filname : string;
BEGIN
      tag := Question ( 'Want a debug switched on ? (Y/N) ', 1);
      if (tag = 'Y')
      then
         Execute ( 'DC2Int.EXE, '+D' )
      else
         Execute ( 'DC2Int.EXE );

      tag := Question
              ( 'Will you be working more on this program ? (Y/N)', 1);
      if (tag = 'N')
      then
         decision := 'ready'
      else
         decision := 'not ready';

      filname := Question ( 'filename to save ( <Enter> if none ) : ', 12);
      if (filname <> '')
      then
         Archive ( filname )
END.
```

Let us explain some constructs of the lesson DC2Interp. Declaration HELP gives a text which is displayed to a student during his overwieving of the teaching schedule. The next one, TRACE, defines what should be stored after the lesson finishes. In this case it is information to the teacher whether the program is ready, finished by the student, or not yet. This information is gained by the teacher while he goes through his students' courses in order to watch the progress they make.

The algorithmic part conducts a small conversation with the student, in order to set interpreter parameters due to student's wish, and after finishing of work asks for his decision concerning future work.

There are quite a lot of other facilities of the language *Lesson*, for example graphical tools similar to Turbo Pascal ones, string operations, other functions and procedures dealing with the operating system and TR mailbox.

5.2 *Course*

The language *Course* constitutes a tool for grouping and synchronizing lessons. Its syntax is similar to Lesson and in general resembles high level programming languages like Pascal. However it does not have an algorithmic part. Instead it has a description of the menu, where entry conditions for individual lessons are defined.

```
COURSE CompArch;
   IMPORT
      Lessons  TestArch;
      Courses  TeachArch;
   HELP
      "Computer architecture course;
       first take basic course, then the final test";
   OPTION
      tbit : STORED integer =
      (   VALUE : 0;
          TITLE : ' special flag at teacher disposal';
          HELP  : ' if the teacher switches it on, the course is passed'
      );
   STATUS
      result : TEMP integer =
      (   VALUE : if (tbit <> 0)
                  then
                     50
                  else
                     TeachArch.points + TestArch.score;
          TITLE : ' final result of the course, 50 points gives the pass';
      );
      MENU
          TeachArch =
             (   READY : true
             );
          TestArch =
             (   PRIOR : (Date >= 30.11.1988) and (Qty (TestArch) = 0);
                 READY : Qty (TestArch) = 0
             );
END.
```

Course attributes OPTION and STATUS are dealt with by the teacher. Those which are declared as STORED may be edited by him, and this can influence the current contents of the menu, which can be parametrized by those vriables. The second meaning of them is that they can decide, if defined in an appropriate way, about the evaluation of student's progress. Variables STATUS are syntactically visible in possible courses which import the given one.

In the menu one declares entry conditions for each lesson. There can be special conditions applied which, if satisfied, make the lesson a priority one, that is the only available to the student. In the above example the deadline for taking teaching course is the end of November. After that day the student is forced to take the final test. The test may be taken only once (function Qty returns number of lesson traces).

As we see, the language tools described above possess a potential to describe extremely wide range of posible situations and needs of didactical nature. We hope that they will find broader application in organization of teaching process in various enterprises.

References

[1] J.Hebenstreit, *Computers in Education—Next Step*, in: F.B.Lovis, E.D.Tagg (eds), *Informatics Education For All Students at University Level*, North-Holland, 1984.

[2] H.Mandl, A.Lesgold, (eds) *Learning Issues for Intelligent Tutoring Systems*, Springer-Verlag, 1988.

[3] K.Nakayama, *Microcomputer based classroom CAI*, J.Sci.Educ.Japan B, 1984, 113–122.

EXPERT SYSTEM BASED TOOLS AND METHODS FOR SCIENTIFIC RESEARCH IN MEDICINE

Mieczyslaw A. Klopotek, Maciej Michalewicz, Andrzej Pacan
Institute of Computer Science
Polish Academy of Sciences
00-901 Warsaw, PKiN, P.O. Box 22, POLAND

Abtract: A complex approach to data analysis in scientific research in medicine is presented. The implemented system supporting this approach allows for storing both data and knowledge and provides with tools for verification of knowledge against data as well as for acquisition of new knowledge from new incoming data.

1. Purpose and Architecture of SYS8688

We understand usually the science as progressive development of theoretical generalizations of observations and experiments leading to new observations and new experiments. So doing scientific research means permanent moving within the cycle observation-generalization-theory-application-observation.
Various tools have been developed to support the researcher in different parts of this cycle, i.e. tools supporting: storing observations and experiments (data base systems), storing the acquired theoretical generalisations (knowledge base systems) and tools supporting knowledge acquisition (enabling to generalize over data base, like statistical data analysis systems, numerous learning-from-example systems) and verification (against new incoming experiment results in the data base: statistical analysis system, or against new single cases: expert systems).

As objectives of various types of tools are different (addressing different aspects of research work, preferential addressing of different data types, amounts of data, data profiles and dependencies, as well as different user groups), it was usually a hard task to achieve cooperation between them when proceeding whith multi-aspect analysis. So the necessity of creating a compound data analysis tool combining the strongs of tools mentioned emerges. We believe that the end effect will be not only quantitative but will mean a qualitative leap as well.

SYS8688 is designed as an expert system for development and testing of knowledge bases with possibility of running current consultations in those subfields of medicine where knowledge prosessed is limitted but data may be successfully collected. The ultimate goal of the system application is to develop well-formed knowledge base delivering an expert support for physicians not thoroughly acquainted with the domain specific task. In that sense, the task of system may be considered as support in scientific research and features of a complex data analysis system mentioned previously are desirable.

One of main features distinguishing numerous medical applications from various other diagnostic systems is the role played by parameter development over time. The point of interest is not solely the duration of a symptom, but also its starting point relatively to main treatment events (e.g. a surgery). These specific requirements influenced the design of the knowledge and data bases.

Whenever we consider obtaining knowledge from data, we are faced with the dilemma of automatic generation versus delivering it by a human expert. While the first way may seldomly provide us with significant new discoveries, the second way may prove hard as the expert frequently acts on a base of "feeling" - non trivial generalizations of previous experience - and finds it difficult to formulate those heuristics in primitive terms of the knowledge base syntax and semantics.

As a compromise, some interactive tools combining expert ideas with computing capabilities of the computer have to be devised. In case of SYS8688 we support three ways in which the expert may be supported in obtaining knowledge for the knowledge base:
- (nearly) fully automatic selection of attributes accounting for a given final diagnosis,
- filling out a partial hypothesis,
- statistical analysis of dependence between selected attributes

Verification of knowledge is done in three ways:
- statistical rule verification,
- experimental consultation using KB debugging facilities for checking deduction tree,
- supposition analysis with reestablishment of certainty factors.

The architecture implied by preceding considerations is outlined in Figure 1.

2. Knowledge representation subsystem and reasoning schema.

The expert knowledge stored in SYS8688 consists of two main parts:
1) declarative knowledge incorporating descriptions of clinical and laboratory parameters, as well as descriptions of conclusions (diseases and disorders),
2) procedural knowledge expressing dependencies between parameters and conclusions in form of inference rules.

Each rule consists of a premise (conjunction of conditional statements) and an action:

IF <premise> THEN <action>.

We have distinguished conditions of two types

1) universal (time independent) and

2) temporal (time dependent)

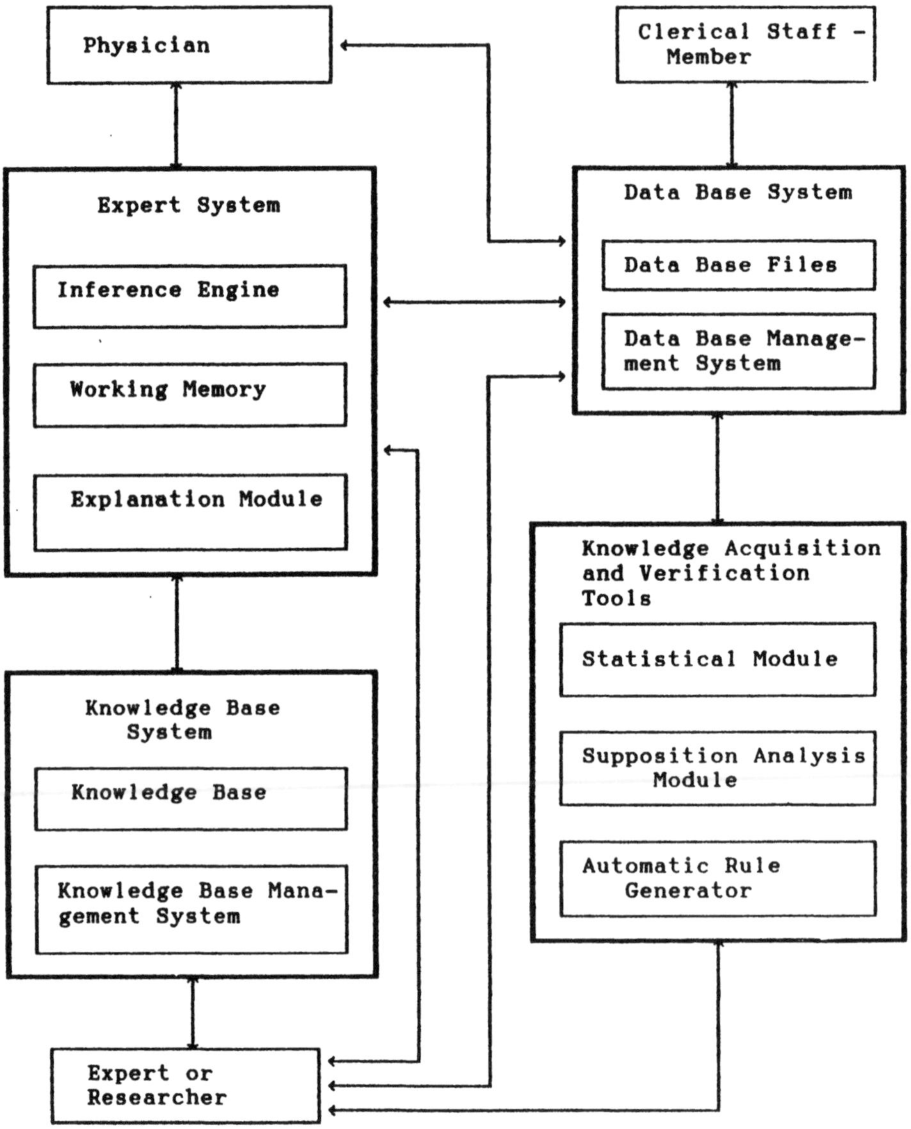

Fig. 1. SYS8688 Architecture
(User Classes Added)

with the following syntax respectively:

1) <attribute name><operator><value>

2) <quantifier><attribute name>[<time specification>]<operator> <value>

An operator belonging to the set { =, <, <=, >, >= } specifies a kind of comparison. A value (literal constant) may be of two types: text or numeric. Time specification describes time point or an interval in which to check the value of an attribute. It is given relatively to so called time constant denoting some significant *event* during patient's disease and treatment. For example, the knowledge base concerned with burns used during the system testing refered to burn and surgery moments.

The current moment is represented by the keyword "NOW". Examples of temporal conditions are:

1) EXISTS temperature [TIME > NOW-2D] = high

2) ALL temperature [TIME > NOW-2D] = high .

They test if temperature of a patient was high during the last two days. They differ in that the truth of the first comparison doesn't preclude existance of other values in that period of time, while the second one does.

The action part of a rule contains some assertions concerning conclusions (terminal rule) or parameters values (non-terminal rule). Assertions are made with some degree of certainty using numbers belonging to [-1.0, 1.0]. The following example presents an inference rule:

```
    IF   leucocyte_level > 9000 AND
         ALL temperature [TIME > burning_moment] > 38.0
  THEN   inflammatory_process = yes  0.8;
```

It expresses expert's 80% belief that the leucocyte level exceeding 9000 and the temperature higher than 38.0 after burn moment are the evidence of inflammatory process.

The reasoning system (rules' interpreter) of SYS8688 includes a working memory and a control structure. The working memory is a collection of facts (conclusions and parameters values). It is loaded based on information about the patient entered by a physician or extracted from data base.

Loading of the working memory initializes reasoning process, which can be considered as a search through conclusions (diagnoses) space. To support a particular diagnosis one or more terminal rules are invoked. If it is possible to match some rule against the working memory it is fired (its conclusion drawn) based on *modus ponens* logical schema. If the information needed is not present in the working memory, other rules (non-terminal) are activated in an attempt to deduce lacking information. Such a recursive invoking may be repeated many times before needed informatin will be found. This method of reasoning known as backward chaining has been involved in many production systems.

One aspect of reasoning concerned with checking of temporal conditions needs comments. In order to match them some extra testing (compared with universal conditions) must be done.

First, the list of pairs (parameter value, time point) is looked through to select those pairs that fall into time interval determined by time specification. Then, parameter values of selected pairs are compared with a constant given in the condition. As a result of each comparison a truth value (true or false) is returned. Finally, the quantification is done to obtain a truth value of a condition. Of course, our approach doesn't involve all possible relations between time points and time intervals, but it proved to be rich enough to handle time dependencies in typical medical applications as precise dates of data collection are usually known.
The control flow is also influenced by the certainty factor (CF) model of inexact reasoning implemented in the system to manage the uncertainty [10]. Such a model assumes the existence of two kinds of uncertainty:

1) static uncertainty, resulting from the expert knowledge incompleteness entered through the CF's associated with inference rules
2) dynamic uncertainty, determined by the data of particular patient entered by means of the CF's associated with facts.

The model supports adequate uncertainty propagation on the terminal conclusions (diagnoses), so those with the greatest CF's are considered as most certain.

3. Knowledge-base debugging facilities.

The *KB construction process* is usually intellectually labor-intensive and time consuming. A lot of bugs and shortcomings appear during transforming the incomplete and inexact knowledge into the formalism of inference rules.
Two modules in SYS8688 serve as knowledge base debugging tools:

1) explanation module (EM) and

2) KB management system (KBMS).

The basic function of EM is to give the user step-by-step explanation how the particular diagnosis was reached. As such, it is possible to review the goal tree for this diagnosis by means of "WHY" and "HOW" commands, corresponding to ascent and descent in the tree structure. Such a browsing is accompanied by visualizing of rules activated, their actual CF's, facts' sources and so on.

The set of explanation facilities is the basis for establishing the error context, while the user feels that the consultation failed. The focusing provided by the context gives him better understanding of the problem, facilitating knowledge transfer [3].

After the error is detected, the user switches to KBMS. His futher actions depend on how well he realizes what the problem is. If he is in a position to make corrections immediately the only matter is to call KB editor and to modify existing or to add new inference rules. If the user has some difficulties in stating his knowledge directly he can use knowledge-acquisition facilities described in the next section.

In both cases, it is possible to make use of KB queries. It gives the possibility to explore the actual state of KB , for example, as an answer for a query the list of rules concerned with given topic will be presented.

4. Knowledge Acquisition Facilities.

The expert (eventually cooperating with a knowledge engineer) has the possibility to add directly a rule to the knowledge base of the system (and then to test it exploiting the debugging facility described in previous section). This will be usually the case if he has definite knowledge and/or experience with a given case.

Otherwise he may wish some support. His state of knowledge and/or experience may be graduated as follows:

- he looks for a possibly small set of attributes out of a larger one classifying objects due to a certain classification parameter,
- he may have an idea on a general form of a rule, but he is not sure of values of parameters (e.g. he has an idea like

```
IF   K_level = high  AND
     temperature = ?
THEN a_surgery_is_not_advisable CF=?
```

with question marks indicating unknown values),

- he may generally know the dependence between attributes and the diagnosis, but he may seek whether or not the dependence really "tells the tale" (that is if it is justified to say that the relation didn't occur by chance).

To support the expert in his decisions, a data base containing representative material must be present. If it is so, then SYS8688 provides him with respective tools described below:
- automatic attribute selector,
- partial hypothesis filler,
- statistical module.

4.1. Automatic Attribute Selector

The idea of the Automatic Attribute Selector is generally based on works [9] and [8]. The idea of Quinlan [9] is to select a sample of objects from the general data base and to construct a decision tree based on requirement of maximum information gain if an attribute is added to this tree and to improve the decision rule performance by checking performance in samples different from the learning one.

This algorithm may be run on the rough database attributes or on more complex attribute compilations. The work [8] is concerned with construction of "elementary decision rules" which constitute those "compiled attributes".

While the algorithm runs fully automatically for rough database attributes, the compiled attribute processing has to be preceded by an interactive search through the (vast) realm of candidate elementary rules.

4.2. Partial Hypothesis Filling

The expert may have defined an inference rule for the expert system but may not be sure of the certainty factor to be assigned. SYS8688 offers the possibility of frequency based evaluation of certainty factor: the IF-part of the rule is viewed then as a query to the data base the results of which are checked on fitting the conclusion of the rule.

Furthermore, some values on the right hand side in an elementary condition of the premise may be missing. In this case the Partial Hypothesis Filler will fill somehow these places (exhausting all possibilities) and then the certainty factor will be evaluated as previously for each "full hypothesis" and those above a certain threshold value will be presented to the user.

4.3. Statistical Module

A "high certainty" in terms of frequency may leave still the question open whether or not any dependence/implication is really a significant one. This question can only be answered when statistical analysis is carried out. The Statistical Module of SYS8688 makes such analysis possible. The reason why no standard statistical package (like SPSS or other) is applied and our own one has been developed instead is not a purely syntactic or linguistic decision (SYS8688 uses Polish as communication language with the user). It is the view of the potential user of the system which was kept in mind.

Perfect application software is usually deemed as one easily operated by "no programmer" users. It is an insufficient requirement for statistical software like this. The expert in a subfield of medicine will seldomly be an expert statistician. Therefore basic expectations of the user have to be translated into expert concepts by the Statistical Module itself.

The expert-like performance of SYS8688 begins with elementary routine operations on data which are frequently ignored by leisure time statisticians just eliminating a large amount of typical errors. Outliers are eliminated automatically, variables with too few data available are dropped from further exploration, variables turning out to be constant are discarded, measurement scale types (compare [2]) predefined by the user (binary, nominal, ordinal, interval) are adjusted if not fitting variable variation requirements. Measures of central tendencies as well as other statistics are evaluated according to the type of measurement scale.

The primary interest of the user is the "significance" of interrelationship between variables. It is no use providing him with a splendid set of statistical tests on significance of correlation and with a thick never-to-be-read manual on how to use them. The user is not interested in what statisticians mean by "significance". He wants to know if a relationship is strong or not and he should not bother whether his data is a large or small sample in the sense of statistics, whether he should concentrate on the results of significance tests, or on magnitudes of the correlation coefficient etc(it is a phenomenon known to statisticians that with large samples we can prove everything significant). The Statistical Module makes such important decisions for him, informing which relationships are to be considered unimportant and warns him on suspectively strong correlation. The basic idea behind the sytem's decision making phylosophy on that subject consists in assumption, that the sample size quality in the above semse is a function of the mean correlation coefficient error. When it falls below a certain threshold value, than the sample is to be considered as large (enough). Such a situation occurs when either the sample size grows enough or the data tend to group in a pattern discovered by the given correlation coefficient. In such a case, it is wiser to consider the correlation coefficients themselves instread of the significance levels to discover the most important relationships. So the user is presented with the list of correlations ordered on decreasing (absolute) values of the correlati9n coefficients. Otherwise, the significance level of the correlation coefficient is the real indicator of the strength of the relationship, so increasing significance level is the the ordering criterion for the display procedure. In both cases, the system delivers an indication whether or not the strength of relationship is to be considered strong, meek or weak. In case of small samples, the usual criterions of significance values intervals is applied, whereas a criterion proportional to the mean correlation value is applied in case of large samples.

The Statistical Module of SYS8688 provides the user with graphic representation of single variables as well as on dependence of two variables. The histograms are drawn using built-in "aesthetic drawing" functions (based on the work [5]). The graphic picture of scattergramm is amended by the "correlation ellipsis" giving the user a feeling of what is meant by the correlation coefficient.

The most important feature of the Statistical Module is its ability to verify expert rules statistically, i.e. to tell the user if the expert rule in use or a rule hypothesis is a significant one as compared with data in the database (whether or not there is sufficient evidence to support the rule) [11]..

5. Implementation Considerations

SYS8688 was implemented for the IBM PC XT/AT computer eqquipped with a 20 MB harddisc and 640 kB main storage and coded in a C programming language. It communicates to the user in Polish, using text, graphics and spoken word. The user is protected from typing as much as possible with his activities limitted to cursor arrows pressing. Multiple Help messages are prepared according to the current state of processing.

The number of attributes is generally limitted by main storage only and is restricted approximately to about 300. The number of expert rules processed may be as high as 5000 with expert system processing not slowed down visibly.

6. Concluding Remarks

The system presented differs from other systems with knowledge base in a number of ways. First of all, the basic concept of combining an expert system with various tools supporting knowledge acquisition and application is to be considered as a novice one. Though several systems are available with possibilities of attaching various environment elements to an expert system in a manner of "EXTENSION SLOTS", SYS8688 is actually a system with those extension slots filled in a consistent way. What is more, this environment communicates with itself, not just with the expert system alone (internal interfaces are provided).

Most of modules included have distinctive features of their own. The inference engine, though based on MYCIN's CF propagation model, is a new development enriching the reasoning scheme by addition of time-dependent conditions. The statistical module fills a gap in the statistical software market. It makes some advanced statistical techniques available to non-professional statistician translating expert experience to system's internal procedures. Hypothesis generation and anwlysis of suppositions are nearly thoroughly based on research work conducted by members of our group.

Our experience with prototype knowledge bases showed the functional capabilities of SYS8688 to be sufficient for solving numerous medical problems. E.g. a subject of our exploration was burn wound treatment. New insights were gained not previously present in the knowledge base, which experts confirmed to be either known to them or anticipated by them. Reasoning on time-dependent data and knowledge acquisition utilities proved useful here.

References

[1] Alty J.L., Coombs M.J., "Expert Systems. Concepts and Examples", National Computer Centre Ltd., 1984

[2] H. Blalock "Social Statistics", McGraw Hill Book Company Inc., 1960

[3] R. Davis, D.B. Lenat, "Knowledge-Based Systems in Artificial Intelligence", McGraw-Hill Inc., 1982

[4] T.L. Dean, D.V. McDermott, "Temporal Data Base Management", A.I. 32 [1987], 1-55

[5] D. P.Doane: "Aesthetic frequency classifications", The American Statistician, Nov. 1976, Vol.30, No. 4, pp.181-183

[6] M. Klopotek, A. Pacan, E. Syropiatko: "Dealing with time-dependencies between events in expert and statistical system of medical diagnosis SYS8688" (in Polish), Symposium on Expert Systems Supporting Decision Making, Poznan, Nov. 1987.

[7] M. Klopotek, A. Pacan, E. Syropiatko: "User's interface for the Expert and Statistical System SYS8688", International Conference on AI: Natural Language Processing and Advanced Dialog Systems, Suwalki, June 1987

[8] M. Michalewicz, S. Wierzchon: "Rule Generation" in "SYS8688 - Introductory Report", Internal Report, Warsaw 1985

[9] J.R. Quinlan: "Learning efficient classification procedures and their application to chess and games" in R.S. Michalski et.al. ed.: "Machine Learning", Springer Verlag New York, Tokyo 1983, pp. 463-482

[10] E.H. Shortliffe, "Computer-Based Medical Consultations: MYCIN", American Elsevier, N.Y. 1976

[11] M. Michalewicz, M. A. Kłopotek: "Environment design for expert system shell in medical knowledge base development system SYS8688" presented at International Workshop on Expert Systems and AI Languages, Berlin(DDR) Nov. 9-11, 1988

An Object-Oriented Language with Parallel Message Passing

Volker Knaack, Hans-Jörg Jäkel, Iavor Antonov, Hans Loeper

bit'89
Dresden University of Technology
Centre of Informatics
Dresden - DDR 8027, Mommsenstrasse 13

Abstract. An object-oriented language is presented which is designed for modelling and describing a wide variety of concurrent problems. Classes and message passing as basic concepts of object-oriented programming allow a natural design of parallel programs and a high degree of concurrency during execution. Flexibility is decisively influenced using three types of message passing, which are determined context-dependently. Some implementation issues of distribution and organization of an object-oriented task on a multiprocessor system are given.

1. Introduction

Special parallel architecture of computers and algorithms have been developed to increase the processing power for some classes of problems (e.g. systolic arrays and algorithms). The paper presented belongs to the research for efficient implementation of universal programming languages on general parallel architectures ([VEEN 85],[MIKLOSKO 84]). A language OPAL was designed, which contains constructs for programming in the large in such a way that their use guarantees easy determination of actions executable in parallel. During program development the programmer doesn't need to consider the questions of concurrency, comprehensively. But it is also possible to influence the degree of concurrency.

The level of parallel actions in the given language is based on notation of complete procedures, which allows a great variability. This is in contradiction with the search for parallelism on the level of single operations based on dataflow analysis. Investigations in this area have shown that this approach causes a low complexity of communication and synchronization, but a very high intensity. In spite of special hardware the expense for communication and synchronization is very high compared with the real performance ([ANTONOV 88]).

2. Objects

The object-oriented programming style is especially well suited for the presented goal because the objects represent the unit of processing power as well as of distribution. The elaboration of such a program is realized through the interaction of independent objects. Since no external access to data of an object is permitted, the exchange of messages is the only way of interaction. This restriction results in a clean interface for every object. The messages are generalized conventional procedure calls and are handled by methods in the target object of each message.

To define the behaviour of an object a specification of the computation must be given for every message it can accept. However, not a single object is the aim of object-oriented program development, but classes of objects. These classes consistently realize the concept of abstract data types. Their definition in the language OPAL has the following general structure:

```
    CLASS Classname [InitialisationParameters] [SUBCLASS OF name]:
        InstanceVariableDeclarations;
    METHOD MethodName_1 [FormalParameters] [Results]:
            LocalDeclarations;
        BEGIN
            Body
        END MethodName_1; ...
    METHOD MethodName_n [FormalParameters] [Results]: ...
        :
    BEGIN
        InitialisationPart
    END Classname.
```

Each individual object belongs to one of these classes and can be dynamically generated by special messages. It contains local data corresponding to the declarations of its class making up its local persistent memory. The contents of the memory represents the state of an object and is initially set during object generation by means of the initialisation parameters and execution of the initialisation part. The possibility to define a class as a subclass of some other class permits a concept of hierarchical inheritance. This aspect will not be discussed here.

The interface of an object is fully described by the methods of its class. An object will only becomes active when receiving messages valid according to the interface. During the execution of a method it can update the contents of the local memory, send messages, create new objects, call local procedures and deliver the results of this method invocation.

The general independance of objects and the limitation of their interaction to the exchange of messages greatly supports the implicit determination of loosely coupled parts in such programs. This allows the description of concurrency independently of a concrete hardware. The adaption to a real multiprocessor, especially the distribution of the parallel program parts to processors and memory, is to be done by the programming system. But there exists no general applicable distribution strategy that ensures an optimal mapping of each algorithm (in particular its dynamic characteristics) to a given hardware structure. Therefore the user should be able to influence the distribution in an explicit manner. But we believe that this will be better done outside of the algorithm.

There are some proposals (ABCL/1 [YONEZAWA 86], POOL [ODIJK 86]) to determine parallel executable parts from an object-oriented program. They differ in concurrency between sender and recei- ver of a message (synchronous/asynchronous message passing) and in possibilities to interrupt the execution of a method. The following studies are deliberately based on a simple computation model to achieve clear semantics for objects and message passing as well as a (relatively) simple implementation.

As discussed above, every object represents an (logical) autonomous process. It is always in one of two states: active or dormant. After generation it will be dormant. When receiving a message it becomes active and a method is executed. If further messages arrive during the execution of a method, they have to wait for the end of the current method activation. The arrival order of all delayed messages is preserved and determines their execution sequence. The only assumption is that two or more messages sent from an object S to an object T arrive in T in the order of their transmission by S.

3. Message Passing

Viewing objects like autonomous processes, which exchange messages, is essential for the good matching of the object-oriented programming paradigm to distributed processing models. The degree of independence among the objects and, thus, the possible concurrency is substantially determined by the concept of message passing choosen.

A synchronous concept (e.g. remote procedure call) allows concurrency if the objects own a permanent activity (like in the task model of ADA [ADA 82] and POOL) with synchronization by a rendezvous only for communication. Another variant is given if an object is capable to deal with several messages simultaneously (Emerald [BLACK 86], OTM [HOGG 87]). The first variant doesn't fully match the object-oriented style because it is necessary to fix the order of message execution by explicit statements of acceptance (ACCEPT, SELECT), which is often unnecessary. The second variant requires additional constructs to realize mutual exclusion for data used by several methods of an object.

The asynchronous message passing ensures maximal concurrency between sender and receiver of a message. However, it is difficult to express such simple problems like client/server-interactions. That is why the language ABCL/1 uses three kinds of message passing:

- past type message passing (send and no wait):

  An object S sends a message M to an object T and doesn't wait for M to be executed by T. It continues its computation after the transmission of M to T. This corresponds to a situation, where one requests someone to do some task and proceeds without waiting for the requested task to be completed. The past type message passing essentially increases concurrency within a system. It is denoted in ABCL/1 by

  [T <= M].

- now type message passing (send and wait; remote procedure call):

  An object S sends a message M to an object T and waits for not only M to be received by T, but also for some returned information caused by the execution of M by T. This is similar to the ordinary procedure call. But the activation of T doesn't have to end with sending back some information to S, i.e. T may continue its computation. Returning information may be the result of the requested task as well as an acknowledgement that the execution of M has reached the required state. The notation

  [T <== M]

  in ABCL/1 denotes both the action of sending M to T by a now type message and the information returned by T, which has to be used in an assignment or like a parameter. The now type message passing synchronizes concurrent activities performed by independent objects.

- future type message passing (send and later wait):

  An Object S sends a message M to an object T expecting some result. But since S does not need it immediately, it continues its computation after the transmission of M. Later on when S needs that result it will only proceed if the result had already been returned. Otherwise S will have to wait. The future type message passing increases a concurrency and is denoted in ABCL/1 by:

  [T <= M$x] where x is a variable for the result.

The different notations of message passing in ABCL/1 force the programmer during program development to steadily choose among these cases. The language OPAL uses all message passing semantics of ABCL/1, but there is only one uniform construct

targetobject <- message (parameters).

The type of message passing is determined for every single class in a context-dependent manner. This results in a maximum of concurrency. The following rules describe the context-dependent choice of the message types:

1) The sender of the message does not want to have any results and

   a) may continue its work independently ---> past type
   b) must wait until the called method is finished or has reached a certain state ---> now type

2) The sender waits for necessary results

   a) just now ---> now type
   b) later ---> future type

An example may demonstrate such decisions:

```
IF car <- MaxSpeedReached                  (* now type    *)
THEN ar := car <- AirResistance;           (* future type *)
     :
     PetrolConsumtion := .... ar ....
ELSE car <- ChangeSpeed(10)                (* past type   *)
FI
```

The choosen strategy decreases the degree of concurrency if context-dependency increases. This obviously conforms to the natural behaviour and is illustrated in the following picture:

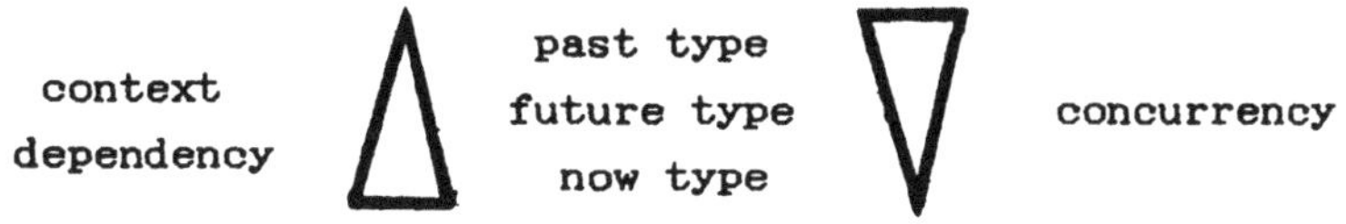

Moreover, figure 1 gives an impression of the different degree of concurrency between sender and receiver of a message attainable for all types of messages.

The execution of messages in their arrival order usually corresponds to the intended system behaviour. But sometimes it will be necessary to override this rule in favour of privileged messages. Therefore the language contains a construct

targetobject <<- message (parameters)

to send an express message. Like in ordinary message passing, the type of express messages is determined context-dependently. If an express message arrives at an active object, it will be delayed. Its execution starts before ordinary messages and after other express messages waiting at the same object. The execution of a method can not be interrupted by an express message, too. This guarantees a sufficient consistency of an object's state.

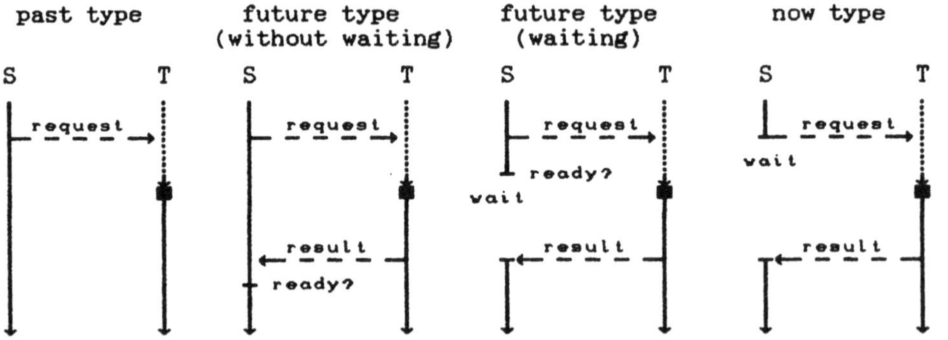

S - sender
T - receiver

⋮ - object is active or dormant
▪ - start of message execution
| - object is active

Fig. 1: Concurrency of the three message passing types

4. Parallel Constructs

Often it is desirable to send and execute several messages concurrently. This is possible for messages of past and future type without loss of concurrency by a sequence of messages. To send now type messages simultaneously the parallel clause is introduced. The semantics of parallel clause does not only comprise simultaneous transmission of all messages within the clause. It is also fixed that the execution of a parallel clause does not end until the completion of all methods executed by messages of the clause. This yields another case of synchronisation and allows the now type even for messages without a result.

An example is given in [YONEZAWA 85] where a robot arm is actuated by three step motors controlled by three objects. All the motors must finish their rotation before the next step. This can simply be expressed by use of the parallel clause:

```
[ motorX <- step(100),
  motorY <- step(150),
  motorZ <- step(-30) ];    (* some action *)
```

A class defines for all of its objects which messages can be received. But in some states of an object, it is (for a time) not possible to execute all methods in a proper way, e.g. to store in a full buffer. Such situations could be signalled by a special result of the message. Later the sender could try to send the message again.

In most cases it will be more appropriate to exclude some methods of an object for a time from execution. Messages for such methods are further received but remain waiting until the methods are released again.

By means of the statement

```
ALLOW { [ NOT ]  <list of method names> }
        ALL
```

methods may both be suspended and released. The execution of an ALLOW-statement gives all named methods the chance of (no) further activations. By default all methods will be released. This can be changed already in the initialisation part of an object. It should be noted that there is no implicit mechanism for method release.

A class definition of a simple buffer demonstrates the use of ALLOW-statements:

```
CLASS BufferManagement:

    VAR Buffer: Message;

METHOD Store (Sentence: Message):
    BEGIN
        Buffer := Sentence; ALLOW Load
    END Store;

METHOD Load RETURNS (Message):
    BEGIN
        RESULT (Buffer); ALLOW Store
    END Load;

BEGIN
    ALLOW Store
END BufferManagement.
```

5. An Example

A further example illustrates some other constructs of OPAL. It is an object-oriented variant of the "Sieve of Eratosthenes" - an algorithm to compute prime numbers. An object of the class checker is generated for every computed prime number. These objects are active sieves of a stream of integers. The stream is produced by the root object and is passed by messages from sieve to sieve. An integer which has passed the whole sequence of current checkers is a new prime number. A new checker is generated for it and is appended to the sequence.

The message NEW is defined for every class and causes the generation of a new object of this class (here: checker). The value of the object's instance variable prime is initialized by the parameter of the NEW message. Generation of an object includes execution of the initialisation part. In the example it causes the output of each new prime number. The result of object generation is a reference to the object, which may serve as the target for message transmissions.

Other constructs of OPAL are similar to languages like ALGOL, PASCAL and MODULA. Their explanation is unnecessary.

```
ROOT CLASS Primes:

    VAR i,n: INTEGER;
          s: Checker;
BEGIN
    Read (n);
    Write (2);
    s := Checker <- NEW (3);
    FOR i:=5 BY 2 TO n   DO s <- Check (i) OD
END Primes.
```

```
CLASS Checker (Prime: INTEGER):
    VAR Next: Checker;
       First: BOOL;

METHOD Check (Number: INTEGER):
    BEGIN
        IF (Number MOD Prime) <> 0
        THEN IF First
             THEN Next := Checker <- NEW (Number);
                  First := FALSE
             ELSE Next <- Check (Number)
             FI
        FI
    END Check;

BEGIN
    First := TRUE;
    Write (Prime)
END Checker.
```

6. Compilation And Program Execution

Different implementation styles of object-oriented languages are known: For example, Smalltalk-80 [GOLDBERG 83] delivers a complete and closed programming environment. Another example is the implementation of ABCL/1 using the LISP environment. Both implementations are interpreters. In such programming systems, the given text is translated into an internal representation and then an interpreter realizes the program execution.

The second variant to implement an object-oriented language is to completely compile the source text. After that a conventional taskbuilding and execution can take place. In such systems the object-oriented approach is not visible outside the task, as the implementation of C++ [STROUSTRUP 86] shows. A C++ program is precompiled to C and then compiled and executed as usually.

In this paper we introduce an implementation with complete compilation. A multipass compiler generates an assembly source. It must then be translated and linked into a task. In this way it will be possible to execute the task in an environment that differs from the object-oriented one. A multiprocessor is used to execute such tasks. Fig.2 shows a possible distribution.

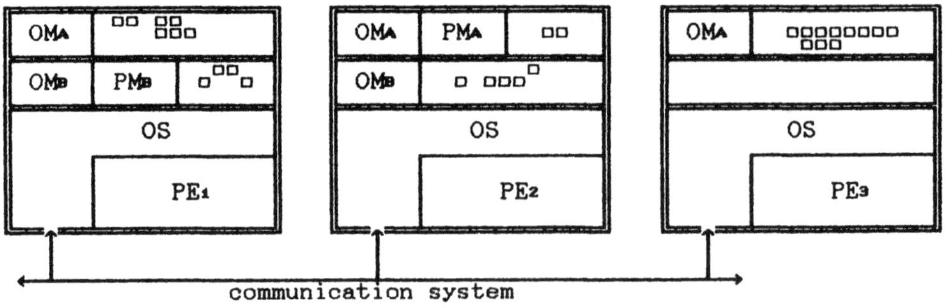

OMA - Object Manager (Task A)
OMB - Object Manager (Task B)
PMA - Program Manager (Task A)
PMB - Program Manager (Task B)
□ - Objects
OS - Operating System Part
PEi - Processor Element i

Fig. 2: Object-oriented multitasking of a multiprocessor

Each processor element PE has a part of the distributed operating system OS. The operating system realizes communication between the processors via the communication system.

An object-oriented task generates for each used processor one process. The process is closely assigned to the processor and is executed sequentially. Time sharing control of several tasks is realized by an independent swapping of processes on each processor.

Each task that works internally object-oriented has for each process of the task an object manager OM. The object manager realizes a quasi parallel control of all objects in this process. One program manager PM for the whole task has to distribute the objects over all processes. The process with the program manager PM is the initial process and can be started on any processor.

Program execution of an object-oriented task begins with load and start on one processor. The distribution over the other processors is supported by the operating system part on each processor element corresponding to the decisions of the program manager. During initialization the program manager has to examine the hardware to get information about the available ressources. This information is used for logical object distribution.

7. The Run Time System

The run time system includes program manager, object managers of separate processes and process internal services for common usage by the objects.

7.1. The Program Manager

The program manager has to control logical object distribution. The decision on which process the object is to be created depends on the one hand on the information derived by compilation and on the other hand on the actual multiprocessor state. By this means, insignificant changes on the hardware (for example: changes of the number of available processors) will not require recompilation.

The program manager is an object that receives all NEW-messages and sends each of them to a choosen processor. If this processor does not have a process of that task the program manager must install it including the object manager.

7.2. The Object Manager

An object management takes place internally to each process with the following actions:

- After each NEW message from the program manager intended to create an object from a given class, the object manager allocates and initializes the memory for all instance variables and internal fields, and executes the initialization part of the object class. All necessary information can be found either in a global storage accessible from all processors, or can be received from the program manager through the operating system;
- The object manager updates a list of all objects in the process in the form of an object table;
- All received messages must be queued according to their priority (normal or express);
- All objects that have a nonempty message queue or are interrupted will be queued to wait for a processor resource;
- After a request to terminate an object, the object manager must release the memory allocated from the object.

7.3. Message Passing

Message passing takes place in packets. If the sending and receiving objects are located on different processes, message passing is realized through the operating system parts of the corresponding processors. Message passing is supported by the following services of the run time system:

- get a send buffer;
- send the message in the buffer;
- receive the packet in the target process.

7.4. Dynamic storage allocation

An efficient memory allocation mechanism is required because the memory portions to be handled with are small. The following memory types must be controlled from the run time system:

- a data memory where the objects are created and dynamic variable allocation takes place. By the termination of an object all its dynamic variables must be released;
- a program memory; The called methods and procedures must be copied into the local memory area (if not always present) before the execution starts. Copying only the necessary methods rather than the whole class reduces run time;
- a stack; It is possible to interrupt method execution of some object if an object of the same process with a higher priority receives a message. In such a case a stack swapping must be done.

Other service routines of the run time system are the access routines for complex data types, memory compaction and garbage collection.

8. Conclusions

The aim of the investigations is an efficient programming system for multiprocessors. At the time of delivery of this paper a language compiler, the run time system, and a distributed multiprocessor operating system are in development. For implementation we use a bus-coupled multiprocessor with up to sixteen 16/32-bit microprocessors. Further research will be directed to parallel compilation of the language, optimization, special run time support and performance measurement.

References

ADA 82 — ADA Programming Language Reference Manual. U.S. Department of Defense, MIL-STD-1815. Washington D.C.: 1982.

ANTONOV 87 — Antonov, J.: Entwurf und Effektivitaetsuntersuchung einer Datenflussrechnerarchitektur. Dresden: TU Thesis Ph., 1987.

BLACK 86 — Black, A.; Hutchinson, N.; Jul, E.; Levy, H.: Object Structure in the Emerald System. in: Proc. of ACM Conf. on Object-oriented Programming, Systems, Languages and Applications. SIGPLAN-Notices, Vol.21, No.11, 1986. Portland: ACM Press, 1986.

GOLDBERG 83 Goldberg, Adele; Robson, David:
Smalltalk-80 - The Language and its Implementation.
Amsterdam: Addison-Wesley Pub.Co.,1983.

HOGG 87 Hogg,J.; Weiser,S.:
OTM: Applying Objects to Tasks.
in: Proc. of ACM Conf. on Object-oriented Programming, Systems, Languages and Applications.
SIGPLAN-Notices, Vol.22, No.12, 1987.
Orlando: ACM Press, 1987.

MIKLOSKO 84 Miklosko,J.; Kotov,V.E.:
Algorithms, Software and Hardware of Parallel Computers.
Berlin(W): Springer, 1984.

ODIJK 86 Odijk,E.A.M.:
The Philips Object-Oriented Parallel Computer.
in: Proc. of the IFIP TC-10 Working Conference on Fifth Generation Computer Architectures.
Amsterdam: North-Holland, 1986.

STROUSTRUP 86 Stroustrup, Bjarne:
The C++ Programming Language.
Amsterdam: Addison-Wesley Pub.Co.,1986.

VEEN 85 Veen,A.:
The misconstrued semicolon.
Amsterdam: TH Eindhoven Thesis Ph., 1985.

YONEZAWA 85 Yonezawa,A.; Matsamoto,Y.:
Object Oriented Concurrent Programming and Industrial Software Production.
in: Lecture Notes in Computer Science, No.186.
Berlin(W): Springer, 1985.

YONEZAWA 86 Yonezawa,A.; Briot,J.-P.; Shibayama,E.:
Object-oriented concurrent Programming in ABCL/1.
in: Proc. of ACM Conf. on Object-oriented Programming, Systems, Languages and Applications.
SIGPLAN-Notices, Vol.21, No.11, 1986.
Portland: ACM Press, 1986.

EDUCATION IN CIM-MASTER CLASS

Wilfried Krug
bit'89
Dresden University of Technology
Mommsenstraße 13
Dresden-DDR 8027

Abstract. As a summary it can be pointed out that all over the world great attention is paid to CIM education of engineers and first experience is available. This refers to both individual education models and education curricula for CAD/CAM foundations with special emphasis on:

- Computer training which takes about 50 - 60 % of total education time

- Independent research work

- System-orientated CIM education

- Spezialization for production automation

- Education in master classes with individual curricula

Conditions for CIM-Engineers

I would like to refer to some aspects of the education of system engineers for CIM in a special master class.
The gradual development of factories with Computer integrated Manufacturing (CIM) urgently requires system engineers working for CIM who are able to introduce/integrated, flexibly automated manufacturing solutions in combines of the metal-working industry with a high economic effectiveness. Therefore, the following aims of training and education are important for our master class:

- Qualification for realization of new forms of organization for CIM in the whole reproductive process

- Management of groups and fields not compiled according to chronological order and special fields of knowledge but in accordance with the corresponding functionalities.

- Qualification for communication readiness of different fields of knowledge in order to eliminate differences in the ideas concerning socialist economic managment, design, production engineering and manufacturing automation on the basis of an uniform CIM strategy.

- Imparting detailed knowledge of sociological processes, manufacturing process organization, manufacturing automation, informatics and CAD/CAM foundations as well as manufacturing measurement technology and factory planning and so on.

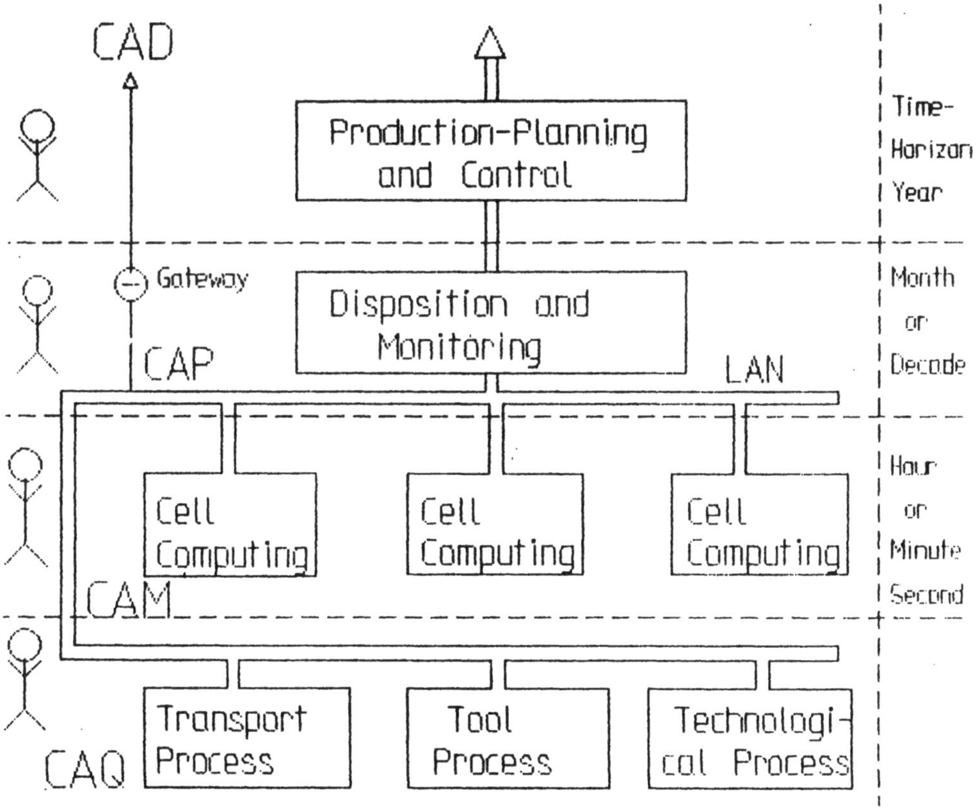

Figure 1 : Computer Integrated Manufacturing Levels and embedding of CIM-Engineers in CAD + CAM + CAQ

Individual Curriculum

The basis is provided by an individual curriculum consisting of four subcomponents as shown in Figure 2.
On the one hand this is a special curriculum with a strongly system-orientated education in four teaching complexes:

- Social sciences

- production automation

- informatics

- CAD/CAM foundations.

Furthermore, there is a supplementary schedule with the spezialization directions for

- computer-aided design processes

- production planning and control

- manufacturing automation

- design and dimensioning tools, etc.

Finally, individual education includes an intensive training on the computer itself which deals especially with the handling of basis software and the operation of all the peripheral devices.
The scientific productive study as the fourth component enables the student already to perform creative work on fundamental problems of research into the computer-integrated factory of future. To this end, he is granted 50-70 % of the individual study time.
The further percentages of the other components are accordingly lower as is also shown in Figure 2 (below).

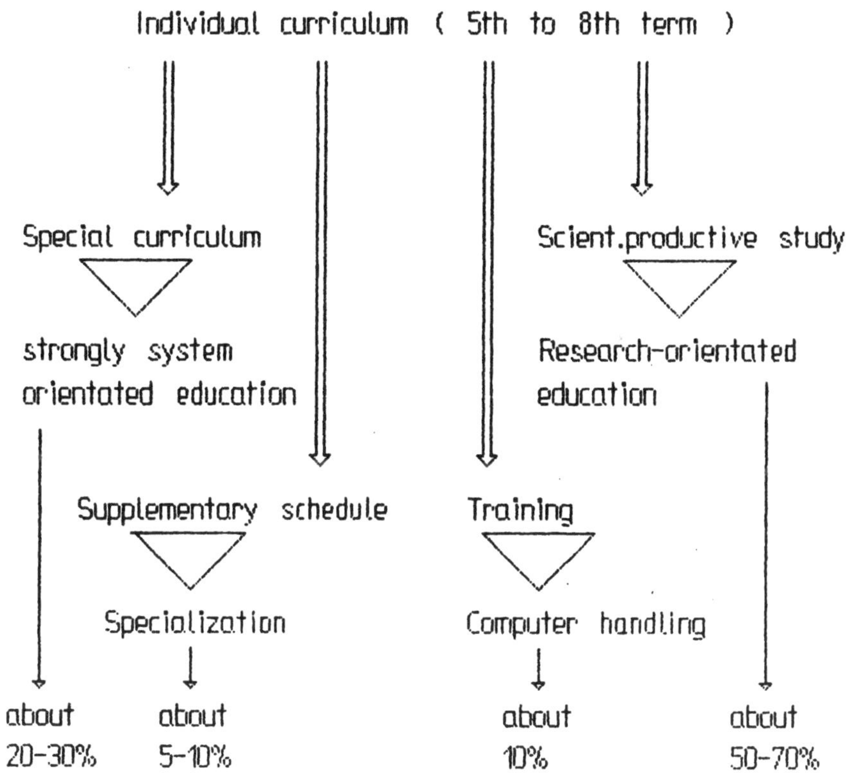

Figure 2 : Masterclass " Production automation "

Example in Research-Orientated Education for System Simulation in CIM

In the Future the system engineer for production automation must be able to develop and test all the system conditions in a CIM-structure as well as in CIM-models. Therefore, the system analysis and simulation is an important field for this education. Therefore, a software was developed which is suitable for carrying out computertraining, as shown in Figure 2, in connection with research-orientated education for CIM applications taking into account the special object. In the following this teaching

software is dealt with in more detail.
The system simulation in CIM is based on a completely modular concept embedded in a frame system as is shown in Figure 3. The Modelling-Simulation-Optimization Kernel System MSOKS contains general software tools for the object-orientated solution of all the simulation and optimization problems in CIM and CAD/CAM. As concerns information, MSOKS corresponds with a model base, data base and possibly with a graphical or geometric kernel as well as with a control kernel by means of the frame system
/2/, /6/, /9/, /10/.
These tools enable the CIM master-class student to carry out the following menu-aided actions on a terminal:

Action 1: model presentation from the model base

Action 2: model manipulation or model validation

Action 3: method presentation from MSOKS

Action 4: method manipulation (only if necessary)

Action 5: simulation experiments

Action 6: experiment evaluation (and possibly back to action 1-5)

Action 7: optimization

Action 8: optimization evaluation (and possibly back to action 1 - 7)

Action 9: geometrical and/or graphical presentation and interpretation (and possibly back to action 1-8)

In each of the above Actions the learning effect of the above students is assessed. If problems arise in the learning process, the students are assisted by appropiate helps in the further learning process. In this case relations are established with the special curriculum according to Figure 2.

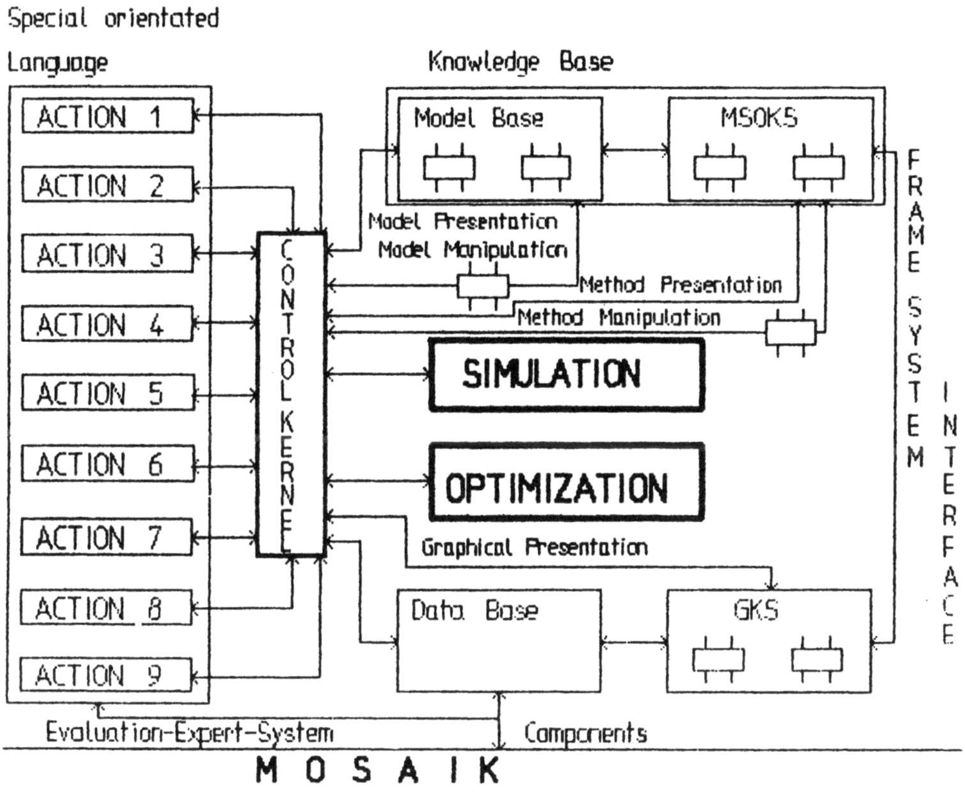

Figure 3: Architecture and tool boxes for system analysis and simulation as well as optimization in CAD/CAM and CIM for education of CIM-engineers

<u>Interactive engineer's workstation</u>

Figure 4 shows the known hardware for an interactive engineer's workstation that offers the master-class student an active training in modelling, computation, simulation, optimization, evaluation and correcting with MSOKS.

In the centre of this workstation there is the computer with its alpha-numerical or graphical display which is available for communication with the other equipment components. This configuration is applied in research, development, design and

planning with different repetition degree.
The automatic drawing table, for example, is used only seldom in the reseach process, whereas in designing and also in planning it is an important equipment component for dimensioning, designing, etc. Here further details of the hardware will not be discussed, however, an attempt is made to represent and explain a relatively universal software conception for the computer-aided model validation, simulation and optimization. In this conjunction, it is supposed that in research, development, design, planning and control, very different modelling problems, simulation problems and optimizations can be solved by the students and, at the end, this leads to uniform software components.
Let us illustrate this by an example of the development of heat exchangers. In the phase of research, a suitable mathematical model is developed from the energy balance, mass and impulse balances. For the investigation or optimization of the heat exchanger behaviour, in the model the heat transfer coefficients, flow conditions, area conditions, etc., play an important role. Therefore, here the model development with a sensitivity investigation is of great importance in order to solve those problems by means of the subsequent simulation for studying the thermal behaviour and for optimizing the exchanger surfaces. If this heat exchanger model is stored in a model bank, in the designing phase the designer can refer to this model in dimensioning and designing the heat exchanger and accordingly resolve his problem. In this connection, simulation and optimization play again a role. However, according to given objective functions a sensitivity analysis is activated by the student which for him graphically represents the sensitivity dependence of any parameters of the model as a function of these independent variables (for example, in unsteady problems).

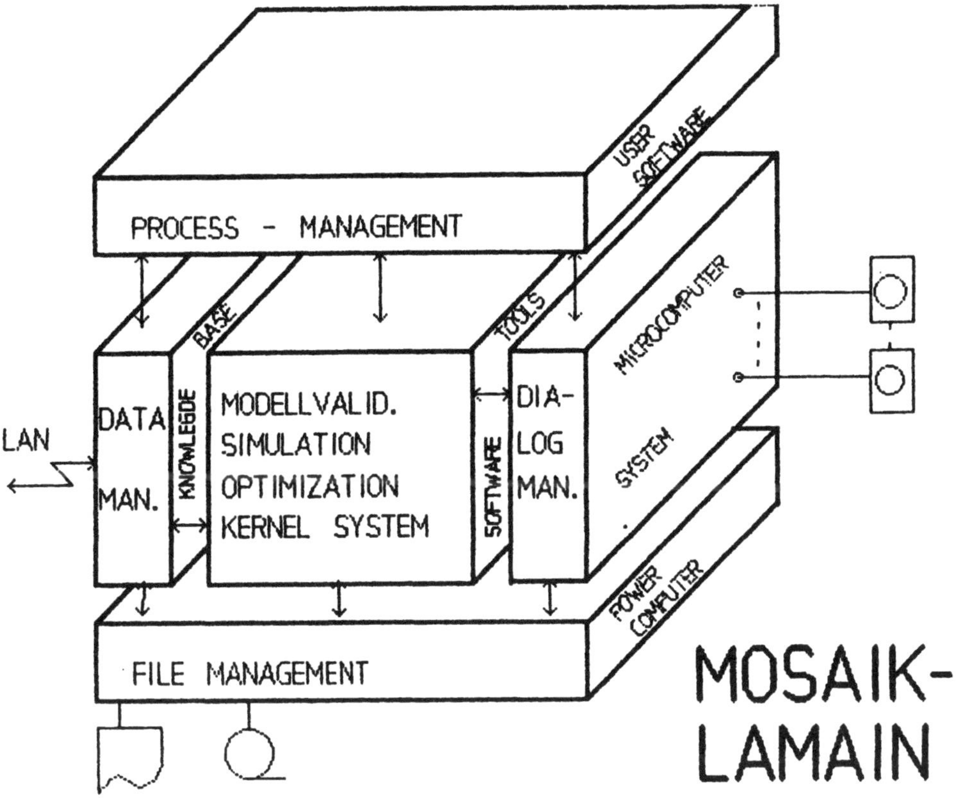

Figure 4 : Interactive engineer s workstation

Experiences with teaching software

First positive experience with this individual curriculum in connection with the teaching software described in chapters above and used by the master-class students at a CAD/CAM workstation was gathered at the centre for production automation of Dresden University of Technology with 13 students and assessment is as follows:

- high readiness to learn

- motivating effect of individual guidance of each student by a university teacher

- participation in research work stimulates readiness to study

- deepening effect of blocked teaching events and intensive computer training

- qualification for independent and creative activities is greatly developed

Reference

/1/ Schwarze, G. and 20 Institutionen : Studie Allgemeine digitale Simulationssysteme. (1980) ZfR-Information 80.08

/2/ Krug, W.: über die Möglichkeiten der Modellierung, Simulation und Optimierung verfahrenstechnischer Systeme. Sammelband zur 4. Tagung der Abt. Mathematik/Rechentechnik der IH Köthen (1980)

/3/ Krug, W.: Software Tools for the Model Validation and Simulation. 1986 EUROPEAN SIMULATION CONGRESS, SEPT. 9.-12.1986 ANTWERP PROCEEDING NSC

/4/ Krug, W.;Jurisch,R.: Zu numerischen Problemen bei der mathematischen Modellierung und Simulation. Preprint TH Köthen, 1985

/5/ Seydel, G.: Zum Simulationssystem USAN für die Feingerätetechnik

/6/ Krug, W.: Systemanalysis and simulation in flexible manufacturing control systems: Paper of INACS WORLD CONGRESS, 1988, Paris

/7/ Frank, N: Tools for Computer Aided Design of Production Processes. Simulation in Research and Development, INADS, 1985

/8/ Krug, W.: Digital Simulation of Partial Differential Equations Syst. Anal. Model. Simul. 1 (1984) 3

/9/ Oeron, T.I.: Simulation and model based methodologics and integrated view. Springer Verlag Berlin, 1984

/10/ Schmidt, B.: Systemanalyse und Simulation. Springer Verlag Berlin, 1986

/11/ Koch, W./Langensiepen, G.: Optimierungssoftware für Kleinrechner und Anwendungen Proceedings, Sellin 1985

SOFTWARE ENVIRONMENT FOR RESEARCH IN DISCRETE MATHEMATICS

Krassimir Nedelchev Manev

Institute of Mathematics, Bulgarian Academy of Sciences
P.O.Box 373, Sofia 1090, BULGARIA

Abstract. In the present paper a general approach to the software environment for research in the field of discrete mathematics is considered. The author's experience in implementing some components of an environment of that type in the UNIX System V is summarized and the results obtained are stated.

1. INTRODUCTION

Nowadays the necessity of applying computers to research in mathematics is obvious. For example, a number of problems in the field of discrete mathematics could be treated through computers to a some extent. Computer experiments become a natural (preliminary or final) step in investigating some discrete configurations namely they could be considered as a part of the reasoning of the new results. Thus the requirements towards software applications to mathematical research are rather complicated.

In this paper a general approach to the software environment for research in the field of discrete mathematics is proposed. Also the author's experience in implementing some of the components of such an environment in the UNIX System V and the results obtained are summarized.

The operating system has been chosen especially for that purpose. UNIX-like systems possess a number of useful features, some of them are listed below:

- practically UNIX-like systems are standardized and they

are installed in almost all wide-spread computer architectures;

- UNIX-like systems have a clear multilevel structure (see the Figure) with appropriate interfaces at the different levels;

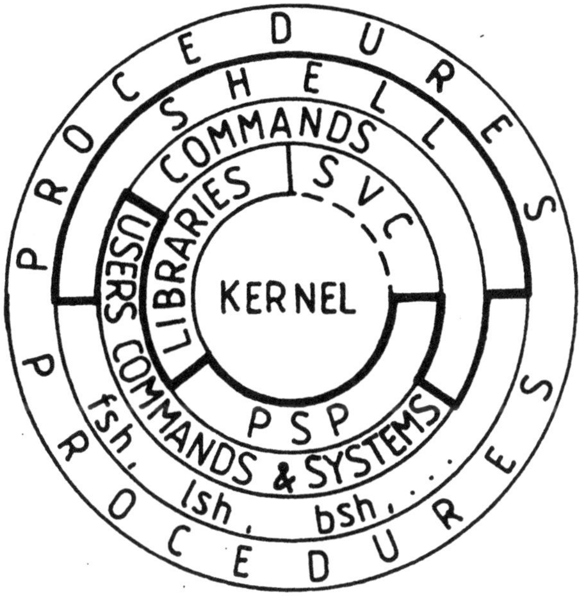

Figure

- in fact UNIX-like systems support standardized compilers from the high-level programming language C. The C language allows the efficient usage of the computer capabilities;

- UNIX-like systems communicate with users in an exclusively flexible way through a command interpreter which controls the running of the executable modules (commands).

2. SOFTWARE ENVIRONMENT

Our general idea is to append some respective tools to the operating system at each of its levels enabling the research in the field of discrete mathematics (see the Figure).

The kernel of the UNIX-like systems suffices for our purposes. It provides the supervisor calls (SVC) needed for constructing the environment directed to scientific research of discrete mathematical objects.

The variety of architectures, operating systems and

versions even for the well standardized programming languages, did not allow a wide-spread usage of packages standard programs (PSP). UNIX-like systems let us create portable PSP. Moreover this portability can be achieved if observing some simple rules, namely:

- to use only standard features of the C language;
- to define all machine dependent constants at a preprocessor level;
- to use as subroutines only standard SVC, standard functions from the system libraries or programs from the package (the latter should observe those rules).

To construct a package by applying a technique of abstract data type (ADT), i.e. to choose such an ADT, which would be appropriate for the package goals and to build the programs in the form of operations with this ADT is very useful. Thus one can easily append new operations (programs) and change the existing ones by implementing better algorithms (without changing the software using the package).

Packages standard programs should be created by experts who know extremely well the features of the operating system, the C language and the object of research.

There exist two possibilities at the next level. First: Any researcher who knows the C language and can formulate a problem in terms of ADT operations can write a program to solve it. He can even create (if helped by an expert) complex systems with appropriate languages for solving a class of problems by using PSP.

Second: Some standard programs could be transformed into commands of the operating system. Though user's systems and commands are at the same level of the structure of the operating system we will distinguish them. The commands are simpler and as a rule they have not a proper language. Usually they perform only one step of the problem solving. The commands usage will be discussed below. Standard programs might be transformed into commands in a very trivial way namely by the provided scheme of processing the arguments.

The construction of new command interpreters is proposed at the next level. The standard command interpreter of UNIX-like systems - *shell*, combines commands with the control constructions of the C language - *for, while, case* and *if*. For researchers who do not know the C language there exsist only one way to solve their problems namely the sequential executing of commands. But mathematicians have a good knowledge of other ways of composing the primitives, such as superposition of functions, logical inference, etc.

That is why we propose new command interpreters to be constructed at this level which would be more appropriate for mathematicians . UNIX-like systems stimulate such activities by providing tools for the automatic generating of lexical analyzers and parsers, by starting from the respective formal grammars. Even a user unexperienced in programming can formulate problems to be solved by computers when having at his disposal such interpreters and enough commands (created at the preceding level) for the special subject.

What about mathematicians who have no experience in working with computers at all. For them we are going to create procedures in the languages of command interpreters. These users can solve some of their problems by executing the procedures (giving appropriate values to the parameters).

Thus, we obtain an environment corresponding to the structure of the operating system which lets each user (according to his experience) work out his problems by appropriate tools. This environment is very flexible. It can be easily modified and developed without changing the existing software.

3. SOME RESULTS

Some of our ideas were implemented in the UNIX System V on the 32-bit (M68010) computer, with 2 Mb operating memory - ICL CLAN and carried out on other computers - IBM PC, PDP-11 etc. rather succesfully. Next the results obtained will be discussed.

The portable package of standard programs COMPACK [1] for combinatorial research was created for the ADT which is called a generated binary matrix (GBM). This ADT is appropriate for representing a very large set of combinatorial objects - graphs, matroids, block-designs, error-correcting codes, etc. It is defined as follows:

```
typedef struct { int n,k;
        unsigned object[MAXROW][MAXCLM];
        int row[MAXROW], column[MAXCLM]; } GBM;
```

where the *object* array is treated as a binary table with *k* rows and *n* columns and it represents the combinatorial object itself. The *row* and *column* arrays contain some integer characteristics of the object.

The programs of the package are divided into some groups. The first of them contains input/output operations either with the whole structure or various parts of it. The values can be represented in a binary, decimal or hexadecimal form. The programs of the second group perform either operations with GBM (including operations between the rows or the columns of the matrix) or operations between two GBM - assignment, transposition, overwriting a part of one matrix by a part of another, etc. A special subgroup contains programs which treat rows of the matrix as big integers and perform the usual arithmetic operations. A large number of programs which might be used in implementing combinatorial algorithms are included in COMPACK. For example programs calculating binomial coefficients and the weight of a binary vector; programs generating permutations, subsets of a given set, Grey's codes, etc. The programs from COMPACK being of some interest were transformed into commands of the operating system.

A package GFPACK of operations having as their arguments the elements of a Galois field, polynomials and matrices over a Galois field is planned to be developed in future.

A special system - LINCOR, was constructed for computer research in the field of error-correcting codes by using COMPACK [2]. For this purpose the package was extended by programs, appropriate for the above mentioned field and we have already got the experience needed to extend the package in other fields as well.

The LINCOR system was designed to avoid the tiresome everyday, routine work. Nevertheless two problems reffering to the covering radius of error correcting codes were solved through it. First the following conjecture was refuted: all binary linear codes, containing all-ones vector meet the lower bound for the covering radius [3]. Second: the covering radius of 73 from 76 cyclic binary codes with lengths 33, 35 and 39 were found [4].

Three languages for new command interpreters were proposed in [5]. The first of them - *fsh* is based on Backus' FP-systems [6]. The functions of *fsh* are the commands and the text files of the operating system. The commands are executed in a natural way and the function is replaced by the results obtained. The text files themselves are searched for lines starting with the given arguments and this search results in obtaining the remaining part of the line. The principal functional form is the superposition but the other forms are implemented too. For example, let the *gf16* file contain in every line an integer *n* and a binary string which is the n-th power of the generator of the field $GF(2^4)$; let the *gfadd* command perform addition of two elements of a given field. Then the functional procedure:

```
<- ( 16 (5)gf16 (7)gf16)gfadd
```

will find the sum of the 5-th and 7-th power of the generator of $GF(2^4)$. The postfix position of the functions names facilitate the user working on an interactive mode.

The second interpreter - *lsh* has as a language an extension of Prolog [7], which treats both the commands and the text files as predicates. The commands are executed and they will have either a *true* value if their exit status is zero or *false* - otherwise. The files are searched for line(s) containing in the respective fields values which coincide with the constant arguments. The values of the fields, corresponding to the variable arguments are assigned to these arguments. The value of such a predicate is *false* only if there is no line corresponding to the given arguments. For example, let the *r* command calculate the covering radius of a cyclic binary code, if the length *N*, the dimension *K* and the generating polynomial *Gen* are given; let the *r1* command calculate the same radius, if the lower bound *R1* and the upper bound *R2* of the radius are given too. Let the text file *table* contain in each line *N*, *K*, *Gen*, *R1* and *R2* for some binary cyclic codes. The following *lsh* procedure finds the covering radius using *table*, *r* or *r1*:

```
radius(N,K,Gen) :- table(N,K,Gen,R1,R2), R1 = R2,
                   write("radius: "), write(R1).
radius(N,K,Gen) :- table(N,K,Gen,R1,R2), not(R1 = R2),
                   r1(N,K,Gen,R1,R2,R),
                   write("radius: "), write(R).
radius(N,K,Gen) :- r(N,K,Gen,R), write("radius: "),
                   write(R).
```

The third interpreter has an original language, which combines commands by applying the usual scheme "backtrack" and it is oriented toward searching combinatorial configurations. Special commands declare the type of the searched structure - array of integers, binary string, binary matrix, integer matrix etc. The other commands are divided into generators and conditions (the exit status zero means that a certain condition holds). The procedure contains one declaration and a list of generators and conditions. The interpreter runs the sequence of commands but at nonzero exit status (a generator cannot generate a new value; a conditition does not hold) it gets back to the last generator which has been executed successfully. The following procedure illustrates the search of three binary vectors with lehgth 25, weight 10 and with Hemming distance 10 for each pair of them:

```
dcl bmatrix 3 25
gen 1 ktuple 25 10
gen 2 ktuple 25 10
con dist 10 2
gen 3 ktuple 25 10
con dist 10 3
con write
```

Here *ktuple m n* generates binary vectors, *dist m n* - checks the condition for the distance between *n* vectors and *write* - outputs the structure found.

All these languages have been experimented in the UNIX System V.

REFERENCES

1. K. N. Manev, A Portable Package of Standard Combinatorial Programs, Proceedings of the Scientific Seminar "Problems of the Portability of Programming Tools", Varna, 1987.
2. K. N. Manev, LINCOR - A System for Linear Codes Researche, in "Mathematics and Education in Mathematics", Proceedings of the Sixteen Spring Conference of the Union of Bulgarian Mathematicians, Sunny Beach, 1987, pp. 500-503.
3. S. M. Dodunekov, K. N. Manev, V. D. Tonchev, On the Covering Radius of the (14,6) Binary Codes, Containing The All-ones Vector, IEEE, Trans. on Inform. Theory, v. 34, No. 3, May 1988, pp. 591-593.

4. E. Velikova, K. Manev, The Covering Radius of Cyclic Codes of Length 33, 35 and 39, Annuaire de l'Universite de Sofia, t. 81, l. 1 - Mathematique, 1987 (to appear).
5. K.N. Manev, Computer Aided Investigations in Combinatorics PhD Thesis, University of Sofia, 1987 (in Bulgarian).
6. J. Backus, Can Programming be Liberated from the fon Neumann Style? A Functional Style and its Algebra of Programs, Comm. of ACM, 21, 8(1978).
7. W. F. Clocksin, C. S. Mellish, Programming in Prolog, Springer-Verlag, 1981.

COMPUTER SUPPORT OF ENTERPRISE ANALYSIS ON PC

Bohumil Miniberger - Miroslav Šimek

bit'89
Computer Center, Charles University, Prague
Malostranské nám. 25
118 00 Prague 1 - ČSSR

Abstract. The paper offers a brief insight into the problems of Enterprise Analysis, which should be a component part of the process of designing the information system for the management of any subject area. In conclusion, a description is made of the program realization for PC's, on which the database system dBASE III Plus is used.

1. ENTERPRISE ANALYSIS. The process of designing Management Information System (MIS) consists of partial processes differing from each other in their complexities and in the rates of unification of their solutions. Standardization efforts in the field of the essential component of MIS - the database system - resulted, in the middle of 1970's, in the creation of a three-level architecture of database system, known as ANSI/SPARC [1] . This approach distinguishes three levels of the view of databases:

- **external** represented by a simplified model of real world satisfying the requirements of one or more applications,
- **conceptual** represented by a limited model of real world maintained for all the applications,
- **internal** represented by a limited model of real world closely linked with the methods of storing and retrieving data from the computer memory.

It is the conceptual view of the database that can be considered principal, because it becomes "mediator" between the external and internal views. Each of these views is represented by a corresponding model. The expression of this model in terms of descriptors relating to the model under consideration will be called **schema.** The conceptual schema constitutes a model of a particular section of the real world. Conceptual objects reflect entities existing in the real world and their interrelations. Designing conceptual schema is the task of the enterprise administrator. The cooperation with him is provided by specialists in the section of the real world concerned as well as by the other administrators. Their efforts result in a description of conceptual schema in some specification language. A specification language should therefore contain not only devices for

- object specification of the conceptual model in terms of object types
- expression of characteristics of specified objects (by specifying the object, object role, admissible value etc)
- specification of the interrelations between objects

but also

- rules providing for object integrity
- automation rule
- other data required for database control and its operation.

The conceptual model described by means of a specification language is then processed by means of conceptual schema processor. The result of processing is the creation of internal and external schemas as well as self-consistency checking.

Among the best known conceptual modeling devices ranks Chen's E-R Model [2] . One of its advantages is the fact that it combines the qualities of three models convenient for database purposes:
- the network model according to CODASYL DBTG
- the Codd's relational model
- the Senko's "Entity Set" model.

This is of a practical consequence, namely that the E-R model can easily be transformed into any of the models mentioned above, as demonstrated in [3] . This work, together with [8] , was underlying to the design of the subsystem for MIS 'University' developed at the Computer Center of Charles University Prague.

2. TRANSFORMATION OF THE CONCEPTUAL SCHEMA ONTO THE INTERNAL dBASE III PLUS

2.1. DESCRIPTION OF THE MODEL USED FOR CONCEPTUAL MODELING

E-R model is based upon the concepts Entity, Relationship and Attribute that promote the principal discrimination of the objects of the world being modeled and their interrelations. Entity is any object (but also event) that exists and can be demonstrably discriminated. Entities of equal type from entity classes or a set of entities (E-set) provided they satisfy the condition of discriminability inherent to the class (set) of entities given. This discriminability condition is considered in designing conceptual model and should result from the analysis of an information system. Similarly, relationship sets (R-sets) can be designed representing relationships between entity sets. A more detailed description of the entity or relationship sets between E-set and R-set is effected by means of attributes, which is the function represented as follows:

$$A_i \text{ (resp. } B_j) : E_i \text{ (resp. } R_j) \rightarrow V_n$$

where E_i resp. R_j is an entity resp. relationship set,

V_n is a set of values that acquire attributes.

For many a user it is more acceptable to express entity resp. relationship sets by means of tables where lines make up entities resp. relationship, columns stand for attributes represented by values of real numbers. For graphic representation of entity set a rectangle will be used, for relationship set a diamond the two being interconnected by edges to which the cardinality of their interrelation is added. Entity and relationship sets, domains and attributes referred to by names reflecting their natures within the conceptual model of the world.

In individual entity sets, distinction is made between the keys K (minimum sets of attributes) the values of which determine unequivocally the elements of entity sets. Each entity set can have even several keys. One of these is then chosen to be the primary key. In each entity set, at least one attribute and one of its primary keys has to be determined. Each relationship set R is characterized by entity sets $E_1, E_2, \ldots, E_n$, which enter it. It must hold at the same time that $n \geq 2$ (hence each relationship has to be binary at least) and it is possible that for two indexes i and j $E_i = E_j$ holds. In relationship sets, their attributes need not be determined.

Furthermore, in each entity set E_j, the cardinality of its participants in the relationship set is determined. It this entity set participates in the given relationship set with the cardinality 1, then to each (n-1)-tuple of elements
$e_1, e_2, \dots, e_{j-1}, \dots, e_n$ there exists at most one element

e_j ($e_i \in E_i$, $i=1, 2, \dots, n$), such that n-tuple of

$e_1, e_2, \dots, e_n$ forms an element of the relationship set R.

If the entity set E_j participates in R with the cardinality N, then to the above-mentioned (n-1)-tuple of elements, there can exist even several elements e_j so that n-tuple $e_1, e_2, \dots, e_n$ forms elements of R.

In each entity set, participating in the relationship set R also its role $\mathcal{R}_i$ in this relation set is determined. For two different indexes i and j, $\mathcal{R}_i = \mathcal{R}_j$ must hold. The above entity and relationship sets are called **regular**. By applying them arbitrary conceptual schemas can be designed, nevertheless, it is impossible to express by them the dependence of the existence of an element of one entity set upon that of elements of some other entity set. In order to do so, we will introduce the concept **irregular relationship** set, which practically constitutes a generalization of the concepts weak relationship set and total relationship set [3]. This concept will be explained to a greater detail below.

2.1.1. IRREGULAR RELATIONSHIP SETS

In E-R model used for transformation from the conceptual schema into the internal schema of the database we introduced the concept **irregular relationship** set.

In irregular relationship sets two and only two different entity sets are required to enter them. One of these entity sets is determined as dependent (let it be E_1) and the other entity set (E_2) is refered to as the determining one. The semantics of such an irregular relationship set R is then as follows:
to each $e_1 \in E_1$ there must exist at least one $e_2 \in E_2$ so that

e_1 and e_2 form the element of R.

2.1.2. WEAK ENTITY SETS

A weak entity set, unlike regular entity set, depends on some of the regular entity sets, not only existentially but also on the key determining the entity set. For each weak entity set it is necessary to use only a regular set as determining information. The relationship set between these two sets is given by the irregular relationship set as stated in the preceding paragraph. If the weak entity set participates in this relationship set with the cardinality 1, then it is not necessary to determine its keys, because identification of a weak entity set element is unambiguously given by the elements of the determining entity set only. In an opposite case, in a weak entity set, it is necessary to determine the primary key at least with the aid of which various elements of the weak entity set related to the same element of the determining set are distinguished. However, a weak entity set must have at least one attribute determined.

2.1.3. **TYPES OF DOMAINS**
Types of domains, i.e. sets of allowable attribute values are chosen, such that are allowed by dBASE III Plus system. Character strings of the lengths 1 to 234, numerical items of 1 to 19 digits and with the number of decimal places 0 - (min (15, number of digits -2)) can thus be used. It is further possible to use logical items, data items and items of memo type (special text data). To one type of domain only one name can be assigned.

2.1.4. **REQUIREMENTS FOR NAMES**
In the E-R model applied, strings of displayable signs of maximum length 10 can be used for the names of entity and relationship sets, attributes and domains. In the resulting relation data base schema, 21-sign names can appear. In the dBASE III Plus database system the requirements for name formation are more rigorous. It is therefore sometimes necessary to change the names in the resulting schema. It holds further that the names of different domains and different attributes must differ from each other. Equally, the names of different entity sets and different relationship sets must differ. Moreover, it is prohibitive to use the same name for an entity set and a relationship set (this helps to avoid making unnecessary errors in describing the conceptual schema and hence to prevent collisions of relation names in the relation database schema).

2.2. **PROGRAM IMPLEMENTATION**
The algorithm of the conceptual schema transformation of thus defined E-R model onto an internal schema of dBASE III Plus relation database system has been programmed at the Computer Center of Charles University Prague in PROLOG [7] and the program can be operated under the interpret of this language on micro-computers compatible with IBM PC´s. The program consists of two parts:

CONCEPT - making it possible to create description of conceptual schema
TRANSF - executing the transformation itself.

The conceptual schema is described by means of Prolog facts of nine types promoting the description of:

1 - the name of the domain and of its type
2 - the name of the entity set and of its type
3 - the dependence of the weak entity set upon the determining entity set through the irregular relationship set
4 - the attributes where its name, the domain concerned and the name of the entity or relationship set, to which the attribute belongs, are determined
5 - the primary entity set key
6 - other entity set keys
7 - the names of the relationship set and of its type
8 - the participants of the relationship set, their roles and cardinalities
9 - existential dependences given by irregular relationship set

At his work, the user, while making the description of the schema, is guided by the CONCEPT program, which controls the sequence of individual operations itself by means of the display output. The conceptual schema described can be arbitrarily changed in the course of the Enterprise Analysis, the consistence of individual data on conceptual schema being checked continually. The description of the schema created is loaded in the file constituting the input into the TRANSF program. The output of the program is then constituted by the description of individual relations and functional dependences. This will enhance the synoptic value of the work of the Enterprise Administrator on the one hand, and detect in advance any inconsistency of the description on the other. Finally, it will simplify the designing of the dBASE III Plus database internal schema. However, the system fails to solve the problem of its automatic creation, and merely plays the part of a supporting device enabling to remove redundances and to achieve a correct design of the schema in BCNF (Boyce-Codd normal form).

Fig.1. The ER diagram of the conceptual schema of a part of warehouse activity

APPENDIX 1: Conceptual Schema

APPENDIX 2: Relations generated by the TRANSF program

Literature:

[1] ANSI/X3/SPARC Study Group on DBMS Interim Report. **FDT-Bulletin of ACM-SIGMOD**, Vol. 7, No2. 1975.

[2] Chen,P.,P.: The Entity-Relationship Model-Towards a Unified View of Data. **ACM of Transactions on Database Systems**, Vol.1, No1, March 1976.

[3] Dogac,A.-Chen,P.,P.: Entity Relationship Model in the ANSI SPARC Framework, In: **E-R Approach to Information Modeling and Analysis**, P.P. Chen (Ed.) ER Institute 1981.

[4] Dogac,1.-Güler,S.-Chen,P.P.: An Entity-Relationship Interface for DMSII: A Software Tool for Database Design. METU Ankara, Technical Report 82-1, 1982.

[5] Machová,S.-Miniberger,B.: Description of Decision Tables by PSL/PSA. In: **Description Methodologies**, D.Teichroew and D.Gábor (Ed.), North-Holland 1985.

[6] Machová,S.-Miniberger,B.: Documentation Metasystem for MIS on SMEP Computers. In: **Proceedings of the 2nd meeting of the 23rd WG**. Tallin, 1988.

[7] Šimek,M.: Automatic transformation of the Conceptual Schema into Internal Schema dBASE III Plus (In Czech). In: **Proceedings "DATASEM 88"**, DT ČSVTS Praha 1988.

[8] Teichroew,D. at all.: Application of the ER Approach. In: **E-R Approach to Information Modeling and Analysis**, P.P.Chen (Ed.) ER Institute 1981.

[9] Webre,N.: An Extended E-R Model and Its Use on a Defense Project. In: **E-R Approach to Information Modeling and Analysis**, P.P.Chen (Ed.), E-R Institute 1981.

[10] Zoc,I.-Eckhardt,P.: Design of the ER Conceptual Specification Language using the IDD of the IDMS. Report of the Computer Centre of Charles University (In Czech), Prague 1987.

Fig. 1 The ER diagram of the conceptual schema of a part of warehouse activity

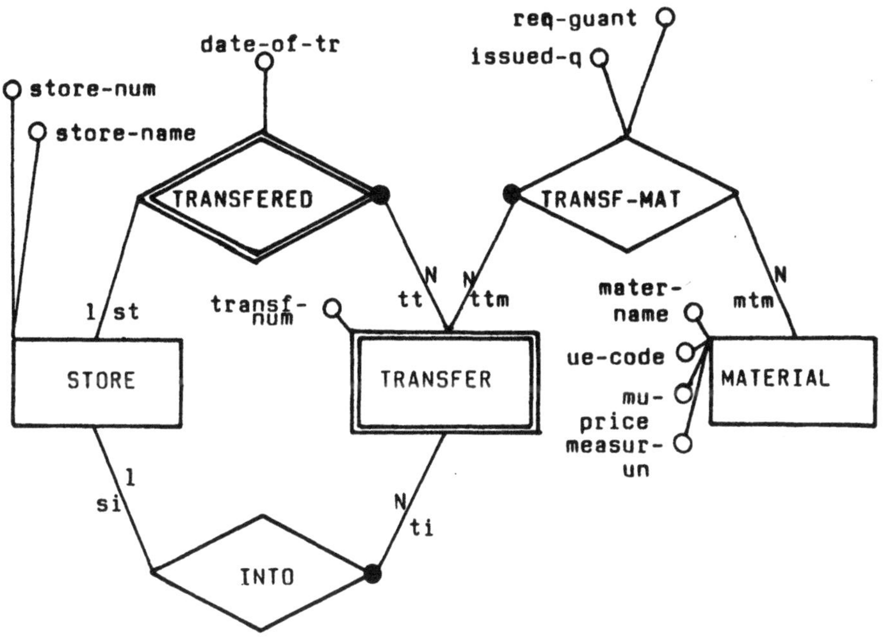

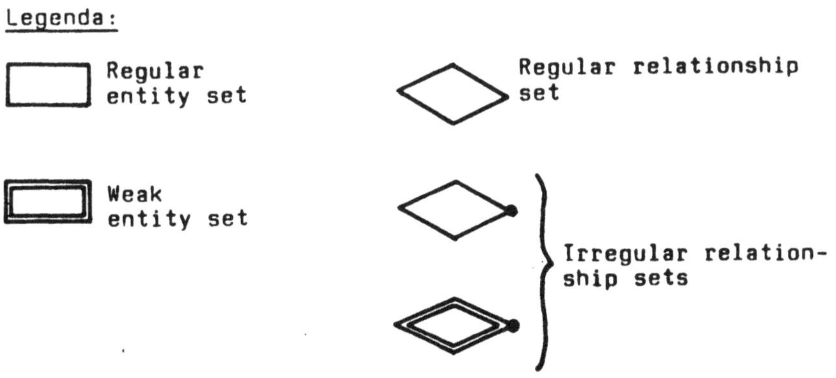

Appendix 1

The description of conceptual schema from Fig 1 using the program CONCEPT

Domains defined:

domain name	domain type
number	numeric(10,0)
price	numeric(9,2)
date	date
name	character(25)
unit	character(9)

***** Press any key. *****

Entities defined:

entity name	entity typ (r ... regular, w ... weak)
store	r
transfer	w
material	r

***** Press any key. *****

Defined identification dependencies of entities:

dependent entity name	independent entity name	name of determining relship
transfer	store	transfered

***** Press any key. *****

Attributes defined:

attribute name	domain name	entity/relationship name
mater_name	name	material
meassur_un	unit	material
uc_code	number	material
mu_price	price	material
store_num	number	store
store_name	name	store
req_quant	number	transf_mat
issued_q	number	transf_mat
transf_num	number	transfer
date_of_tr	date	transfered

***** Press any key. *****

Defined primary keys:

entity name	primary key
material	[uc_code]
store	[store_num]
transfer	[transf_num]

***** Press any key. *****

Defined keys:

entity name	key
material	[mater_name]
store	[store_name]

***** Press any key. *****

Defined relationships:

relship name	relship type (r ... regular, tw ... irregular)
tramsfered	tw
into	tw
transf_mat	tw

***** Press any key. *****

Relationship elements defined:

relship name	entity name	role	cardinality
into	store	si	1
into	transfer	ti	n
transf_mat	transfer	ttm	n
transf_mat	material	mtm	n
transfered	store	st	1
transfered	transfer	tt	n

***** Press any key. *****

Existencial dependencies defined:

relship name	dependent entityname	determining entiy name
transfered	transfer	store
into	transfer	store
transf_mat	transfer	material

***** Press any key. *****

Appendix 2

The output generated by the program TRANSF

```
Relation name: store

attribute name      primary key element      domain type

store_name             0                     character(25)
store_num              1                     numeric(10,0)


Functional dependencies:

[store_num] -->  [store_name, store_nume]
[store_name] -->  [store_name, store_num]

                        *****      Press any key.      *****
```

```
Relation name: material

attribute name     primary key element     domain type

mater_name         0                       character(25)
meassur_un         0                       character(9)
mu_price           0                       numeric(9,2)
uc_code            1                       numeric(10,0)

Functional dependencies:

[uc_code]  -->  [mater_name, meassur_un,mu_price,uc_code]
[mater_name]  -->   [mater_name, meassur_un,mu_price,uc_code]

                        *****      Press any key.      *****
```

```
Relation name: transfer

attribute name      primary key element      domain type

store_num           1                        numeric(10,0)
transf_num          1                        numeric(10,0)
date_of_tr          0                        date
store_num*si        0                        numeric(10,0)

Functional dependencies:

[store_num,transf_num]                                          -->
[date_of_tr,store_num,transf_num,store_num*si]

                        *****      Press any key.      *****
```

Relation name: transf_mat

attribute name	primary key element	domain type
store_num	1	numeric(10,0)
transf_num	1	numeric(10,0)
uc_code	1	numeric(10,0)
issued_q	0	numeric(10,0)
req_quant	0	numeric(10,0)

Functional dependencies:

[store_num,transf_num,uc_code] --> [issued_q,req_quant,store_num,
transf_num,uc_code]

***** Press any key. *****

A TUTORING SYSTEM WHICH EXPLAINS IN NATURAL LANGUAGE

Ruslan Mitkov

Institute of mathematics
Sofia, P.O. Box 373

ABSTRACT The paper describes a tutoring system, which explains in natural language (Bulgarian) concepts of elementary geometry (planimetry). The system is designed as a pure tutor - it gives eplanations about concepts and has not been designed to exercise drill and practice.

The present paper will first sketch an overview of the system and will then introduce the tutor model, which is based on both natural human dialogue and organization of concept explanation. Next the work will proceed to differentiate domain knowledge from linguistic knowledge. After that the concept representation will be discussed in connection with the formalism of functional descriptions, which enables easy expression of all kinds of knowledge. The following sections will examine the sublanguage of school geometry (planimetry) and text organization of concept explanation, the production of preliminary surface structures and the production of final survace struktures will be also discussed. Finally, future continuation of the present work will be proposed.

OVERVIEW OF THE SYSTEM

As already mentioned, the described system gives explantions about geometrical concepts upon user's questions. The user is supposed to ask a question in natural language, which is "decoded" by the analyzer (Fig.1). The analyzer makes use of the comparatively simple analysis techniques "pattern matching", which meets completely our practical demands. After the system has realized the user's question, it checks for the relevant information in the knowledge base. Some facts, that are not explicitly available in the knowledge base are concluded by means of lagical rules. However, we should point out, that since the major efforts have been made on developing a sophisticated generator which explains in good quality natural language, a great deal of the facts are represented explicitly in the knowledge base: therefore not too much inference is done by the program. Once the information for the response has been retrieved or concluded, the generator has the task to formulate it in a good quality natural language. Its work will be described in detail in the last chapters of the paper.

A sample dialogue between the system and the user is given in Fig.2. As visible, our tutoring system can be regarded as an intelligent question-answering instructional system with its generator as most developed component.

Fig.1

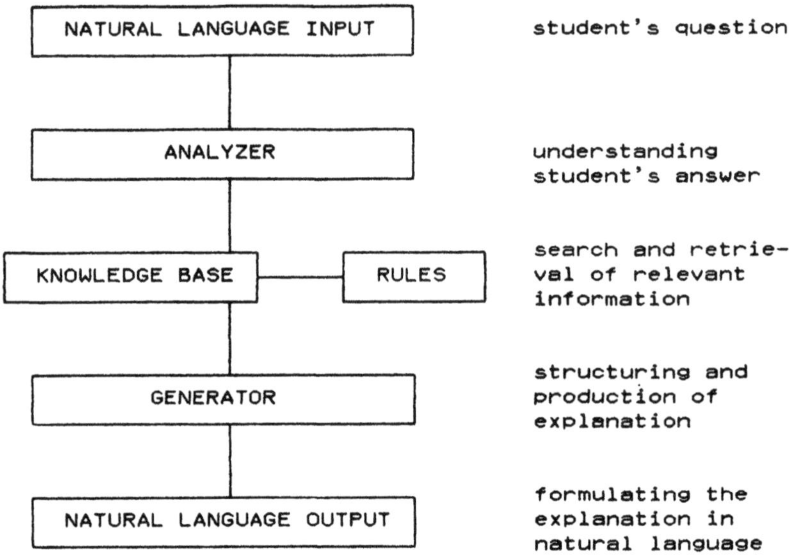

THE TUTOR MODEL

Suppose that a student would like to ask for information on certain geometrical object (concept). In this case the most general questions, he may ask, are "What is X", "What types of X are available", "Is X a Y?", (X and Y are concepts in geometry), "(Explain) What is the difference between X and Y ("Compare X and Y"), " Explain Z" (Z part of X) etc., which are "understood" by the tutor.

There are two main ways to explain a concept in its entity: to explain it by describing it (descriptive approach) or by comparing it to other concepts (contrastive approach). The system has adopted both ways of explanation, depending on user's question.

The system presumes, that each new user is a novice (at the present stage of our research, the system is not supposed to evaluate the initial konwledge level of the student) and behaves as a tutor is expected to do: given a question about a concept, it introduces the user in detail into it, but if he forgets what this concept was and asks again (Fig.2), the system reminds him in brief (as in human dialogue) what it was about (using past tense - specific at least of Bulgarian). It is also possible, that the user has forgotten only a part of the initial information and for instance after being introduced into the concept "triangle" (Fig.2), he may ask "What types of triangles exist according to its sides". In this case our system selects the relevant information from the knowledge base and "translates" it into a conncted natural language text.

Fig.2

USER: What is a triangle?
SYSTEM: The triangle is a convex straightlinear plane geometrical figure, which has 3 sides. According to its sides the triangle can be equilateral, isosceles and scalene and in according to its angles - rigt-angled, acute-angled and obtuse-angled.
....

USER: What types of triangles exist according to its sides?
SYSTEM: According to its sides the triangle can be equilateral, isosceles and scalene.
....

USER: What is a triangle?
SYSTEM: The triangle was a convex, straightlinear and plane geometrical figure, which has tree sides.

SYSTEM KNOWLEDGE

Both domain and linguistic knowledge are represented in the knowledgebase. Domain knowledge includes concepts, their relations as well as text organization strategies for explanations of concepts in the sublanguage of school geometry. Concepts are described formally as a set of a superordinate, critical and variable attributes and an animate object indicator. Relations between concepts are presently represented by "part-of" and "is a" relations. Linguistic knowledge includes the functional unificational grammar rules which produce preliminary surface structures after unifying with the input, linguistic operations such as coordination, pronomilization, ellipsis etc. and linguistic principles (such as place of focus or logical emphasis) for the choice of sentence voice or complexity, aiming at producing the final surface structures.

CONCEPT REPRESENTATION AND THE FORMALISM OF FUNCTIONAL DESCRIPTIONS

The concept knowledge representation model, proposed by the author is an extension of Tiemann and Markle's model [Mitkov,1988] for concept semantic knowledge representation. The proposed model describes each concept as a set of critical and variable attributes, superordinate and animate object indicator.

Consider the concept "triangle". Our semantic knowledge representation model will describe it formally as follows:

Triangle (geometrical figure / plane, convex, straightlinear, three sides / acute-angled, right-angled, obtuse-angled; equilateral, isosceles, scalene/0).

which is a particular example of the general semantic knowledge representation of a concept given as:

Concept: (superordinate / critical attribute 1,...,
critical attribute n / variety 1 of variable attribute
1,.., variety m of critical attribute 1;...; variety 1
of critical attribute k,..., variety r of critical
attribute k / an animate
mate object indicator)

The concept representation is notated in the formalism of functional descriptions, developed by Rousselot [Rousselot,1985]. This formalism enables the representation of all types of knowledge. A functional description represents a list of attribute-value pairs. Attribute-value pairs may represent the constituents and features of a sentence grammar (syntactic knowledge), but also objects with their characteristics (semantic knowledge). Rousselot's formalism is a very extended form of the functional grammars [Kay,1980]. The word "Triangle" would be described within the notation of functional description in the following way:

Fig.3

word	triangle
gender	neutral
number	singular
cat	substantive

We can now state, that more than one description may apply to the same object. For instance, we can describe the triangle also as follows (using our concept semantic representation approach):

Fig.4

	word	triangle
	is a	geometrical
figure		
	straightlinear	yes
	plane	yes
	convex	yes
	number of sides	3
		angle
rightangled		
	example	angle
acuteangled		
		angle
obtuseangled		
		side isosceles
	example	side
equilateral		
		side scalene
	animate object ind.	0

The value of a functional description may be itself a functional description. The power of this formalism consists in its ability to unify two or more functional descriptions. If functional descriptions from Fig.3 and Fig.4 are unified, a new functional description is obtained, which combines all the available in both descriptions knowledge.

SUBLANGUAGE OF SCHOOL GEOMETRY AND EXPLANATION DISCOURSE ORGANIZATION

As in parsing, generation is only efficient, if it is limited to a peculiar subdomain, referred to as "restricted domain". The language, which describes this restricted domain is called sublanguage. Our system has to do with the sublanguage of scool geometry (taught in Bulgarian schools). This sublanguage uses a comparatively restricted lexicon and not too great variety of syntactic constructions. Its text (what is to be read in the textbooks), however, are often overloaded with very complicated complex sentences. Good school geometry texts are presented in balanced way by simple and complex sentences.

Studying discourse peculiarities of school geometry textbook texts helped us to design discourse rules which the system uses when ordering the contend within a text. Generation of text requires the ability how to organize individual sentences. A reasonable writer does not randomly order the sentences in his text, but rather plans an overall framework or outline, from which the individual sentences are produced. Consider the following sample text:

> "School geometry is a highschool subject, comprised of three separate domains: planimetry, stereometry and trigonometry. Planimetry studies plane concepts. Space concepts are examined in stereometry. Trigonometry introduces the trigonometric functions with respect to their application in planimetry and stereometry. School geometry is taught within 5 years at the highschool."

The author has chosen an organisational framework, that is appropriate for providing definitions. Here, he first identifies school geometry by describing its superordinate (highschool geometry) and then introduces its three constituents (planimetry, stereometry and trigonimetry). Next, characteristic descriptive information about each of these constituents is given and finally the autor presents an additional information about school geometry in the last sentence.

We have chosen a similar approach also for explaining of geometrical concepts. The system would explain a concept descriptively first by identifying it and its superordinate, then by introducing its components (which possibly characterising them sortly) and finally by providing supplementary information (which is available in the knowledge base). So when describing the concept "quadrilateral" the program would first identify it, then introduce its superordinate (polygon), its constituents (four sides which are not concave and lie in one plane i.e. conve, straightlinear, plane polygon having four sides) and finally its varieties. The contrastive explanation introduces both concepts (possibly by common superordinate), and after searching and comparing in the knowledge base gives first their similarities and then their differences.

PRODUCTION OF PRELIMINARY SURFACE STRUCTURES

The grammar used to produce the preliminary surface structure of the explanation sentences is the functional unification grammar (Kay,1985). It is termed functional, because it assigns equal status to terms which describe functional role elements play in a sentence (e.g. protagonist) and to terms, which describe the syntactic category an element belongs to (e.g. noun phrase). A functional description may describe legal strings of the language using both these terminologies. For instance in the TEXT system (mcKeown,1985) Kay's functional categories protagonist (PROT), sometimes called agent in case formalisms, and goal (GOAL), sometimes called agent, were adopted. Beneficiary (BENEF) is used for verbs which take an indirect object. A sentence grammar is defined for passive and active sentences by identifying the subject of the sentence as protagonist if the voice is active or as the goal if the voice is passive.

The grammar is termed also "unification(al)", because the sentence is produced by unifying the grammar with the input, which is represented in the same formalism as the grammar (here the formalism of functional descriptions). The input, which is represented in the same formalism as the grammar (here the formalism of functional descriptions). The input is a deep structure of what is to be generated. The output is a surface syntactic representation of the sentence, which is linearized using the pattern it contains (e.g. PATTERN = (SUBJECT VERB OBJECT); each element of the pattern is a string to be generated by an auxiliary grammar, for instance SUBJECT = [SUBJECT GRAMMAR]).

Thus if the following input (functional description represented as in the program in Ksi Prolog notation)

```
r(relation(have),
  numerus(N),
  protagonist(ob(concept(triangle),
                 numerus(N),
                 modifier([]))),
  goal(ob(concept(side),
                 numerus(pl),
                 modidier([three])).
```

is unified with the sentence synthesis rule

```
sysnthesis(prot,Verb,3,Tense,act,r(relation(R),
                                   numerus(N),
                                   protagonist(Prot),
                                   goal(Goal)),Clause):-
            object(gen,def,Goal,Obj),
            subject(gen,indef,Prot,Subj),
            predicate(Pred,Verb,3,N,Tense,act,R),
                append(Obj,[Pred$Subj],Clause).
```

(logical emphasis on protagonist)

the following result will be obtained

[Three,sides,has,the_triangle]

(possible Construction in Bulgarian)

while its unification with the sentence synthesis rule

```
synthesis(goal,Verb,3,Tense,act,r(relation(R),
                                   numerus(N),
                                   protagonist(Prot),
                                   goal(Goal)),Clause):-
            subject(gen,def,Prot,Subj),
            object(gen,indef,Goal,Obj),
        predicate(Pred,Verb,3,N,Tense,act,R),
            append(Subj,[Pred$Obj],Clause).
```

(logical emphasis on goal)

yields the result:

[The_triangle,has,three,sides]

(in Bulgarian the definite article is part of the word as an inflection; the subject, predicate and object synthesis rules are for the sake of bervity not explicitly presented).

PRODUCTION OF FINAL SURFACE CONSTRUCTIONS

The sentence generated by unifying the functional unification grammar with the input and representing a fact about or related to a concept is not the final sentence the system offers to its users. Although the resulting sentences of the previous examples sound quite reasonably, the system would not be able to impress always its users if it accepts the sentence as final. The problem is that each explanation of a concept is not a single sentence, but discourse. To illustrate our position assume that the system has to give a detailed (initial) description of the concept "triangle" (such description is actually given by our system, see Fig.1 first answer). After consecutive unifications of the grammar rules with the relevant inputs (see semantic representation of "triangle" in Fig.4), the system would generate in the best case the following text:

Fig.5

> The triangle is a geometrical figure. The triangle is straigtlinear. The triangle is plane (plane as adjective). The triangle is convex. The triangle has three sides. The triangle can be isosceles, equilateral and scalene according to its sides. The triangle can be right-angled, acute-angled and obtuse-angled according to its angles.

This is a clumsy text, that no reasonable man would write. The three main linguistic operations (part of the system's linguistic knowledge) that will process this text are coordination, pronomiloization and ellipsis. Note that coordination has worked on the first sentences, pronomilization - on the fifth sentence and ellipsis - on the sentence obtained from coordination of the last two sentences (before these three operations a rhetoric rule has operated, which says, that "according to" sounds better at the beginning of the sentence and is not subject to deletion during coordination). The processed text will be:

Fig.6

> The triangle is a straightlinear, plane and convex geometrical figure. It has three sides. The triangle can be isosceles, equilateral and scalene according to its sides. The triangle can be right-angled, acute-angled and obtuse-angles according to its angles. According to its sides the triangle can be equilateral, isosceles and scalene and in according to its angles - right-angled, acute-angled and abtuse-angled.

There are also further linguistic decisions to be made: should the sentence be in an active or in passive voice, should two or more simple sentences be comined into a single complex one (In Fig.6 the first sentence is generated by combining the first four sentences of Fig.5 into a complex one), should gerundium be used etc. Such decisions are made on the basis of linguistic phenomena as focus, logical emphasis (exclusively for Bulgarian), causality etc. and are not to be discussed in the present paper. To sum up the pruduction of a natural language explanation we propose the following figure:

Fig.7

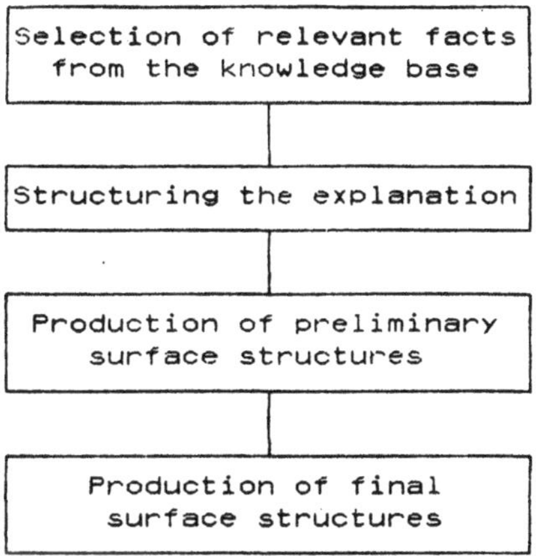

FUTURE WORK

We regard the system also as possible explanation module of a student expert system, which is being now designed.

REFERENCES

Derr, Marcia and McKeown, Kathleen - Using focus to generate complex and simple sentences, COLING, 1984

Kay, Martin - Parsing in functional unification grammar. In Zwicky et al (eds): Natural language parsing, Cambridge, 1985

McKeown, Kathleen - Text generation: using discourse strategies and focus contstraints to generate natural language text. Cambridge university pres, Combridge, 1985

Mitkov, Ruslan - A knowledge representation model and its applications. Paper presented at the "Models of meaning" conference, Varna, 1988

Roesner, Hannelore - Generierung von Erklärungen aus formalen Wissensrepräsentationen, Bericht No.3, Verbundvorhaben WISBER, 1986

Rousselot, Francois - Un systeme comprenant des textes en utilisant un formalisme unique. T.A. Informations, N.2, 1985

An EDP–System Reference Model and its Application to Solve Compatibility Problems.

Dr.-Ing. H. Petersen
Technical University Aachen, FRG

1 Introduction

EDP Systems (Electronic Document Processing Systems) or "Computer Assisted Document Processing Systems" are used in various application areas under different names and different implemention characteristics. There are applications in the graphic industry, for scientific publications, technical documention, office publications in administrations and industry, etc. So far, processing and handling of documents has grown up and become one of the most interesting application fields of computer systems seen from market considerations, as well as from the challenge concerning the development of modern software tools. In the beginning of computerized typesetting systems and the desktop publishing business, EDP systems were preferably considered as stand–alone applications. Today the user understands that one is confronted with system environments, which makes it necessary to consider their requirements and properties. Some reasons are as follows:

- the connection of EDP systems in larger units, which is often desirable in research institutes, industrial plants, administrations, universities, etc.
- the necessity of interchanging documents between different applications, such as DTP systems, textprocessing systems, typesetting systems, mainframe applications, etc.
- to support the useful sharing of specialized functions such as text recording, typographic make up, picture processing and graphic arts.
- the evaluation and selection of EDP systems, which should be used for certain applications within existing environments.
- the improvement of EDP systems by additional functions or the expansion of the application areas.

In all cases, compatibility problems arise very soon, which appear similar to those problems according to the beginning of the computer–to–computer communication. It is therefore obviously necessary — with respect to the OSI model (Open Systems Interconnection) of the ISO — to develop a reference model, which allows to

- render the complex structure of EDP systems more transparent,
- define interfaces,
- describe functions,
- realize for the users a common base for understanding and discussion.

The relation between the reference and the OSI model is beyond that which is based solely on the fact that documents in their various forms of realisation are used as media for information interchange. In this sense, the related layers of the OSI model are especially layers 6 and 7.

2 Document and Preparation Process

First, it is necessary to define and delineate the item "document". In our case, a document is to be understood as any physically recognizable form of information (for which a suitable internal representation has to exist because of the processing by computer systems). We particularly consider text, graphics, pictures, formulas, tables etc. as information types. In a closer sense, we mean the visible representation of information on paper, screens, photomaterial, printing plates, etc.
In modern EDP-systems, especially in the field of office automation and the production of technical and scientific publications, we distinguish between the "logical" structure, the "physical" structure (often designated as typographical structure) and the content portions of a document. The reason for this consideration is the fact that the same content (for example the text of a lecture) can be represented, i.e. designed, in different forms (as report or as a magazines article). Content and logical structure, consisting of, for example, title, chapters, subchapters, paragraphs, footnotes and marginals, remain identical, but the representation can be performed in different forms (fig. 1). This approach shows that a document exists in different "states", whereby one state can be transformed into another.

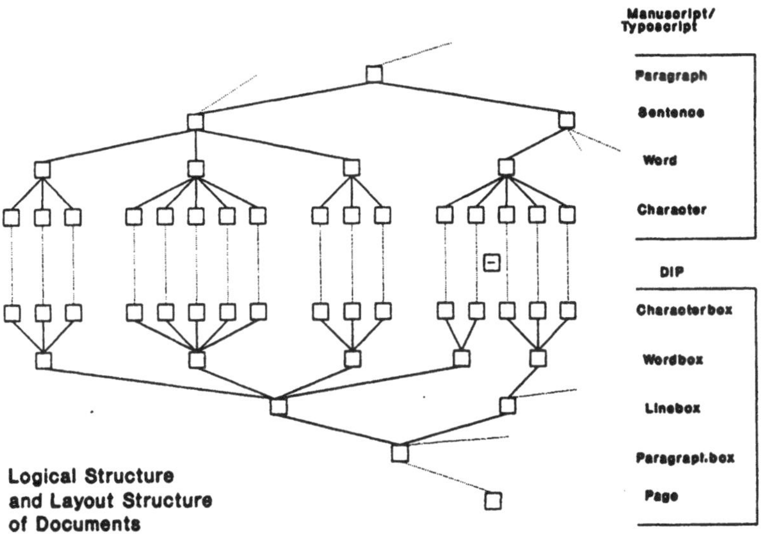

fig. 1

The basic functionality of an EDP system with respect to its environment is shown in fig. 2. In general, an EDP system is embedded in its environment without any on-line interface, i.e. documents exist in a printed form as input and output information. This means that a document within an EDP system has to be available in four different forms in relation to the special application or the proposed processing steps:

- form 1 is the document representation which is directly gained by the copy and allows the further processing by computer.

- form 2 is the representation which is necessary to perform a programmed and/or interactive processing.
- form 3 is the result of various processing steps and enables the immediate documents visualization in printed form or on a screen.
- form 4 is used for storage, archiving and retrieval of documents and in our case (for simplification) we assume that this form can also be used for the exchange of documents (send and receive).

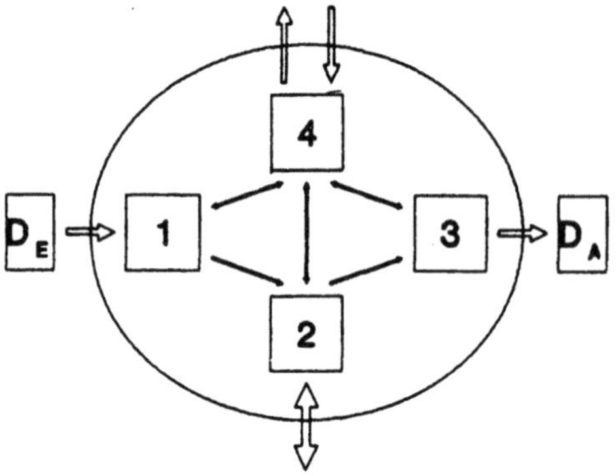

fig. 2

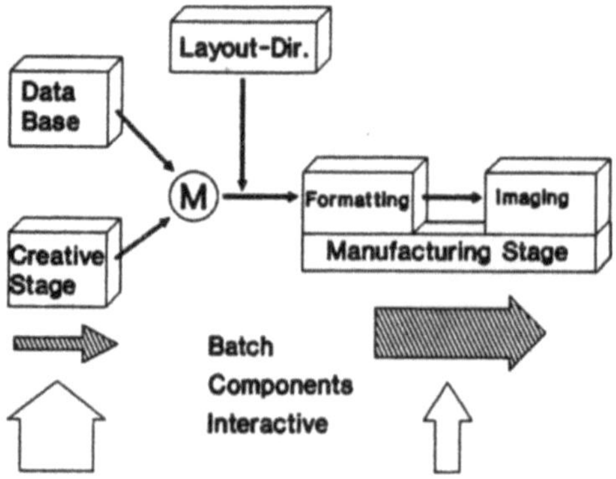

fig. 3

Depending on the specific application these forms of representation are not necessarily different. In practice, different forms are implemented in order to solve the problems in an optimal way (compression methods for memory saving storage and time saving interchange of documents, different data structures for dialogue and batch processing, etc.).

This structure shows that there are also four types of relationships between and EDP system and its environment, which are important if we want to study integration problems:

1. Transformation of the visible and (or machine readable) document into a processable form, generally performed by device controllers (scanner, OCR reader).

2. Transformation of the electronically represented document into a visible form, also performed by device controllers (printer, typesetter, screens).

3. Dialog-oriented interface as an EDP system user interface to support different functions of the document preparation process (editing, designing, structuring, retouching).

4. Interfaces for document interchange protocols and services (teletext, telefax, ODIF, EDIFACT). Since EDP systems have to communicate, the related system- and state-specific interchange protocols have to be implemented.

Processing of documents can be performed similar to other information processing tasks, batch oriented as well as dialogue oriented. Batch oriented means the stepwise execution of subprocesses with a maximum of system support and a minimum of user interruptions. Dialogue-oriented processing means current user control and the possibility of user interaction between any subprocess at anytime. These different operating characteristics do not change anything concerning the basic system structure, but affect in particular the implementation of data-structures, user interfaces and the level of typographic languages. The following disclosures therefore are based on a batch oriented operation as far as examples are shown.
A further basic aspect of EDP systems is shown in form of a top-down description in fig. 3. The document preparation process can basically be divided into two stages: the creative stage and the manufactoring stage. The result of the creative stage is the manuscript. This is the documents stage consisting of content portions and the logical structure. In the case of data base publishing applications the creative part is changed by a data base, which contains the manuscripts.
In general, the creative stage is the author's desk, i.e. tools for interactive editing of content portions (text editing) as well as logical structure (structure editing) should be available. Batch oriented functions are, in this case, in minor relevance available.
The following production oriented part should not require interactive functions and consists of the formatting and visualisation process. Restricted to those cases where conflicts can arise, by, for example, arranging footnotes, hyphenation problems and the change of presentation parameters, interactive access must be possible and the batch process is interrupted and restarted.
This overlook describes the logical relationship between EDP system functions. A specific implementation can contain such a structure, but depending on the application, editing operations on the visualized state of the document is possible (WYSIWYG-systems). Both system types have advantages and disadvantages, so one can suppose that the related disadvantages can be eliminated by combining the properties of both types. The difficulties and subsequently related problems shall not be discussed here.

3 Reference model

The next refinement of an EDP system functionality description should enable the discussion of compatibility problems and serve as basis to evaluate EDP systems. Therefore a more precise desription of relevant components is necessary. These components belong (besides the technical compatibility of interfaces) to the set of data-objects and user interfaces. In fig. 4 these details are shown by the CUPIDO model (Complete and User Oriented Processing of Integrated DOcuments). Files are data-objects and are shown as squares, functions as arrows, editors as circles and user interfaces are tagged with "U". The naming of the model shall express that all system functions are contained in the model, that not only text documents have to be processed and that all possible user activities are taken into account, i.e. independence of the operation types "dialogue" and "batch". By the stepwise processing, a document takes different states, which are available as data-objects inside the system. This modularity is either enforced by the application or leads to specific advantages during the preparation process. In order to avoid an unnecessary model complexity, storage and interchange functions are bound together.

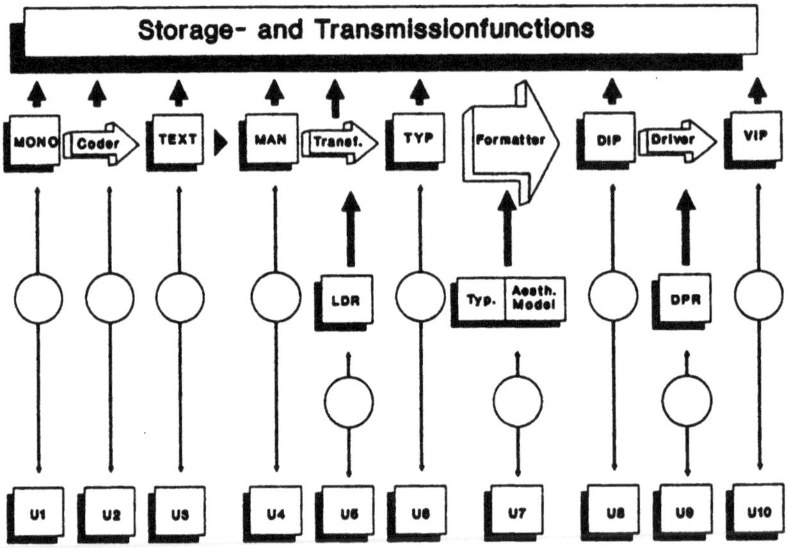

fig. 4

3.1 Data Objects

It is assumed for the following considerations, that a document passes all processing steps, i.e. it could be available as a printed sheet, will be produced and printed again. In this case, when the document first passes the preprocessing stage, it will be scanned and a data-object "monogram" is produced. A character recognition module produces the data object "text" (a vectorizer realises a similer function in case of graphics). The document consists in the form of "text" essentially of unstructered text in coded form, because character recognition methods cannot apart from specific exceptions classify logical structure elements in documents.
The following data object "manuscript" contains-besides the content portions-information about the logical structure in the form of markers (i.e. no layout information) and therefore can be produced in three ways:

1. editing text and structure information by the author or a typist,
2. by inserting markers into the unstructured text,
3. by data base input, the text portions are stored in a suitable structured form.

At this point it is obvious that the differentiation between manuscript and the following states is very important. On the one hand, only the author is able to formulate the content and give it the appropriate structure (paragraphs, chapters, sub–chapters, footnotes etc.); on the other hand, he need not carry out the layout, page make up and production of the document, which can differ depending on the intended application. A further advantage is the fact that sub–documents or parts of documents, which are produced by different authors, can simply be integrated and produced as homogeniously designed documents.
Transformation of a manuscript into a typoscript means that markers, which describe the logical structure, are now replaced by statements, which describe the desired design of the document. Instead of the "title" marker, we now find information about font, character size, highlighting, underline etc. The manuscript to typoscript mapping is done by using the "layout directives". Systems, which allow the separate storing and editing of layout directives support the preperation of standardized documents by organising specific libraries. Additionally, variations of laying out document classes are very simple to achieve.
The typoscript is exactly that state of the document which is edited by the user of classical typesetting equipment (in this case, layout directives are formulated by himself or the preparations for work).
The formatting process (or the typesetting process) produces the state "device independent page" (DIP) from the typoscript. This is performed by the formatter, using a typographical model and — in only a few cases of existing systems — quality values are generated. These values are based on an aesthetic model and allows to mesure the quality of the formatting results. The question of the generated page description device independance has to be answered very differentially with respect to existing systems. It is necessary to have the DIP state because the production of the "visible page" (VIP) is not only necessary for devices like screens, printers, typesetters etc., but there exist various technical differences within these classes or devices. These differences are represented by device parameters, which are considered for the DIP → VIP transformation.

3.2 Functions

The functions, which are contained within a complete system can roughly be devided into two classes:

1. Editors, which realise the interchange or information between user and system.
2. Transformations and mappings, which realize the state transition functions between the particular document states. A third class of functions, which have to be used for protocol conversions between incompatible data objects, are not considered here. It should be just noted at this point that the term "mapping" is used, if the coordinate systems or source and target are different.

3.2.1 Editors

The structure of the editors consists basically of the same elements which form an EDP system, because it is necessary to produce a physically recognizable presentation on a screen out of an internal form. In this case, specific conditions exist, such as the typographical design, which has to suffer the criteria of user interfaces or the device attributes, which are designed for this special work. Nevertheless, it is possible to derive editor standard functions and to use them as tools.

3.2.2 Transmition functions

It is essential for modern EDP systems, that all these functions really do exist and that they are controlled by parameters.
If these parameters can be influenced by the user, we get systems which can easily be adapted to various application requirements. The experience has shown that EDP systems can be realized as professional typesetting systems with highest quality requirements as well as office systems for

production of standardized documents with minimal expert knowledge, depending on their special characteristics.

3.3 User interfaces

The user interfaces together with editors form the interactive "paths" into an EDP system. Today's systems are distinguished by supporting a subset of interfaces with respect to the reference model. Some systems, for example classical typesetting systems, are restricted to one interface and are offered for editing text and typesetting commands (U4 as part of the model). In the model we assume that one data object can be affected by only one user interface. The fact is that there are systems with editing functions which can work on several data objects. These constructions are not considered here.

By using the set of available user interfaces, one can classify EDP systems very well, also because these interfaces affect at first the user's experience and training efforts. Nevertheless, these user interfaces also characterize the internal data structure of the systems dialogue quality.

4 The meaning of data objects

The number and characteristic properties of data objects which are available are specified by their functions, which they have to carry out within an EDP system. These function and the operation mode additionally affect the object's internal representation.

4.1 Manuscript

The manuscript is the device– and layout independant state of a document and consists of structure and content portions description. It follows that functions concerning this state can only refer to input, completion and change of content portions (realized by texteditors) or structure (structure editor). The logical structure elements can be tied up with (logical) attributes, such as, for example, identification of the language within citations. Changes of structure are the re–ordering of paragraphs and chapters, footnotes into marginals, etc.

The quality of editors is defined:

1. by the possibility to refer to certain logical elements as characters, words, sentences, paragraphs, etc.
2. by the existence of various functions as delete, insert, search, replace, move, etc.
3. by the user interface concerning the manuscript representation (content portions with or without markers) and the editor functions (command oriented, menu driven, graphic).

The device– and layout independance of the manuscript allows the documents visual representation in different forms (one column, multicolumn, various fonts and formats etc.).

4.2 Typoscript

The typoscript consists of the same content portions as the manuscript, but instead of structure information (logical markup) we find typographical statements (or commands). The typographical statements represent the "desired design and layout" which produces the device independant physical document representation. The set of typographical statements represent the typographical language of the system and can be ordered into language levels (sometimes named as microtypographics, macrotypographics and layout). The functionality of an EDP system is basically determined by the range of the typographical language. Language elements which are in use within a specific typoscript form together with typesetting parameters and layout information the so called "typogram".

The typoscript is the formatting process (or typesetting program) input information. The formatter calculates the position and modification of the content portions and eventually generates new ones (pagination, column titles, references, etc).

4.3 DIP (Device Independent Page)

This state consists of the complete description of all content portions (i.e. those which are contained in the manuscript and those which were generated) and their position on a page, which is understood as a plane of arbitrary dimension. The description of such a page is performed by a page description language (PDL). The independence of any output device requires the definition of a virtual coordinate system, which has to be mapped into the real device coordinate system when the VIP is generated.

4.4 VIP (Visible Page)

This document state is transformed immediately by hard- and grayware (more exactly the device controller) into the visible form of the document. The importance of this state is determined by the fact that the visible form can fulfil different functions:

1. It is the ultimate representation of the document and will not be changed in any way (e.g. output on typesetters and printers, i.e. the document is fixed on film, paper, overheads or printing plates).
2. The document can be retouched, for example, by its representation on a screen with the resolution of a laserprinter. The retouching can be performed pixelwise just before the output process is started.
3. Preview function, i.e. approximated representation of the document before the output for control purposes. Eventually necessary corrections are independently done in the manuscript or typoscript.
4. Interview function. In this case, the VIP state supports correction activities in all other states. The orientation within the document is much more easier by the VIP and the correction results can immediately be shown and controlled. It is therefore necessary to establish references between the particular document state according to the interview functions in order to achieve this "synchronisation" (for example cursor movement control). This functionality is essential in case of dialogue mode.

5 Model and Implementation

The investigation of existing (or desirable) EDP systems show that they can assume very different properties, depending on specific applications. These differences are determinded by the fact that the reference model elements can be implemented more or less completed and with different characteristics. Integration of different systems requires compatibility, whereby one should distinguish between data compatibility, function compatibility and interface compatibility.
Considering the system structure we find that data compatibility can be required on several levels, depending on the state in which document interchange is being carried out. In particular:

1. Manuscript level:
   Standarized coding of content portions, logical markers and logical attributes. At this level there exists presently the sole standard in the form of SGML (Standard Generalized Markup Language).

2. Typoscript level:
   Compatible systems would require — besides the content coding — a standardized typographical language. Presently there is no standard at all. Perhaps a standard could be achieved by the development of the ODA/ODIF standard (Office Document Architecture/ Interchange Format). At this level, all existing systems are not compatible.

3. DIP level:
   An officially supported standard concerning a page discription language does not exist. There is a project in process at the ISO called SPDL (Standard Page Description Language). This standard is of more interest with respect to the DIP–VIP mapping. Concerning the DIP level, one has to consider that a standard restrains the further system development, e.g. in case of implementation of new formatting functions or content elements.

4. VIP level:
   Defacto standards (or industry standards) are at this level the large printer and typesetter manufacturer's PDL or those of widely used graphic systems. One can expect the SPDL development to be widely based on PostScript resp. Interpress, i.e. if the page discriptions would be standardized on both levels, the mapping could be performed with minimum (or no) expense.

6 Experiences, Applications, Conclusions

The development and application of the CUPIDO model has led above all to the following results:

1. The evaluation and functional description of existing systems is much more simplified and improved.

2. To compare different systems is possible by evaluation of their structure elements.

3. Inhouse standards can be developed by defining the size and formats of language levels, user shells, font libraries, macro libraries, etc.

4. The interchange of information and the understanding between users of different systems is improved.

5. For further system development there is a good basis which was not available until today.

6. The implementation of protocol converting modules, i.e. the integration of incompatible components as distributed EDP systems was performed very successfully.

The experiences generally have shown that — based on the CUPIDO model — much "lower" system layers can be described and structured. The developments are still in progress.

References

[1] Martin Bryan: *An Author's Guide to the Standard Generalized Markup Language.* Addison–Wesley Publishing Company 1988

[2] ISO 8613: *Office Document Architecture and Interchange Format, (ODA/ODIF).*

[3] XEROX Corporation: *Introduction to Interpress.* XEROX Publication number: 610P72581 1984

[4] Peter Egloff: *Dokumente mit Format (Projekt DAPHNE).* DFN–Mitteilungen Nr. 15, p. 22–25

[5] Richard Rubinstein: *Digital Typography.* Addison–Wesley Publishing Company 1988

[6] Leslie Lamport: LaTeX — *A Document Preparation System.* Addison–Wesley Publishing Company 1986

[7] Adobe Systems: *Postscript, Vol. 1–3.* Addison–Wesley Publishing Company 1988

[8] O. Abeln: *Referenzmodell für CAD–Systeme, Bericht aus einem Arbeitskreis der GI.* Informatik–Spektrum Bd. 12, Heft 1 1989, p. 43–46

DISTRIBUTED OBJECT-ORIENTED KNOWLEDGE PROCESSING ENVIRONMENT DIPROTALK

A. Petkov, A. Simeonov, D. Dimitrov, Tz. Tzonev

Bulgarian Academy of Sciences
Institute of Mathematics
P.O.Box 373
1090 Sofia, Bulgaria

Abstract

This paper describes an environment for building distributed intelligent information system based on remote object interaction.

1. Introduction

We define the distributed knowledge processing systems as a group of decentralised and loosely coupled knowledge sources working in co-operation as in [4]. Knowledge sources have to work in co-operation because the information in any of them isn't enough to give the rigth solution of the whole problem. The knowledge should be or is distributed among the members of the group. The decentralisation concerns both the management and the data which can be logically and/or physically distributed. The term loosely coupled means, that the communications are not a considerable part of the task execution.

Distributed knowledge processing requires specialized architectures of distributed systems with following features:

- addition of new knowledge sources;
- addition of new knowledge users;
- the knowledge representation models on different machines does not influence on interaction among these sources;
- migration of some knowledge sources.

The proposed architecture is based on the intelligent agent's concept, an abstraction on knowledge source in case of determined topics. Such group agents is described with the following properties [6]:

- it is impossible (or very difficult) an agent to know in details the whole problem;
- the agents execute their own jobs concurrent so a synchronization among them is needed;
- every agent has a set of rules (methods) used to solve certain problems. It is possible two agents to satisfy the same goal trough different methods;
- every agent executes its job using set of inputs and output the results for other agents in the system;
- the agent can ask for an additional information to satisfy its goal.

In order to build an architecture with the above properties we propose the object-oriented approach based on a system of loosely coupled abstract machines. So the distributive nature of the building components can be hidden.

The object oriented paradigm is a programming and design style by which the system is modelled as a collection of selfcontained program modules having a unified interface for message passing and interacting one with another by sending messages. These modules are called objects. An object has a set of operations and a state that saves the operations effects.

Recent development of object-oriented approach permit its successfully application in languages and programming technology, for creating of distributed systems, data bases and knowledge representation. All of these domains are based on interaction between encapsulated data and programs although each of them accents in particular properties in term object. These consideration leads us to develop an integrated environment for knowledge processing called **Diprotalk**. This paper represents a distributed environment considering infrastructure of interaction between servers and clients of knowledge.

2. General view of Diprotalk.

The general view of **Diprotalk** is showed at fig.1.

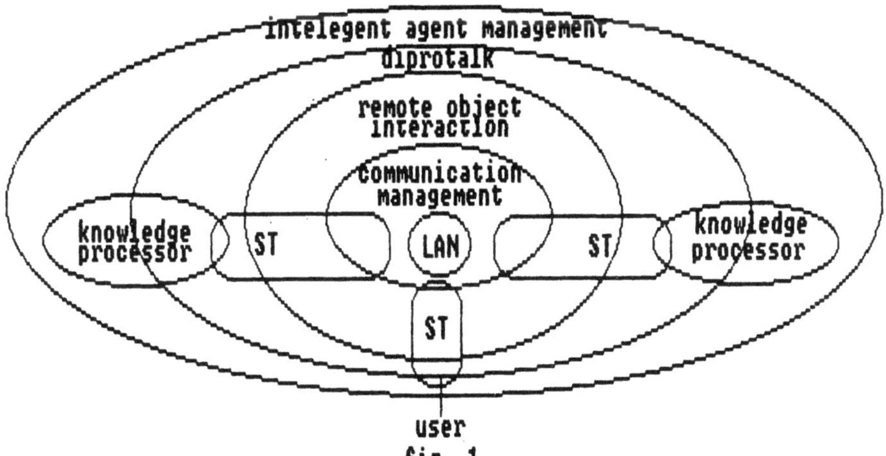

fig. 1

The system for information exchange management is based on specialized communication interface. On its top is the remote interaction among the objects, residing in different virtual object spaces. Trough the interaction mechanism is built a distributed environment for object-oriented programming, including following features:

- to define new classes of objects as a part of the class hierarchy;
- to create instances of these classes;
- to define global object for the system;
- to create programs for treatment that objects;
- to execute object programs;
- error processing.

The management of intelligent agents is created using distributed object oriented programming. The intelligent agent could be created using the tools of object-oriented programming or another programming systems (logical, relational etc.) which are encapsulated as object. The architecture building components are set of **Smalltalk** station making loosely coupled system. Every station represents an environment for applications creation and implementation. It consists of:

- a virtual object machine;
- a virtual image space;
- a compiler generating code sequences which can be dynamic bound and executed on the virtual machine;
- an user window interface.

An essential feature of **Smalltalk** station is a rich class hierarchy which is contained in virtual image space. Certain classes are integrated with virtual machine in order to build object-oriented environment.

We define some new classes and modify some existing classes of the ordinary **Smalltalk** image. They enable a **Smalltalk** station to send messages transparently to objects residing in remote machines and to receive the resulting objects in return. The defined model of interaction between stations enables a **Smalltalk** station to send several messages to multiple remote **Smalltalk** stations concurrently.

3. Diprotalk environment

Diprotalk adds some new capabilities to **Smalltalk** environment. Using these capabilities the programmers can write programs which access objects residing in more than one station.

Smalltalk is a quasi concurrent language. The virtual machine is defined to hold only one active context at a time. When a message is sent,the sending context is suspended ,a new context is created to execute the methods, a result is produced and then the sender context is activated again. The mechanism of interaction between objects is defined to have the same semantics as procedure calling. The computation is done sequentially.

In **Diprotalk** some virtual machines work in cooperation to perform a common task. In this system more than one active context exist at a time in the system as a whole. This enables the message sending context to remain active parallel with the message executing context. The message sending process is suspended not at the time of the sending of the message but at the time when the resulting object becomes necessary for further computations (fig. 3). This model of interaction enables the objects to send several messages to multiple remote objects concurrently.

The model of interaction is transparent to the programmer. The kind of method invocation is determined by the locations of the objects at the time of the message sending. If the objects reside in the same station then the method call is synchronous. If they reside in different stations then the method call is asynchronous. The source code does not depend on the location of the objects. The changes in the locations of the objects do not have to be reflected in the source code. The implementation of our model also allows the migration of objects at run time.

3.1. Mail management

3.1.1. Need of communications

A **Smalltalk** target system is constructed as a collection of objects residing in a common virtual object space. This enables the interaction between the objects to be implemented using **shared variables**. The sender object and the receiver object share the message object.

In a set of **Smalltalk** stations objects reside in different object spaces. The approach **shared variables** is inadequate to implement message passing between remote objects. Some communications are needed to implement message passing. The communications in the system described here take place over a special LAN based communication subsystem.

3.1.2. Communication subsystem

The **Communication subsystem** includes primitives for maintaining the global name space; establishing, using and disconnecting links for reliable data exchange (sessions); and some other services.

Communication names

In the object-oriented language **Smalltalk** messages sending from one object to another is a basic paradigm. These messages include name of destination object and method (procedure) to be performed. In the distributed environment for object-oriented programming messages are carried by the **Communication subsystem** and objects are known to it by their names. Servicing the objects' names have to be completely done by the **Communication subsystem**. Names are global - i.e. they are known in the whole system. Names are of two kinds - unique names and group names. Each pair of unique names can be used to establish a link for reliable data exchange (session) between them, or to send single, nonacknowledged messages (datagrams). Group names can be used for sending messages simultaneously to a set of objects. Group names cannot be used to establish a session.

It is possible to have a large number of objects in a **Smalltalk** station. For this reason the communication subsystem and its name service should maintain a large number of objects. Another requirement arises from the dynamic characteristics of the objects - while the system is active, objects are being continuously created, used and destroyed. It leads to the necessity operations of creating and deleting the names associated with objects to be handled with high efficiency. This requires functions, related to objects names, to be carried out by the communication subsystem. Implementing this functions at higher logical level will increase system overhead.

Name support primitives are:

DefineName(Name, Type, G)
DeleteName(Name)
ReportName(Type, NameList)

Data exchange

In the distributed environment for object-oriented programming data exchange takes place mainly in the form of sending messages to remote objects. The **Communication subsystem** is in charge of delivering messages reliable. For this purpose it provides primitives for establishing using and terminating sessions - bi-directional links for reliable data exchange.

Session support primitives are:

Listen(RemoteName, LocalName)
Connect(RemoteName, LocalName)
Receive(Connection, Buffer, Length)
Send(Connection, Buffer, Length)
Close(Connection)

Sessions offer simultaneous a two-way connection. All primitives can be executed in either synchronous or asynchronous mode.

3.1.3. Naming.

The naming in **Smalltalk** virtual machine is a mechanism for designating objects without any concern with their physical locations. It is maintained by using **object oriented pointers** (OOPs) [3]. An object table is implemented to hold the relations between **OOPs** and the locations of the objects in the virtual object spaces.It is impossible to use an **OOP** as a unique object name in the distributed system as a whole, because the object tables in the different machines are independent. We can not make changes in the implementation of the table because it is a private part of the virtual machine.

Because of that we define an additional scheme to maintain the naming in the distributed system. An unique network name is assigned to every object which well receive messages from remote objects. A part of a global dictionary is created as an ordinary **Smalltalk** object in every station to hold the relations between OOPs and the network names of the objects. At some level of abstraction it is possible to consider a single dictionary in the distributed system. But in fact the parts of the dictionary are distributed over the **Smalltalk** stations.

3.1.4. Proxy objects.

It is impossible in the **Smalltalk** station to use a network name to identify the remote receiver object because an **OOP** is used to identify the object which receives the message. To avoid this problem a special kind of objects (**proxy objects**) are used to represent the receiver objects in the virtual object spaces where the senders reside. Any message to a proxy object is forwarded via the network to its corresponding remote object (the object which is represented by the proxy object) (see fig.1).

Any proxy object is an instance of the new class **Proxy**. **Proxy's** behaviour is implemented by using the **doesNotUndersstand** mechanism of the **Smalltalk** interpreter.

This mechanism consist in the following: if the interpreter can not find a message selector in the message dictionary of the class of the receiver object or its superclasses then it creates a new instance of the class **Message**. This message instance holds the selector and the arguments array of the original message. A **doesNotUnderstand** message is sent to the receiver object with the newly created object as an argument. When an object receives a **doesNotUnderstand** message it invokes the which reports an error.

In the class **Proxy** the method **doesNotUnderstand** of the **Object** class is overridden by a method in which the argument of the message is forwarded to the remote object via the communication subsystem. Since the **Proxy** class has been defined as a subclass of Nil, the **doesNotUnderstand** mechanism is activated always when a message is sent to an instance of the class **Proxy**.

3.1.5. Mail **agent**.

As stated above an asynchronous model is used to introduce interaction between objects residing in different object spaces. To implement the asynchronous interactions an asynchronous model of communications between remote objects is defined. In this model any object which will receive messages from remote objects is defined as a global network object by assigning to its an unique network name. An empty mailbox is assigned to the network object too. Any message which arrives to an object is saved in its box.

In order to implement this model, the new class **MailAgent** is defined in every station. A instance of class **MailAgent** encapsulate the state of the communication subsystem and provide operations for communications over the **LAN**. Any object which has to communicate sends messages to this instance.At some level of abstraction it is possible to suppose that only one object of the class **MailAgent** exists in the distributed system as a whole. This abstract object is represented as a set of instances of **MailAgent** which communicate over the communication subsystem.

The messages which can be accepted by the objects of class **MailAgent** are the following:

- **at:aName put:anObject** - This message is sent to the **MailAgent** when anObject has to be defined as a global network object in the distributed system;
- **nameOfObject:anObject** - If anObject has already been defined as a global network object then the message result is the global network name of anObject; otherwise **MailAgent** determines anObject as a global object by assigning a service network name to it. This service network name is returned as a result;
- **objectWithName:aName ifAbsent:aBlock** - If an object with the global network name aName exists then this object is returned as a result; otherwise aBlock is evaluated. When the object resides in the station , in which the method is evaluated then this object is returned as result; otherwise a proxy object is returned;
- **send:aMessage to:aName** - The message aMessage is saved in the mail box of the object with name aName if there exists an objects with this name.

This implementation of the communication model from a process point of view is represented by fig. 2.

The specialized interface of the communication subsystem is described in detail in [5].

The mail server process buffers all arriving data from remote stations and interrupt the **Smalltalk** virtual machine to inform it about the mailing.

Then the active **Smalltalk** process is suspended and the **Mail manager Smalltalk** process is activated.It sends messages to **MailAgent** and it stores them in the mailboxes of the objects.

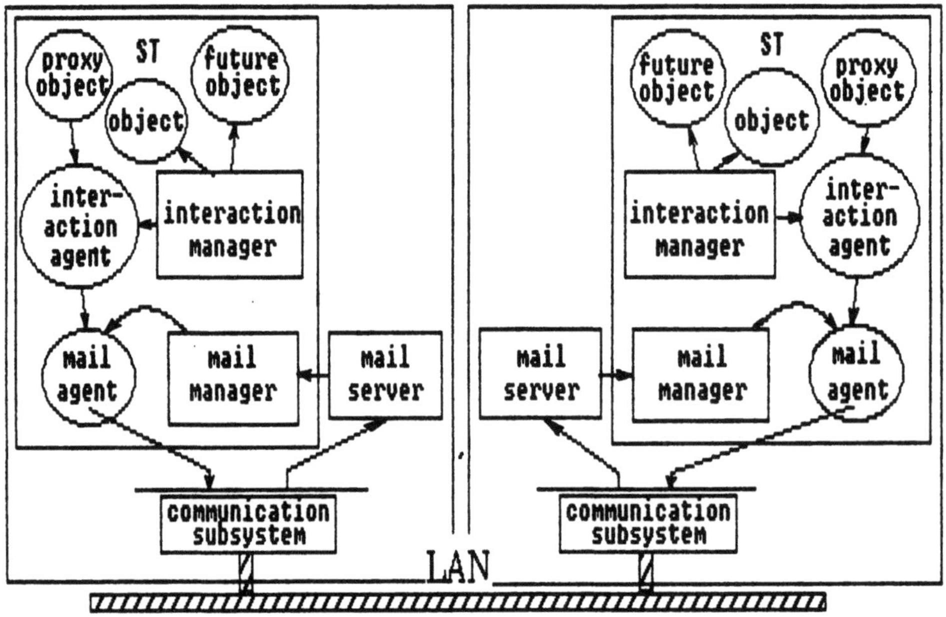

proxy object
ST
future object
object
interaction agent
interaction manager
mail agent
mail manager
mail server
communication subsystem
LAN

fig. 2

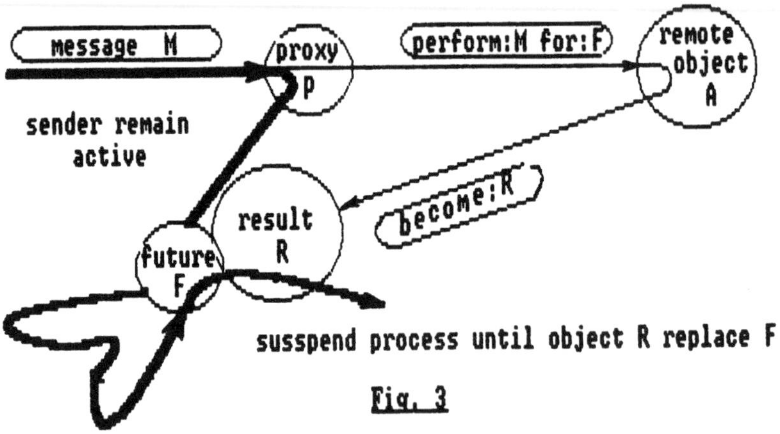

message M
proxy
P
perform:M for:F
remote object
A
sender remain active
result
R
become:R
future
F
susspend process until object R replace F

Fig. 3

3.2. Remote Objects Interaction.

3.2.1.Future objects.

In our model of interaction between objects residing in different machines the sending process is suspended not at the time of message passing but at the time the resulting object is required for further computations.

To implement that we define the new class **Future** in every **Smalltalk** station. Whereas an object of the class **Proxy** represents the receiving object in the sending station, an object of the class **Future** represents the result object in the virtual image of the station from which the message is sent.

Let some object send a message M to the proxy P which represent the remote object A (see fig. 3).

When P receives the message M as an argument of the message **doesNotUnderstand** then it creates an instance F of the class **Future**,defines F as a global network object in **MailAgent** by assigning it an unique network name , forwards M to the remote object A via **MailAgent** and returns F as a result of the operation. The sender process remains active. It is suspended when any message is send to the object F.

MailAgent saves the message M' (see fig. 3) in the mail box of the object A. Let R be the object which has been returned as a result of evaluating the method M in the station containing A.

After R has been produced the interaction service process in the station of A constructs a message **become** with an argument **R** and sends it via **MailAgent** to the object F. When the **become** method is evaluated then the object R replaces the object F in the image containing F. The suspended process, if any, is activated.

Two phases of the message passing mechanism are distinguished. During the first phase the message is sent to the remote object and a future object is returned as a result. During the second phasé a become message is sent to the future object. The future object is used to synchronise the send and receive processes.

The behaviour of the class **Future** is implemented by using the **doesNotUnderstand** mechanisms of the **Smalltalk** interpreter. The **doesNotUnderstand** is overridden to suspend the sending process.

3.2.2. Parameter Passing.

Messages in **Smalltalk** have parameters. The parameters are used for exchanging information between the sender and the receiver. When the sender and the receiver reside in a common object space the OOPs of the parameter objects are passed. This is impossible when the sender and receiver reside in different object spaces.

There are two possible solutions of the problem:

- create a deep copy of the object in the virtual image of the receiver - **pass by value**.
- create an instance of the class **Proxy** which represents the parameter object in the virtual space of the receiver - **pass by remote reference (pass by Proxy)**.

We use **passing by value** when the parameter objects are immutable.

It is difficult to use pass by value for mutable objects because the passed object is accessible from the sender and from the receiver processes after message sending. We must treat the object and its copies in remote stations as a replicated distributed database. Because of that we do not use passing by value for mutable objects. For mutable objects we use passing by proxy.

Another mechanism for parameter passing is defined in our work too. We call it **pass by migration**. The parameter object is passed by value and a proxy object is created in the sender station to replace the migrating object.

3.2.3. Remote Object Interaction Management.

Using the communication services the **Remote Object Interaction Management** enables sending messages to remote objects and receiving results of the appropriate method executions. The basic parts of this layer are **Interaction Agent** and **Interaction Manager**. When proxy object receives a message it interacts with the local **Interaction Agent** and requests the execution of the service remoteInteraction with arguments:

- the name of the remote object;
- the service name of the future object which represents the result object;
- the message which is to be executed remotely.

After receiving a request the Interaction Agent makes decision how to pass the parameters and forms a request to the remote Interaction Manager with following arguments:

- the service name of the future object which represents the result object;
- a **Smalltalk** program. After its execution on the remote station this program creates the message object.

This request is saved in the mailbox of the remote receiver. The **Interaction Manager** scans the local mailboxes for messages and executes these messages localy. The result objects of this executions are sent to the appropriate future objects. To do this the **Interaction Manager** use the services of the **Interaction Agent**.

4. Intelligent Agent Management

An application based on knowledge can be treated as a collection of two components: knowledge and control [1]. Knowledge is relatively the static component whereas the control is the dynamic one.

The knowledge is extracted from general application semantics and then decomposed into a set of semantic models in the **Diprotalk** environment. Each static semantic model is implemented as an intelligent agent in an appropriate **Smalltalk** server station. The decomposed parts describe the particular semantic elements of the whole knowledge component. These semantic models are relatively independent and are presented as class hierarchies in the appropriate **Smalltalk** station.

The dynamic part of knowledge is a set of production rules and relationships between intelligent agents. It is a **Smalltalk** program residing on user **Smalltalk** station which manages remote intelligent agents through message exchange and satisfies application goals using inserted production rules. This means that general knowledge for an application is represented as a distributed cooperating intelligent agents.

Knowledge sharing (or inheritance) is the main feature of **Smalltalk** [3]. In this scheme, knowledge is shared among classes. A class can be declared as a subclass of another class, called the superclass. The subclass will then inherit the structure and properties of its superclass. The superclass/subclass hierarchy is usually represented as a tree called the inheritance tree.

Smalltalk supports complete unification - all language elements are objects and each object belongs to a particular class. On the one hand the class has its own variables and methods that determines it as object. On the other hand the class has variables and methods that give the characteristics of the instance objects of the class. The class code is shared by all its instances, thus an instance needs a link to its class. The inheritance of variables of a object (class or instance) is static and performed only once when the class is created.

Furthermore, the inheritance of the method dictionary is dynamic. When one activates a method which is not explicitly specified in the definition of the class, the lookup process for the method begins in the method dictionary of the class the object belongs to. Then it propagates along the subclass/superclass hierarchy until the method is found.

The adventures of the **Smalltalk** scheme for knowledge sharing are :

- enables high modularity of the knowledge by general methods sharing;
- classifies the knowledge in hierarchies;
- enables knowledge specialization;
- separates the knowledge in general one (knowledge about the class) and particular one (knowledge about particular instances of the class).

5. Conclusion

Diprotalk project has been implemented as a set of **Smalltalk** stations connected over two different networks: **a 115 KB/second network** and **a 10 MB/second Ethernet**. **Smalltalk** virtual machines and other processes of this implementation are executed on IBM-PC compatible computers.

References

[1] Abbott, R., "Knowledge Abstraction", CACM, August 1987, Vol. 30, Number 8.

[2] Corkill, D., V. Lesser, "The use of meta-level control for coordination in a distributed problem solving network", in Proceeding of IJCAI 8

[3] Goldberg, A., D. Robson, "Smalltalk-80: The Language and Its Implementation", Addison-Wesley, 1983.

[4] Davis, R., R. Smith, "Negotiation as a Methaphor for Distributed Problem Solving", Artificial Intelligence 20, 1983

[5] Petkov, A., Al. Simeonov, "Communication Support for Distributed Object Oriented Systems", Information Systems Problems, Moscow, 1989 (to be published in Russian)

[6] Woo, C., F. Lochovsky, "Supporting Distributed Office Problem Solving in Organizations", ACM Transactions on OIS, Vol 4, No. 3, July 1986

Module concepts and object-oriented features for PROLOG for the interface-specification in modular architectures of advanced knowledge based systems

Jürgen Pitschke

Dresden University of Technology
Center of Informatics
Department of Applied Informatics

Mommsenstraße 13
DRESDEN - DDR 8027

Abstract: The paper deals with the problem of interface specification in an advanced knowledge based system. A complex architecture is introduced. The second part deals with module concepts and object-oriented features for PROLOG. The fitness of these concepts for the interface specification in a complex architecture is discussed. A new object-oriented concept called "channel" is introduced to guarantee the horizontal and vertical structurization of the system.

1. Introduction

One important shortfall of existing knowledge based systems (KBS) is the lack of a complex modular architecture. Most of the existing KBS have a simple internal structure. So they are used in practice only in a small range. An intrinsic growth of the performance is to be expected in the next years by the following causes:

- The functionality of the systems will be enlarged by the integration of various knowledge representation methods and problem solving methods and by the integration of components for the realization of operating system functions (e.g. the external management of parts of the knowledge base).
- Comfortable connections to "classical" software systems will be realized, especially to data base systems.
- The efficiency will be increased by the improvement of current implementations of problem solving methods and the development of new methods.
- Existing systems will be rectified with regard to transparency, extensibility and safety.

In difference to the structure of simple KBS as sketched in /Appelrath 85/ advanced KBS will possess a more complex architecture. First solutions are given by blackboard-architectures, but a general solution hasn't succeeded till now. That's why principle attributes of a architecture of an advanced KBS will postulated in the second chapter. These principles are taken as the base for the implementation of the system ETA-P (see /Petersohn 89/) developed on the Dresden University of Technology.

2. A proposal for a modular architecture of advanced knowledge based systems

An advanced KBS should possess the following attributes:

- The system encloses a big diversity of components, e.g. system components for knowledge representation, for the user interface or for the external management of parts of the knowledge base.
- Especially different knowledge representation methods and problem solving methods should be integrated into the system.
- The user should be able to include his own components and to exclude components not necessary for his purposes. This means the system has to be configurable and extensible.
- The user must be able to encode the specific knowledge and procedures of the area of discourse.
- The communication between the individual components must be realized in a simple and transparent way.
- The system have to handle very large knowledge bases, especially by using data base systems and intelligent strategies for the external management.
- Validation and verification of the knowledge bases and the several system components should be supported.
- Large data sets will be exchanged between several components.
- The system must include a comfortable environment.

It is difficult to realize the properties pointed out within the architecture sketched in /Appelrath 85/. On that account a system architecture must be developed, which is characterized as follows:

- The architecture has a high modularity.
- The system components are independent of other system parts.
- Unique interfaces are organized between the components. So a simple and transparent communication will be possible.
- Name-conflicts should be avoided. It should be possible to select names free within one component.

- Different heterogeneous subsystems must be integrated in the system, particularly components with different internal representation forms.

To reach the listed properties and a high transparency and efficiency a three level architecture was developed for the system ETA-P (see figure 1). This architecture has the following characteristics:

- The system includes various problem solving components.
- The knowledge base is partitioned, caused by using various knowledge representation methods.
- Control components to coordinate the work of the system parts are integrated.
- The system components are assigned to the levels according to their function during the problem solving process (horizontal structurization). So the system consists of the object level, the methods level and the control level.
- The object level contains the whole knowledge base of the system. Different knowledge representation methods for the representation of domain specific knowledge, but also for the representation of system internal knowledge are available.
- The methods level contains all components which operate over the object level. These are e.g. the typical parts of a KBS, as the problem solving component and the knowledge acquisition component. But also components for the realization of operating system functions belong to this level.
- A set of components of the methods level are attached to one knowledge representation method on the object level (vertical structurization).
- The components of the control level coordinate the work of the several components of the methods level according to the state of the problem solving process.
- Every component disposes of a set of procedures, which are only usable within the component, and over a set of procedures, which are also usable by other components.
- The levels form a hierarchy. The control level is the highest level and the object level is the lowest level.
- Every component can only use the own procedures or procedures of the direct superordinated or subordinated level.
- Initially the control level has the control.
- The control level activates one component of the methods level for the solution of a subtask. The activated component searches for a solution and gives the solution (if found) and the control back to the control level. With other words: Between the control level and the methods level subtask management will be realized (see also /van Harmelen 87/).

- If an error (or a crisis) occurs during the problem solving process (e.g. if a needed block of the knowledge base is on the external storage medium) the control will given to the control level. The activated control component activates an other component of the methods level to overcome the error. After this control is given back to the component, where the error occurs, and the work will be continued. In short: Between the methods level and the control level crisis-management will be realized.
- The components of the object level have only declarative character. They posses procedures for adding, deleting or reading of elements of the knowledge base. These procedures are used by the components of the methods level.

For the system ETA-P PROLOG is used as the implementation language. That's why chapter 3 deals with module concepts for PROLOG and discusses their suitability for the specification of unique interfaces between the components in the ETA-P-architecture.

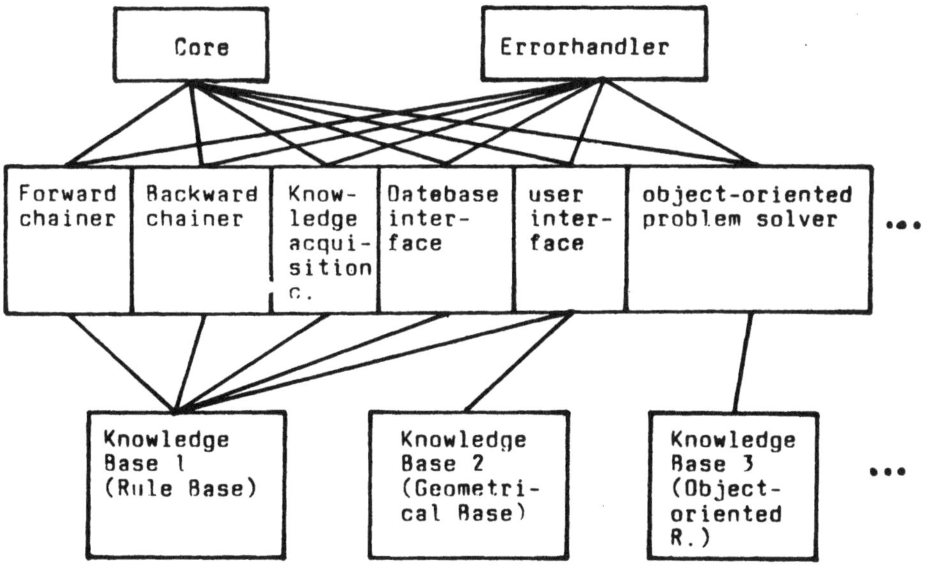

Figure 1: Architecture of a advanced knowledge based system

3. Module concepts for PROLOG and their usage for the interface specification in the ETA-P-architecture

PROLOG contains three basic statements (/Sterling&Shapiro 86/):

- facts
- rules
- goals (queries).

Facts and rules with the same functor (with the same name and the same arity) form a predicate. The only data structure of PROLOG is the logical term. Predicates and terms are named by their functors (name/arity).
A PROLOG-module contains a set of predicates. The predicates have arguments which are terms. Then a program consists of a set of modules and goals. The computation of a goal can include the computation of subgoals in different modules. These subgoals must be known (or visible) in the other module. So it is important to specify which predicates should be known only within one module (invisible to other modules) and which predicates should be known to other modules (visible predicates).
A subset of the terms is equivalent to facts, rules and goals or can be transformed easily to these statements. They can be used as a fact, a rule or a goal. Especially the usage of arguments as goals (meta-call feature) makes it necessary to specify also the visibility of terms (see also /Szeredi 82/).
The interface specification of a PROLOG-module includes definitions of the visibility of predicates and terms. Further the classification of module concepts by Szeredi (see /Szeredi 82/) will be introduced. A detailed discussion and the reflection of other aspects of using modules is to seen in the named paper of Szeredi.
Szeredi distinguishes the following models:

a. The name based model
b. The visible meta-call model
c. The meta-call separation model
d. The hidden information model.

He starts from the following assumptions:

"1. The quoted meta level operations are compatible with the unification (i.e. two most general terms are unifiable if and only if they result in calling the same procedure when used in a meta-call, furthermore the built in procedures for term decomposition and composition will produce unifiable terms if and only if applied to unifiable arguments).

2. Any occurrence of a term in a module can be used as a data-structure or a template for meta-call (or both).

3. It is always possible to make a meta-call to a procedure defined in the same module independently of its visibility properties."

a. The name based model

All three assumptions are valid in the name based model. The visibility of predicates and terms with the same name are always the same. So predicates and terms are not distinguished in the interface specification. If a term with the name 'foo' is declared visible all predicates with the name 'foo' and any arity will also be visible. Are all terms declared visible (e.g. as a standard) all predicates that are meta called are visible automatically. The name based model is used e.g. in micro-PROLOG.

b. The visible meta-call model

In this model assumption 3 is denied. Only predicates which are declared visible can be meta-called. In the interface specification predicates and terms are distinguished. The visible meta-call model is taken as the base of the module concepts of PROLOG-2 and SD-PROLOG. But in PROLOG-2 only the visibility of predicates is specified, while all terms are visible as standard. A predicate is named by it's functor (name/arity). So it is possible to make foo/2 visible whereas foo/1 is invisible. The same holds for SD-PROLOG. In both versions it is possible to make a meta-call to a specified module (with call/2). In this case the called predicate can be invisible but the module name have to be known.

c. The meta-call separation model

For the meta-call separation model the second assumption is dropped. Terms which are used by a meta-call will be distinguished from other terms. Exactly this means that PROLOG becomes a multi-sorted language. A special type of terms will be introduced, which is usable in meta-calls. This makes the semantic of PROLOG more complicated and requires the introduction of special built-in-predicates for handling these type of terms. PROLOG-implementations which use this model are not known.

d. The hidden information model

The first assumption is denied for the hidden information model. Terms can carry some additional information referring to the module they originated from. This additional information isn't used in unification or in the most built-in-predicates. Only the meta level predicates (e.g. call or '=..') can use this information. As in the meta-call separation model the semantic of the programs is more complicated and transparency is lost. Implementations which use this model are not known.

For practical use only the name based model and the visible meta-call model are relevant.
A further difference between various implementations of module concepts for PROLOG consist in a distinction between an import and an export interface specification. The interface specification can consist of the definition which predicates should visible to other modules (which predicates should be exported) and which predicates defined in other modules should be known within the module (which predicates should be imported). This is realized e.g. in micro-PROLOG and SD-PROLOG.
In other versions as in PROLOG-2 the interface specification consists only of the declaration of the predicates which should be visible to other module (the export specification). All visible predicates are automatically known (imported) in any other module. In some cases this can cause an inefficiency.
All models offer some features for the implementation of the ETA-P-architecture. The following problems appear:

- Predicate names of visible predicates can not used in other modules. This means the selection of names within a module is restricted. This is especially a problem if all visible predicates will be imported automatically as in PROLOG-2.
- If it is necessary to specify the visibility of all terms which should be used in different modules, the exchange of large data sets is very difficult. This is the case in micro-PROLOG. Especially it is difficult to exchange terms whose name is known only at runtime.
- The interface between the modules is implicitly realized by the call of predicates. So it is not possible to ensure the hierarchical structure of the architecture.

Especially the last two points avoid the realization of a efficient and transparent architecture. The next chapter shows how the use of object-oriented features and extensions of such features can help to overcome these shortfalls.

4. Object-oriented features for PROLOG

The object-oriented paradigm is shown to be very useful in knowledge representation (/Pitschke 89/). But the object-oriented paradigm offers also many advantages for the realization of operating system functions. These point should discussed in the next chapter. The introduction of new features based on the object-oriented paradigm shows a new way to realize the ETA-P-architecture.
The following object-oriented principles are the starting point:

- The basic unit is the object.
- Every object is characterized by it's internal state and by it's behaviour.
- It is not possible to inspect an object or the internal state of an object from the outside.
- The behaviour will be described by a set of procedures which are called methods.
- The only way to use an object is to send a message. A message consists of the message sign, the name of the object the message is sent to, the name of the method which should be performed and some arguments.
- If an object receives a message it becomes active. It performs one of it's methods according to the received message. In this it can send messages to other objects. This means: The modeled world is described by a set of communicating objects.
- The protocol of an object is characterized by the set of all methods the object can respond to. The object can also own methods which are only usable within the object.

For the implementation of the ETA-P-architecture it is assumed that every module is a object. So it is necessary to implement predicates for creating and changing objects (including the specification of the protocol) and for sending messages with attention to the principles pointed above. Every meta-call will be substituted by a message. The following advantages result:

- It is possible to select names free within one component.
- The interface between the objects (modules) is represented by the message handling routine.
- The transparency of the system will be improved.
- The localization of errors is more easy.
- Configuration and verification of the system can be supported.

The problem of ensuring the hierarchy can not be overcome because every object can send a message to any other object. For this purposes it is necessary to restrict the communication between objects or groups of objects.

One way to fulfill this is to introduce a so called "world concept" as in KEEworlds (/Filman 88/). Sets of objects are grouped together in worlds. The worlds are arranged in a tree structure. Every object can communicate with the objects within the same world or with the objects in a world higher in the tree structure. This means the communication between the objects is restricted according to the (hierarchical) tree structure. It is a comparatively strong restriction that the worlds have to form a tree structure. For example: In ETA-P a set of components of the methods level is assigned to one component of the object level. Every object of the methods level can communicate with different components of the control level. So the tree structure is violated.

That's why a new concept called "channel" is introduced. A channel is a passive object which mediates the communication between two objects. Two objects can only communicate if a channel is created between them. So general message passing between objects is restricted to message passing by channels. A channel represents explicitly the interface between two objects. It is possible to distinguish two cases:

1. The channel is not directed. If a channel exists between a object "A" and a object "B" both objects can pass messages to the other object ("A" to "B" and "B" to "A").

2. The channel is directed. If a channel from object "A" to object "B" is created only object "A" can send a message to object "B" but not vice versa.

It should be possible to create and delete channels between objects at runtime.

The additional advantages of using channels are:

- A channel represents explicitly the interface between two objects. Through attached procedures (demons) and methods it is possible to restrict the communication and to guarantee the horizontal and vertical structurization of the system.
- The efficiency of the system will be improved as theoretical results and a prototypical implementation show. This is caused by the (strong) restriction of the search space.
- A high security is reached.
- The configuration of the system by a (naive) user can be supported by special methods.

A first prototypical implementation of undirected channels is done for SPROLOG. Further practical work has to be done for the implementation of directed channels. Further research work will be done in the field of using object-oriented programming and the ideas of channels for program transformation and for connecting world concepts and channels. The use of the channel concept for other purposes (e.g. for access control) can offer further advantages.

Literature:

/Appelrath 85/ Appelrath, H.J.:
Von Datenbanken zu Expertensystemen,
Springer-Verlag, Berlin, Heidelberg, New York, Tokyo, 1985

/Filman 88/ Filman, R.E.:
Reasoning With Worlds and Truth Maintenance in a Knowledge Based Programming Environment,
CACM, April 1988, volume 31, Nr.4, S.382-401

/Petersohn 89/ Petersohn, U.:
Entwicklungsumgebung und Toolsystem zur Projektierung wissensbasierter Systeme ETA-P,
submitted to IX. Kolloquium "Mensch-Maschine-Dialog", TU Dresden, 1989

/Pitschke 89/ Pitschke, J.:
Entwicklung und Anwendung einer objekt-orientierten Erweiterung von PROLOG - OPE,
TU Dresden, appears 1989

/Sterling&Shapiro 86/
Sterling, L.; Shapiro, E.:
The Art of PROLOG,
MIT Press, Cambridge Ma.,London, 1986

/Szeredi 82/ Szeredi, P.:
Module concepts for PROLOG,
in MPROLOG Collection of papers on logic programming, SZKI, Budapest, 1988

/van Harmelen 87/ van Harmelen, F.:
A categorisation of meta-level architectures,
DAI Research Paper No. 297, Department of Artificial Intelligence, University of Edinburgh, 1987

NEWTON: An Intelligent Training System for Differential Calculus

M. Prieto, G. Loret de Mola, T. Guerra, L. Pacios
Department of Computer Science, University of Havana

Introduction

The application of intelligent tutoring systems (ITS) to the developing of skills and the removement of bugs in mathematical knowledge has been our main goal for years. The Newton system is one of the first results of our group in this context. Created as a single terminal-single user. Prolog-based software; with a very straight modularity, it contains all the classical modules of an ITS, namely:

- an interface, with graphics and natural-like language facilities;
- a matter expertise, which contains all the knowledge expressed as rules and the entire definition of Algebra and Trigonometry;
- a student model, where student behaviour in solving any given task is simulated including those mechanisms for dealing with uncertainty;
- a stage of knowledge model, provided with external storage of historical records of every student;
- a coach, which decides, creates and explains concepts, theorems, tasks, etc, with a given complexity degree.

A detailed explanation of different system components will be given with some applied techniques wich allow to accomplish important tasks.

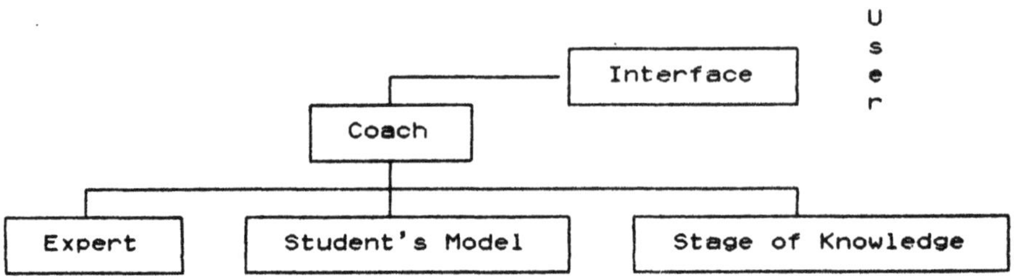

Figure 1. Structure of NEWTON

The Interface

The goal of interface is to understand student's intentions or answers and to perform such actions as showing graphical sequences about theorems proofs. By mean of its graphics tools the user can write functional expressions on the screen in the same way he does on paper. It means he can write $\frac{sin(x)}{x}$ instead of sin(x)^2/x. The answers of the system are produced in the same way. To achieve this goal we have used a tree structure to store the hierarchy of the operands. Later on a parentized form is produced from wich the linear form could be derivated. Through this process backwards we transform the linear form in The so called two-dimensional form (2D-form). To speed up the transformation we used some compilation-like techniques. On the other hand, to process natural-like language, we must analyse the syntactical structure of the statements. Once all components are recognized, we proceed searching keywords which implies the system must perform some actions, i.e. generation of an exercise. This recognition is supported by a Definite Clause Grammar, which brings more flexiblility in dialog. In any way we work only on a subset of natural language and we eliminate, through a chain of questions, the potential vagueness in student's answers. At the beginning of a given task this module should catch the information showed in following graph:

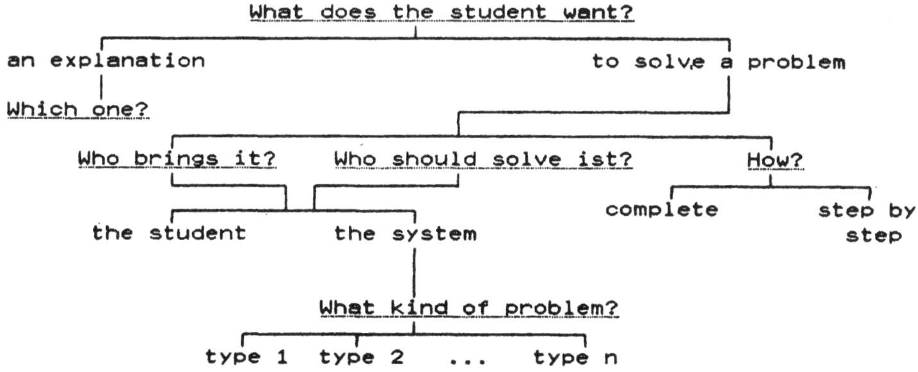

Once the problem is completely characterized the next modules could be activated.

The Expert

The system s knowledge base is the expert module. All the knowledge about the matter must be stored as rules. In our particular case it begins with differentiation rules. To express this knowledge by rules is not a very difficult work.

```
  deriv(1,X,X,1).
  .......
  deriv(10,X+Y,Z,W) :- deriv(N,X,Z,X1),deriv(M,Y,Z,Y1),
                       simplif(X1+Y1,W).
  .......
  deriv(20,sin(X),cos(X)).
 .......
deriv(31,X,Y,0).
```

Figure 2. Some differentiation rules from NEWTON's expert

Rules for the manipulation of algebraic and trigonometrical expressions also belong to this module, thus the results of calculations may be simplified. We considered the generation of exercises in this module too. Then, exercises will be generated just only to be solved; and solving exercises in this particular case always involves derivatives calculation. Thus it is useful to have both mechanisms in the same memory segment at execution time. Conceiving a simplification strategy for symbolical expressions is one of the hardest tasks in this step. Symbolical simplification could be very time expensive, because of the amount of particular cases that can arise. For this reason there must be sometimes a cut decision in simplification process. With a trial and error method we have designed a symbolical simplifier conjugating time and memory needs. It was the hardest part of system programming.

```
simplif(X+Y,Z)  :- simplif_sum(X,Y,Z).
.......
simplif_sum(X,Y,Z)  :- number(X),number(Y),Z is X+Y.
simplif_sum(X,Y,Z)  :- number(X),express(Y),Z = Y + X.
```

Figure 3. Structure for simplification rules

The Student Model

For simulating the student's behaviour in solving a particular task, an ITS needs a student model. We choose Sleeman's Configuration System [1]. This model needs not only the right rules from the expert but also "wrong rules", which must be incorporated to the expert too. These wrong rules represent in our case common bugs detected in derivatives calculation by human expert tutors. The differentiation rules from the knowledge base could be interpreted as a procedure to calculate a derivativ for a particular type of functions. So we can have for every of these rules so many wrong rules as wrong procedures to do this calculation. So there exists a relationship between a differentiation rule and its wrong rules. We emphasize that only rules that represent tasks to be solved by the student are considered to generate wrong rules.

```
deriv(11,X*Y,Z,W)   :- deriv(N,X.Z,X1),deriv(M,Y,Z,Y1),
                       simplif(1*Y+*Y1,W).
mderiv(110,X+Y,Z,W) :-  deriv(N,X,Z,X1),deriv(M,Y.Z.Y1),
                        simplif(X1*Y1,W).
```

Figure 4. An example of a rule and one of its wrong rules

The steps performed by the system to solve a problem are considered the ideal behaviour. The debugging process is based on the comparison of student's and ideal behaviour. When the student's result agrees with the one from the system, it could be assumed that he chooses the ideal way to solve the task. Otherwise the error scanning predicate must be activated. It begins with the generation of configurations. A configuration is a sequence of

rules (right or wrong). The application of this sequence to one specific task gives one specific result. For us are relevant all those configurations which produce the same result as the student's one. To avoid the analysis of all possible configurations, we introduced some modifications in Sleeman's model. Starting from the ideal configuration (supplied by the expert) we consider new ones, where one right rule is substituted by one of the wrong rules associated to it. If the error hasn't been cought yet, the process is repeated with two-rule substitution.
If only one configuration is capable of leading us to the student's answer, we assume it was the one followed by him. If there are several configurations we must select one of them. The choice is made on the basis of a probabilistic system and combination rule designed ad hoc [3], different from all commonly used systems (Bayesian, MYCIN, Dempster-Shafer, etc).
The basical idea is to assign to every rule in the knowledge base a weight. These weights represent how probable is the choice of any rule. On the other hand we have designed a combination rule for the weights of the rules in a configuration. It takes in account the position of the rule in the invocation tree.
Finally we will have whether a configuration (containing a wrong rule) or none. In the later we assume we have a configuration beginning with a wrong rule. The next step is to start the bugs-removing algorithm. It begins at the point where the first error was detected, and it tries to remove the bug through a sequence of questions.

The Stage of Knowledge Model

All the information about a particular student and his work with the system is stored in this module. It is conceived as a frame with fix slots in the sense of Minsky. The total number of sessions and exercises, the number of correctly solved, of times he needed to apply a given type of rule, and the number of times he took the right (wrong) one, etc, are stored. These all are important data for the chracterization of a given student.
This information is a big help to optimize the generation of configurations, it can vary the probability distributions defined

over the rules for duality cases, and based on it the development of a given student could be evaluated. To keep this information appart from the system body, it has been stored on an external medium. One file on disk corresponds to one student, so there are no restrictions imposed by our system regarding the number of students that could be controlled.
This module constitutes the basis of the intelligence of the system. It consists of the learning possibilities of the system from student's behaviour and it's ability to handle him in a different way, depending on the results obtained in early sessions and tasks.

The Coach

The management of the system must be made in accordance with certain pedagogical criteria. To decide teaching strategies, deepness of explanations, etc, are very complex problems. We have attempted to express some teaching strategies in form of rules and have actually obtained 6 different coaching strategies. This are activated directly by the student in the way he choses how the system should give it's answers. One of them includes the Sleeman's model for the case the student wants to solve himself a task.
To obtain a detailed information about the work of the student at any moment, a lot of meta-programming is done. The main goal was to obtain all the subtasks from the one the student should solve. This allowed us to perform a step by step simulation of a solving algorithm, and to generate detailed explanations about the problem.

Conclusions

The construction of ITS in more complex knowledge domains, demands the creation of generic tools for a number of modules, except the expert. It is the same idea as a shell for an expert system. Some of the here described modules are conceived in this way (interface, stage of knowledge, coach), while other must be reformulate. Our goal for the next two years is to build an Intelligent Training System Development Tool. With such a tool a

user would be able to build his own application on some expert domain.
This system runs on IBM-XT or compatibles with at least 256 Kb RAM under MS-DOS 3.10 (or later).

References

[1] D. Sleeman and J. S. Brown: Intelligent Tutoring Systems, Academic Press:New York, 1982
[2] D. Servan-Schreiber: From Intelligent Tutoring to Computerized Psychotherapy, IJCAI-1987 Proceedings, pp.66-71.
[3] Loret de Mola: Tratamiento de la Incertidumbre en Sistemas Tutoriales Inteligentes, Consideraciones sobre la Construccion de Entrenadores Basados en Sistemas Expertos, Direccion Docente Metodologica, UH, monografia.
[4] Loret de Mola: EXALGEBR: Un instrumento para la manipulacion del algebra y la trigonometria, idem.
[5] K. Swigger, H. Burns, . Loveland, T. Jackson: An Intelligent Tutoring System for Interpreting Ground Tracks, IJCAI-1987 Proceedings, pp.72-76.

KNOWLEDGE BASED USER GUIDANCE IN A STATISTICAL PACKAGE FOR TESTING BIVARIATE DEPENDENCE

Egmar Rödel, Robert Wilke

Humboldt University
Computational Centre
P.O.B. 1297
Berlin - DDR 1086

Summary.

An expert system for the choice of appropriate tests of independence in bivariate distributions is presented. This choice depends upon user inputs on the type of the underlying bivariate distribution, on the character of the observed data and on the alternative hypothesis to test against independence.
The knowledge base consists of if-then relations and has been implemented by a PROLOG-program. Additionally we have tested the knowledge base with some shells.
Interfaces for data input and numerical processing of the selected tests are in preparation.

Zusammenfassung.

Ein Expertensystem für die Auswahl geeigneter Unabhängigkeitstests in zweidimensionalen Verteilungen wird vorgestellt. Diese Auswahl erfolgt in Abhängigkeit von Angaben des Nutzers über den Typ der zugrundeliegenden Verteilung, den Charakter der Beobachtungsdaten und die Alternativhypothese, die gegen Unabhängigkeit getestet werden soll.
Die Wissensbasis besteht aus if-then-Beziehungen und wurde durch ein PROLOG-Programm realisiert. Zusätzlich wurde sie mit einigen Shells getestet.
Schnittstellen für die Dateneingabe und die numerische Durchführung der ausgewählten Testverfahren werden vorbereitet.

I. EXPERT SYSTEMS IN STATISTICS.

Statistical analyses are needed in many fields of scientific research and production. They have a rate of about 60% of all mathematical applications.

But only few users of statistical methods are able to select the correct statistical procedures in all situations.

Also the standard packages of statistics do not contain in detail all necessary models in order to solve sufficiently all statistical problems.

The construction of expert systems in statistics has the following aims,

- to help in selection and application of statistical methods in special fields of statistics,
- to provide rare special knowledge and ability to solve statistical problems,
- to avoid severe errors in handling statistical models and procedures,
- to aid the interpretation of the results .

There are many approaches to implement expert systems in statistics [Gale (1985)].

On the other hand, only few really existing systems are known. Most of them do not use methods of artificial intelligence, but they work by conventional programmes [Streitberg (1988)].

Our first approach to construct an expert system is the following.

The system contains two main components,

- a guidance component for model and method selection written in PROLOG

and

- a progamme package of statistical procedures written in FORTRAN and PASCAL.

The first component yields a list of appropriate methods with weights of their correctness based on user inputs to the system. The default is to process the method with the highest weight. But the user has the option to start another procedure of the list by cursor motion.

This approach is only implementable for subfields of statistics. Our knowledge base and statistical procedures are concentrated on " Testing Bivariate Dependencies between Random Variables ", i.e. on the detection of interactions between random variables.

The spectrum of possible users reaches from beginners with elementary knowledge to highly qualified statisticians.

II. THE GUIDANCE SYSTEM.

The guidance system consists of three components:

1. The "Knowledge Base" -
   a Rule System, giving the relations between

Facts (user s information on properties of his statistical data , e.g. continuity , distribution assumptions and so on)

and the weight of Choices (that means the degree of applicability of the statistical procedures for processing the user data).

2. The "Knowledge Acquisition Component" – at the start of the system, the knowledge on facts is empty.

3. The "Dialogue Component" – prompting the user by means of windows to input the facts, and finally giving him the decision of the system, that is, an overview of the appropriate statistical procedures with their computed weights.

   The procedure selected by the user is then called via the COMMAND interface of the PROLOG interpreter.

(4.) An explanation component is not (yet) included.

The rule system represents the real "Expert Knowledge".

It contains relations between the data type, the underlying bivariate distribution and the alternative hypotheses and rules between them and statistical procedures for testing independence.

The structure of rules becomes clear by the following examples.

```
value(correlation_coefficient,10) :-
                          data(continuous),
                          distribution(normal),
                          hypothesis(dependence_in_any_sense).

data(continuous) :-
    distribution(normal),
    not(data(bivariate_ranks_of_cont_distributed_sample_points)),
    not(data(dichotomized)).
```

Thereby the weights have values from zero to ten, where zero and ten mean absolutely false and absolutely correct, respectively. If a test procedure has been derived more than once then the resulting weight equals the average of weights, but the extreme weights 0 and 10 are not changed.

Our system at present contains 58 rules and gives correct answers in all cases tested so far.

All of these rules are static, i.e. they do not include variables, but only atomic parameters.

Also, except for a list of all possible choices,

```
choice(C) :- (C=1;C=2;...);true.
```

there is no rule with fixed right side, i.e., we have no facts.

The goal of the guidance system is then simply

```
goal :- init,choice(C),value(C,V),result(C,V),fail.
```

By successive instantiation of the variables the system reaches a state where facts will be needed in order to find nontrivial solutions.

For that reason rules are added at the end of the knowledge base in order to guarantee knowledge acquisition. They consist of predicates with same names as the rules of the Expert Knowledge, but the parameters are variables.

The user will be prompted via the dialogue/window system to input the facts, e.g. his knowledge on the data types. The user input is tranformed to PROLOG facts, i.e. rules with right sides of the form "!" or "!,false", respectively, and added to the rule system.

These new rules are located between the "Expert" rules and the "Acquisition" rules.

If the user input is done, the acquisition is cut off by including a catch rule.

The rule system before input:

```
            .
            .
data(mixed) :- data(binary),                          knowledge
               data(continuous).
            .
data(X) :- ...,(dialogue(data_type),
                add_facts(data_type));               acquisition
               add_catch(data_type),
               data(X).
```

The rule system after input "data type: continuous" :

```
            .
            .
data(mixed) :- data(binary),                          knowledge
               data(continuous).
            .
data(continuous) :- !.                                input fact
data(Y) :- !,false.                                   catch rule

data(X) :- ...,(dialogue(data_type),                 acquisition
                add_facts(data_type));                (cut off)
               add_catch(data_type),
               data(X).
```

All possible choices and their weights will be "computed" by backtracking the goal and the choice rule, respectively.

Because of the fact that the knowledge rules are "static", the same technique of memoisation as for the user input is used for storing intermediate results as facts, in order to avoid repeated execution of such rules, which will not change their result after user input is done.

III. CONCLUDING REMARKS.

It is remarkable that during the construction of the knowledge base we found several gaps in existing statistical procedures.

E.g., we could not find numerical procedures for testing independence in the very important classes of exponential and gamma-distributions.

Theoretically and practically we must introduce various adaptive procedures for all situations where the underlying distribution of the observed data is unknown.

For instance, the standard situation in practice is uncertainty on the underlying probability distribution of the observed data.

We have implemented so-called adaptive procedures for such cases. These procedures automatically approximate the test known as optimal from the viewpoint of Mathematical Statistics.

The use of expert system shells is efficient in our opinion only for a first check of the knowledge base.

The implementation of suitable user interfaces, of programs for data input and data control, for the numerical calculation of statistical procedures and for the interpretation of their results is easier done in the frame of self-tailored programs.

Our inference engine is now a PROLOG program putting into practice our ideas on the process of the "statistical dialogue".

Some difficulties occuring in connecting commercial shells and user programs have been avoided in this way.

In the future we aim to develop a third component of the system, namely an interpreter of the results using graphical output.

IV. ENVIRONMENT.

The program is running under MS/DOS. At least 350k main storage and hard disk is recommended.

The numerical routines are being written in FORTRAN 77 and PASCAL.

The data input is performed via ASCII files and will be extended to other usual file types.

V. REFERENCES.

Büning, H.; Trenkler, G. (1978).
Nichtparametrische statistische Methoden.
De Gruyter, Berlin.

Gale, W.G. (1985).
Preliminary Papers of the Workshop on Artificial Intelligence and Statistics.
Princeton.

Hájek, J.; Sidak, Z. (1967).
Theory of Linear Rank Tests.
Academia, Prague.

Mardia, K.V. (1970).
Families of Bivariate Distributions.
Griffin, London.

Rödel, E. (1988).
Expertensyteme für die Anwendung der Mathematischen Statistik.
Schriftenreihe " Informationsverarbeitung im Hoch- und Fachschulwesen ", Heft 2, Teil 5.

Rödel, E. (1989).
Linear Rank Tests with Estimated Scores for Testing Independence.
To appear in statistics 20 xx -xx.

Streitberg, B. (1989).
On the Nonexistence of Expert Systems. Critical Remarks on Artificial Intelligence in Statistics.
Statistical Software Newsletter 14(2), pp 55-62.

DISTRIBUTED TRANSACTION MANAGEMENT: ANALYSIS TROUGH DISTRIBUTED SIMULATION

Elen K. Stancheva

Institute of Mathematics
Bulgarian Academy of Sciences
G. Bonchev Str., 8 - Sofia 1113, Bulgaria

Abstract. An idea is proposed to apply distributed discrete-event simulation to the functional and performance analyses of distributed database systems. The presented approach can be conformed to the design of some other distributed systems as well. The accepted notion of distributed simulation includes the Chandy-Misra-Bryant approach. A major concern of the study is the potentiality of the distributed discrete event simulation to the analysis of such distributed systems whose degree of inherent parallelism is high enough to be embedded into the simulation system. The distributed database systems are considered an appropriate representative of such systems. The reason is that the sites always have autonomous processing capabilities. A performance and a simulation models and a corresponding distribution algorithm have been developed. They capture, in a distributed environment, the functioning of concurrency control and recovery mechanisms, and the local database processings, i.e., the processing, storage, and communication resorces of the whole distributed database system. The approach also favours the simultaneous consideration of several database design stages in the system performance measurement.

1. INTRODUCTION

During the last several years there has been an increasing interest in the homogeneous and heterogeneous distributed database systems, as well as systems applying mixed technologies, including the technology of the distributed databases [Ceri84]. In designing such systems, a concurrency control and a recovery mechanism must be selected from the field of candidates. The decisive criterion for choosing a combination of particular algorithms is their individual and integrated performance. Unfortunately, the importance of this issue is not supported by analogous advances in research.

In the studies on quantitative analysis of the performance of single concurrency control and recovery mechanisms analytical modelling and/or simulation are usually applied under limited operating conditions [Garc78, Lin81]. Such performance studies are very difficult to compare. They make use of different assumptions about the application environments, and different measures for system performance. Moreover, the interference of the adopted different purpose algorithms is neglected, as it makes the models too complex to be workable.

The idea we propose is to apply distributed discrete event simulation (DDS) to the design analysis of distributed database management systems (DDMSs).

Our notion of distributed simulation includes the Chandy–Misra–Bryant approach. We study the applicability of DDS to the design analysis of distributed database systems. Our approach includes a conformation of distributed simulation algorithms with a proved correctness. The presented experiments are based on the Basic distribution algorithm of Chandy, Misra and Bryant with null masseges for deadlock avoidance. We present an integrated algorithm for DDS of some of the well–known transaction management techniques, namely the basic 2–phase–commitment protocol (for recovery) and the basic timestamp mechanism with prewrites (for concurrency control). In the same way, versions of the 2–phase–commitment protocol for different communication structures, and versions of other concurrency control, as well as deadlock detection and resolution algorithms can be developed. The approach is also applicable to the different techniques which have been proposed in the research literature but have not been implemented in real systems. It is not clear how such techniques perform and how they affect each other. Therefore, a performance evaluation could also be reasonable.

To the author's knowledge, there are not any reported works on the application of distributed simulation to the design analysis of DDMSs.

The paper includes two main sections devoted to: distributed simulation, and performance evaluation of distributed transaction management.

2. DISTRIBUTED DISCRETE EVENT SIMULATION:

All the classical discrete–event simulation techniques suffer from a common drawback: there is a strong limitation on the duration and size of such simulation when executed on a single processor configuration. It is widely recognized that the only way out of this situation is to use distributed discrete event simulation techniques on a shared memory multiprocessor or on a network of processors.

The first ideas of distributed simulation were proposed by Chandy [Chan79a] and independently by Bryant [Brya77]. The approaches differ mainly in the memory requirements and the deadlock considerations.

Not many studies in this field have appeared in the literature. Most of them adopt the process view of simulation [Chan79a, Peac79, Jeff85, Bezi87]: a system being simulated is assumed to consist of a finite number of physical processes, which interact at discrete instants of time. The process interactions are called events and the time instants at which they occur, event times. Each physical process of the system is simulated by a logical process. Events appear to happen in a consistent order at all processes in the system, even though they may not physically be executed in that order. The simulation system consists of a finite number of logical processes and directed channels connecting some pairs of them. Communication is permitted only by passing messages between processes; in the messages the physical time and the event type are encoded; each process maintains its clock; different clocks are associated with the channels which move forward in an asynchronous manner.

Most of the algorithms that have appeared in the literature employ this classical Chandy–Misra–Bryant scheme, and they differ mainly in the way of deadlock resolution. For the purposes of the study a distribution simulation scheme is necessary to be adopted and conformed. We have considered reasonable to start with the Basic distribution simulation algorithm [Chan79a, Misr86], described below. The correctness proof of the algorithm and of its variant with null messages, for deadlock avoidance, are provided by Misra in [Misr86]. The proof that there is no deadlocks in the situation is essentially contained in [Chan79b]. The same results hold if the buffers are not unbounded. The buffer spaces can be decreased by introducing annihilation rules. The number of the sent null message could be limited if null messages are transmitted after a proper time–out.

Basic distribution simulation algorithm: Consider n logical processes $p_1, p_2, \ldots, p_n$ simulating the behaviour of n physical processes $P_1, P_2, \ldots, P_n$, respectively. A channel c_{ij} exists from P_i to P_j if P_i can send messages to P_j. p_i can simulate P_i up to time t if it knows the initial state and all the messages that the P_i is to receive up to time t. If message m is sent by P_i to P_j at time t, message (t, m) has to be sent by p_i to p_j at some point during simulation. If p_i sends a sequence of messages to another p_j, a requirement the time component to increase is stated. The channel clock value of a channel c_{ij} is the t component of the last message received along that channel; the channel clock value is 0 if no message has been received along that channel. The clock value of p_i is the value $T_i = min_j\{t_j\}$, where t_j's are the channel clock values of all incoming channels to p_i. If p_i has no incoming channels, it is the source process; if p_i only receives messages without affecting the simulation, it is the sink process. Null message (t, null) is sent by p_i to p_j when P_i sends no message to P_j between the current c_{ij} clock value and t.

The scheme is the following: ***whenever p_i receives a message it properly updates T_i, and if T_i changes in value, then p_i advances the simulation of P_i to T_i. At this point p_i predicts for each outgoing channel a sequence of messages that P_i would have sent.***

3. PERFORMANCE ANALYSIS OF DISTRIBUTED TRANSACTION MANAGEMENT

We consider the subject of distributed simulation of DDMS performance. In the case of a high degree of site autonomy, i.e., a degree of parallelism high enough to be embedded in the simulation model [Stan89a], we are interested in whether the physical system performance would lend itself to DDS.

In designing a distributed database system, distributed transaction algorithms must be selected from the field of the candidates. The decisive criterion for choosing a particular algorithm is its performance. Some researchers have attempted performance studies of different concurrency control algorithms using analitical modelling and simulation [Garc78, Lin81, Than88]. These and other authors comment on the difficulties to compare such studies and to generalize the results, because different algorithms are compared, different assumptions about system and application environments are used, different measures for system performance are applied.

Most of the performance studies consider and compare techniques based on 2–phase–locking. Very few researchers have attempted to study the performance of timestamp–based concurrency control algorithms and to compare their performance with that of the 2–phase–locking algorithm. The presence of recovery algorithms heavily affects the DDMS performance and, for that reason, is also avoided. Assuming the presence of a recovery algorithm together with a concurrency control makes the transaction processing model too complex to be adequately comprehended with analitical or conventional simulation tools.

To comprise the performance of different concurrency control and recovery mechanisms and the overall structure of a DDMS, we experiment on applying DDS methods to the distributed transaction management.

3.1. The performance model

A reference architecture of DDMSs. Consider a DDMS to consists of a collection of n sites $S_1, S_2, \ldots, S_n$ connected by a communication network and communicating by sending messages. Each site consists of a computer running both, a Transaction Manager (TM), and a Data Manager (DM). The Transaction Manager coordinates the execution of the transactions. The Data Manager manages a local database. There are a finite number of transactions, issued from the site terminals and running on the overall distributed database. A transaction presents a resource request to the TM in the form of a sequence of read and write operations and special messages. A resource request can be local, i.e. served by the local DM, or can refer to a resource at another site, in which case the transaction is distributed and the local TM is responsible for its distributed perfornance by communicating with the corresponding DMs. Neither TMs not DMs intercommunicate.

The architecture of the system model resembles that of SDD-1 and some other DDMSs [Roth80].

Concurrency control and recovery mechanisms. As was already mentioned, the application of recovery algorithm together with a chosen concurrency one makes the processing model rather complex to be workable. But we are interested in the potential of the proposed DDS tools, that is why we include them both in the performance model.

The synchronization of the operations among the sites, to avoid explicit conflicts between concurrent operations, may be performed by such techniques as: 2-phase-locking, timestamps, optimistic methods [Ceri84]. Consider chosen the timestamp mechanism with prewrites, controlling the concurrency of transactions, for the model under description. With this method a unique timestamp is assigned to each transaction at the time of its creation. Each resource data item carries the timestamp of the last transaction, which read and wrote it. When a transaction attempts to read or write a data item about a resource, the DM compares the timestamp of the resource item with that of the transaction. In the case of a read operation, the timestamp of the transaction must be greater than the write timestamp of the data item, if the order of the timestamps is to remain a valid serialization order. In a write operation, the timestamp of the transaction must be greater than the read timestamp of the data item , for read-write synchronization, and greater than the write timestamp, for write-write synchronization. For all other cases, the operation is rejected and the transaction will be restarted.

A version of this mechanism applies "prewrites", i.e., the write operations are buffered and not applied directly to the database, before the transaction is committed.

The correct commitment of a distributed transaction requires that all its local representatives (local transactions) commit locally even in the case of failures. It is not acceptable that a subtransaction is locally aborted because of a failure and the other subtransactions commit. For allowing the return to normal operation of a distributed system after a failure, different recovery algorithms have been proposed

Suppose the classical 2-phase-commitment protocol is also chosen, i.e., there is one process, which has a special role for the final commit or abort decision, called coordinator, and other processes, participants, which must commit together and are responsible for performing the write actions at its local database. The basic idea of the protocol is to determine a unique decision for all participants with respect to commiting or aborting all the local transactions. If a participant is unable to locally commit, then all participants must locally abort. The first phase of the protocol is reaching a common decision. The second phase is implementation of the decision.

We choose the mentioned mechanisms for the performance model under development, but it is possible other versions of the two-phase commitment protocol, as well as different concurrency control mechanisms to be simulated in a similar manner.

Model parameters. Typical groups of parameters which can be considered in the model are: communication parameters (concerned with the concurrency control and recovery mechanisms, and deadlock resolution); application parameters (request type, average local processing time, degree of interference, transaction size, average interarrival time of transactions, maximum number of transactions running concurrently, etc.); network parameters (number of nodes, type of communication, network transmission time, etc.).

3.2. The simulation model

The structure of the site processes. A DDMS can be modelled as a collection of n site processes $s_1, s_2, \ldots, s_n$ running in parallel on the different sites and communicating through messages. Each site process s_i, representing a site S_i, consists of internal processes, such as: the input and output interface processes (ip_i and op_i); transaction manager process (tm_i); data manager process (dm_i); transaction generation process (tg_i) and transaction sink process (ts_i) (Fig. 1.). All of them include statistics collection for the corresponding internal processes.

The physical processes inside the sites can be simulated by conventional dicrete–event simulation techniques. For the site communication simulation we propose that DDS method be applied.

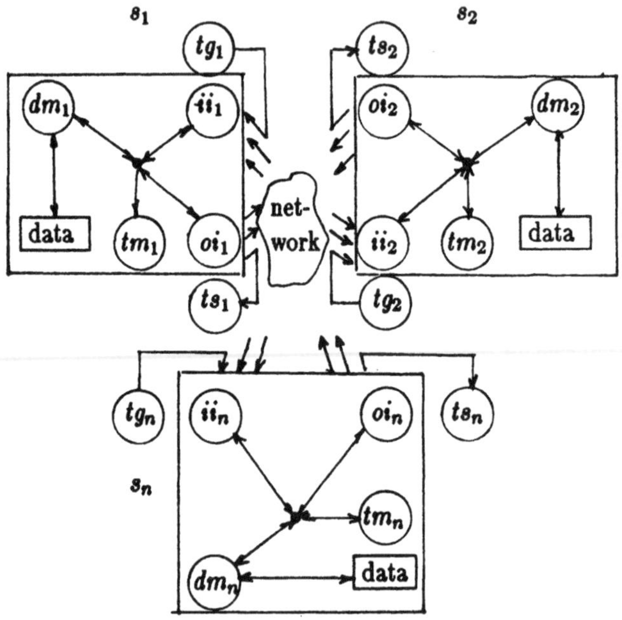

Fig. 1. *Site processes model*

The performance simulation algorithm. To simulate the described environment we choose to conform the Basic distribution simulation algorithm, with null messages for deadlock avoidance.

The scheme for the distributed simulation of the transaction management in the simulated system can be presented as a distributed algorithm.

```
/*   Si local subsystem process, i = 1,2,...,n   */
/* si corresponding logical process; Ti clock value of si */
Ti := 0;
prepare NULL messages to be sent along the output channels;
input local simulation data for the purposes of tgi;
while simulation completion criterion is not met do
/* simulation of Si up to Ti */
   prepare for each outgoing channel a sequence of messages for sending;
   send the messages whose times has come;
/* receive messages and update Ti until changes value */
   Ti' := Ti;
   while Ti' = Ti do
      wait to receive messages along all incoming channels into si buffers;
      update Ti, the minimum over all incoming channel clock values;
      upon accepting of a message, add it to the list of events;
/* si plays "participant" in the basic 2PC protocol */
      if the message is READ then
         dmi applies the timestamp mechanism with prewrites and READY or ABORT
         messages are prepared to be sent, or the request is simulated buffered in dmi until
         the timestamp conditions allow READY message to be prepared to be sent in reply;
      else if the message is PREPARE then
         dmi applies the timestamp mechanism with prewrites and according to the result the
         request is simulated rejected (ABORT message is prepared to be sent), or buffered
         (READY message is prepared to be sent);
      else if the message is COMMIT command then
         dmi converts the buffered prewrite operation into a write operation, and application
         to the database is simulated (ACK message is prepared to be sent back), or the
         operation is kept on simulating buffered until the timestamp condition sets in and
         ACK message may be prepared to be sent;
      else if the message is ABORT command then
         dmi simulates clearing up the buffer space from the corresponding operation and
         ACK message is prepared to be sent;
/* si plays "coordinator" in the basic 2PC protocol */
      else if the message is ABORT, or the coordinator's timeout expired then
         tmi prepares ABORT command message to be sent along all the participants' chan-
         nels;
      else if the message is READY then
         according to the responses of the rest participants, tmi prepares ABORT or COM-
         MIT command message to be sent along the participants channels;
      else if the message is ACK then
         tmi considers the rest participants' responses and prepares COMPLETE or FAIL_-
         COMPLETE messages to be sent to tsi;
      else if the message is from the tgi then
         a timestamp is attached to it (the value of the current Ti), and according to the
         event type (local or global request) it is sent to dmi or tmi, and PREPARE message
         is prepared to be sent along the participants' channels;
      else /* the message is a NULL one */
   endwhile
endwhile
consider the model validation;
output the simulation results;
```

Fig. 2. *Distribution algorithm for a site process S_i*

Consider the simulation of the site process S_i. At the initialization phase, the corresponding logical process s_i inputs the local simulation parameters. In the main simulation phase s_i

prepares for each outgoing channel sequences of messages (at the beginning, null ones), to be sent when their times comes. After that s_i waits to obtain messages along all incoming channels; updates its clock value T_i; accepts a message; advances the simulation of S_i up to T_i. The dm_i applies the timestamp mechanism and controls the concurrency of the operations, when the message comes from a coordinator process; the tm_i controls the execution of the subtransactions in two-phase commitment mode, if s_i is a coordinator process itself. When the message comes from the local *tg* process, the execution is controlled by dm_i or tm_i (for local and remote data processings, respectively). At the point when T_i changes in value, for each outgoing channel a sequence of messages that S_i would have sent is prepared, and the messages are sent at their times. When the simulation completion criterion met, a validation test can be performed and all the results are released.

Distributed simulation algorithm for a subsytem process S_i is presented (in a pseudo-code) in Fig. 2. It is clearly seen that the simulation of other concurrency control mechanisms (for instance, 2-phase-locking instead of timestamp mechanisms) together with the whole system functioning, does not changes the algoritm. It is enough to change the corresponding local process module (*dm*, in the case). By changing the *tg* process module different application needs and politics can be expressed.

Simulation parameters. The simulation model permits parameters describing the transactions, site processes, network, recovery and concurrency control mechanisms, communication structure, etc., to be considered.

3.3. Simulation of different communication structures

Models corresponding to different communication structures, linear, centralized, hierarchical, and irregular, may be developed with the same tools, provided that, appropriate synchronization mechanisms are chosen and simulated in a manner similar to the exposed in Fig. 2.

3.4. Deadlock considerations

We have chosen a distributed simulation technique that avoids deadlocks, using null messages. Nevertheless deadlocks may occur, because of the simulated control mechanisms, or because of real or simulated hardware failures. Corresponding deadlock-resolution simulation algorithms, developed in the demonstrated way, can distinguish and process them in an appropriate manner.

4. CONCLUSIONS AND FUTURE WORK

It has been shown how recovery and concurrency control techniques could be modelled together in a distributed environment, capturing the processing, storage, and communication resources of the whole system, for the purposes of DDMS performance evaluation. A performance and a simululation models have been developed, as well as a reference distribution algorithm, obtained by conformation of an existing distributed simulation method. The same approach holds if other deadlock free DDS methods are embedded. Other transaction management mechanisms can be simulated only by replacing *dm* and *tm* modules with new ones from a local library. Different local simulation conditions can be applied only by changing the *tg* process module.

We plan to continue our study towards the distributed simulation of distributed database systems with a low site autonomy, and to regulate the application of the different DDS approaches by a cost-effective analvsis, based on quantitative measures for the inherent parallelism.

It is essential to note, that decisions on the rest DDMS design stages (not only on distributed transaction management) can be included in the system performance. No other approach can provide a possibility for performance studies of the integration of some or all DDMS design stages.

The observations being in the paper can have practical importance in developing adequate tools in the performance measurement of different types of distributed applications [Stan89].

The research reported here is a part of a more extensive study aimed at supplying quantitative indications of the effects and impact of concurrency control mechanisms on DDMS performance. A distributed simulation system is under development, but is still at an early stage to be reported. It is being developed as a system engineering tool for the design of distributed system. A main aspect in the architecture organization is the development of libraries for local use, with software modules containing: 1) different versions of the distributed control units, corresponding to different communication stuctures, and 2) distributed control techniques, for which it is supposed to be of interest for quantitative studies.

REFERENCES

[Bezi88] Bezivin, J. 1988. "An Evaluation Environment for Concurrent Object-Oriented Simulation." In *Proceedings of the 1988 Distributed Simulation Conference* (San Diego, CA, Feb. 3-5). SCS, San Diego, CA, 149-153.

[Brya77] Bryant, R.E. 1977. "Simulation of Packet Communication Architecture Computer System." Technical Report MIT/LCS/TR-188, Massachusetts Tech, Cambridge, MA (Nov.).

[Cery84] Ceri, S.; and G. Pelagatti. 1984. *Distributed Databases: Principles & Systems.* McGraw-Hill.

[Chan79a] Chandy, K.M.; V. Holms; and J. Misra. 1979. "Distributed Simulation of Networks." *Computer Networks* 3, no. 2 (Apr.): 105-113.

[Chan79b] Chandy, K.M.; and J. Misra. 1979. "Distributed Simulation: A Case Study in Design and Verification of Distributed Programs." *IEEE Transactions on Software Engineering* SE-5, no. 5 (Sep.): 440-452.

[Jeff85] Jefferson, D. 1985. "Virtual Time." *ACM Transactions on Programming Languages and Systems* 7, no. 3, 404-425.

[Garc78] Garcia-Molina, H. 1978. "Performanse Comparison of Two Update Algorithms for Distributed Databases." In *Proceedings of the 3-rd Berkeley Workshop on Distributed Data Management and Computer Networks*, Berkeley, CA.

[Lin81] Lin, W. 1981. "Performance Evaluation of Two Concurrency Control Mechanisms in a Distributed Database System." In *Proceedings of the ACM-SIGMOD*, Ann Arbor, MI.

[Livn85] Livny, M. 1985. "A Study of Methodology of Parallelism in Distributed Simulation." In *Proceedings of the 1985 Distributed Simulation Conference.* (San Diego, CA, Jan. 24-26). SCS, La Jolla, CA, 94-98.

[Misr86] Misra, J. 1986. "Distributed Discrete-Event Simulation." *Computing Surveys* 18, no 1 (Mar.): 39-65.

[Peac79] Peacock, J.K.; J.W. Wong; and E. Manning. 1979. "Distributed Simulation Using a Network of Processors." *Computer Network* 3, no 1 (Feb.): 44-56.

[Roth80] Rothnie, J.B.; P.A. Bernstein; S. Fox; N. Goodman; M.Hammer; T.A. Landers; C. Reeve; D.W. Shipman and E. Wong. 1980. "HSDD-1: A System for Distributed Databases." *ACM TODS* 5 no 1, 1-17.

[Stan89a] Stancheva, E.K. 1989. "Distributed Discrete Event Simulation to Design Analysis of Distributed Database Systems." In *Proceedings of the Summer Simulation Conference* (Austin, Texas, July 24-27). SCS

[Stan89b] Stancheva, E.K. and J.K. Pavlov. 1989. "Computer Network Integrated Manufacturing: Performance Evaluation using Distributed Simulation." In *Proceedings of Advanced Information Processing in Automatic Control Conference* (Nancy, France, July 3-7). IFAC/IFORS/IMACS/IEEE.

[Than88] Thanos, C.; E. Bertino; and C. Carlesi. 1988. "The Effects of Two-Phase Locking on the Performance of a Distributed Database Management System." *Performance Evaluation* 8, 129-157.

Vatterrott, H.-R.; Department of Informatics of Rostock
Wilhelm Pieck University

Wetzenstein-Ollenschläger, E.; Department of Psychology of
Berlin Humboldt University

INRA-I: an information system for tutoring user interface design

The establishment of mandatory rules governing the design of human-computer interfaces has long been regarded as an important means of increasing computer use efficiency. The standardization of internal system interfaces is therefore a major condition for ensuring software portability. This realization forms the basis of both programming language and graphic standardization.

The recognition of the economic importance of a rapid and competent use of interactive systems led to world-wide efforts being made to lay down rules on the design of user interfaces.

While as a result of, e g, graphic standardization internationally binding standards began to be adopted in the mid-1980's, the systematization of the knowledge gained in software ergonomics has so far led to nothing but the publication of a large number of recommendations, from which several rules - some of them internationally binding - have by now been derived (cf Table 1).

Table 1: Standards of human-computer interface design

Graphic standardization			Standards of user interface design		
GKS	7/85	(IS)	Smith, Mosier	1986	USA
GKS 3 D	2/88	(IS)	DIN 66234	2/88	FRG
PHIGS	6/88	(DIS)	TGL 44690	12/88	GDR

The German Democratic Republic adopted regulations of this kind in TGL 44690, making them binding in late 1988.
TGL 44690 is in five parts:

(1) Terms and definitons;

(2) Ergonomic requirements and hardware;

(3) Ergonomic requirements of design for the work stations;

(4) Perceptibility of characters; and

(5) User inferface design.

What does the entry into force of TGL 44690 mean? Does it mean that after internal system interfaces have been defined that can be checked in formal terms, human-computer interfaces are now clearly defined as well?

To answer the question, we have to remember that the issues involved in the design of human-computer interfaces are related to matters of equipment and terminals design and also to matters of software design. In accordance with the latest international research findings (cf Table 2), the question has to be answered partly in the affirmative and partly in the negative: while the statements in Parts One to Four of TGL 44690 are framed in a way that allows them to be checked in detail in formal terms, those in Part Five are more recommendations and do not immediately allow deriving methods of software evaluation.

This being so, Part Five is radically different from the other four parts of the TGL and also from programming languages and graphic standards.

This means that the implementation of Part Five cannot be expected to lead to any standardization of user interfaces. What can be expected instead is that more use will be made of reliable software-ergonomic knowledge and that this will improve user interfaces, without any restrictions being placed on the opportunities offered by new hardware solutions in matters of user interface design.

Table 2: Stages of the progress made in the research done into various aspects of design (after Gaines 87)

	1956–1964	1964–1972	1972–1980	1980–1988	1988–1996
Software ergonomics			E	T	A
Programming languages		E	T	A	
Hardware	E	T	A		

E: empirical stage
T: theoretical stage
A: stage of application

Parte Five of TGL 44690 was contributed to by the Sub-Department of Industrial and Engineering Psychology of the Department of Psychology of Berlin Humboldt University. Its application on software products is, however, a matter to be dealt with by the informatics experts engaged in system development.

If we wish to create software aids that serve to apply Part Five, we will find that these aids can be:

- information and teaching systems;
- evaluation systems; and
- knowledge-based author systems.

The basis of the two last kinds of system is a large fund of formalizable knowledge on user interface design. In view of the findings that have hitherto been made in software ergonomics research, the provision of this knowledge base will prove very difficult indeed (cf Wetzenstein, Wandke 89 a, 89 b). Not even on

the international plane have satisfactory solutions been found so far.
It is even possible today to provide systems that supply information on TGL 44690 and rely on examples to demonstrate the implications of some of the rules laid down in the TGL. With this idea in mind, the Department of Psychology of Berlin Humboldt University and the Department of Informatics of Rostock Wilhelm Pieck University have been cooperating to begin implementing a teaching system on user interface desing.

The system can be run on IBM-PC compatible equipment under MS-DOS-compatible operating systems. It is mainly programmed in TURBO-PASCAL 4.0; and in terms of its graphic components, it is therefore adaptable to quite a variety of graphic cards. The present first stage of the system operates as follows:

The user can have himself led through a sequence of teaching units referring to a number of different key words. A teaching unit consists of up to three explanatory texts, to each of which one or two rather detailed explanations can be attributed, which may be presented on request. Additionally, examples can be called up that give a illustrative demonstration of some of the design instructions given in the texts. This is done with the help of both alphanumeric or graphic pictures and small dialogs.

The texts are displayed on a specially provided section of the screen - the working window. The user can take his bearings from three windows giving status information. Looking at the windows, he can at any time find answers to three questions: Where am I?, Where am I coming from?, and Where can I go?

There are keys that allow selecting the service that the system is to provide. The functions of the keys are shown in a menu window, which, in accordance with the WYSIWYG principle, presents the keys that it makes sense to press at any particular time.

If the user wishes to obtain information on certain definite aspects of design, he can consult two catalogues - one alphabetical, the other systematic. The systematic catalogue lists teaching units in the order in which they are offered to the user when he is being led through the system. The alphabetical catalogue does not only give the key words contained in the systematic catalogue, but also adds synonyms of these words so that the user has less difficulty in finding the information he is looking for. The two catalogues can at any time be made visible in a catalogue window, which overlaps part of the working window. The search is pursued with the help of cursor keys.

The key word in question is made to stand out from the rest by an area cursor. The catalogue presentation disappears as soon as the user has made his choice or presses a key to show that he wishes to stop locking at the presentation. In other words, the catalogue window is of a pop-up nature.

The teaching system was so conceived that it can easily be extended. For this purpose, an author system was developed that allows generating and changing any kind of data structure as well as storing it on, an reading it from, a floppy disk. The author can also consult the above-mentioned catalogues to obtain information on the contents of the data structures being processed; and he can have additional services randered, e g the determination of foreground and background colours for the various windows, and the generation of a PASCAL skeleton program, which simplifies the integration of the data structure-named illustrative programs into the teaching system.

Neither the author system nor the control system underlying the teaching system is linked to the teaching subject of user interface design. They can each be made to present others kinds of teaching subjects.

The current teaching system on user interface design cannot be considered as perfect for the following two reasons:

(1) Up to now the system can only provide information on approximately 30 key words; and

(2) progress in hardware is constantly opening up new opportunities for user interface desing, so that the contents of teaching will, for the next few years, continue to require constant updating.

The system should, therefore, be seen as an interdisciplinary attempt at publicizing rules on computer-aided human-computer interaction design. It will, as a result, be telling people about the existence of rules of this kind, which we regard as a very important thing to do if Part Five of TGL 44690 is to be observed.

References

Gaines'87: Gaines, B.: A methodological framework for the design and evaluation of software in systems involving complex human-computer interaction. In: Schönpflug, W.; Wittstock, M.: Software-Ergonomie'87, Teubner, Stuttgart 1987, pp 55-73

Smith 86: Smith, S.; Mosier, J.: Guidelines for designing user interface software; ESD-TR-86-278, MTR 10090, 1986

TGL 88: Amt für Standardisierung, Meßwesen und Warenprüfung (Board of Standardization, Metrology and Goods Testing of the German Democratic Republic): TGL 44690 Bildschirmarbeitsplatz (Visual-Display Terminal), Teil 1 bis 5 (Parts One to Five), 1988

Wetzenstein 89 a: Wetzenstein-Ollenschläger, E.; Wandke, H.: Zu einigen psychologischen Problemen bei der Gestaltung der Mensch-Rechner-Schnittstelle (On some psychological issues involved in human-computer interface design). In: Rostocker Informatik-Berichte 1989 (Rostock Informatics Reports of 1989) (forthcoming)

Wetzenstein 89 b: Wetzenstein-Ollenschläger, E.; Wandke, H.: Toward adaptive human-computer interfaces. In: Ackermann, D.; Tauber, M. J. (eds.): Mental models and human-computer interaction I. North-Holland 1989

New Developments in Computer Aided Mathematics

Roman E. Maeder
Department of Mathematics
and
Center for Supercomputing Research and Development
University of Illinois, Urbana-Champaign

Abstract

We give an overview over recent developments in computer aided mathematics teaching and research. The use of advanced software for symbolic computation has influenced the teaching of mathematics. Students are introduced to tools for mathematical computation that have gone largely unnoticed so far by the mathematical community in general.

In the first section we talk about some design issues for the new computer mathematics system *Mathematica* that has been available since June 1988 and is being used in an increasing number of places. We then give an example of combining symbolic, numeric and graphic computations to draw pictures of minimal surfaces.

The next section deals with examples of the use of *Mathematica* in teaching on a graduate and undergraduate level. We conclude with a section on *mathematical programming*.

1 A Tool for Doing Mathematics by Computer

In the Fall of 1986 *Stephen Wolfram* began the development of what is now known as *Mathematica*. He was later joined by *Dan Grayson* and the author. With the help of a small number of additional people the first version of the program was released in June, 1988. A variety of software for doing mathematics in one form or another has been available earlier. There are programs for *symbolic computation* or *computer algebra* in particular (Macsyma, Reduce, SMP, μ-math, Maple, SAC-2, Cayley, Macaulay). Most of these required larger machines to run on. Other programs specialized in doing simpler mathematical calculations in a more user-friendly setting ("mathematical spreadsheets", among them MathCAD and MathStation). Statistical analysis packages are a third type of mathematical software (SPSS, SAS).

One of the design goals of *Mathematica* was to provide a tool for most of the applications imaginable. Since no program can possibly implement all known algorithm—and even if that were possible, the resulting program would be much too large—the most important ingredient is a flexible programming language that allows to extend the system. Conventional programming languages are not very well suited for expressing mathematical formulas and algorithms. LISP and other functional languages have offered alternatives. Another important tool is the ability to specify mathematical relations or rules in an easy way. This requires good pattern matching capabilities. PROLOG has shown how this can be done. Another important area is the easy manipulation of structured data. APL showed how this might be done. Object oriented elements and modularization are important when developing larger applications. Ideas came from SMALLTALK and C++. *Mathematica*'s programming language has most of the features just mentioned. This does lead to a rich language with several hundred built-in functions but it can be done in a uniform and consistent way. The key is the exclusive use of pattern matching and rewrite rules underlying all other programming constructs, control structures, procedure- and function definitions. Another benefit of this approach is that the language is easy to use interactively and allows rapid prototyping.

Apart from the programming language there are three key areas in which a program can help doing mathematics. The one that comes to mind first is numerical computation. For many applications the usual floating point or double precision numbers are good enough but especially for applications within mathematics itself we need more. Arbitrary precision approximate calculations and exact calculations with integers, rational numbers and Gaussian integers of any size are essential. For applications in the sciences a library of special functions is most welcome. It could one day make the unwieldy tables and handbooks obsolete. In *Mathematica* all the built-in special functions can be evaluated to arbitrary precision anywhere in the complex plane.

The second area is symbolic computation and computer algebra. These two terms are often used interchangeably even though there can be symbolic computation without any algebra (LISP) and libraries of computer algebra algorithms don't need extensive symbolic manipulation capabilities (SAC-2). *Mathematica* follows the tradition of Macsyma, Reduce, SMP and Maple in providing good symbolic manipulation with some key algebraic algorithms built-in (polynomial factorization, integration in finite terms, solving systems of equations).

It does not (yet) provide much in the direction of modern computer algebra systems, such as Cayley or Scratchpad II, although algebraic data types and algorithms can be added easily.

The third area is the presentation of results. Good graphics is essential for the presentation of experimental results and the illustration of mathematical concepts. Today's advanced hardware and software allow for device-independent graphics output, colour and animation (the latter two unfortunately still beyond the scope of a printed paper).

Apart from all the requirements outlined, another major concern is that a modern software package should interface properly with other programs and the computer on which it is running. It then becomes a tool that can be used by other programs, for example. The present paper is an example of such interfacing. The manuscript was written in LaTeXwith a few additional macros. It contained only the input of the *Mathematica* examples in the next sections. As part of the formatting process, *Mathematica* was run as a subprocess, reading the input lines and doing the computations. The output was then put back into a macro for typesetting with LaTeX. The pictures were automatically saved as POSTSCRIPT code and then combined with the output of LaTeX.

2 Combining Symbolic, Numeric and Graphic Computation

As an example of combining symbolic and numeric computation and graphic output let us look at minimal surfaces. We will use the *Weierstrass* parameterization. Given two holomorphic functions f and g we can express the three cartesian coordinates of points on the surface in terms of a complex parameter z by the real part of

$$(\int f - fg^2dz, \int i(f + fg^2)dz, \int 2fgdz) \tag{1}$$

If we express the complex parameter z as either $z = x + iy$ or $z = re^{i\phi}$ we get the usual parametric representation of a surface in 3-space in terms of two real parameters (x, y) or (r, ϕ).

To plot the surface we evaluate (1) for a grid of points and then connect the resulting points with quadrilaterals. In the following verbatim *Mathematica* dialogue, the `In[n]` lines are the user input and the `Out[n]` lines are the results of evaluating that input. First we define f and g and then perform the integration. The choice $f(z) = 1$ and $g(z) = z$ gives *Enneper*'s surface.

```
In[1]:= {f, g} = {1, z}
Out[1]= {1, z}
```

```
In[2]:= Integrate[{f - f g^2, I(f + f g^2), 2 f g}, z]

                3
               z         I  3   2
Out[2]= {z - --, I z + - z , z }
               3         3
```

Next we replace z by $re^{i\phi}$. Then we use the command `ParametricPlot3D[]` to generate a table of values of the real part of the expression in the range $0 \leq r \leq 1.2$ and $0 \leq \phi \leq 2\pi$ and plot the resulting surface.

```
In[3]:= coords = % /. z -> r Exp[I phi]

                      3 I phi  3
         I phi      E          r        I phi      I  3 I phi  3    2 I phi  2
Out[3]= {E      r - ---------------, I E      r + - E        r , E        r }
                           3                       3
```

```
In[4]:= ParametricPlot3D[ Re[coords], {r, 0, 1.2, 0.12}, {phi, 0, 2Pi, Pi/18} ]
```

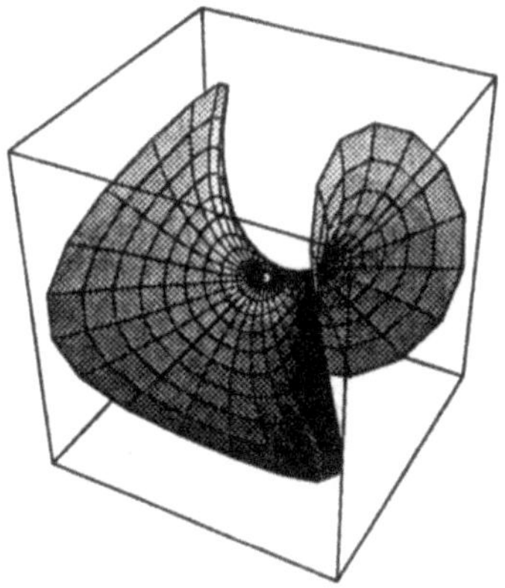

If the parameterization involves logarithms, for example, we run into problems when we evaluate the result of the integration in (1) purely numerically. Let us again derive a parameterization, now for $f(z) = z, g(z) = 1/z$ in polar coordinates. This time we use the auxiliary function `Parameterize[ ]` from the package **MinimalSurfaces.m** to compute the parameterization. A package is a collection of functions written in *Mathematica*'s programming language. This package is in a file that is read into the current *Mathematica* session.

```
In[1]:= <<MinimalSurfaces.m

In[2]:= Parameterize[z, 1/z, z]
          2
         z               I  2
Out[2]= {-- - Log[z], - z  + I Log[z], 2 z}
         2               2

In[3]:= % /. z -> r Exp[I phi]
          2 I phi  2
         E        r            I phi       I  2 I phi  2            I phi         I phi
Out[3]= {--------------- - Log[E      r], - E         r  + I Log[E      r], 2 E      r}
               2                        2
```

The expression `Log[E^(I phi) r]`, when evaluated numerically, will always choose the principal branch of the logarithm, with $-\pi < \mathrm{Im}(\log z) \leq \pi$. The values will therefore be discontinuous if the plot range for ϕ includes odd multiples of π. Symbolically it is straightforward to simplify `Log[ E^(I phi) r]` to `(I phi + Log[r])`. The imaginary part will now be equal to ϕ without any discontinuities. (Note that it would be wrong to always automatically simplify $\log e^z$ to z.) In *Mathematica* such simplification rules are expressed as rewrite rules. The notation `x_` denotes a pattern that matches anything and is referred to as `x` in the right hand side of the rule.

```
In[4]:= Expand[ % //. {Log[a_ b_] :> Log[a] + Log[b], Log[E^x_] :> x} ]
                      2 I phi  2
                     E        r                       I  2 I phi  2                   I phi
Out[4]= {-I phi + --------------- - Log[r], -phi + - E          r  + I Log[r], 2 E      r}
                        2                            2
```

```
In[5]:= ParametricPlot3D[ Re[%], {r, 0.0005, 2.0005, 0.2}, {phi, -Pi, 3Pi, Pi/16},
                Boxed->False, ViewPoint->{-2.1, -1.1, 1.2} ]
```

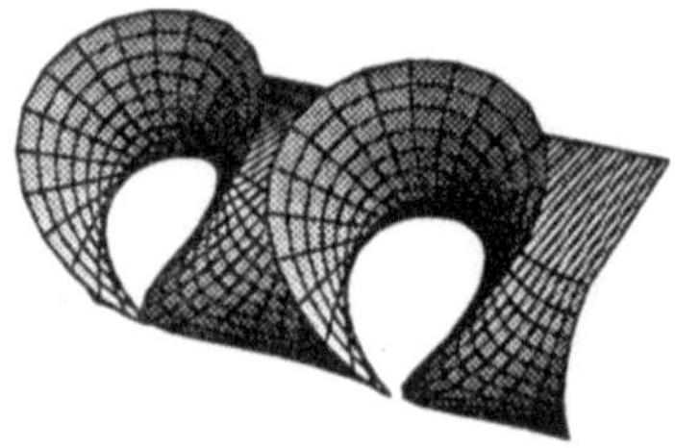

The package **MinimalSurfaces.m**—part of which is reproduced in the appendix—does many such simplifications and automates the process of generating pictures from the given two functions f and g. As a last example, here is *Henneberg*'s surface:

```
In[6]:= PolarSurface[2-2/z^4, z, z, {0.4, 0.9, 0.05}, {-Pi, Pi, Pi/12}]
```

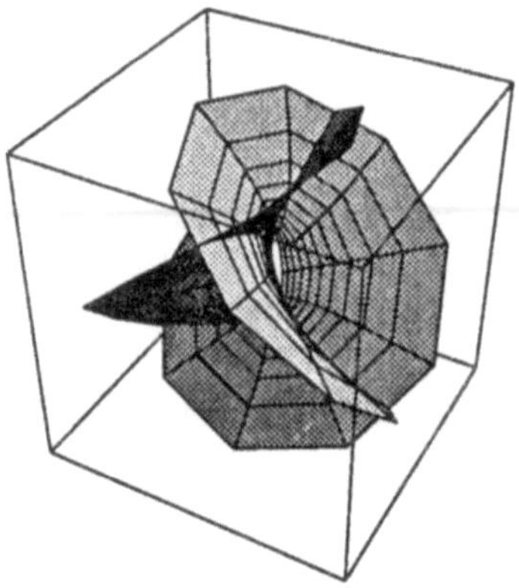

3 Teaching with *Mathematica*

Mathematica allows a simplification of the approach to teaching the use of mathematical software presented in [EM85]. The goal of the course described there is to introduce students to computer aided mathematical computation. It uses a variety of software packages. The students work on "projects", that pose problems in a certain area of mathematics or physics that can be solved with one of the programs available.

With *Mathematica* the use of many incompatible software packages can largely be avoided. This greatly reduces the overhead involved in teaching such a course and lets us focus on the mathematical ideas instead. In a course taught at the University of Illinois graduate students in mathematics and the sciences are introduced to *Mathematica*. After looking at the basic capabilities of *Mathematica* the course progresses rapidly towards teaching how to write programs that implement algorithms from a variety of fields in mathematics and other areas of interest to the students. The second half of the semester is devoted to developing a larger application in a field chosen by each student. The goal is to show the students how to use a tool like *Mathematica* to solve the problems in their area of interest and to judge the suitability of a computer-oriented approach.

The background of the students influences their programming style significantly. Most of them are familiar with traditional procedural programming languages and tend therefore to use this programming style throughout, even though for most applications a functional approach should be preferred. *Mathematica* allows to compare different programming styles to solve the same problem [Maeder89]. It is hoped that in the near future skills in the use of mathematical software will be developed on an undergraduate level to be available in higher level courses for problem solving, much like calculators today.

Another course—beginning calculus—uses *Mathematica* mostly as a tool for computer aided instruction [PU89]. On many computers *Mathematica* supports so-called *Notebooks*, which are structured documents containing text, *Mathematica* input and output and graphics. A notebook is live, students can change *Mathematica* input lines and recompute the results or add their own computations. Homework assignments are distributed on floppy disks and students return the solutions on the same disk.

4 Mathematical Programming

The use of pattern matching and rewrite rules greatly simplifies the programming of mathematical transformations. Most formulas found in mathematical handbooks can be entered more or less directly into *Mathematica*. It is not necessary to write a program to parse expressions. Instead one merely defines replacements for patterns. The left hand side of such a rewrite rule can be arbitrarily complicated. We have already encountered the rule

```
Log[a_ b_] :> Log[a] + Log[b]
```

that writes logarithms of products as sums of logarithms.

```
In[1]:= f[ Log[2 r s^2] ] //. Log[a_ b_] :> Log[a] + Log[b]

                                      2
Out[1]= f[Log[2] + Log[r] + Log[s  ]]
```

The operator `//.` applies the rules on its right repeatedly to its left argument. Pattern matching is basically syntactic, so it does not recognize `s^2` as the product `s s` and this was therefore not simplified. But it knows that multiplication is associative and so it did combine the argument of the logarithm into two terms, apply the rule and then went on simplifying those terms that were still products (In the rule we only defined what to do with a product of *two* terms). We can give another rule to deal with powers inside logarithms:

```
In[2]:= % //. Log[a_^n_] :> n Log[a]
Out[2]= f[Log[2] + Log[r] + 2 Log[s]]
```

When writing a pattern, certain parts of it can be declared as optional. If they are missing, the pattern will nevertheless match with the missing part taking on a default value. If we wanted to teach *Mathematica* that the derivative of cx^n is cnx^{n-1} then the simple rule

```
diff[c_ x_^n_, x_] := c n x^(n-1)
```

will not match the cases where $c = 1$ or $n = 1$ because these are syntactically different. (The notation := defines a global rule. It will be applied to all expressions automatically.)

```
In[3]:= diff[c_ x_^n_, x_] := c n x^(n-1)

In[4]:= diff[ 2 y^5, y ]
             4
Out[4]= 10 y

In[5]:= diff[ y, y ]
Out[5]= diff[y, y]
```

We can make c and n optional by using the notation c_. and n_.. We also need to restrict the application of the rule to cases where c is independent of x. This is done with a side condition in the form

```
diff[c_. x_^n_., x_] := c n x^(n-1) /; FreeQ[c, x]
```

```
In[7]:= diff[c_. x_^n_., x_] := c x^(n-1) /; FreeQ[c, x]

In[8]:= diff[x, x]
Out[8]= 1

In[9]:= diff[2 a y, y]
Out[9]= 2 a

In[10]:= diff[ f[x] x^2, x]
                    2
Out[10]= diff[x  f[x], x]
```

Note that it did not apply the rule in the last case even though the pattern did match with c becoming f[x]. But the condition at the end of the rule was not satisfied.

For a more sophisticated example of rewrite rules, here are a few basic rules for Laplace transforms. They were taken almost verbatim from a handbook. They implement the following formulas:

$$
\begin{array}{lll}
\mathcal{L}(c,t,s) & = c/s & \\
\mathcal{L}(a+b,t,s) & = \mathcal{L}(a,t,s)+\mathcal{L}(b,t,s) & \\
\mathcal{L}(ca,t,s) & = c\mathcal{L}(a,t,s) & \\
\mathcal{L}(t^n,t,s) & = \frac{n!}{s^{n+1}} & n>0 \\
\mathcal{L}(at^n,t,s) & = (-1)^n \frac{d^n}{dt^n}\mathcal{L}(a,t,s) & n>0 \\
\mathcal{L}(ae^{b+ct},t,s) & = \mathcal{L}(ae^b,t,s-c) &
\end{array}
$$

Here is the *Mathematica* code needed to define these rules. In the formulas above it was implied by convention that the symbols c and n denote constants. There are no such assumptions in *Mathematica*. It is therefore necessary to constrain the rules to the cases where c and n are independent of t.

```
Laplace[c_, t_, s_] := c/s /; FreeQ[c, t]

Laplace[a_ + b_, t_, s_] := Laplace[a, t, s] + Laplace[b, t, s]

Laplace[c_ a_, t_, s_] := c Laplace[a, t, s] /; FreeQ[c, t]

Laplace[t_^n_., t_, s_] := n!/s^(n+1) /; (FreeQ[n, t] && n > 0)

Laplace[a_ t_^n_., t_, s_] :=
    (-1)^n D[Laplace[a, t, s], {s, n}] /; (FreeQ[n, t] && n > 0)

Laplace[a_. Exp[b_. + c_. t_], t_, s_] :=
    Laplace[a Exp[b], t, s-c] /;FreeQ[{b, c}, t]
```

And here is an example of their use.

```
In[1]:= <<Laplace.m

In[2]:= Laplace[Pi Exp[omega t + phi] t^3, t, s]
               phi
            6 E    Pi
Out[2]= ---------------
                      4
        (-omega + s)
```

5 Conclusions

Early experience in teaching mathematical computation with *Mathematica* shows that the system is easy to learn and very useful in many different areas. Its flexible programming language that encompasses most of the different programming styles found separately in other languages allows code to be written that matches closely the natural formulation of the problem to be solved. Its range of capabilities make it suitable in many areas from pure mathematics to financial analysis and computer aided instruction.

Appendix: The Code of MinimalSurfaces.m

The code reproduced below provides the basic functionality. Advanced features, such as defaults for arguments and error checking have been omitted.

```
BeginPackage["MinimalSurfaces`", "ParametricPlot3D`"]

PolarSurface::usage = "PolarSurface[f, g, z, {r0, r1, dr}, {phi0, phi1, dphi}, opts...]
    plots a minimal surface with parametric representation
    Integrate[{f - f g^2, I(f + f g^2), 2 f g}, z] in polar coordinates."

CartesianSurface::usage = "CartesianSurface[f, g, z, {x0, x1, dx}, {y0, y1, dy}, opts ..]
    plots a minimal surface with parametric representation
    Integrate[{f - f g^2, I(f + f g^2), 2 f g}, z] in cartesian coordinates."

Begin["`Private`"]

Parameterize[ f_, g_, z_ ] := Integrate[ {f - f g^2, I(f + f g^2), 2 f g}, z ]

logRules = { Log[a_ b_] :> Log[a] + Log[b], Log[E^x_] :> x }
```

```
PolarParameters[ f_, g_, z_, r_, phi_ ] :=
    Block[{complex},
        complex = Parameterize[f, g, z];
        Re[ complex /. z -> r Exp[I phi] ] //. logRules
    ]

CartesianParameters[ f_, g_, z_, x_, y_ ] :=
    Block[{complex},
        complex = Parameterize[f, g, z];
        Re[ complex /. z -> x + I y ] //. logRules
    ]

PolarSurface[ f_, g_, z_, {r0_, r1_, dr_}, {phi0_, phi1_, dphi_}, opts___ ] :=
    Block[{list, r, phi},
        list = PolarParameters[f, g, z, r, phi];
        ParametricPlot3D[Release[N[list]], {r, r0, r1, dr}, {phi, phi0, phi1, dphi}, opts]
    ]

CartesianSurface[ f_, g_, z_, {x0_, x1_, dx_}, {y0_, y1_, dy_}, opts___ ] :=
    Block[{list, x, y},
        list = CartesianParameters[f, g, z, x, y];
        ParametricPlot3D[Release[N[list]], {x, x0, x1, dx}, {y, y0, y1, dy}, opts]
    ]

End[]
EndPackage[]
```

References

[EM85] Engeler, E. and Maeder, R., "Scientific Computation: The integration of Symbolic, Numeric and Graphic Computation", in *Proceedings of Eurocal '85 Vol. I*, ed. B. Buchberger, SLNCS **203**, Springer-Verlag, New York, 1985.

[Maeder89] Maeder, R., *Programming in Mathematica*, Addison-Wesley, 1989 (*to appear*)

[PU89] Porta, H. and Uhl, J., "Calculus&Mathematica: Background and Future" in *Proceedings of the First Annual Conference on Technology in Collegiate Mathematics*, ed. F. Demana and B. K. Waits, Addison-Wesley, 1989 (*to appear*)

[Wolfram88] Wolfram, S., *Mathematica: A System for Doing Mathematics by Computer*, Addison-Wesley, 1988

Human-Computer Interaction - its Role in Dutch University Level Education

Gerrit C. van der Veer, Ted N. White*#

*Department of Cognitive Psychology,
Department of Computer Science, Free University, Amsterdam

#Ergonomics Group,
Twente University of Technology, Enschede.

1. Introduction

It is generally accepted that scientific theory and research are indispensible as a basis for the design and development of interfaces between a computersystem and the end-user (e.g. Norman & Draper, 1986). For the design of user interfaces, both ease of use and efficiency are strong requirements. Moreover, end-users need education and information regarding the system they are going to use. In the current situation there is a general trend towards increasing use of computers by "professionals", people who apply a computer system as a tool in their professional environment, without being a computer scientist. There is therefore an increasing demand for designers of user interfaces and for qualified instructors. We address the question whether there is one specific faculty in which education and training on this topic is or should be concentrated, and how in general the education regarding human-computer interaction (HCI) is structured. In the international literature, few sources on this subject can be found. As far as we know, the current study is the first of its kind in the Dutch situation.

The designer of an system for end-users has to think about the user having abilities as well as limitations. He has to keep in mind for which circumstances the system is applied, by whom and even why the system is used. The central question is what does the system add to what has allready been obtained? In the short history of automation systems the examples are numerous about projects lasting longer than planned, products which had less impact than expected, or systems promising to solve all problems but finally lacking quality. One may ask why is the case. The computer is a fast machine which looks very intelligent but can behave rather stupid in comparison with human beings, and in fact stupid with the high speed promised by the manifacturer. What is wrong is that the information technologist has, in general, not been educated to weight the value of the meaning of the information. He has been tought only to manipulate information to search structures and to generate models about related data. In fact the information technology student is thought to search for hard facts and structured information.

If a system engineer, novice in the field with clientele, happens to built a system for a customer, there is a fair chance that the customer complains about the fact that he has not got what he wanted, and that the technologist reasons that the specifications where too fague. If the architecture is built as a truly open system, to adapt for wishes from the customer, the chance is substantial that system development is unacceptably slow. Besides, the longer the construction of the complete system takes, the larger will be the chance that changes have to be accepted in the specifications, required from developments in the outside world. Besides, the more complicated the system becomes, the more time it takes to add all issues in a logical and coherent way.

So next to teaching the students Information Technology from the technological side, one should also teach design and software engineering with reference to the human part in HCI.

In the United States of America the ACM (Association for Computing Machinery) is the forum for recommandations on educational curricula. In 1978 the program recommended for Undergraduates in Computer Science hardly included HCI (Austing et al., 1979). The course on Software Engineering contained only technical design methods and a unit on organisation and management in relation to project teams. The course "Computers and Society" contained a section on "the Computer and the Individual" of which the content, however, was not elaborated. In 1985 this was the base for the recommendations of the Chines Computer Federation (Wilson et al., 1988). Here we find a section on user interfaces, regarding mainly graphics and character set translation. Human factors do not seem to be involved. Recently SIGCHI (the Special Interest Group on Computer and Human Interaction of ACM) is actively involved in a discussion on curriculum development (Carey, 1988, 1989, Baecker, 1989, Mantei, 1989, Strong, 1989). In Carey's proposal the three main parts of an undergraduate program (with the tentative name "Information Systems and Human Behavior") are Computer Science, Psychology, and Sociology. Human-Computer Interaction is a separate unit from Software Engineering, and both are parts of the course on Computing and Information Science. Besides there is an important course on Psychology, containing among other subjects cognitive processes and perception. These recommendations are a topic of discussion at this moment.

2. Objectives

In this study we present an overview of the current situation in HCI education at the Dutch university (undergraduate) level. In order to elaborate on our investigations we need a description of the concept "HCI education". We developed a structured list of possible topics. This list is not complete, reflecting the content of existing courses, and the available literature on HCI curricula.

2.1. A tentative description of HCI education

In our framework a destinction is made between (a) design and evaluation (of application systems, of user interfaces, and of documentation), (b) input and output, (c) communication between user and system, and (d) motivational aspects. The complete structure of topics envisaged, is as follows:

DESIGN AND EVALUATION

design of application systems
- *tasks analysis (what can be done with the system, what not)*
- *functionality (quality of task delegation, time constraints)*

evaluation of applications (requirements, checklists)

design of user interfaces (user friendliness, ease of use, adaptation)
evaluation of user interfaces

design of end-user documentation
evaluation of end-user documentation

standards and guidelines
- *for user interfaces*
- *for end-user documentation*
- *for end-user languages*
- *for human computer interaction*

INPUT AND OUTPUT

input
- *keyboard ergonomics (posture, movement, skill)*
- *ergonomics of the working place*
  - *(spatial arangement, adaptation to individual differences)*
- *speech recognition*

other media (mouse, drawing tablet or writing pad, etc.)

output

VDT ergonomics (visual aspects, health)
speech generation

COMMUNICATION

dialogue styles (menu, command language, object manipulation, etc.)
languages for end-users
natural language processing

MOTIVATIONAL ASPECTS

computer literacy
mental load
work satisfaction

This list was used to structure the inventory sent to the relevant educational institutes. We indicated clearly that the list was not complete, but merely functioned as a guide. In fact the list aimed at helping the respondents to identify which parts of a course or curriculum could be considered to be part of the field of HCI.

2.2. The target population

In the Netherlands higher education is provided in different types of institutes. There are a relatively small number of Universities and comparable institutes, which provide scientific education in a variety of faculties. On the other hand there is a larger number of institutes for "Higher Professional Education". of which some aim at a relatively small set of professions, although there is a strong tendency for these institutions to fuse, resulting in large schools with a diversity of curricula.

type of institute	name/location	code
University	U of Amsterdam	UA
	Free University	UF
	Groningen	UG
	Leiden	UL
	Nijmegen	UN
	Tilburg	UT
	Utrecht	UU
U of Technology	Delft	UoTD
	Eindhoven	UoTE
	Twente	UoTT
Post Academic Education	PAO computer science	PA
Open University		OU

Table 1. The Dutch population of institutes for university level education

In this study we concentrate on the university situation. Educational institutes in this field traditionally are of two types: (a) the classical Universities and (b) the Universities of Technology. The latter originally concentrated on technical education of the university level, but currently there is a tendency to broaden the scope of education and of establishing departments that traditionally would only be found in the classical Universities.

In the Netherlands there are 7 universities of the former type, and 3 universities of technology. In table 1 we list their names and the code we will use to indicate them in this publication. Apart from these institutes, we investigated the situation on HCI education at the Dutch Institute for Post Academic Education in Computer

Science), the Dutch Open University, and some commercial institutes at the level of post-higher professional education (this last category is fragmentarily represented, only to provide some comparison to university education in this field).

3. Method

An inventory was sent to all teachers of relevant courses. In order to locate these, course descriptions, department guides and comparable documents were collected. Some non-university institutes did not react even on repeated requests for documentation, so they were left out of the report.

A thorough reading of all material collected provided us with a nearly complete list of all courses that (according to title, to description of contents, or by referring to relevant literature) might contain even a small amount of HCI knowledge. We tried to be very carefull, and included e.g. a course of which the title did not show any relation to the subject, but for which one of the books listed as compulsary reading contained a single chapter on user-interface design.

As completeness was not guaranteed, all teachers approached were asked to mention any comparable course knewn, or formally related to their course (in the way of being prelimimnary to it or a possible continuation to it). In this way some additional courses were added to the list.

The second phase of the search consisted of the actual data collection by sending a questionnaire to teachers responsible for all known courses. In case more than one teacher was mentioned, we usually chose the first one. A letter was sentexplaining the goal of our project, the list of HCI topics (see section 2.1) and a 2-page questionnaire. Filling these two pages took between 15 and 30 minutes. Teachers responsible for more than one course, were sent a list for each course.

The questionnaire covered the following information:

a. identification of respondent, office address, name of the course;
b. content of the course, to be indicated by a short description of objectives and a list of units that were related to HCI;
c. prior knowledge required, supplementary courses, target students (department, curriculum), and year;
d. estimate of total time spent, classified in lecture hours, practical sessions, and self-study. Moreover we asked to estimate which part of this time was spend on topics directly relevant for HCI;
e. compulsory and recommended literature, including, if applicable, a table of content of the reader composed by the teacher;
f. final assesment if any (written exam, oral exam, piece of work, thesis);
g. "age" of the course, i.e. calendar year in which the course was given for the first time.

All university departments and institutes approached, responded, as did three of the five commercial institutes addressed (one respondent made use of the same external educational institute as one of the non-respondents). Some university institutes returned an incomplete reaction, and three teachers failed to meet the deadlines, but in these cases we tried to complete the information frome the department guides and other sources available.

4. Results

4.1. HCI as part of a curriculum

In most universities Education on HCI is part of a curriculum in Social Sciences. This education is provided by institutes in the Departments of Social Sciences known as "Social Science and Information Technology" (UA, UG, UL, UN), or in sections for "Educational Technology" or "Psychonomic Science" (UF. UU. UoTT).

HCI education is part of a curriculum in Computer Science in three universities (UF, UL, UoTD). Mainly in Universities of Technology there are courses in the Departments of Ergonomics (UoTD, UoTT, UT). and in curricula on "Technology, Labour and Organisation" (UoTD, UoTE).

Both the Open University, and the Dutch Institute for Post Academic Education in Computer Science, present a course on HCI, and a course on "Designing Modern Software / User Interfaces" is provided by two commercial institutes. Courses in this last group are not part of an official curriculum, but there are clear descriptions of prior knowledge required, that indicate at least University level.

The majority of these courses have originated within the last five years, some were given this year (1988-1989) for the first time. Only two curricula originated between 1970 and 1980 (UoTD - product-ergonomics, UoTE - Technology and Organisation). PA and commercial courses started in 1987, and the Open University plans to present the course on MCI in 1990 (in cooperation with the British Open University).

4.2. Target students

Parts of the curriculum that cover HCI aspects are normally not a part of introductory courses. With a single exception the topics are treated from the 3th year in university.

Courses that are part of a curriculum in Social Science and Information Technology and related institutes, are offered as a free choice for all students in the Department of Social Sciences, or, alternatively, are a compulsory course for students specialising in Social Science and Information Technology. Educational Technology institutes provide their education in HCI mainly for students graduating in this field.

Ergonomics Departments and Departments for Technology, Labour and Organisation provide education for a broad range of students, in fact these courses are open for students of all kinds of technical curricula.

Departments of Computer Science present their courses on HCI partly as an option for various departments, but at the same time they provide specialised courses as a compulsory part of curricula in Software Engineering.

4.3. Content of HCI courses

From the description of content and objectives differences in curriculum in the different disciplines involved have become clear. The name of the course, in the first place, shows a clear difference between departments. Departments of Ergonomy list courses like "Ergonomy of Office Automation, of Telecommunication, or of VDU", "Ergonomics and Information Technology", of "Methods of Systematic Analysis of Labour Situations".

Courses in institutes for Social Science and Information Technology contain "Human-Computer Interaction", "Human Factors", but we also found "Dialogue Design". Educational Technology courses often refer to "Computer Aided Education" or "Educational Programming".

Titles of relevant courses in Departments of Computer Science are "Software Engineering" or "Very Interactive Software", but also plain titles like "Human-Computer Interaction".

Looking at the actual content of the courses, design and evaluation of user interfaces is almost always addressed, but there is a differential attention to applications. Educational Technology focusses on Computer Aided Education (as does one curriculum in Ergonomics), on Intelligent Tutoring Systems, and on Artificial Intelligence. Ergonomics and the non-university institutes in our sample pay a lot of attention to general problems of design and evaluation of applications. Standards and guidelines are among the topics treated in some Departments of Computer Science, and in institutes for Technology, Labour and Organisation. Documentation is only mentioned in courses in the Departments of Computer Science, and in Social Science and Information Technology (and in one single course in Technology, Labour and Organisation). These same Departments stress the importance of models of human information processing, and pay attention to modes of representation, knowledge, and mental models, as developed by users of computer systems.

Input and output technology in relation to human users is mentioned in Departments of Social Science and Information Technology, and in Ergonomics, Educational Technology, and sometimes in Computer Science or in Technology, Labour and Organisation. The non-university institutes show a clear specialist character in this respect (interactive video or VDU ergonomics).

Communication and dialogue styles are mentioned in curricula in Social Science and Information Technology,

Psychonomics, and Educational Technology (these latter stressing natural language interfaces), and in a more general sense also in the other curricula. Motivational aspects are solely mentioned in some courses in Social Science and Educational Technology.

4.4. Time aspects of the courses

Of the courses described, the part that is devoted to HCI varies considerably, from about 10 per cent in "Software Engineering", 20 to 40 per cent for courses in "Knowledge systems" and "Tutor Systems", to 100 per cent in courses named "Human-Computer Interaction" or "Human Factors". These data, however, are not always very clearly reported, so it is dangerous to draw conclusions.

Stand-alone courses spend from 1 to 60 hours to HCI teaching. Departments that offer an integrated curriculum containing HCI components (Ergonomics, Social Science and Information Technology, Educational Technology) claim to devote 40 to 200 lecture hours to HCI education, including practical sessions. If these are part of the course, they require normally more than half of all teaching hours and of all hours students spend.

Final assessment for lectures normally is of the written examination type, sometimes requiring students to produce an essay. Practical sessions are concluded by the presentation of piece of work or a written report on the session.

4.5. Literature

Many teachers produce their own syllabus or lecture notes, the contents of which reflect the content of their course. Readers are often mentioned, but, alas, the content is hardly ever mentioned in the questionnaires returned (we recorded a striking number of reprints from the International Journal of Man-Machine Studies, and from the book "Man-Computer Interaction MACINTER I, eds. Klix and Wandke). Apart from these a multitude of books are mentioned. Some titles clearly show the intention to introduce a programming language (like "Turbo PASCAL", or "PROLOG programming for Artificial Intelligence").

Specialised courses refer to titles like "Educational application of computers", "The role of HCI in intelligent tutoring systems", "Computer simulation as a teaching aid", "Knowledge systems in services", "Management information systems", "Ergonomics at work", or "VDU ergonomics" (a publication of the Dutch Ergonomic Society, referred to several times), or "Computer graphics".

General literature stressing the design of user interfaces is mentioned with titles like "User centered system design" (Norman & Draper, referred to by four different departments), "Designing the user interface" (Shneiderman, mentioned three times), "Applying cognitive psychology to user-interface design" (Gardiner & Christie), "Human factors in engineering and design" (McCormick & Sanders), "Software engineering concepts" (Fairley), "Software engineering" (van Vliet).

A general theoretical approach is supported by works like "The psychology of HCI" (Card, Moran & Newell) or "HCI - a multidisciplinary approach" (Baecker & Buxton), both mentioned twice.

5. Summary and conclusions

The general picture of Dutch curricula that include HCI aspects is very unsystematic. Both the duration and the content vary considerably, partly in connection with the discipline that provides the course. The literature recommended is also strongly dependent on the department, but here there is some systematic relation: some sources are mentioned in several comparable situations.

We would like to stress the interdisciplinary character of the field, in which mainly software engineering, ergonomics, and applied cognitive psychology participate. Each of these disciplines contributes specific theories and specialised methods. The integration of these contributions will lead to new models and methods that are unique for the new discipline of HCI. This requires a dedicated curriculum at the level of scientific education.

5.1. HCI as part of a curriculum

It seems to be possible to incorporate courses on HCI in several departments and curricula. The content of these courses has to be tuned to the anticipated careers and jobs of the students. In some curricula HCI is compulsory, in other situations it is recommended as a useful possibility for specialisation.

a. Social Sciences (and Information Technology)
Application of cognitive psychology, possibly complemented with organisational psychology, in situations of HCI seems to fit well in a specialisation. Students may draw a link to other courses in the field of "cognitive science" (artificial intelligence issues), or to educational technology. Post graduates may apply for jobs related to the design of application systems, user interfaces, documentation or training. In these situations they will need some knowledge of software engineering theory and methods.

b. Ergonomics
The ergonomy of HCI may be seen as a relatively independent domain separate from "hardware ergonomics". This makes sense if we interpret ergonomics as a professional discipline that provides knowledge on behalf of experts in a different field. In this sense ergonomics may support a technical designer. The ergonomist should be able to communicate in the language of the discipline concerned (e.g. software engineering). At the same time he may be considered to supply guidelines and methods on behalf of the designer.

c. Computer Science
Education on HCI can be an integral part of a curriculum on software engineering. In this way a direct link is provided to methods of user-interface design, and to the development and use of UIMSs (user-interface management systems). In this case a selection of cognitive psychological theories and methods have to be included in the curriculum.

5.2. Cognitive ergonomics as a separate curriculum

As an alternative structure, education in HCI may develop into a separate specialised curriculum Cognitive Ergonomics (the label Software Ergonomics refers to a somewhat too narrow concept: spatial and physical aspects of HCI need to be included, mainly in relation to perception and motor skill). The scientific research community preceeded education in this respect. A number of specialised international journals of high standard allready exist (International Journal of Man-Machine Studies, Behaviour and Information Theory, Interacting with Computers, and Human-Computer Interaction). Organisations such as IFIP, IEEE, and ACM have their own journals, bulletins, and conferences in this field. One can hardly keep up with the number of international conferences and workshops, and with the stream of literature.

5.3. Some examples of instruction

For the benefit of stimulating discussions about the necessity and possibility of HCI-education in university curricula two examples of instruction will be worked out.

a. Example on the visual display of trends
Suppose a designer / software engineer acts in team of control engineers. These have described the control loops, the control settings ect. The software engineer is requested to design all software including the user interface. In bulletins the software engineer read about userfriendliness of interfaces and he has even seen a checklist during college education. It sayd things like "present as few information on one screen as possible", and "don't use too much colours". The problem now encountered is that there is a technical systems with hundreds of loops, all supplying a multitude of information. In this situation the checklist does not give any help. Straight forward questions on what kind of information the operator requires at what time. and what kind of additional information does support the operator during the supervision of the multidimensional and complex system are not answered by ordinary checklists. Scientific research could answer some of the questions by laboratory experiments. However. the information should be available within a short time frame. Therefore knowledge about HCI on the level of defining the problem and posing the right questions is the first step in such a case. Thereafter the level of expertise of the operators and supervisors has to be known and with their help and participation the interface can be designed. Quick experiments and well specified literature scans belong to the design of the interface, but still seldom tought on a level to be of any practical use in itself.

If we focus on only one topic of layout design it becomes clear what kind of problems may be encountered.

Suppose the software engineer concludes that graphical trend representation is needed in order to see the present values of system outputs as well as their recent history. He designs representations by defining time and amplitude axis and determines whether trends share the same baseline or, alternatively, are displayed separately. Then he counts how many trends will fitt on one screen and concludes that colour will help to distinguish the different trends. If then several alternative representations are written in software and showed to the operators to give their opinion, trend representations which show the output signal rather smoothly may well be selected as best representation by the operators.

Students of the second author have performed trend scaling experiments, and they have seen that subjective preference and face validity are not valid determinants for the design of trend lay-out. In contrast, these factors contradict objective performance on trend prediction. These experiments, including preparation, data analysis and writing a scientific report, take about 50 hours of student time.

b. Example on colourblindness

Suppose a software designer is working for a Workstation/PC manifacturer. One of the advantages of this manifacturer's hardware is that a hudge amount of different colours can be displayed. Unfortunately some of the future users are diagnosed as colour deficient and have difficulties in colour selection. In fact 8% of the male European population has defects in colour perception. Although not digging to deeply into this matter, still it can be said that ergonomic guidelines can be misleading in this sence especially in the hands of naive users. The checklist that our designer may remember from college might have guidelines like "don't use too much colours on your screen (prevent a christmas tree effect)", but also "use preferably green as the colour to indicate a safe condition and red as an indication of a nonsafe or danger condition. If no indication is needed don't use any. Select grey for the background colour (no attention attractor)".

But a "deuteranopian" (5% of the male population) confuses red and green and perceives them both as some sort of grey, which indicates the hazard of some of the ergonomic guidelines. As a matter of fact, the increase of distance to the screen will increase the effect of confusion. Moreover, colour deficiency is not only a matter of congenital defect but that it can also happen temporally, Temporal deficiency may occur when people are ill or use drugs, when they have consumed much alcohol or when they are suffering a (not necessarily noticed) brain tumor. Regarding the use of colours in the user interface, designers have a responsability.

Once again students may be explained these aspects of colour vision. As the second author showed in his classes, some experimentation, based on the concepts and theories of colour perception, may reduce the 8% of colour deficients to less then 0.01% having trouble with the misperception or confusion of colours on well designed user interfaces.

We propose to incorporate in the education of Information Technologists some practical instruction based on experimental psychology, cognitive ergonomics, technology assessment and impact studies, and industrial engineering. Both authors have experience in the field of social sciences and technology and feel that the necessary practical knowledge can be supplied.

5.4. Concluding remarks

The main problem, as it turned out from our review, is that much of the available knowledge on HCI education is unevenly spread over the universities. Many faculties are not yet aware of the existence of practical knowledge, or they do not appreciate the benefits of sharing this knowledge with others. Our primary aim is to make the inventarisation available for all who might be interested in HCI-education in the field of information and technology.

6. References

Austing R.H., Barnes B.H., Bonnette D.T., Engel D.T., and Stokes G. (1979) Curriculum '78 - Recommandations for the Undergraduate Program in Computer Science. *Communications of the ACM*, 22 (3), 147-166.

Baecker R. (1989) A vision of education in user-centered system and interface design. *SIGCHI Bulletin*, 20 (3), 10-13.

Carey T. (1988) Education. *SIGCHI Bulletin*, 20 (2), 16-17.

Carey T. (1989) Position paper: the basic HCI course for software engineers. *SIGCHI Bulletin*, 20 (3). 14-15.

Mantei M.M. (1989) An HCI continuing education curriculum for industry. *SIGCHI Bulletin*, 20 (3), 16-18.

Norman D.A. & Draper S.W. (1986) *User centered system design.* Lawrence Erlbaum Associates, Hillsdale, NJ.

Strong G.W. (1989) Introductory course in human computer interaction. *SIGCHI Bulletin*, 20 (3), 19-21.

Wilson J.D., Adams E.S., Baouendi H.P., Marion W.A., and Yaverbaum G.J. (1988) Computer education in the People's Republic of China in the late 1980's. *Communications of the ACM*, 31 (8), 956-964.

LIBRARY INFORMATION SYSTEMS

Sigrid Reinitzer

bit '89
Universitätsbibliothek Graz
Universitätsplatz 3
A 8010 - Graz

Abstract: Library information systems are complex computer systems of hardware and software components comprising all functions of library activity, such as, e. g., cataloguing, accessions records, periodical administration, book charging, interlibrary loan, or information services, as well. The ideal of the seventies, embodied in the conception of large integrated library systems could be realized almost nowhere in Europe, one of the few exceptions being the Dutch system PICA: The recent communication technology with its open networks and personal computers of high storage capacity opens up new prospects that appear to promise better and more flexible methods in finding proper and individual answers to the needs of a single library.

In 1980 F.Machlup defined the professional intermediary of knowledge as follows:
"...one that involves activities, gainful or costly, that are designed chiefly to aid in the generation, transmission, or reception of knowledge of any type, sort, or quality, including giving, directly or through instruments, visual, aural, or otherwise sensible signals, and ranging from carrying messages to creating new knowledge...". This definition of information by Machlup was complemented by the following classifcation scheme: "General - education - research and development - print media of communication - addressed telecommunication - artistic creation and communication-theater, music, dance, cinema, museums, and art galleries - libraries - science information services - technological information services - medical and health information services - other professional information services - financial information services - business information services and management - government information services - advertising and public relations - information

machines and equipment." (in: Machlup, F.: Knowledge: Its creation, distribution, and economic significance. Princeton, Univ.Press 1980.)
So there are information systems in all walks of life: in the public administration they supply data about demography, the utilization of the soil for the community, or the development of exports and imports; in the private sector of the economy data are stored, offering intelligence about products, staff members as well as on rival business. These information systems can be kept by hand or by means of automatic data processing.

Libraries also have at their disposal information systems which have been both produced and used for inquiries by hand for centuries, while automated production and interrogation in libraries is now in its third decade. The invention of letter-press printing having, as a result an increased reading capacity, brought about a dramatic increase of knowledge. This led to the creation of broad classification systems by which kwowledge was arranged in classes. At the same time tools were produced, such as encyclopaedias, that made it possible to render the whole of the existing information in a logical order of relations. Thus it was possible to adjust human knowledge into a classification system that was comprehensible for the individual mind. In the late 19th and the early 20th centuries libraries were established as substantial repositories of knowledge. Here, likewise, classification systems were arranged according to the specific ruling fashion. The further accretion of knowledge in the 20th century resulted in abolishing the classification systems as a means for organizing knowledge. The use of and the interest in, these systems was replaced by specialized techniques and tools for the use of specific disciplines, such as, by example, thesauri, these being used as a means both for vocabulary control and access to information. This style of laying emphasis upon specialized techniques and tools was continued, keeping pace with the growth of information. At the present time information is accompanied by other methods of extraction, such as the use of full text systems in natural language as a new electronic form of storing, organizing and passing on information, and the like.

Now stress is laid upon how to offer information without referring to classification systems in electronic systems. Information specialists depend upon the electronic memory in like wise as we have relied upon human memory. Information is stored without using classifications, but by means of

"particular identifiers". These are a special kind of search terms, such as for example, a subject term or the author.
But here we shall solely treat library information systems set up and used by means of data processing. These information systems serve the administration of the libraries on the one hand, on the other hand they enable the quick supply of documents and information to the users.

Libraries are centres of information, documentation and communication. It is their task to pass on all kinds of information existent all over the world as quickly as possible and in best quality to those users who need this information in their work in science, economy and technology or for their training and further education. This is done by utilizing up-to-date technology in the best possible way. The services offered by the libraries to their users are known as "**Library Information Service**". The software technology as a whole by means of which this service is developed by computer specialists together with librarians and information and communication specialists can be referred to as the "**Library Information System**". During the past 25 years data processing brought a revolutionary developemt for all spheres of information and communication. The libraries are included in this process, and they must respond to this technological progress with regard to their financial situation, but also to their academic, economic and educational functions.

The library users expect better and quicker service by reason of the manifold opportunities offered by data processing in connexion with information and communication technology. What the librarians expect is gaining better facilities for their work. The ministry which makes funds available anticipates a success manifesting itself quickly for all library users and library personnel, at the same time expecting that the always slender budget is being used as economically as possible.

The advantages and drawbacks of the use of data processing are so manifold, though, that the authorities often find it hard to decide what technology should be brougt into action in their own country or library. One can always learn from the variety of experiences made in other countries and libraries, but choosing a definite strategy and technolgy in most cases involves a certain amount of risk for the ministry, but particularly for the libraries and their users.

Many of those responsible for library affairs and librarians, too, think that the ideal library information system is the totally integrated library system, making an online-realtime data input, data processing and data output feasible. At the same time it should be possible to provide the users in the library and on the university campus via the local area network (LAN) with information, but also to satisfy the needs of the users in other libraries and universities of the country through the wide area network (WAN).

But in everyday practical work it often becomes apparent that every integrated library system can only be used efficaciously, when similar types of libraries that have a not too great variety of requirements are united. An excellent circulation system does not simultaneously afford an equally good cataloguing system; a circulation system for books in open access or closed stack cannot be compared with interlibrary loan; a good online public access catalogue (OPAC) can on no account be lumped together with an information retrieval system, neither allows it that, under the same conditions, a printed bibliography or a microfiche catalogue can be produced; book processing of a single library does not correspond with the multifarious administrative assignments of a hierarchically organized university library with all its faculty, special and departmental libraries which for the most part are accommodated in separate buildings, while their funds come from a common budget; a periodical data bank ist not simultaneously a fitting instrument for the administrative work with periodicals; using secondary data and bibliographic data from an integrated network does not necessarily imply that advantages only are to be expected, in particular, if there are long response times. For many EDP projects in the library information system it appears to be more purposive to develop small, easy to survey subareas that can be linked with other subareas. Then only will it be possible to utilize up-to-date technology. The great integrated overall concept for all types and sizes of libraries is an unattainable ideal that in most cases will bring rather limitations and impediments than advantages for all types of libraries, the large ones and the small special libraries, as well.

The future path of the large libraries appears to be most promising when they will develop of their own really good subsystems, offering a homogeneous system for the whole, too, when an integrating user interface is added. If need be, several systems may be linked with one another by means of computer-computer communication through open system interconnection (OSI). In this case an exact interface definition is necessary. On the other hand, small and special libraries can successfully use integrated PC solutions or small-sized computer (minicomputer) systems available on the market. But they should also have the possibility of using the data of other systems through open communication networks and common interfaces.

A **complete library information system** comprises the following constituant parts:

- **Cataloguing:** This is the gathering of data of the newly acquired book holdings, including the creation and use of standard files for corporate and personal names; in addition, the persons doing this kind of work will have to decide, whether the holdings of monographs, series and periodicals should be treated separately or in the lump; every volume will have to be made certain in its physical individual entity, as this is the only guarantee for the interface towards the charging desk to be effective; for the OPAC (online public access catalogue) and OKAPI (online keyword access to public information) or the online catalogue respectively the exact title of the work will have to be specified. It is significant, though, whether a library holds a work in a single volume or in several separately bound parts.

- **Retrospective conversion:** This term means computer aided data collection of the library's stock that had already formerly been catalogued in book or card form; interfaces to the online catalogue for the staff and to the OPAC or OKAPI respectively will have to be provided for the users.

- **Use of external data:** application is feasible through national or international data centers or by means of CD-ROM for complete cataloguing and for retrospective conversion as well as for accessions records. The external data of several millions of titles, integrated within the entire system, occassionally lead to a peak load that may exceed the capacity of the computer, thus thwarting the benefit of making use of external data.

- **Accessions records:** interfaces to national and international booksellers will be necessary here, furthermore to the external data, to the cataloguing and finance departments, but also to the charging system, where titles of books requested are to be reserved on the spot.

- **Loans:** the charging system will have to deal with issues both from open access areas and closed shelves, comprising the complete holdings and not only those represented by a catalogue entry; for issues of closed stack books arrangements will have to be made, regarding clear standards for borrower requests to be executed by the borrower himself; a basic requirement for the user will be the integration of at least the online short title catalogue.

- **Online catalogue information** for the staff
OKAPI: Online Keyword Access to Public Information and
OPAC: Online Public Access Catalogue; with anonymous and personal or corporate name entries with an integrated interface to book charging, cataloguing and accessions.

- For the **administration of periodical issues** the data of the periodical titles kept in a library are a basic requirement. It cannot be compared either with the cumulated dataset of a periodical data bank or with handling and controlling the single volumes of the charging system, but it should be provided with adequate interfaces towards these data. All single issues will be recorded at their arrival, and preset patterns will be used for the intervals at which the issues are published. Interfaces to accessions and finances are essential.

- The personnel occupied with **interlibrary loan** will access the centrally stored data of all or several libraries of a country, a region, a town or a university campus having several libraries, such as faculty and departmental libraries. The personnell will draw on the material that is to be forwarded by having access to the open communication networks, and standardized options will be available for selecting the items needed.

- **CD-ROM:** Compact disc - Read Only Memory for the utilization of data in cataloguing work, for retrospective conversion and acquisitions, as well as for special information services to be used by the library's clientele. Till 1992 joint standards for CD-ROM are expected. The first CD-ROM produced through international collaboration of three national bodies is being given financial aid by the European Commission. Query languages are English, French and German, and all European and international standards, such as ISO, CEN/CENELEC, are incorporated.

- **Online Information Retrieval** for various fields in national and international data centres and specialized information centres, to which the library is linked through communication networks, such as DATEX-P, Tymnet, Telenet or Euronet.

Some additional aspects regarding components of library information systems in Europe:

Comparing some statistical figures taken from the IM, Information Market, the journal published by the Commission of the European Communities, DG XIII, we find out that in Europe there are about 20 million **personal computers**, but less than one million only are connected to modems for communication at speeds up to 1200 baud (bit/sec.). Only a small fraction of these belong to users of online data bases. On the other hand the number of information or knowledge workers is far greater. The explanation for this probably lies in the phenomenon that specialists more often than not find themselves confronted with technically complex systems, the access to networks being rather too difficult for them. Many managers and knowledge workers still prefer to receive information printouts - even from databases. The way out of this difficulty might be to bring information to the user rather than to compel him or her to do complicated searches in different online databases. In this connexion in the University Library of Graz we could find out that students and very young academics more or less prefer easy-to-handle CD-ROM-searches and clearly structured OPACS, which they can use almost without any assistance of library personnel. They usually gather quite a lot of citations on printouts or diskettes, in most cases more than a hundred at a time, and feel much more satisfied than they are with a limited but very precise online-search that had been prepared in collaboration with the information specialist, using the thesaurus or lists of subject headings. These searches have the nature of information browsing and may produce many new ideas in the minds of the young scientists. Besides, professionalists like to use selective dissemination of information, the so-called SDI-services, where they regularly will find answers to their standardized inquiries. They also want their information requests to be accepted at any time of the day, finding the completely processed information output on their desks some hours (or days) after, at the latest. In consequence American database managers offer "bring-services". Dow Jones, for example, has a special service for its customers. These are supplied with messages through conversational communication instead of having to use poor computer language for their retrievals. Charging policy has also been revolutionized last year. One of the databases that has done so is, by way of example, ESA/IRS, the European Space Agency/Information Retrieval Service. This agency does no longer charge institutions subscribing the new service by means of a time-based scale, but for the number of searches and the number of computers in a local area network. By the introduction of bring-services the information market will probably grow rapidly now, the specialists, who need better information in order to do their jobs better, getting this information in a form in which they can make the best of it.

Computer-computer-transfer via international data networks is not the only way of communication of importance for exchange of data and information and for the transmission of full texts on the market. Transfer of the complete documents by means of **telefax** is revolutionizing interlibrary loan to a much greater extent than transmitting requests by online-dialling has done so far. While in Germany, for example, the number of telefax subscribers redoubles in a year now, telex subscribers remain stagnant. There are as many as 84.000 already, as against 170.000 telex numbers. There are already 33.000 main subscribers for **Datex-P**, this number being exceeded by far by the number of persons entitled to use it. In Germany this boost was made possible when the post licenced private modems, too, while modems owned by the post itself increased only slightly in the same period. This small growth rate prevails in Austria, too, where post-owned modems are permitted only.

The **BTX-market** is in a spectacular boom in Germany during the last few months. In contrast to this no substantial progress is perceptible in Austria. This is caused mainly by the slow formation of the BTX-page, a shortcoming that is worsened by the excessive insertion of pictures. In Austria the focus of actual progress is now on database inquiries and on home-banking. This can also be said in respect to the Austrian land register and the database for legal information, either being ready for interrogation through BTX.

All telecommunication systems offer **mailboxing** functions through LANs or WANs. These services are to some extent used by researchers for so-called computer conferences, by means of which new findings can be swiftly exchanged and mutually utilized, provided that the mailbox is used at regular and short intervals. If this is not the case, information by letter is still the better alternative. Moreover, mail is not menaced by LAN insecurity. Technological naivite on the part of the communication managers is one of the main factors of this insecurity. The technology for tapping into LANs is now widely available and can be used by industrial spies.

Reflecting on the European and American library information systems as they have been presented in specialist meetings of **LIBER**, **ELAG** or **IFLA**, one can observe that the individual characteristics of all library systems is making progress. The extensive integrated solutions are disappearing from the market, being replaced by smaller individual answers to requirements, the small systems being able to communicate with one another. These small solutions have been developed for functional spheres of application, such as the charging system, cataloguing, information center services or interlibrary loan. Along with and in addition to, these there are also trends of providing for newly developed systems which are to be applied by spheres, where the aspect of organization is in the foreground of discussion. This applies to special and professional libraries or detached libraries without any dependencies, such as departmental or faculty libraries, whose needs are quite different from those of large general libraries. Inflexible universal concepts can no longer satisfy the needs of both library users and librarians.

Any library information system that is being developed for the nineties of this century is based upon a **networked PC technology** making possible the use of different hardware- and software components.

1 **Inverse and Improperly Posed Problems in Differential Equations**
Proceedings of the Conference on Mathematical and Numerical Methods, held in Halle/Saale (GDR) from May 29 to June 2, 1979
Edited by Gottfried Anger
296 pages, 1979

2 **Fundamentals of Computation Theorie FCT '79**
Proceedings of the Conference on Algebraic, Arithmetic and Categorial Methods in Computation Theory, held in Berlin/Wendisch-Rietz (GDR) September 17–21, 1979
Edited by Lothar Budach
576 pages, 1979

3 **Decidability and Generalized Quantifiers**
By Andreas Baudisch, Detlef Seese, Hans-Peter Tuschik, and Martin Weese
XII, 235 pages, 1980

4 **Zur Elastizitäts- und Thermoelastizitätstheorie**
Potentialtheoretische Methoden in Anwendung auf verschiedene Modelle
Von Lothar Jentsch und Johannes Maul
157 Seiten, 1980

5 **Systems Analysis and Simulation 1980**
Proceedings of the International Symposium held at Berlin (GDR) September 1–5, 1980
Edited by Achim Sydow
496 pages, 1980

6 **Nichtlineare diskrete Optimierung**
von Eberhard Girlich und Michail M. Kowaljow
218 Seiten, 1981

7 **Completeness Problems in the Structural Theory of Automata**
By Jürgen Dassow
148 pages, 1981

8 **Darstellung von Lösungen linearer elliptischer Differentialgleichungen**
Von Günther Wildenhain
92 Seiten, 1981

9 **Introduction to the Spectral Theory of Operators in Spaces with an Indefinite Metric**
By I. S Iohvidov, M. G. Krein, and H. Langer
120 pages, 1982

10 **Nonlinear Time-discrete Systems**
A General Approach by Nonlinear Superposition
By Michael Gössel
115 pages, 1982

11 **Preprimal Algebras**
By Klaus Denecke
162 pages, 1982

12 **Ergodic Theory and Related Topics**
Proceedings of the Conference held in Vitte/Hiddensee (GDR) October 19–23, 1981
Edited by Horst Michel
232 pages, 1982

13 **Singularly Perturbed Differential Equations**
By H. Goering, A. Felgenhauer, G. Lube, H.-G. Roos, and L. Tobiska
176 pages, 1983

14 **Leben wir in einer Volterra-Welt?**
Ein ökologischer Zugang zur angewandten Systemanalyse
Von Manfred Peschel und Werner Mende
233 Seiten, 1983

15 **Markov Decision Problems with Countable State Spaces**
Optimality Criteria – Algorithms – Clustering
By Hans Michael Dietz and Volker Nollau
174 pages, 1983

16 **Stochastische Verfahren zur Suche nach dem Minimum einer Funktion**
von Ryszard Zieliński und Peter Neumann
133 Seiten, 1983

17 **Invertibility and Asymptotics of Toeplitz Matrices**
By Albrecht Böttcher and Bernd Silbermann
200 pages, 1983

18 **Structural Induction on Partial Algebras**
Introduction to Theory and Application of Partial Algebras – Part II
By Horst Reichel
205 pages, 1984

19 **Algebraic Methods for Toeplitz-like Matrices and Operators**
By Georg Heinig and Karla Rost
212 pages, 1984

20 **Frege Conference 1984**
Proceedings of the International Conference held at Schwerin (GDR), September 10–14, 1984
Edited by Gerd Wechsung
408 pages, 1984

21 **Numerical Analysis of Selected Semilinear Differential Equations**
Edited by Christian Großmann, Thomas Riedrich, and Hartmut Schönheinz
203 pages, 1985

22 **Singular Ordinary Differential Operators and Pseudodifferential Equations**
By Johannes Elschner
200 pages, 1985

23 **Lotka-Volterra-Approach to Cooperation and Competition in Dynamic Systems**
Proceedings of the 5th Meeting of UNESCO's Working Group on Systems Theory held on the Wartburg, Eisenach (GDR) at March 5–9, 1984
Edited by Werner Ebeling and Manfred Peschel
271 pages, 1985

24 **Convergence Structures 1984**

Proceedings of the Conference on Convergence held in Bechyně (Czechoslovakia), September 24–28, 1984
Edited by Josef Novák, Werner Gähler, Horst Herrlich, and Jan Mikusiński
254 pages, 1985

25 **Parcella '84**

Proceedings of the II. International Workshop on Parallel Processing by Cellular Automata and Arrays held in Berlin (GDR), September 25–27, 1984
Edited by Wolfgang Händler, Tamás Legendi, and Gottfried Wolf
239 pages, 1985

26 **Multiobjective and Stochastic Optimization Based on Parametric Optimization**

By Jürgen Guddat, Francisco Guerra Vasquez, Klaus Tammer, and Klaus Wendler
175 pages, 1985

27 28 **Systems Analysis and Simulation 1985**

I: Theory and Foundations

II: Applications

Proceedings of the International Symposium held in Berlin (GDR), August 26–31, 1985
Edited by Achim Sydow, Manfred Thoma, and Robert Vichnevetsky
per volume 495 pages, 1985

29 **Parcella '86**

Proceedings of the III. International Workshop on Parallel Processing by Cellular Automata and Arrays held in Berlin (GDR), September 9–11, 1986
Edited by Tamás Legendi, Dennis Parkinson, Roland Vollmar, and Gottfried Wolf
279 pages, 1986 ISBN 3-05-500175-3

30 **Fuzzy Sets Applications, Methodological Approaches, and Results**

Proceedings of the International Workshop on Fuzzy Sets Applications cosponsored by IIASA and convened in cooperation with IAEA held on the Wartburg, Eisenach (GDR), at March 3–8, 1985
Edited by Steffen Bocklisch, Sergei Orlovski, Manfred Peschel, and Yasushi Nishiwaki
233 pages, 1986 ISBN 3-05-500016-16-1

31 **Mathematical Methods of Specification and Synthesis of Software Systems '85**

Proceedings of the International Spring School, held in Wendisch-Rietz (GDR), April 22–26, 1985
Edited by Wolfgang Bibel and Klaus P. Jantke
245 pages, 1986 ISBN 3-05-500018-8

32 **A Model Theoretic Oriented Approach to Partial Algebras**

Introduction to Theory and Application of Partial Algebras – Part I
By Peter Burmeister
319 pages, 1986 ISBN 3-05-500176-1

33 **Finite Difference Method on Irregular Networks**

A Generalized Approach to Elliptic Problems of Second Order
By Bernd Heinrich
206 pages, 1986 ISBN 3-05-500328-4

34 **Modern Algorithms for Large Sparse Eigenvalue Problems**

By Arnd Meyer
125 pages, 1987 ISBN 3-05-500332-2

35 **Parametric Optimization and Related Topics**

Edited by Jürgen Guddat, Hubertus Th. Jongen, Bernd Kummer, and František Nožička
407 pages, 1987 ISBN 3-05-500337-3

36 **Discretization in Differential Equations and Enclosures**

Edited by Ernst Adams, Rainer Ansorge, Christian Großmann, and Hans-Görg Roos
250 pages, 1987 ISBN 3-05-500362-4

37 **Factorization of Measurable Matrix Functions**

By Georgi Semenovich Litvinchuk and Ilya Matveyevich Spitkovskiĭ
372 pages, 1987 ISBN 3-05-500368-3

38 **Parallel Algorithms and Architectures**

Proceedings of the International Workshop on Parallel Algorithms and Architectures held in Suhl (GDR), May 25–30, 1987
Edited by Andreas Albrecht, Hermann Jung, and Kurt Mehlhorn
205 pages, 1987 ISBN 3-05-500397-7

39 **Parametric Integer Optimization**

By Bernd Bank and Reinhard Mandel
138 pages, 1988 ISBN 3-05-500398-5

40 **Computer Analysis of Images and Patterns 1987**

Proceedings of the II. International Conference CAIP '87 on Automatic Image Processing, held in Wismar (GDR), September 2–4, 1987
Edited by Leonid P. Jaroslavskiĭ, Azriel Rosenfeld, and Wolfgang Wilhelmi
282 pages, 1987 ISBN 3-05-500451-5

41 **Multivariable Control**

A Graph-theoretic Approach
By Kurt J. Reinschke
274 pages, 1988 ISBN 3-05-500452-3

42 **Equilibrium Distributions of Branching Processes**

By Alfred Liemant, Klaus Matthes, and Anton Wakolbinger
240 pages, 1988 ISBN 3-05-500453-1

43 **Andreotti-Grauert Theory by Integral Formulas**

By Gennadi Markovič Henkin and Jürgen Leiterer
270 pages, 1988 ISBN 3-05-500510-4

44 **Continual Means and Boundary Value Problems in Function Spaces**

By Efim Mikhailovich Polishchuk

164 pages, 1988 ISBN 3-05-500512-0

45 **Advances in Mathematical Optimization**

Invited papers dedicated to Prof. Dr. Dr. h. c. F. Nožička on occasion of his 70th birthday

Edited by Jürgen Guddat et al.

332 pages, 1988 ISBN 3-05-500543-0

46/47 **System Analysis and Simulation 1988**

Proceedings of the International Symposium held in Berlin (GDR),
September 12–16, 1988
I: Theory and Foundations
II: Applications

Edited by Achim Sydow, Spyros G. Tzsafestas, and Robert Vichnevetsky

426/425 pages, 1988 ISBN 3-05-500654-2
ISBN 3-05-500655-0

48 **Parcella '88**

Proceedings of the IV. International Workshop on Parallel Processing by Cellular Automata and Arrays, held in Berlin (GDR), October 17–21, 1988

Edited by Gottfried Wolf, Tamás Legendi, and Udo Schendel

379 pages, 1988 ISBN 3-05-500656-9

49 **Algebraic and Logic Programming**

Proceedings of an International Workshop held in Gaussig (GDR),
November 14–18, 1988

Edited by Jan Grabowski, Pierre Lescanne, and Wolfgang Wechler

278 pages, 1988 ISBN 3-05-500655-8

50 **Asymptotics for Elliptic Mixed Boundary Problems**

Pseudo-Differential and Mellin Operators in Spaces with Conormal Singularity

By Stephan Rempel and Bert-Wolfgang Schulze

418 pages, 1989 ISBN 3-05-500676-3

51 **Geobild '89**

Proceedings of the 4th Workshop on Geometrical Problems of Image Processing held in Georgenthal (GDR), March 13–17, 1989

Edited by Albrecht Hübler, Werner Nagel, Brian David Ripley, and Günter Werner

198 pages, 1989 ISBN 3-05-500677-1

52 **Splines in Numerical Analysis**

Contributions to the International Seminar ISAM-89 held in Weissig (GDR),
April 24–28, 1989

Edited by Jochen W. Schmidt and Helmut Späth

198 pages, 1989 ISBN 3-05-500679-8

53 **Complex Methods on Partial Differential Equations**

Aspects in Complex Analysis

Edited by Claudio I. Withalm

258 pages, 1989 ISBN 3-05-500680-1

54 **Markov Processes and Control Theory**

Edited by Heinz Langer and Volker Nollau

234 pages, 1989 ISBN 3-05-500754-9

55 **Computer Analysis of Images and Patterns**

Proceedings of the III. International Conference CAIP '89 on Automatic Image Processing held in Leipzig (GDR),
September 8–10, 1989

Edited by Klaus Voss, Dmitry Chetverikov, and Gerald Sommer

259 pages, 1989 ISBN 3-05-500755-7

56 **Quaternionic Analysis and Elliptic Boundary Value Problems**

By Klaus Gürlebeck and Wolfgang Sprößig

254 pages, 1989 ISBN 3-05-500756-5

57 **Computers in Science and Higher Education**

Contributions to the Conference BIT '89 held in Berlin (GDR), June 1989

Edited by Jan Grabowski

321 pages, 1989 ISBN 3-05-500774-3

58 **Wissenschaftliches Rechnen mit Ergebnisverifikation**

herausgegeben von Ulrich Kulisch

VI, 262 Seiten, 1989 ISBN 3-05-500816-2

This volume contains the contributions to the international conference "Computers in Science and Higher Education", which was held as the third conference in the series "Berliner Informatik-Tage" (BIT).
Invited papers and communications submitted by authors from 10 countries were included. The topics are:

Computers in Education
Computer Networks
Document Processing
Problem Solving Environments and Expert Systems
Languages, Tools, and Technology
Human Factors

Dieser Band enthält Vorträge der internationalen Tagung „Computer in Wissenschaft und Hochschulbildung", die im Rahmen der jährlich durchgeführten „Berliner Informatik-Tage" (BIT) stattfand.
Die Beiträge von Autoren aus 10 Ländern sind folgenden Themen gewidmet:

Computer in der Ausbildung
Computernetzwerke
Dokumentation und Information
Umgebung von Problemlösungen und Expertensystemen
Sprachen, Werkzeuge und Technologien
Mensch – Maschine – Beziehungen

ISBN 3-05-500774-3
ISSN 0138-3019

Bei Fragen zur Produktsicherheit wenden Sie sich bitte an:
If you have any questions regarding product safety,
please contact:

Walter de Gruyter GmbH
Genthiner Straße 13
10785 Berlin
productsafety@degruyterbrill.com